THE MYTH OF REPRESSED MEMORY

False

Memories

and

Allegations

of

Sexual Abuse

THE MYTH OF REPRESSED MEMORY

Dr. Elizabeth Loftus and
Katherine Ketcham

St. Martin's Griffin
New York

Design by Junie Lee

Library of Congress Cataloging-in-Publication Data

Loftus, Elizabeth F.
The myth of repressed memory : false memories and allegations of
sexual abuse / by Elizabeth Loftus and Katherine Ketcham.
        p.   cm.
Previously published: 1994.
Includes bibliographical references and index.
ISBN 0-312-14123-8
1. False memory syndrome.   2. Recovered memory.
I. Ketcham, Katherine.   II. Title.
RC455.2.F35L64   1996
616.85'83690651—dc20   95-46232   CIP

D 10 9 8 7 6

Dedicated
to the
principles of science,
which demand that any claim to "truth"
be accompanied by proof

CONTENTS

ACKNOWLEDGMENTS

We would like to express our deep gratitude to the many people who offered their help and support during the three years we worked on this book. We are especially grateful to:

—the families and individuals who told us their stories. Many of the people we interviewed asked to remain anonymous in order to spare their families further pain; thus, while we cannot mention them by name, we honor their contribution;

—Raymond and Shirley Souza, Lynn Price Gondolf, Laura Pasley, Melody Gavigan, Phil and Susan Hoxter, Chuck and June Noah, Jennifer and Pamela Freyd, and Paul Ingram who taught us so much about the anguish of both accuser and accused;

—Steve Moen for legal insights and advice;

—Richard Ofshe, whose wit, wisdom, and plain speaking frequently lifted our sagging spirits;

—Lawrence Wright, author of *Remembering Satan* (Knopf, 1994); Harry N. MacLean, author of *Once Upon a Time* (HarperCollins, 1993); and Stephanie Salter (San Francisco *Examiner* columnist and co-author of the *Examiner*'s April 4–9, 1993 series "Buried Memories/Broken Families"), for generously sharing their ideas and research;

—Ellen Bass, Lucy Berliner, Karen Olio, Gerald Bausek, David Spiegel, George Ganaway, Paul McHugh, Joseph Barber, Gayle Gulick, Nelson Cardwell, Ricardo Weinstein, Marsha Linehan, and Margaret Hagen for illuminating discussions about psychotherapy;

—William Calvin, who reviewed various sections dealing with the physiological mechanisms of memory;

—the National Science Foundation and the National Institute of Mental Health, for supporting Elizabeth Loftus's research efforts in the area of the malleability of memory;

—the student members of the Repressed Memory Research Group at the University of Washington;

—Jane Dystel, our indefatigable and delightful literary agent;

—Charles Spicer, our editor at St. Martin's Press, who proves that the substantive editor is alive, well, and energetically active in New York. We are grateful for that, and for him;

—Ilene Bernstein, Lonnie Rosenwald, and Diana Arnold, for their friendship and support;

—Melinda Burgess, who helped frame the direction of this book and constantly affirmed its central purpose;

—Tracee Simon, for careful readings of the manuscript and suggestions for improvement;

—Sharon Kaufman-Osborn, Chris Anderson, and Delores Humphreys, for their insights into the therapeutic process;

—Callie Walling, Jacquie Pickrell, and Michelle Nucci, for valuable research assistance;

—Geoffrey Loftus, Maryanne Garry, and Steve Ceci, who were unfailingly generous with their time and compassion whenever the letters, calls, or e-mail took a hostile turn;

—Robyn, Alison, and Benjamin Spencer, who continually bring home to their mother, Kathy Ketcham, the knowledge that family matters more than anything;

—Patrick Spencer, who proves through his patience, sense of humor, and loving attentiveness that the near-perfect husband and father does indeed exist;

—the family of Elizabeth Loftus (the Fishman, Breskin, and Loftus family members), who deserve enduring gratitude and affection for all they have taught her about the importance of protesting injustice. It was her family who first introduced her to the writings of Elie Wiesel. "There may be times when we are powerless to prevent injustice," Wiesel wrote, "but there must never be a time when we fail to protest."

AUTHORS' NOTE

In our research for *The Myth of Repressed Memory* we conducted hundreds of interviews with accusers and accused, therapists, lawyers, psychologists, psychiatrists, sociologists, criminologists, and law enforcement personnel. We read thousands of pages of scholarly and popular books and articles on the subjects of memory, trauma, therapy, and recovery. The stories we tell in this book rely on the recollections and reconstructions of those involved in the separate dramas, as well as on our own personal memories of the events described. Certain scenes and dialogue have been dramatically re-created in order to convey important ideas or to simplify the story; some letters and other written materials have been paraphrased (in particular, *Megan Patterson*'s letters in Chapter 10); and trial transcripts and testimony were edited in places to make the material more understandable and readable.

Although we have tried to correct obvious biases and base our accounts on the known and undisputed facts, these retrospective interpretations will undoubtedly contain inaccuracies. While we struggled throughout for balance and fairness, we may have misremembered or, through our own biases, misreported the facts. We apologize in advance for any distortions of memory that remain after all the editing and polishing stages involved in writing and publishing a book. We hope the reader will understand and forgive.

The names and identities of certain individuals were changed, at their request, to protect their privacy; in those cases, the name is italicized the first time it appears.

As a final note, we offer our respect and appreciation for the efforts of the many talented and devoted therapists who help victims of incest and sexual abuse cope with the aftermath and long-lasting memories of these traumas. We trust that they will understand that our purpose is not to attack therapy, but to expose its weaknesses and to suggest ways that it might better help those who enter its doors seeking help for their problems. We are not therapists, and any criticisms we offer come from the perspective of our research and experience in the field of memory.

We hope readers will remember that this is not a debate about the reality or the horror of sexual abuse, incest, and violence against children.

This is a debate about memory.

John Proctor: There might also be a dragon with five legs in my house, but no one has ever seen it.

Reverend Parris: We are here, Your Honor, precisely to discover what no one has ever seen.

—Arthur Miller, *The Crucible*

1

SUCH STUFF AS DREAMS
ARE MADE
OF

What we are really, and the reality we live, is our psychic reality, which is nothing but—get that demeaning nothing but—the poetic imagination going on day and night. We really do live in dream time; we really are such stuff as dreams are made of.
—James Hillman, *We've Had a Hundred Years of Psychotherapy and the World's Getting Worse*

Shirley Ann Souza was a mother's dream. "She was the sweetest, most darling, delightful, brilliant child," her mother remembers. In high school, Shirley Ann was on the softball team and captain of the basketball and volleyball teams. A member of the National Honor Society, she graduated nineteenth in her class.

After graduation, Shirley Ann worked in a mental health facility and began studying for a pharmacy degree. Then, when she was twenty-one years old, Shirley Ann was violently raped. In the months after the assault, her grades plummeted. She transferred to a school closer to home, and her parents bought her a car so that she could visit them on the weekends. Less than a year later, in the summer of 1988, Shirley Ann was again the victim of a sexual attack; in August 1989, her assailant was convicted of assault and battery and sentenced to eighteen months in prison.

Therapy seemed to help her cope with feelings of grief and rage, but she was plagued by recurring nightmares. In these terrifying dreams, her mother, who had a penis, molested her, her brother raped her, and her father sodomized her with a crucifix. With her therapist's help, Shirley Ann attempted to analyze and interpret her nightmares. One morning in June 1990 she understood with sudden, shocking insight what the dreams were trying to tell her: Her parents had sexually abused her when she was a child, and in an attempt to protect herself, she had repressed the memories. Shirley Ann immediately called her sister and sister-in-law, begging them to keep their children away from their grandparents, Raymond Souza, a retired lineman for the Massachusetts Electric Company, and Shirley, a nurse.

Like black ink on absorbent paper, the fear spread. Shirley Ann, her sister, Sharon, and her sister-in-law, Heather, read *The Courage to Heal.* "If you don't remember your abuse, you are not alone," they learned. "Many women don't have memories, and some never get memories. This doesn't mean they weren't abused."

Checklists and symptom lists confirmed their suspicions. Fearing the worst, they questioned their children and took them to therapists for diagnosis and treatment. In November 1990, five-year-old *Cindy*'s therapist noted that the child's "information was repetitive and somewhat confused . . . It seems that there might be mother pressure." Several weeks later, Cindy's mother switched therapists, taking her child to a specialist in childhood sexual abuse. In their very first session, the therapist diagnosed Cindy's problem as post-traumatic stress disorder, a classic indicator of sexual abuse. When four-year-old *Nancy* began having nightmares featuring frightening creatures she identified as her grandparents, she began counseling with the same therapist.

On the basis of the memories reported by their children and grandchildren, Raymond and Shirley Souza were indicted. The prosecutor immediately offered them a deal: If they agreed to plead guilty, they could walk away without a prison sentence. The Souzas refused the arrangement, and a trial date was set.

At the trial, held nearly three years after Shirley Ann began to suffer from nightmares, Nancy testified that her grandparents made her touch their genitals, put "their whole hand" in her vagina, and even stuck "their head" into her. She described a machine as big as a room that her grandparents operated by pushing a button; the machine had hands that "hurt" her. Cindy testified that her grandparents stuck their fingers into her vagina and anus, put her in a giant cage in the basement, forced her to drink a foul green potion, and threatened to stab her mother in the heart if she told.

No physical evidence whatsoever existed to corroborate the charges, but on February 12, 1993, Raymond and Shirley Souza, both sixty-one, were convicted of multiple counts of rape and indecent assault and battery. If their appeal fails, they will spend nine to fifteen years in prison because of memories that did not exist until a grown woman had a bad dream.

2

A STRANGE TIME

This is a strange time, Mister. No man may longer doubt the
powers of the dark are gathered in monstrous attack upon
this village. There is too much evidence now to deny it. You
will agree, sir?

—Reverend Hale, *in Arthur Miller's The Crucible*

The great enemy of the truth is very often not the lie—
deliberate, contrived and dishonest—but the myth—
persistent, persuasive, and unrealistic.

—John F. Kennedy

I am a research psychologist who has devoted her life to the study
of memory. For twenty-five years I have conducted laboratory studies, su-
pervised graduate students, written books and articles, and traveled
throughout the world attending conferences and delivering speeches.
My vita is filled with research papers with titles like "Distortions of
Recollection After Misleading Information," "Information-Processing
Conceptualizations of Human Cognition," and "Misinformation Effect:
Transformations in Memory Induced by Postevent Information."

I am considered an authority on the malleability of memory. I've testified in hundreds of court cases where a person's fate depended on
whether the jury believed the eyewitness's sworn testimony and pointing
finger of blame: "He's the one." "I saw him." "He did it." I take the witness stand and speak my academic truths, cautioning the court that our
memories are flexible and superimposable, a panoramic blackboard with
an endless supply of chalk and erasers. I try to impress the jury with the
mind's vulnerability, its inherent permeability. I think up metaphors, hoping to better convey my point. "Think of your mind as a bowl filled with
clear water. Now imagine each memory as a teaspoon of milk stirred into
the water. Every adult mind holds thousands of these murky memories. . . . Who among us would dare to disentangle the water from the
milk?"

I like this particular metaphor because it defies the oft-heard explanation that memories reside in a certain part of the brain, like coded computer disks or crisp manila folders carefully placed in a file drawer for safekeeping. Memories don't sit in one place, waiting patiently to be retrieved; they drift through the mind, more like clouds or vapor than something we can put our hands around. Although scientists don't like to use words like "spirit" and "soul," I must admit that memories are more of a spiritual than a physical reality: Like the wind or breath or steam rising, the cirrus and stratus of memory exist, but when you try to touch them, they turn to mist and disappear.*

This view of memory has been a hard sell. Human beings feel attached to their remembered past, for the people, places, and events we enshrine in memory give structure and definition to the person we think of as our "self." If we accept the fact that our memories are milky molecules, spilling into dream and imagination, then how can we pretend to know what is real and what is not? Who among us wants to believe that our grasp on reality is so provisional, that reality in fact is impenetrable and unfathomable because it is only what we remember, and what we remember is rarely the literal truth?

No, this is too much like science fiction, hocus pocus, magic . . . and we humans like to deal with the real, the physical, the material. We seek terra firma under our feet, and we send thick roots downward into the soft soil of our history, seeking to embed them in something called the truth. Ambiguity makes our hair stand up on end.

I know the prejudices and fears that lie behind the resistance to my life's work. I understand why we want to believe an eyewitness who says, "He did it, he's the one." I sympathize with the need to *own* the past—that is, to make it one's own truth. I have my own reasons for wanting the past to be solid and immovable rather than quicksand under my feet.

But memory surprises me again and again with its gee-whiz gullibility, its willingness to take the crayon of suggestion and color in a dark corner of the past, giving up without any hint of an argument an old ragged section of memory in exchange for a shiny new piece that makes everything glow a little brighter, look a little cleaner and tidier. In my experiments, conducted with thousands of subjects over two decades, I've molded peo-

*This metaphorical explanation obviously oversimplifies the complex neurological and biochemical processes involved in memory storage and retrieval. Neuroscientists are currently mapping out the brain and identifying the specific sites that are activated when we engage in different types of remembering. While this research will eventually give us a more detailed picture of the brain's memory circuitry, it is already obvious that whole memories—for example, the memory of your wedding day or your tenth birthday party—are not stored in one particular place but distributed throughout the brain. For more information on the physiology of memory, see pages 73–75.

ple's memories, prompting them to recall nonexistent broken glass and tape recorders; to think of a clean-shaven man as having a mustache, of straight hair as curly, of stop signs as yield signs, of hammers as screwdrivers; and to place something as large and conspicuous as a barn in a bucolic scene that contained no buildings at all. I've even been able to implant false memories in people's minds, making them believe in characters who never existed and events that never happened.

My work has helped to create a new paradigm of memory, shifting our view from the video-recorder model, in which memories are interpreted as the literal truth, to a reconstructionist model, in which memories are understood as creative blendings of fact and fiction. I've changed some minds, helped to save some innocent people from being sent to prison, inspired new research, and provoked some heated arguments. My plan for my life was to keep working away, designing studies, pursuing grants, giving speeches, training graduate students, all in the hope that my accumulated life's work would instill a sense of the wonder and mystery of memory-making and promote a healthy skepticism about holding up any memory, even a piece of memory, as the literal truth.

But recently my world has been turned upside down. I find myself casually tossing out acronyms—MPD, DID, PTSD, SRA, DSM-IV—while my colleagues regard me with concern and amazement. I answer hate mail and struggle to defend my work from a rapidly enlarging and increasingly hostile band of critics. My feminist friends accuse me of defection. Fellow professors wonder out loud if I've abandoned the scientific method.

As the grant applications pile up in the corners of my hopelessly cluttered office, I spend my days talking on the phone to strangers accused of the most loathsome crimes imaginable. They write long, emotional letters, entrusting me with the intimate details of their lives. The letters start off calmly enough:

"My family is currently in a state of disruption."

"I have a very serious problem."

"I feel a great need to know about your work."

But the succeeding paragraphs quickly reveal the extent of the horror.

"One week before my husband died after an 8-month battle against lung cancer," writes a woman from California, "our youngest daughter (age 38) confronted me with the accusation that he had molested her and I had not protected her. This has broken my heart; it is so *utterly* untrue."

"I am a seventy-five-year-old retired obstetrician," a man from Florida writes, "and I am being sued for six million dollars by my forty-nine-year-old daughter who claims that I sexually abused her during her early childhood and teen years."

"We were suddenly and inexplicably accused four years ago," a woman from Maryland writes, "by our now 28-year-old daughter of having sexually and incestually [sic] abused and molested her, i.e., her father raped her as of age 3 months, I raped her repeatedly as of a very young age, one of her two older brothers raped her consistently. It is like a nightmare situation, where I feel that my daughter's mind has been replaced with another's."

"Please help us," a woman from Canada writes. "We were a normal, caring family, and we would like to become normal again."

And a man from Texas writes: "Our youngest son is in a seminary and as part of his training he went through an intense two-week counseling session. It was shortly after this that he accused my wife and myself with not only condoning his sexual abuse by others, but also accused us of sexual abuse. He spoke of memories floating up like bubbles."

Each of these stories, and hundreds more like them, began when a grown man or woman walked into a therapist's office seeking help for life's problems. Each of these stories involves memories of childhood sexual abuse recovered while in therapy—memories that did not exist, or at least were not remembered, before therapy began. Each story tells of a family wrenched violently apart.

I put the phone back in its cradle, place the letters in their files, and sit back, staring out the window, wondering how human beings can endure such anguish, wondering where this is in my job description, wondering how I will find the time to deal with their requests. "Do you have any additional knowledge or research that might help families like us?" the letter writers inquire. "Are there any support groups you know of that can help families bereft of a child who is not dead, but is as good as dead?" "Do you have any literature dealing with this phenomenon of false memories?" "Where can we turn, who can help us, how did this happen?"

I used to think of time as a solid, unyielding reality—an hour to read a journal article, three hours to write a review, one and a half hours in seminar, three-day conferences, two-day trials. But time has gone soft, and I feel overwhelmed by all these anguished appeals for help.

If I had known what my life would be like now—the frantic phone calls, the tearful confessions, the paranoid thoughts of conspiracy, the gruesome stories of sadistic sexual abuse, torture, even murder—would I have beaten a hasty retreat back to the safety and security of my laboratory? No. Never. For I am privileged to be at the center of an unfolding drama, a modern tale filled with such passion and anguish that it rivals the pathos of an ancient Greek tragedy. Who would not be captivated by these tales of hypnotic trances, sadistic rituals, and bloody sacrifices? Oedipus would walk onto this modern stage and feel right at home, as would Medea, Hamlet, Macbeth, and Lear. So would Reverend Parris, John Proctor, Abigail Williams, and the others accused and accusing in

Salem. Sigmund Freud and Carl Jung would have a field day with these stories of incest, lust, and forbidden desire.

Mark Twain once said, "The past may not repeat itself, but it sure does rhyme." And Hegel, ever the pessimist, said, "What history teaches is that men have never learned anything from it." What is happening on this particular stage in this final decade of the twentieth century has happened before in other cultures and at other times. Much larger and more significant than any of its separate parts, this story rises above and beyond itself to raise questions that have haunted human beings for thousands of years.

The central question—"Who am I?"—has been reduced by modern psychotherapy to "How did I get this way?" To understand who we are and why we are the way we are, many therapists encourage us to go back to our childhoods and find out what happened to us there. If we are in pain, we are told there must be a cause; if we cannot locate the cause, we have not looked deep enough. And on goes the search to find the truth of our lives in the memories we have and the memories we have lost.

When we begin to look for memories we have lost, we enter a strange psychic realm called repression. The concept of repression presumes a certain power of the mind. Those who believe in repression have faith in the mind's ability to defend itself from emotionally overwhelming events by removing certain experiences and emotions from conscious awareness. Months, years, or even decades later, when the mind is better able to cope, these "repressed memories" can be dredged up piece by piece from the watery grave of the past, studied and painstakingly analyzed like ancient scrolls filled with literal truth.

Believers claim that even while the traumatic memories are safely buried, the emotions entombed with them seep into our conscious lives, poisoning our relationships and undermining our sense of self. This is why we must go back to the past, excavate the buried memories, and expose them to the light of day. Only through this encounter with the dark truth of our past can we discover understanding, knowledge, healing, and release.

Skeptics point to the reconstructive nature of memory and ask for evidence and corroboration. Without proof, they wonder, how can we be certain that these long-lost memories represent fact and not fiction?

I study memory, and I am a skeptic. But this story is much more important than my carefully controlled scientific studies or any specific argument I might have with those who cling so fervently to the concept of repression. The modern-day unfolding of the drama known as repression is rooted in the very depths of the human psyche—that inner place where reality is primarily symbolic, where images are alchemized by experience and emotion into memories, and where meaning becomes possible.

3

ENTRANCED

*I never knew it before. I never knew anything before. . . .
But then—then she sit there, denying and denying, and I feel
a misty coldness climbin' up my back, and the skin on my
skull begin to creep, and I feel a clamp around my neck and
I cannot breathe air; and then—entranced—I hear a voice, a
screamin' voice, and it were my voice—and all at once I
remembered everything she done to me!*

—Mary Warren, in Arthur Miller's *The Crucible*

He sat her down on the bench seat of his 1965 shortbed pickup and made her watch as he took out his pocket knife and slit the fish up the middle of its belly. "That's yucky," she cried, screwing up her face in horror and disgust as the fish guts spilled out onto the dusty Texas soil. He smiled and wiped his bloody hands on his jeans. With one hand he unbuckled his belt and with the other pushed hard against her chest, pressing her body flat against the seat. She stared up at the water-stained ceiling and thought about her legs hanging outside the truck. They felt funny; thick with blood and muscle, heavy and disconnected, going numb.

He pushed up her dress and she felt something warm and sharp against her belly. Pressing hard, he cut a line from her sternum to her pubic bone. She screamed in terror and jerked up, sure that she would see her insides spilling onto the rusted-out floor of the pickup, gutted just like that dead fish. He laughed; then, slapping the blunt side of the knife against the palm of his hand ("Thought I'd cut ya, didn't ya?"), he threw the weapon down and unzipped his pants, all of it happening in seconds. Then there was the familiar pain and pushing, the ripping-apart feeling, the hot vinyl scraping against her bottom, and the strange sensation of floating up to the sky and staring down at this scene, which always looked and felt the same.

When it was over, they drove back through the Texas oil fields, nothing out there but the burning sun, the swirling dust, and her uncle smiling at some private joke.

Lynn Price Gondolf never forgot this memory of her uncle raping her when she was six years old. She could call up other memories of similar scenes throughout the years: concrete and detailed pictures of fondling, sodomy, sadistic teasing, even torture. Twenty years later she could still feel the warm, bloody edge of the knife pressing against her belly. She could remember the color of her sandals and the blister on her heel, the white-hot sky and the dust in her teeth. She could see in her mind the dead, unblinking eye of the fish . . . like her eyes, she thought, as she drifted upward and stared down at her uncle's heaving body and the helpless child trapped beneath him, her legs hanging out the door. The years passed, but the memories stayed on, unwelcome guests with no intention of seeking out another resting place.

[handwritten margin note: Detail of Reality]

Thirteen years after the last time her uncle raped her, Lynn picked up the phone and dialed the number of a local therapy clinic. Fifty pounds overweight, she had suffered from an eating disorder for years, binging on junk food and then using diuretics, laxatives, and ipecac syrup to purge her body. Each episode of binging and purging added to her feelings of guilt and remorse. She was depressed, anxious, filled with shame, and tired of feeling out of control of her own body. She wanted to be "normal." She explained all this to the counselor who returned her phone call. He listened to her story, was silent for a moment, and then said, "Tell me, Lynn . . . have you ever been sexually abused?"

"Yes," she said, surprised by the counselor's ability to read her past from her symptoms. Briefly, she related the abuse by her uncle.

"Was he the only one?"

She laughed. "He was enough."

Lynn started therapy that week, and right from the beginning her counselor was preoccupied with uncovering the explicit details of her childhood sexual abuse. He insisted that she recount in excruciating detail exactly what happened in the pickup, even to the point of describing the size and shape of her uncle's penis. Over and over again she was asked to relive those painful memories. At the end of the second or third session, the therapist's questions shifted, not so subtly, to her parents.

"Where were your parents during these episodes of abuse?" he asked. "Didn't they know that your uncle was abusing you?"

"I never told them," she said, "not until this year."

"Are you sure? Think about it, Lynn . . . think about all the times you went off with him—what were there, twenty or thirty separate episodes of abuse? What did your parents think was going on when your uncle drove away with you?"

She argued with him. "They didn't know," she said, "because I didn't tell them. I was too ashamed. They were dirt poor, they both worked twelve hours every day of the week, they had three other kids to think about. I was the oldest, and they just assumed that I could take care of myself or that I would tell them if someone hurt me."

"All I want you to do is think about it," he said in a gentle and reassuring tone. "Try to imagine the scene in your mind. You were a little girl, just six years old, going off with your uncle for several hours and coming back dirty, sweaty, probably scared to death. You must have cried, acted out, misbehaved, clung to your mother. Do you really think they didn't know that something was wrong? Just think about it, Lynn. Keep trying to remember exactly what happened."

She thought about it; after a while, she couldn't think about anything else. Her counselor kept encouraging her to sift through her memories, suggesting that she keep a daily journal and regularly hypnotize herself by relaxing, breathing deep, and trying to imagine what might have happened. After a few weeks of intensive therapy and "soul-searching," she weakened. "Maybe you're right," she said. "Maybe they did know."*

Her therapist shifted focus again. "If your parents knew," he said, "why did they let it go on?" She shrugged her shoulders, causing him to put a slightly different spin on the question. "Now that we know they knew, and we know they didn't do anything to stop it, don't we have to wonder: Could they have been part of this? Is it possible that you were also abused by your father or mother, perhaps both?"

Once again she was on the defensive. Maybe they didn't want to think about it, she argued. Maybe they knew but didn't want to believe it was true. Maybe they didn't know how to protect me. Maybe they just did the best they could, even if they didn't protect me, even if they weren't able to stop the abuse. They weren't perfect, but they did the best they could.

She tried switching the subject back to her eating disorder. "I'm still having trouble with feeling out of control," she said. "I just don't seem to be able to stop myself from binging and purging."

"You're trying to vomit up a flashback," her counselor concluded. "Once you remember the truth about your past, the need to purge yourself will stop and your eating disorder will gradually fade away."

"My mother and father never touched me!" she said, suddenly angry.

"Lynn, Lynn," he said, using the exasperatedly patient voice a parent would employ with a rebellious child, "your symptoms are too severe and long-lasting to be explained away by your uncle's abuse, as awful as that was. You remember those incidents, you've faced what he did to you and come to terms with it. But your eating disorder persists, you continue to feel out of control, and you don't understand why. I believe there

---

*In fact, Lynn's parents did not know about the abuse until many years after the fact. "My parents didn't know what happened at the actual time—they found out later," Lynn would subsequently recall.

must be something else back there in your past, something much, much worse that you have not been able to face."

Think, he told her, write, dream, imagine. Dig down into your unconscious and pull these memories out. If you can only remember, he assured her, you'll feel so much better.

After a month of searching desperately for the memories and coming up empty-handed, Lynn agreed to join a group of eight women for weekly therapy sessions, in addition to her private sessions. "You're in a safe environment here, with people who care a great deal about you," the therapist told the women, whose problems ranged from eating disorders to depression to sexual abuse. "Let the memories come, don't be afraid of them. If you can recover these long-lost memories, they will lose their power over you, and you will be free to become yourself again."

He liked to talk about the mind's "gateway." Everyone, he explained, has a little gateway in the mind, secured by a latch-type mechanism that keeps painful and traumatic memories locked away from consciousness. When we are "safe"—emotionally prepared, physically protected, and surrounded by people who care about us and want us to get well—the latch will spontaneously spring open, and the memories will be released. "Let the gateway open," he encouraged the women. "Don't be afraid."

Lynn *was* afraid. She was, in fact, scared to death. Everything she believed in and cared about was being challenged. She had always believed that her mother and father had loved and protected her—but why hadn't they saved her from her uncle? Could her therapist be right? Could it be that the people she loved most in the world, the parents she had trusted for all those years of growing up, had abused her? But if they had molested her, her whole life had been built on fantasy and denial. How could she have deluded herself for so many years? How could her mind have cast away such important pieces of her past?

As these questions circled around and around in her mind, Lynn began to wonder if she might be going crazy. If she didn't know the truth about her own past, then how tenuous was her grip on reality? If she didn't know the truth about her own parents, then how could she trust herself to understand anyone's motives? If she was so easily deceived, who would take advantage of her next?

Concerned about her erratic mood swings and increasingly severe bouts with depression, her therapist referred her to a physician who prescribed antidepressants and sleeping pills. The drugs seemed to help, but it was only when she was in therapy with her counselor and the other group members that she felt real and substantial; only in therapy did she feel understood and appreciated. Her therapist seemed to know exactly what was going on in her mind. He was so confident and self-possessed as he assured the group that they would find this mysterious truth, and that when they did, all their current problems would fade away.

"Together we will find the truth," he intoned, "and the truth will set you free."

The search for the truth began in earnest. Eight women sat in a tight circle, telling their stories, encouraged by their therapist's verbal prodding to expand and elaborate on the details. One day in group Lynn talked for an hour and a half, sharing the details of being raped by her uncle. Afterward, one of the women broke down in tears. "I can understand why Lynn is having so much trouble," she sobbed. "She has a good reason for her problems. But what's the matter with me? Why am I so unhappy?"

"Keep looking for those lost memories," the therapist reassured her. "Something in your past is trying to make itself known. Keep listening, waiting, watching, imagining. The memories will come."

The first memory flashed into Lynn's mind when she was driving to the grocery store. As she waited impatiently at a red light, her mind suddenly filled with an image of a man standing in a corner of a dark room. That was all she could see. It was as if someone had taken a faded black-and-white photograph, ripped off the corner, and stuck it in her head. Shaken, she drove straight home and called her therapist.

"Can you identify the man in the memory?" he asked.

"I think it's my father," she answered. As they talked, the image became less grainy, more focused in her mind. "Yes, yes, I'm sure it's my father."

"What is he doing?"

"He's standing in the corner. I can only see his head."

"Not his body?"

"No, just his head in the corner."

"Is he moving or gesturing?"

"No, he's just standing there."

"Where are you? How old are you?" Her therapist sounded excited.

"I'm probably about six or seven," Lynn said. "It looks like I'm lying down on a bed or something, watching him."

"Imagine that your father is walking toward you," her therapist suggested. "Picture him approaching the bed. Can you tell me what happens next?"

Lynn started to cry as the ripped-off corner of the picture suddenly matched up with another jagged piece. "He's right above me," she whispered. "I can feel him touching me. He's touching me. He's touching my legs."

Another piece of the memory slid into place, joined by another and then another. She could see it all now.

"He's pulling my legs apart. He's standing over me. He's on top of me." She was sobbing uncontrollably, and her voice was hoarse as she struggled to talk through the tears. "Oh God, oh God, Daddy, no, Daddy, no!"

Several weeks later, another memory emerged. Lynn was talking to the group about a time in fourth grade when her mother gave her a bath and rolled her hair up on hard pink curlers. "She pulled my neck hairs," Lynn remembered. "I hated that. It hurt."

Her therapist wanted to talk about the bath. "Did anything happen in the bathtub that seems significant to you?" Lynn said no, nothing else happened, all she could remember was the rollers and that pinching feeling. Her therapist suggested that perhaps she was subconsciously blocking out a traumatic memory. "Think about what happened in the bathtub," he said. "Go home and think, write, imagine, do some soul-searching."

coersion

Three days later, Lynn had another flashback. She was in the bathtub. Her mother was washing her hair when her hand began to move slowly and methodically down Lynn's chest. She began to rub Lynn's breasts, and then her hand continued downward, touching, poking, probing into forbidden places.

As Lynn related the memory to the group, she flushed with embarrassment and shame. "Your body is remembering the shame you felt twenty-five years ago," the therapist explained. "A body memory is a powerful sign that your body has stored this memory as a kind of physical energy. Now that you are ready to face your past, the forgotten memory emerges spontaneously, triggering a strong physiological reaction. What must be felt again *is* felt, both physically and emotionally."

Lynn had been in therapy for less than two months when her therapist suggested that she confront her parents with the truth about her past. Only by facing them and speaking openly about the abuse she suffered at their hands, he assured her, would she be able to release herself from the past. The idea filled Lynn with horror, but her therapist reminded her that he would be there with her, helping her every step of the way. A face-to-face confrontation was the only sure way to move through and beyond her pain, he insisted.

Lynn called her parents and told them she was in therapy for her eating disorder. She explained that she was taking three different prescription medications for depression, anxiety, and insomnia, and she had been feeling suicidal. Her therapist was worried about her and thought it might help to meet with her parents. Would they be willing to drive down for a meeting? Yes, of course, they said, just tell us when and we'll be there.

The week before the "conjoint session" Lynn practiced for the confrontation with her parents. "You're being too nice," the women in the group told her. "You need to be more forceful about your feelings."

"You're in denial," her therapist said, "because your inner child still has this loyalty to your parents. Remember, they must have known about the abuse, and if they knew, that means they were participants. Be strong, and don't back down."

Lynn walked into the session with a list of all the injuries and abuses her parents had committed. Her therapist began by explaining that Lynn was seriously ill; she had been suffering with an eating disorder for many years, and she had recently developed a major depressive disorder.

"Your daughter's survival depends on you," he concluded. "Please listen carefully and without interruption to the things she is about to say."

Lynn read down her list: You never understood me. You never really loved me. You didn't come to my basketball games. You were never interested in what happened at school. You used to yell at me and spank me. Once Dad called me a heifer. My uncle sexually abused me, and you did nothing to stop him.

"We didn't know he was abusing you," her father said, stumbling over his words. "But maybe we should have known. If we had known, honey, we would have protected you."

"Please don't interrupt," the therapist said. Lynn's mother was crying. The therapist handed her a box of tissues.

Lynn continued to read down her list. At the very end she hesitated. In group therapy the week before, she had discussed a traumatic memory involving her father's sister, a woman who had been in and out of mental hospitals. When Lynn was about seven years old, her aunt took her aside and said: "Your parents were married two weeks after you were born. That means your daddy may not even be your daddy. For all we know, you may be another man's child."

When the group reviewed the list Lynn would read to her parents, they insisted that she discuss her fears with her parents. "You'll never get well if you don't," her therapist agreed.

She had written down a simple question. Looking right at her father, Lynn finally blurted it out: "Are you my dad?"

Her father mumbled something like, "Think so."

Lynn stood up and left the room, her therapist following right behind her. In the hallway he gave her a big hug. "You were wonderful," he said. Behind the closed door she could hear the sound of her mother's strangled sobs.

In the next year, Lynn tried to kill herself five different times. After one attempt, she was hospitalized for two days. She was taking several different prescription medications at once including Xanax for anxiety, Mellaril to control her flashbacks, Lithium for mood swings, Zantac and Carasate for ulcers, Restoril to help her sleep, and Darvocet for headaches. Her therapist kept changing the diagnoses. In less than a year Lynn was diagnosed with schizoid affective disorder, bipolar disorder, major depressive disorder, neurotic depressive disorder, chronic post-traumatic stress disorder, clinical depression, dissociative disorder, dysthymic disorder, and borderline personality disorder.

The other women in the group were also going downhill fast. In their first meeting together, when they had introduced themselves and briefly discussed their problems, only one woman identified herself as a victim of sexual abuse. After three months of weekly sessions, every woman in the group had recovered memories of being abused by one or more family members. They were all "Survivors."

Once the therapist established that every woman in the group had been abused by someone in her family, he suggested that they would be better off avoiding all family get-togethers. "The family's denial system is well-entrenched," he explained, "and only by removing yourself from the family system can you ever hope to get well."

One day, one of the women broke down in tears. "I want to talk to my brother," she sobbed. "I miss him so much. Please, all I want to do is call him and tell him how much I love him."

"It's too dangerous," the therapist said. "Your brother is in his own denial about what happened to you. If you try to reestablish a relationship with him, you'll get caught up in that denial all over again. You're too vulnerable right now, you need to get strong. Remember ... we're your family now. We're the only people you can trust."

When group members received cards or letters from their families, they brought them to the group to be read and analyzed. Lynn shared a short note from her father that was signed "Love, Dad." After a long discussion, the group concluded that her father was trying to convince her that he was, in fact, her father and thus lure her back to the family. Stay away from him, she was warned. Watch yourself. Don't let your guard down.

Efforts to recover the buried memories intensified. One day Lynn's therapist asked her to close her eyes, breathe deeply, and relax; after a few moments he tried to "age regress" her to the day she was born. Lynn closed her eyes and concentrated, trying hard to bring back the memories of her birth. But the images wouldn't come. Her therapist encouraged her to keep trying. "If you can't remember any details, just try to imagine what it must have been like," he said. "Visualize the womb, picture yourself as a tiny, helpless baby inside, think about what it must have felt like to emerge into the world."

When age regression didn't work to bring back the buried memories, other techniques were employed. "Trance writing" was a favorite exercise used in group therapy. The therapist would begin with standard relaxation techniques, asking the women to close their eyes and breathe deeply; whenever a thought or image appeared in their minds—no matter how trivial or bizarre—they were instructed to describe it in their journals. One woman filled several pages with a graphic description of sexual abuse, but ended her narrative with the words "This isn't real." When the therapist read what she had written, he explained that all sexual-abuse victims believe that their suffering isn't "real," because they don't want to admit that these terrible things actually happened. All survivors, he said, are in denial.

"Denial" was the buzzword that reverberated throughout the room, the quick diagnosis that explained everything. If one of the women expressed doubts about being abused, she was "in denial." If you are in denial, the therapist explained, that is further proof that you were, in fact, abused. If a parent or sibling resists your story, accuses you of getting your facts wrong, or asks for external proof or corroboration, then they are "in denial." Most likely, they have repressed memories of their own.

The group sessions were becoming more unpredictable and emotionally chaotic. In a typical session, one of the women would describe a "flashback" in which she was sodomized and tortured by her father, brother, or grandfather. Sitting in a circle around her were three or four women holding hands, tears streaming down their faces. On the other side of the room a woman was beating the wall with an "encounter bat"—a soft, foam rubber club—while another sat moaning in the corner, her hands pressed against her ears, and yet another hunkered down in the middle of the floor methodically ripping the pages out of a telephone directory.

Adrenaline surged, emotions seethed, abreactions abounded. Just being in this room filled with high drama and wild emotional breakthroughs became addictive, for only here was it possible to let go of everything and scream, cry, curse, howl. No one ever told you to stop, to grow up, to behave yourself, to get a grip. After a ninety-minute session, the outside world seemed tame, inconsequential, almost manageable.

In May 1987 Lynn became suicidal, and her therapist admitted her to an in-patient hospital psychiatric ward. Three months later, she was still there, still suicidal, still plagued by flashbacks so brutal and bizarre that she knew she was losing her mind. Each new memory of abuse, sodomy and torture seemed to eat away at her dwindling sanity. Months earlier she had cut off all ties with her family; now she had no friends outside her therapy group. She had been out of work for six months, her car had been repossessed, and she was so doped up with sedatives, relaxants, anti-psychotics and sleeping pills that she felt as if her life consisted of one blurry dream after another.

The last straw came on the day her therapist received a letter from Lynn's insurance company explaining that the latest diagnostic codes were unacceptable and all additional claims would be denied. Her therapist marched into her hospital room and read the letter to her.

"What are you going to do now?" he asked, his voice tight with anger.

"I don't know," she said miserably.

"How are you going to pay your hospital and therapy bills?" he demanded.

"I have no idea." She began to cry.

He kept asking her the same questions: What are you going to do? How are you going to meet your obligations? Where will you go from here? Feeling abandoned by the person she trusted more than anyone else in the world, Lynn finally said, "I guess I'll have to go home and rot."

The next day sheriff's deputies arrived at the hospital with an order for protective custody signed by her therapist and a psychiatrist. Lynn was handcuffed and escorted to the mental diagnostic center to be evaluated for admission to a state institution. Lynn remembers the diagnostic center as a vision of hell. Men and women hammered their heads against the wall, masturbated openly, urinated and defecated on the cement floor. Cries of terror shattered the fetid air. Lynn sat sobbing in a corner of the large, crowded room; after twelve hours her body began to shake and convulse with withdrawal symptoms. When she begged for help, an attendant told her to stop crying and get control of herself. "You're headed for the institution for sure," he said, looking at her in disgust.

When the attendant allowed her to call her therapist, she begged him to sign an order for her release. "I'll do anything, anything," she pleaded with him. "I promise I'll work hard, I'll find a way to pay you, I'll do anything you ask."

"I'm sorry, Lynn," he said. "But what can I do? You don't have a job, you don't have any insurance, and you're suicidal. I can't just allow you to go home and kill yourself. Your only option is the state mental institution."

Her tears seemed to move him. "It's the only solution," he said. "But I'll make a deal with you. If you agree to be institutionalized for two years, I promise to accept you back as a patient when you're released."

"I can't go to an institution," Lynn cried. Her aunt had been involuntarily committed to a state mental institution, and Lynn remembered the stories about the barred windows, the stench, the shuffling feet, the wild-eyed stares. "Please help me, please, I'm begging you, I'll do anything you want me to do, anything . . ."

"I'm sorry," he repeated, hanging up the phone.

Seventy-two hours later Lynn was interviewed by a state psychiatrist. Heart racing, hands shaking uncontrollably, she watched as he read through her chart. After a minute, he looked up at her. "You don't belong in an institution," he said. Advising her to go home and get on with her life, he signed the order for her release.

Lynn doesn't remember much about the next weeks. She recalls being taken to a friend's house where she lay in bed unable to sleep, sweating and shaking from withdrawal symptoms because she had no money left to pay for her medication. And she remembers calling a therapist whom she had seen several years earlier, and begging for his help. He agreed to accept her as a patient and waive all fees until she could afford to pay him. Concerned about her withdrawal symptoms, he referred Lynn to a physician, who prescribed mild tranquilizers and provided her with free samples.

Several months passed. Lynn found an apartment, bought an old car, and got a job as a computer programmer. Over time, as the memories of abuse began to fade away, she decided that she was strong enough to live her life without drugs, and entered an alcoholism and drug-treatment program. Something very strange happened there. She was told to forget about the past and get on with her life.

What was she going to do about now, today, this moment? the counselors asked her, over and over again. When she said she couldn't stop thinking about the past because she still wasn't sure what happened back in her childhood, the counselors advised her to stop looking in the past for the answers to her present pain.

"Who promised you that life wouldn't hurt? So what if you're depressed?" they said. "We all have days when we feel lousy, but we get up and go to work. We sleep, eat, take a shower, comb our hair, walk out the door and down the street. You have to keep moving forward, putting one foot in front of the other."

Lynn didn't know how to respond to this advice. In her previous therapy she had been told that she didn't have to do anything she didn't want to do. If she felt sad, sick, depressed, or just unwilling to face the demands of the day, she was told to call her therapist who would help her "get in touch with her feelings," write in her journal, or get out her frustrations by pounding the furniture with her fists. But these counselors were telling her to stop trying to "fix" herself and start taking "responsibility" for herself. She wondered what the word "responsibility" meant.

She struggled to understand what had happened to her in therapy. Where did all those vivid, terrifying memories come from? Were they real? As time went by the memories became almost cartoonlike, colorful animations that gradually lost their power to hurt. After she had been sober and drug-free for several months, she knew the truth. All those detailed memories of her parents abusing her were the fantasies of a confused, drug-saturated mind. She began to understand that these imagined memories were created from fears, dreams, and desires, along with bits and pieces of real life. The massive doses of drugs, the preoccupation with sexual abuse, the paranoia inspired by her therapist, and the mass hysteria of the group worked together to create a traumatic but wholly fictional world. The memories had actually created the trauma.

What had she done to her parents? How could she ever face them? The questions caused her physical pain. She ached to put her arms around them and beg their forgiveness, but she could not find the courage. Every week she called her sister, who kept her informed about the family. "Mom and Dad are desperate to see you, Lynn," her sister said. "They miss you so much." But for two more years Lynn was too filled with shame for what she had done to them.

Then, one day, the pain of being separated from her parents over-whelmed her fear of facing them. She was at her sister's house when they walked in the door. Seeing their daughter for the first time in three years, they opened up their arms and hugged her as if they would never let her go. They never asked Lynn to explain what happened, nor did they re-quest an apology. They had what they wanted, and what for years they had believed would never be theirs again: their daughter, safe, sane, alive.

What a story, you may be thinking . . . what an amazing, bizarre, fantas-tic story. Perhaps, like many people I know, you find yourself wondering about Lynn. Why did she come to accept memories that she initially in-sisted were false? Was there something inherently wrong with her—a mental weakness of some kind, a psychological flaw, an inability to sepa-rate fact from reality? Surely only a fragile, troubled individual would allow herself to become convinced that a false memory was actually real . . . and if she were so vulnerable, so easily misled, wouldn't that indicate that in fact something terrible had occurred in her past?

Or perhaps you are thinking: All those memories that Lynn recovered in therapy were true, if not in all the particulars then at least in the gen-eral outline. For how could the mind create such visual, emotionally charged memories out of thin air? Lynn later retracted her accusations not because the memories were false but because she could no longer stand the pain of being separated from her family. She was back, to use the familiar words, in denial.

Perhaps you are not prepared to put the blame on Lynn: She simply had the misfortune to run into a misguided and overzealous therapist. Or perhaps the problem is with therapy itself: a profession that has become our new religion, offering quick and easy answers for life's complex and essentially unanswerable problems. In its zeal to ameliorate our suffering, has therapy reduced all our problems to symptoms, equating suffering with abuse, and holding forth the false hope of redemption through the resurrection of lost innocence?

How *do* we make sense of this story? Is Lynn a fragile and disturbed individual whose memories represent a distorted but basically accurate representation of the past? Is her therapist to blame? Was the group like gasoline on a smoldering fire, a volatile mixture of depressed and depen-dent women urging each other onward and upward into a conflagration of false memories? What can we learn from the bizarre twists and turns of this tale of therapy gone berserk?

4

LOOSE SPIRITS

There is prodigious danger in the seeking of loose spirits.
I fear it, I fear it.

—Rebecca Nurse, in Arthur Miller's *The Crucible*

I can say this with conviction: Lynn is not the only person who has suffered through such an experience; her therapist is not the only clinician who has suggested the presence of long-buried memories; and her therapy group is not the only assemblage of lonely, confused individuals transformed within a period of months into suicidal "survivors" obsessed with graphic memories of sexual abuse and sadistic tortures.

I talked to five women—Elizabeth, *Pamela,* Melody, Laura, and Erin—with stories so similar to Lynn's that I think it is fair to say that there are themes here, coarse and rugged with awkward truth, and we do not have to dig very deep to find them. Troubled, depressed, anxious, or frightened, these women (ranging in age from seventeen to thirty-five) turned to a therapist for advice and guidance. Pamela and her husband contacted a licensed social worker for help with their marriage problems. Melody was hospitalized for depression. Elizabeth was depressed and experiencing marital problems. Laura had an eating disorder. Erin, who was clinically depressed, entered therapy hoping to improve her relationship with her father. "I wanted to feel closer to him," she explains. "I was angry with him because he had always favored my older brother."

Within a few months (in two cases, within the first hour), the therapist asked: "Were you sexually abused as a child?" For Pamela the matter was stated simply as fact. "My husband and I had been in therapy for two months, and we were feeling really positive and hopeful about our marriage. We had learned how to communicate with each other, to express our feelings and vent our anger in constructive ways. Then, out of the blue, the therapist turned to me and said, "Now, Pamela, your father sexually abused you, didn't he?"

Pamela's initial reaction was typical. "I was just floored," she says. "I couldn't understand what the therapist was asking me. I didn't know if he had me confused with another client or was somehow accusing me of lying, or what. I told him that I didn't remember anything about being sexually abused; the thought had never crossed my mind. He said that didn't mean anything, it was irrelevant. I was probably 'dissociating,' which he explained was my mind's way of protecting me. He said that sexual abuse was his area of expertise, he had worked with hundreds of women who had been abused, and he felt ninety-five percent sure I had been abused. He told me to go home and see if I could remember anything. He said the memories would just come to me, they would suddenly come pouring out if I would only let myself remember."

For each of these women the suggestion of abuse had several immediate emotional effects. The first reaction was shock and disbelief. "My therapist asked me point blank if my brother had abused me," Erin says. "I told her that I had never been abused by my brother or anyone. 'Are you sure?' she asked. 'Yes, I'm sure,' I answered. She looked up at the ceiling, then, as if she were doubting me. I began to hyperventilate and had a panic attack. I couldn't handle the emotions connected with the idea that I might have been abused."

The second response was a strange sensation of relief edged with hope. "I felt a desperate need to remember what happened to me so that I could get well and get on with my life," Melody says.

"Maybe this is the explanation for my pain and distress," they all speculated. "Maybe this is why I feel out of control, moody, depressed, and anxious. If I was abused, and if I can find these memories, maybe all my problems will go away, and I can start a new and better life."

The search for the memories began in earnest. The women read *The Courage to Heal,* by Ellen Bass and Laura Davis, in which they learned that many people who were abused as children don't have memories of the abuse, and some people are never able to retrieve their memories. But the memories don't really matter, not in the sense of proving to yourself or anyone else that you were abused. What matters is how you feel. "If you think you were abused and your life shows the symptoms, then you were."

"I memorized *The Courage to Heal,*" Erin says. "I used to take it with me everywhere—to the doctor's office, to babysitting jobs, whenever I went out with friends—because I was afraid I might have a flashback, and I knew the book would help me through it."

Erin also memorized whole sections of therapist E. Sue Blume's book

Secret Survivors. On the very first page, even before the title page, she discovered something called "The Incest Survivors' Aftereffects Checklist." The checklist begins with this question and statement: "Do you find many characteristics of yourself on this list? If so, you could be a survivor of incest." The "characteristics" include the fear of being alone in the dark; nightmares; poor body image; headaches; arthritis; adult nervousness; fear of losing control; guilt; shame; low self-esteem; feeling crazy; and feeling different.

"I kept comparing myself to those symptoms," Erin says. "With each symptom that fit—and virtually every one did—I had more evidence to convince myself that I was an incest survivor."

The women worked their way through the twenty questions of the twelve-step group Survivors of Incest Anonymous, matching their own experience with the questions intended to reveal abuse. Among the questions:

- Do you feel you have to control your emotions?

- Currently, do you over-react or misdirect your anger in situations that frustrate you? Are you afraid of anger?

- Do you have blocks of your childhood you can't remember? Do you have a sense that "something happened?" Do you have memories of abuse with no emotions associated with those memories?

- Do you have a problem with alcohol, drugs, food, migraines, or back pain?

The questions seemed to fit, but where were the memories? Melody read through *The Courage to Heal* dozens of times. "I did little besides reading *The Courage to Heal* and crying and feeling depressed and angry," she explains. "I tried all the 'tricks' in that book and *The Courage to Heal Workbook,* but still I could not remember anything concrete, although I was convinced that it had happened. I was always thinking and trying, trying hard to remember."

Pamela sat down with her old photo albums, carefully looking at each picture, hoping that the image of a hand resting on her shoulder or the flowered pattern of a favorite childhood dress would suddenly liberate a long-buried memory.

Elizabeth appealed directly to God. "I was praying all the time, just praying to God to give me the memories." Pamela also turned to God, begging him to help her find the long-lost memories. "I fell down on my knees and called out to God: Please, God, give me the memories!"

They searched and prayed and thought of little else, because their therapists insisted that their current pain was so severe that only repressed memories of traumatic abuse could explain it. "The abuse in your life is always at least as great as the emotional pain you suffer now," they were told. "If your pain is extreme, the abuse must have been severe; and if you don't remember being abused, you must have repressed the memory."

"In the beginning of my therapy, I brought with me some very real hurts and disappointments," Laura wrote. "I had lost one of the most important relationships of my entire life. My life seemed out of control. I had external problems that caused me great distress, but my therapist didn't seem too concerned with those. The pain had to be *deeper,* had to be buried, 'repressed.' For me to have a 'death wish' of the magnitude I had and to be so self-destructive, I had to have repressed something so horrible and so traumatic that only a lengthy therapy, hypnosis and hard work were going to make me better."

They wanted so desperately to get better, to feel better, to be better, but their agony only seemed to get worse. And so they gave themselves up to therapy, surrendering their will, their reason, their control. Laura's life became "so enmeshed and intertwined" with her therapist's life that she could no longer think for herself. "I thought what he wanted me to think. I believed what he wanted me to believe. I became what he wanted me to become."

"My therapist had my picture on her desk," Erin recalls. "In every session she would tell me many times that she loved me. She explained that she felt I needed more nurturing."

When their therapists suggested that joining a group might help them recover their lost memories, they agreed to give it a try, even though several of the women initially resisted. "I did not want to go," Laura explains, "but my therapist said I was just transferring the fear of my family onto the group. He said I must go." Pamela's therapist encouraged her to enter group therapy in order to overcome her loneliness. "In the group you'll make lots of friends," he said. "And you'll be amazed at how much work you can get done, piggybacking with other women."

Sure enough, just being in the group seemed to speed things up. "I cut myself off from everything else except my group," Elizabeth says, "and in group we were all talking about the same stuff—child abuse, incest, sodomy, torture—and we were all verifying it with each other. I wanted to belong somewhere, and in the group I finally got the feeling that I belonged."

"The main denominator in my group was loneliness," Pamela agrees. "We were all lonely, and confused and afraid, and we were all desperately searching for memories. I figured this search for long-lost memories must be real if all these women were looking for the same thing."

In group they tried several unusual techniques to recover the buried memories. Laura's therapist relied on a procedure called trance work. He told her to shut her eyes, imagine what might have happened back in her past, and then write down in her journal "whatever pops into your head." The theory was that uncensored journal writing would tap into unconscious memories. Afterward the therapist would read the entries aloud. "This is real," he would say. "These events really happened."

If someone in the group insisted that she had been fantasizing or making things up, the therapist would argue with her. "You did not make this up," he would say. "Your mind has difficulty accepting the reality of the horror, and so you deny the truth in order to protect yourself. These are memories, and they are real."

In one of Laura's journal entries she expresses her fear that her memories might not be real.

> I have a hard time believing the dreams I have. My shoulders ache, my arm hurts, even to the point of having to take pain medication. Real pain or memories of real pain? Could it have been as bad as I am dreaming? Are the dreams symbolic maybe? Can bad dreams be mistaken for flashbacks? How could so much happen and no one notice or care? I wish I could figure out what is real and what is programmed from T.V., horror stories, or imagination. Is it real or is this some kind of game my mind is playing?

Is this real? Am I making it up? the women would ask. "No," their therapists gently reassured them, "crippling disbelief, accompanied by self-hatred and guilt, often affects survivors. The existence of doubt and skepticism is an indication that the memories do, in fact, exist. Ignore your doubts. Trust your feelings. Let go of denial. Don't seek external proof, because in most cases it won't be available."

The women were warned in great detail about anyone who might question or doubt their memories. The most obvious target of the therapist's distrust was the patient's family. "Your families have a huge investment in making sure your memories stay buried. They will try to discredit you because they are caught up in their own denial."

Denial was the ever-present word, the inherent, unalterable, indisputable truth. Survivors are in denial. Families are in denial. Child abusers are in denial. "Denial" is the answer to every question. If accused family members have nothing to say, it's because they are guilty; if they claim innocence, they are trying to hide something; if they don't remember an event the way the survivor remembers it, they are in denial. There was always an answer, and the answer always involved the word "denial."

"Your whole family is in denial," Erin's therapist told her.

"But wait a minute," Erin said, feeling angry and defensive. "You're proceeding as if you're certain that I'm an incest survivor, when I still don't know what happened to me."

"Many of my clients who are incest survivors don't know what happened to them," her therapist responded. "Most of them are in denial."

If you were "in denial," you simply had to work harder. When Elizabeth questioned the need to spend so much time searching for memories that might not even exist, her therapist said, "You're getting sicker because you're not trying hard enough." When Laura refused to participate in some of the trance writing sessions, her therapist told her she was running away from her problems. "You're not willing to work hard," he said. Later, when Laura had a flashback of a young boy holding a pillow over her face when she was an infant, her therapist kept asking her the same question—"When are you going to accept the fact that your brother tried to kill you?"—until she finally agreed with him that her brother once tried to suffocate her.

"My therapists encouraged and pushed me to 'remember' more and more, even though I was starting to show signs of psychosis during the treatment sessions," Melody says. "I was rapidly losing the ability to differentiate between my imagination and my real memory."

Because Pamela was putting so much pressure on herself to remember, her therapist tried a different approach. "You're working too hard to recover the buried memories," he counseled. "Be patient. Often just being in therapy is enough to begin the retrieval process. The memories will come when they are ready."

As the internal and external pressure to remember intensified, the women began to crack under the strain. Melody had a mental breakdown. Elizabeth tried to commit suicide. Pamela's marriage began to fall apart. Erin's depression deepened. Laura was consumed with anger, fear, and suspicion. Could anyone in the whole world, they wondered, be trusted?

Four of the five women were given drugs to relieve their depression, rage, anxiety and suicidal tendencies. Melody was taking four different medications. Erin was on Prozac. Laura was taking pills to sleep, pills to fight depression, pills to "mellow out my rage, pills for literally everything." Elizabeth was taking Ativan for anxiety and such a high dosage of the antidepressant Desyrel, one of whose side effects is drowsiness, that she was sleeping fifteen to twenty hours a day.

It wasn't long, then, before the memories began to invade and encroach. They started as flashbacks, sudden intrusive images or visions that jolted the mind out of its complacent routine, and they came without warning—while the women were vacuuming the floor, brushing their teeth, pulling a chair back to sit at the dinner table, dozing off for a nap. Afterward, with the distorted images firmly lodged in their minds—a leering grin, a hand reaching out, a scream of terror, a breast, an erect penis, an aborted fetus—the women would wonder what was real and what was imagined. Were these grotesque flashes of horror real? If they weren't real, what were they?

"They're real," the therapists insisted, "and they're only the beginning." In group and in private sessions, hour after hour, week after week, the women worked with the flashbacks, writing, thinking and dreaming about them, discussing and analyzing them at every opportunity. The strobelike images were interpreted as pieces of memory; with a little more time and effort the "memories" became focused and three-dimensional. What began as a shapeless form, vaguely outlined, with no discernible features, became a brightly lit scene in which details like the texture of a bedspread, the pattern of the wallpaper, or the scratchy discomfort of a man's beard against a smooth, hairless cheek could be seen, felt, heard, and experienced all over again.

"I was doing deep relaxation exercises at home, and I'd get myself into these trance states," Erin says. "But I was worried about my flashbacks because they weren't like the flashbacks described in *The Courage to Heal* that hit you so hard you can't breathe. They were more like stories unfolding and developing in my mind."

Every one of these women eventually recovered memories of sexual abuse. At first the pictures in their minds included one abuser, usually a father, mother, or brother; but eventually the images enlarged to include uncles, aunts, cousins, grandparents, ministers, friends, neighbors. In the beginning, when the memory was developing, the abuse involved touching, fondling, probing; but as time went by the panorama of images expanded to include penetration, rape, and sodomy. Eventually, for several of these women, the mental spectacle included satanic cults, sadistic tortures, blood-drinking rituals, even murder.

As the memories swelled and thickened, congealing into a solid block of horror, the women in Laura's group bonded more tightly together. Loyalty to the group was fundamental, and contact with family members was considered the ultimate violation of the group's integrity. "I was constantly berated and verbally attacked because I lived near my family," Laura says. Another woman in Laura's group was repeatedly warned by her therapist that her parents were high-ranking members of a satanic cult; the therapist believed that if she tried to contact them, she would be killed for betraying their secrets. Birthday and Christmas cards from family members were interpreted by the group as subliminal messages intended to lure them back into the cult or, failing that, to create a state of mental unrest that would eventually lead to suicide.

Although Erin wasn't in a group, her therapist encouraged her to move out of her parent's house. "She kept telling me that I was a helpless, defenseless, vulnerable little girl," Erin explains. "In my mind I could hear her voice repeating those words over and over again."

Cut off from their families, besieged by flashbacks, paralyzed by suspicion and fear, the women clung to their therapists as a lost child clings to a rescuing parent. They trusted their therapists more then they trusted themselves. "I idealized him," Pamela says. "He had all the answers. He didn't talk like there was any chance the abuse didn't happen. He had such authority and confidence, and I didn't trust myself. I was afraid of myself."

"He was the expert, the Ph.D.," Melody explains. "I trusted him. I assumed he must be right."

"She was my own personal guru," says Elizabeth. "I believed that she would help me figure everything out."

"She was my saviour," Erin says. "I trusted her completely."

"I trusted this man with my innermost soul," writes Laura. "I shared my dreams with him, confessed my sins to him. He was my mother, my father, my brother, my sister, my best friend, my husband, boyfriend, decision maker, choice maker, teacher and pastor. He had become *everything* to me."

As therapy continued and the women were encouraged to stockpile memory upon gruesome memory, they became consumed with fear and rage. "I was filled with anger," Erin says. "I wanted to break glass and rip apart phone books."

"My anger was constant," Laura writes. "I would drive down the street and throw Coke bottles out the window. When they shattered, it was like a sedative. But the more anger I expressed, the madder I got. I was in a constant state of rage."

"I went on disability because I could not work without having flashbacks," Melody says. "The 'memories' became increasingly more shocking and violent, and I became more ill with each therapy session. I began *Ditto* showing signs of multiple personality disorder. My symptoms grew much worse with therapy until I finally suffered a mental breakdown and was hospitalized."

Pamela became so obsessed with thoughts of incest and sexual abuse that she avoided physical contact with her children. "I was afraid to bathe or hug them, because I feared some perverted image from my subconscious would suddenly overwhelm me. I forced myself to touch them, but I felt guilty and I was afraid that people were watching me to see if I was abusing them. I was afraid to leave my house, I was afraid to even go outside. I was falling apart."

Elizabeth convinced herself that she was going to end up in a mental hospital and lose custody of her children. Better for me to die, she thought. She tried to kill herself several times, getting her ideas for the drug overdoses from careful readings of the *Physicians' Desk Reference* in her therapist's office.

The horror ended in strange and unpredictable ways. Hospitalized after her mental breakdown, Melody was treated by two psychiatrists who questioned the wisdom of literally interpreting memories that had not existed before therapy began. "They helped me to understand that my memories were not real but some kind of hallucination or figment of my imagination," Melody says.

One day, after more than three years in therapy with her psychiatrist, Elizabeth received a phone call informing her that her next appointment was cancelled. No reason was given. Elizabeth called the office and insisted on speaking to her psychiatrist, who told her that she believed the group members were "conspiring" against her, and so she had made the difficult decision to dissolve her relationship with all of them. The next day Elizabeth received a certified letter in which her psychiatrist offered to extend her medications and refer her to another therapist because she was terminating her therapy.

Erin began to doubt her memories after a childhood friend called her. "I've known you since you were four and your parents never abused you," her friend said. "You've been a victim of bad counseling. I haven't heard from you for two years—what kind of counselor would make you ignore your friends?"

After that phone call Erin experienced moments of panic. I've given up everything for this, she thought. What if I bought into a total lie? Several months later, while working as a counselor at a summer camp, she took a young camper for a boat ride on the lake.

"Counselor, I have something to tell you," the eight-year-old girl said after a long silence. "My daddy's sleeping with me."

Erin turned to look at the child, who was staring down at the bottom of the boat, hands tightly clasped together, a look of total despair on her face. The truth hit Erin hard. "I wasn't withdrawn like that," she thought, "I wasn't depressed and hopeless. I was a happy kid." In that moment of insight she knew that she had adopted a false identity. She was not an incest survivor.

Pamela's minister stopped by her house one afternoon and listened patiently to her long story of abuse and survival. As gently as he could, he told her that he feared she had been misled and mistreated by her therapist. "Forgive me, Pamela," he said, "but I don't think there is any question that you are getting worse, not better. Whatever happened to you in the past, this is the wrong way to go about fixing it."

At first Pamela was angry and defensive, but when he left the house two hours later, she was laughing for the first time in years. "He gave me permission to end it," she understands now. A few days later she told her therapist about the meeting with her minister. The therapist, who was placing a folder in the filing cabinet, suddenly slammed the drawer shut. "How dare that man deny your pain?" she said.

Pamela believes that God answered her prayers in an unexpected way. "I never stopped praying. Sometimes when I felt like I could not go on because I was in so much agony, I would fall down on my knees and cry out to God: Protect me, help me, please give me these memories! Whenever I prayed, I always felt in my heart the answer: 'Be patient, it is about to come to an end.' I think God answered me but not in the way I expected."

Years have gone by, and Elizabeth, Pamela, Melody, Laura, and Erin are recovering their strength and their sanity. But the healing is far from over. They all mourn for the time they lost, years spent in a futile effort to discover a past that never actually existed. They grieve for the pain they caused their husbands, children, parents, and friends. They ache for their lost innocence and misplaced trust. And they blame their therapists.

"I'd cut myself off from my family because of my therapist," Erin says. "When I quit therapy two years ago, I apologized to my father, and my brother, both of whom I had accused of molesting me. They don't blame me for what happened in therapy, but I suffer from a horrible sense of guilt. Waves of sadness and anxiety overwhelm me, and I often feel as if I have no control over my life."

"This therapy has snatched years from me that I can never get back, years where I was emotionally distant from my family," Laura writes. "I have problems trusting anyone. Professionals scare me to death. My daughter and I still have no financial security and nearly lost our home. I do not have a car that runs. I am a single parent and I should have been there emotionally for her. I wasn't. All my energy, all my being, everything I had went to my therapist."

"I lost my job, my husband divorced me, I lost my family," Melody says. "I feel better emotionally since I quit therapy, but I remain disturbed and perplexed: How did this happen to me?"

Elizabeth struggles with feelings of despair and problems with self-esteem. "I feel stupid, embarrassed, and enraged. How could I have let this happen to myself, my family, and my children?"

Pamela echoes the sentiment. "How could this have happened?"

"How could a relationship with a therapist become the sole focus of my life for four long years?" Laura asks. "How could I have sold my soul to a mere human being?"

The answers to these questions continue to elude the women, and they struggle with feelings of shame, embarrassment, grief, and rage. They berate themselves for trusting so freely and openly. They swear they will never be so foolish again. And they fear for others who are innocently looking for answers to unanswerable questions.

Families, they say, are being "torn asunder" by "injudicious advice" from "misguided" and "overzealous" therapists. "Extreme gross negligence" and "unethical, unprofessional treatment" are contributing to the "senseless destruction" of families. Friends are still trapped "in the bewildering labyrinth of lies and deception," still caught up in the therapists' "paranoid delusions," still "bound by their beliefs."

Perhaps the cruelest irony of all is the fear Elizabeth, Pamela, and Laura feel for their own children. They know how easy it is for the innocent and guileless to trust in an authority figure, and they know how quickly that trust can be abused. Recently Elizabeth sat down with her twenty-year-old daughter and read through the checklist of symptoms in a popular book written for incest survivors. "You know, Mom," her daughter said with a laugh, "this list describes me and every one of my friends."

"We laughed about it then," Elizabeth says, "but that conversation frightened me. How do I know that in ten or fifteen years my daughter won't look back at her childhood and wonder: What *did* happen back there? Did I repress some memories? Maybe someday she'll call me and say, 'Mom, I've been seeing this therapist, and I suddenly recovered this memory . . .'"

Elizabeth's voice catches. She takes a deep breath. "How do I know that someday she won't accuse me?"

5

GOD'S BEARD AND THE
DEVIL'S HORNS

---

*Ours is a divided empire in which certain ideas and
emotions and actions are of God, and their opposites are of
Lucifer. It is as impossible for most men to conceive of a
morality without sin as of an earth without "sky." Since
1692 a great but superficial change has wiped out God's
beard and the Devil's horns, but the world is still gripped
between two diametrically opposed absolutes. The concept
of unity, in which positive and negative are attributes of the
same force, in which good and evil are relative, ever-
changing, and always joined to the same phenomenon—such
a concept is still reserved to the physical sciences and to the
few who have grasped the history of ideas.*

—Arthur Miller, *The Crucible*

*Mass movements can rise and spread without a belief in
God, but never without belief in a devil.*

—Eric Hoffer, *The True Believer*

Something has gone wrong with therapy, and because that something
has to do with memory, I find myself at the center of an increasingly bit-
ter and fractious controversy. On one side are the "True Believers," who
insist that the mind is capable of repressing memories and who accept
without reservation or question the authenticity of recovered memories.
On the other side are the "Skeptics," who argue that the notion of repression is purely hypothetical and essentially untestable, based as it is
on unsubstantiated speculation and anecdotes that are impossible to
confirm or deny. Some skeptics are less circumspect, referring to repression as "psychomagic," "smoke and mirrors," or just plain "balder-
dash."

The True Believers claim the moral high ground. They are, they insist, on the front line, fighting to protect children from sexual predators and assisting survivors as they struggle through the arduous healing process. The implication, unspoken but not unheard, is that anyone who refuses to join the True Believers in their quest to uncover the hidden past and to gain legitimacy for the concept of repression is either antiwoman, antichild, antiprogress, or, at the worst extreme, "dirty," i.e., a practicing pedophile or satanist.

The Skeptics attempt to evade these accusations with talk of proof, corroboration, and scientific truth-seeking, but they are not afraid to hurl some deadly grenades of their own. According to the most outspoken and vituperative Skeptics, therapists specializing in recovered memory therapy operate in a neverland of fairy dust and mythic monsters. Woefully out of touch with modern research, engaging in "crude psychiatric analysis," guilty of oversimplification, overextension, and "incestuous opinion citing," these misguided, undertrained, and overzealous clinicians are implanting false memories in the minds of suggestible clients, making "therapeutic lifers" out of their patients and ripping families apart.

This is obviously more than an academic discussion about the mind's ability to bury a memory and then bring it back into consciousness years later. The issues evoked by the simple notion of repression are among the most controversial concerns of cognitive and clinical psychology: the role of hypnosis in therapy and courts of law; the power of suggestion; social influence theory; the currently popular diagnoses of post-traumatic stress disorder (PTSD) and multiple personality disorder (MPD, labeled in the fourth edition of the American Psychiatric Association's *Diagnostic and Statistical Manual* as dissociative identity disorder, DID); the inner child and the dysfunctional family; pornography; satanic cults; rumor mills; moral crusades; alien abduction; media-inspired hysteria; and, of course, the question of political correctness.

I watch the bullets fly, and I duck for cover. My research into the malleability of memory aligns me with the Skeptics, but I am also sympathetic to the True Believers' concerns. I do not want to see a return of those days, not so very long ago, when a victim's cries for help went unheard and accusations of sexual abuse were automatically dismissed as fantasy or wish-fulfillment and shunted away into the backwaters of the public conscience. Nor can I automatically accept the idea that significant numbers of fanatical therapists are carelessly implanting memories in their clients' vulnerable minds.

I don't believe the world is so purely black and white. And so I insist on entering the gray areas of ambiguity and paradox, asking questions, listening carefully, struggling to sort out the conflicting and contentious points of view. I answer ten-page, single-spaced letters from the True

Believers; I talk to them for hours on the phone; I meet them in airport coffee shops and hotel restaurants where they tell me their stories and plead with me to come over to their side.

"Can't you see the damage you are doing?" they ask.

"All the gains the feminist movement has made in the last twenty years will be destroyed if you and others like you continue to question these memories," they insist.

"If you could only see the pain that I see, if you could only witness the intensity of my clients' anguish," a therapist pleads, "you would know that these memories arise from real, not imagined, events."

I listen and try to balance their passion with the pain I have witnessed in the stories of "the accused." A balding man in his seventies hands me a letter he recently received form his daughter's lawyer. He and his wife hold hands and wait patiently as I read through the official-looking document with "Attorneys at Law" embossed in scrolled script at the top. "Dear *Mr. Smith*," the letter begins:

> I have been retained by your daughter, who is prepared to file a lawsuit against you for severe emotional damage inflicted during her childhood. She has recently recovered memories of perverse physical and sexual abuse perpetrated upon her by you, her father, when she was a minor. We are prepared to settle this case for $250,000. If we do not hear from you within four weeks from the date of this letter, we will file a lawsuit requesting a substantially larger sum of money.

An accused mother shows me the fading color photograph of her "baby," the youngest of five children, whom she hasn't seen in more than three years. "She went to a therapist for help after she was severely beaten by her alcoholic husband," the gray-haired woman explains, cradling the thirty-year-old photograph in her arms. "While she was in therapy, she left her two young children with us. But after a few months she began to have flashbacks of her father sexually abusing her, beginning when she was just five months old. She wrote us a letter and said she never wanted to see us again. She has forbidden us to see or talk to our grandchildren."

"I'm not a baby-raper," an accused father tells me, tears running down his cheeks. "How could my daughter say these things about me? Where did these memories come from?"

I pick up the phone and call the accusing children, hoping for—what? Reconciliation?

"I can't take back the truth," the voices tell me.

"He did what he did, and he needs to admit it and ask for my forgiveness."

"I'm not responsible for my parents' pain."

"People need to believe the children."

"The world is an unsafe place."

"I only want to protect other children."

"The truth has set me free."

"Parents lie," a child-abuse advocate tells me, her face red with anger. She quotes me the oft-repeated but always shocking statistic: One in three women have been sexually abused by the time they reach the age of eighteen.

"But those statistics," I interrupt gently, "are based on a very broad definition of sexual abuse that would include grabbing at breasts or buttocks covered with clothes, stroking a leg, or snatching a sloppy, unasked-for kiss at a drunken wedding reception."

"If you doubt the statistics"—the woman's voice rises—"why don't you visit the county rape center or the battered women's shelter? These women and children are not statistics; they are real people in real pain."

I have stopped arguing statistics.

"I can't describe the pain," an accused mother tells me. "If a child dies, you learn how to deal with the grief, but every morning I wake up to this nightmare, and every night I go to bed with it, and in between nothing changes."

"I think, My God, could this have happened? Did *I* repress the memories of abusing my children?" her husband says, waiting patiently for his turn to put words to his anguish. "And then I think: How could you forget something like that, how could I have touched my child and repressed all knowledge of it? No, no, *no*. I didn't forget this because it never happened. It simply never happened."

They look pleadingly at me. *Do you understand? Do you believe me?*

One of the most heartbreaking stories I've heard was told by a thirty-year-old woman who happens to be trained as a therapist. Her story is, perhaps, more complicated than most because she was a victim of childhood sexual abuse.

I know a lot about victimization, because I have been a victim. When I was in grade school, I was sexually molested. For the record, it was not my parents. And also for the record, I have never forgotten it, not for one day. But out of a deep sense of shame, just as many other victims experience, I remained silent for more than twenty years.

Then, one day, I shared my story of my abuse experience with my sister. Eventually she began to suspect that she, too, had been abused. She had no memories, no clues, no reason, no faces, no names, not one shred of evidence. She and my other sister began discussing their ideas and suspicions. As they bounced their thoughts and feelings off each other, they began having dreams about being molested.

They accused my grandfather, my uncle, and then my father. Their allegations became more bizarre and included my mother and older brother, aunts, uncles, cousins, friends, and neighbors. My parents stood by and watched as their family went down like dominoes, and they could do nothing.

My six-year-old nephew, who had been in therapy for more than a year and was now seeing his second counselor because his first counselor couldn't find any evidence of sexual abuse, began to make some disclosures. He said that my mother, my father, and my older brother, whom he had not seen in four years, had sexually molested him. Two weeks after my parents were named, I began my career as a therapist. I worked for three days, and on the fourth day, my supervisor called me into the office to inform me that my nephew had named more people who allegedly molested him. I was among the people he named. I was fired on the spot and was investigated by the Children's Services Board and the police. The investigation took almost four months before my name was cleared.

Having been a victim of sexual abuse, I would rather be found standing with a bloody knife next to a corpse than be accused of sexually molesting a child. Not a day goes by when I don't feel the emptiness of all the things and all the people that I have lost. But in the deepest part of my soul, I know the truth—the fact of my innocence, known only for certain to me and to God. No one can take that from me.

"These people are in denial," therapists counter.

"You are being used by them," a friend tells me. "They need your expertise to give their denials some kind of legitimacy. You're just a pawn in their hands."

"Get out of this whole field before your reputation is destroyed," another friend warns.

The skeptics tell me to stop being so wishy-washy. "This is not a fence-sitting issue," they say.

"Naive patients are being led like lambs to slaughter by incompetent therapists."

"These therapists are worse than misinformed, poorly trained fools," a sociology professor fumes. "They are dangerous zealots, and they must be stopped."

Both sides tell me to watch my step. "Take very good care of yourself," a therapist writes.

"Watch yourself," a colleague warns.

"Be careful," a journalist cautions.

An anonymous letter postmarked from a mid-sized city in the Midwest accuses me of collaborating with satanists. "Please consider your work to be on the same level as those who deny the existence of the extermination camps during World War II," the letterwriter concludes.

"Is this the memory doctor who hates children?" a soft female voice inquires when I pick up the phone.

"I have an opinion about Dr. Loftus," a caller to a local radio program announces. "I think she's connected with the right-wing Christian groups who are trying to advance the cause of male patriarchy . . ."

I open the newspaper to read that a man I testified for in a child molestation case was brutally murdered. Two years earlier Kaare Sortland and his wife Judy had been charged with sexually molesting three young children at their day-care center. They were acquitted of one charge, and the judge dismissed the other two charges, noting that the children had originally denied that they were abused and only changed their minds after numerous therapy sessions and intensive interviews with interrogators.

On the night Kaare was murdered he heard noises outside his home and went outside to investigate. His wife heard him shout, "I didn't do it!" Seconds later he lay dying in the gravel driveway, shot three times in the chest with a large caliber handgun.

I remember—was it just a few years ago?—sitting in a hotel coffee shop in Washington, D.C., with Herb Spiegel, a giant in the field of psychiatry and hypnosis, and Ed Frischholz, a young cognitive psychologist with a clinical practice in Chicago. Over coffee and Danish, we were having a lively discussion about memory, the media, and the amazing rebirth of the phenomenon known as repression. I related some of the odd stories and bewildering legal cases I'd become involved in, and we talked about the media frenzy that began with *People* magazine's cover stories featuring the repressed memories of Roseanne Barr Arnold and of 1958's Miss America, Marilyn Van Derbur.

During a lull in the conversation, Ed leaned back in his chair and said. "What do you suppose is going on out there?" By "out there" he meant, of course, the real world.

We were genuinely confused and caught a bit off guard. I couldn't know then where that question would take me, how far I would wander from the ivory tower of safe, scholarly pursuits. I remember laughing a bit nervously, hugging my friends good-bye, and, as I rushed out to catch my plane, promising to mail reprints of my recent papers. It was a familiar routine. But my world and my life were already in the process of a radical and irrevocable shift.

I want to understand "what is going on out there." I live, breathe, eat, and sleep repression. I have surrendered to this obsession because I believe that what is going on in the real world is vitally important to an understanding of how memory works and how it fails. I have been willing to step out of my role as a laboratory scientist and into this messy field experiment because I believe that this is where science begins: with puzzled questions about the causes of a phenomenon and the meticulous untangling of coincidence and design.

What is repression? Where do repressed memories come from? Are they authentic relics dredged from a forgotten past, or are they "smoke and mirrors" images that develop when a suggestion is implanted in a vulnerable person's mind? Whatever the answers turn out to be, these are critically important questions. I believe that the phenomenon of repression holds up a mirror in which we can catch glimpses of our own psyche. If we are willing to look without prejudice and preconception, we may be able to discover profound truths about our need to belong, to be loved, to be accepted, to be understood, to recover.

To recover—from what? That, of course, is the question.

6

THE TRUTH THAT
NEVER HAPPENED

*When you lose someone you love—that person keeps
changing. And later you wonder, Is this the same person I
lost? Maybe you lost more, maybe less, ten thousand
different things that come from your memory or
imagination—and you do not know which is which, which
was true, which is false.*

—Amy Tan, *The Kitchen God's Wife*

My memory is the thing I forget with.

—a child's definition

In his novel *The Things They Carried,* Tim O'Brien distinguishes between two kinds of truth: story-truth and happening-truth. Happening-truth is the indisputable black-and-white reality of "at such and such a time this happened, and then this, and then that." Story-truth is the colorized version, breathing luminous life into the inert shell of the past, waking up the dead, sparking emotion, inspiring a search for meaning.

Making up stories about the past is "a way of bringing body and soul back together or a way of making new bodies for the souls to inhabit," O'Brien explains. Writing about his experiences as a soldier in Vietnam, he offers two versions, both "true," of his past.

> Here is the happening-truth. I was once a soldier. There were many bodies, real bodies with real faces, but I was young then and I was afraid to look. And now, twenty years later, I'm left with faceless responsibility and faceless grief.
>
> Here is the story-truth. He was a slim, dead, almost dainty young man of about twenty. He lay in the center of a red clay trail near the village of My Khe. His jaw was in his throat. His one eye was shut, the other eye was a star-shaped hole. I killed him.

Stories make the past come alive. We can reimagine our younger selves, feel the emotions we once felt (or were afraid to feel), battle the demons we could only run from because we were too frightened, too young, or too helpless, dream a new ending, even bring the dead back to life.

But there is a hitch. As we put meat and muscle on the bare bones of the happening-truth, we can get caught up—captured, if you will—within our own stories. We become confused about where the happening-truth leaves off and the story-truth begins, because the story-truth, which is so much more vivid, detailed and *real* than the happening-truth, becomes our reality. We begin to live our own stories.

I remember a summer many years ago. I was fourteen years old. My mother, my aunt Pearl, and I were on vacation, visiting my uncle Joe in Pennsylvania. One bright sunny morning I woke up and my mother was dead, drowned in the swimming pool.

That is the happening-truth. The story-truth is something quite different. In my mind I've returned to that scene many times, and each time the memory gains weight and substance. I can see the cool pine trees, smell their fresh tarry breath, feel the lake's algae-green water on my skin, taste Uncle Joe's iced tea with fresh-squeezed lemon. But the death itself was always vague and unfocused. I never saw my mother's body, and I could not imagine her dead. The last memory I have of my mother was her tiptoed visit the evening before her death, the quick hug, the whispered "I love you."

Thirty years later, at Uncle Joe's ninetieth birthday party, a relative informed me that I was the one who found my mother in the pool. After the initial shock—*No, it was Aunt Pearl, I was asleep, I have no memory*—, the memories began to drift back, slow and unpredictable like the crisp, piney smoke from the evening campfires. I could see myself, a thin, dark-haired girl, looking into the flickering blue-and-white pool. My mother, dressed in her nightgown, is floating face down. "Mom? Mom?" I ask the question several times, my voice rising in terror. I start screaming. I remember the police cars, their lights flashing, and the stretcher with the clean, white blanket tucked in around the edges of the body.

Of course. It all made sense. No wonder I was always haunted by the circumstances of my mother's death . . . the memory had been there all along, but I just couldn't reach it. Now, with this new information, everything fit together. Perhaps this memory, dead and now revived, could explain my obsession with memory distortion, my compulsive workaholism, my unfulfilled yearning for security and unconditional love.

For three days my memory expanded and swelled. Then, early one morning, my brother called to tell me that my uncle had checked his facts and realized he'd made a mistake: His memory, it turned out, had temporarily failed him. Now he remembered (and other relatives confirmed) that Aunt Pearl found my mother's body in the swimming pool.

After that phone call I was left with my shrunken memory, pinpricked and deflated, and a sense of wonder at the inherent credulity of even a skeptical mind. All it took was a suggestion, casually planted, and off I went on an internal snipe-hunt, eagerly searching for supporting information. When my memory was revealed as a false creation, I experienced a strange yearning for the crisp colors and narrative drive of my invented story-truth. That elaborate but completely fabricated memory comforted me with its detail and precision, its utter lack of ambiguity. At least I knew what happened that day; at least my memory had a beginning, a middle, and an end; at least it all hung together. When it was gone, all I had left were a few somber details, a lot of empty spaces, and an aching, endless grief.

Eileen Franklin, a red-headed, freckle-faced fourth-grader, and her best friend, Susan Nason, lived in Foster City, a middle-class suburb eighteen miles south of San Francisco. On September 22, 1969, five days before her ninth birthday, Susan disappeared. Two months later her body was discovered in a wooded area near Half Moon Bay Road, approximately five miles west of Foster City; her skull had been crushed by a heavy object.

For two decades the murder remained a mystery. Then, in a case that made "repression" a household word and Eileen Franklin an overnight celebrity, the police charged George Franklin, fifty-one, with Susan Nason's murder. The only evidence against him was the testimony of his daughter, who claimed that she witnessed the murder but had repressed the memory for more than twenty years.

That is the happening-truth of the Eileen Franklin story. Other facts, also indisputable, will be discovered in this story of sexual abuse, murder, and repressed memories, but they are so skillfully woven within the tapestry of a once-upon-a-time story that no one, not even Eileen Franklin, can say for sure what really happened. The "real truth" is buried with a little girl who was murdered a long time ago.

It all began in a room bright with sunshine. Eileen Franklin, a beautiful twenty-nine-year-old woman with long red hair, cuddled her two-year-old son in her arms and watched as he contentedly sucked at his bottle. Her daughter and two playmates sat on the carpeted floor at her feet, surrounded by crayons and coloring books. Every once in a while they would hum along with Raffi on the stereo system. It was a warm, sunny day in a California winter, and as Eileen looked out the window of the family room, it occurred to her that it might be warm enough to let the children swim in the pool.

"Isn't that right, Mommy?" Six-year-old Jessica's sweet, freckled face turned up to her mother for confirmation. The sunlight filtered through the curtains, highlighting Jessica's strawberry-blond hair and creating intricate patterns of light and shadow on the floor. In that moment, as she looked into her daughter's eyes, the memory returned, and Eileen Franklin's carefully ordered world plunged into chaos.

In the vivid, visual scene that flashed into her mind,* Eileen saw her best friend, eight-year-old Susan Nason, sitting on a rock in a wooded setting. Behind her, silhouetted by the sun, a man held a heavy rock above his head. Lifting her hands to protect herself as the man moved toward her, Susan glanced at Eileen, her wide eyes conveying her terror and helplessness. Seconds later the man's arms came down with tremendous force. The rock crushed Susan's skull, and Eileen covered her ears against the sound of flesh tearing and bones shattering.

In that burning flash of memory Eileen believed she had made contact with the forgotten past. A memory she had buried for two decades, almost two thirds of her life, had returned without warning or premonition to reveal the shocking truth: She had witnessed her best friend's murder. But the flashback disclosed another shocking fact: The man who murdered Susan Nason was George Franklin, Eileen's father.

For months Eileen tried to avoid the memory, but despite her efforts to push it back beneath consciousness, it kept returning and gaining detail and precision. Terrified of the emerging memories, Eileen was even more afraid that she was going crazy. She finally divulged her secret to her therapist, who assured her that she was not insane; eventually she confided in her brother, her three sisters, and her mother. In November 1989, ten months after her memory first returned, Eileen decided to tell her husband, who insisted that they call the police. After several conversations with the San Mateo County District Attorney's office, in which Eileen revealed a detailed knowledge of the murder, assistant district attorney Marty Murray decided her story was sufficiently credible to begin an investigation. Detectives Robert Morse and Bryan Cassandro were assigned to the case.

On November 25, 1989, Eileen Franklin sat down in her living room with Morse and Cassandro to relate the astonishing details of a playful outing that ended in rape and murder. Her memory was perfectly formed, filled with colors, sounds, textures, emotions, and word-for-word conversations. As she added detail to detail, faltering only occasionally, the detectives exchanged looks. As amazing as it seemed, this woman seemed to be telling the truth.

Her story began early on a Monday morning—September 22, 1969—

---

*According to Harry MacLean, author of *Once Upon a Time*, this is only one of five different versions Eileen offered to explain how the memory came back to her.

when she was in the fourth grade. George Franklin was driving Eileen and her sister Janice to school in the family's beige Volkswagen van when Eileen spotted Susan Nason. She asked her father if they could give Susan a ride. Eileen recalled that when Susan jumped into the van, her father asked Janice to get out.

George Franklin drove Eileen and Susan around for a while, and at one point pulled up to the front of their elementary school as if to drop them off. But instead he announced that they were going to play hooky. They continued driving around, eventually heading up into the hills on Half Moon Bay Road and pulling off the highway to stop in a wooded area. Eileen and Susan played outside in the brush and trees for a while and then climbed back into the van. They ran back and forth from the bucket seats in the front to the back of the van, where they bounced on a plywood platform bed covered with a mattress.

George Franklin climbed into the van and started playing with them on the bed. Eileen was in the front seat when she saw her father climb on top of Susan. "My dad pinned Susan down," Eileen told the detectives, "with her legs hanging off the edge of the bed, up toward the front seat, and he held her two arms up with both of his hands and with his elbows straddling either side of . . . her body, he began to, um . . . to rub back and forth on her, in a humping motion . . . and, um, he continued to do this, and I walked from the front seat back to where they were, and I got really scared when I looked directly at Susan." When her father pulled up Susan's dress, Eileen saw "something white underneath," perhaps a slip or an undershirt.

Eileen rolled herself up into a ball next to the bed until her father was finished with Susan. Then she and Susan, who was crying now, got out of the van. Susan walked over to "a point or a peak," where she sat down. Eileen stayed next to the car and picked up a leaf that had fallen off a tree. When she looked up, she saw the sun streaming through the trees and her father standing above Susan, holding a rock above his head, his right arm and leg forward. Susan looked up, then quickly glanced at Eileen and brought both hands to her head. The rock came crashing down. Eileen screamed when she heard the sound of rock crushing bone.

Then her father grabbed her and knocked her to the ground, pushing her face into the leaves, telling her that he would kill her if she ever told anyone, that no one would believe her anyway—they would take her away and put her in a mental home. When she stopped screaming, he pulled her up and sat her on his knee. He told her to forget all about it; it was over. He took a spade or shovel out of the van and began digging. With Eileen's help, he pulled the mattress out of the car, swearing at her for her clumsiness. She climbed into the van, put her head down, and curled up next to the seat. The sliding door closed, and they drove off. She begged her father not to leave Susan because she would be afraid, and she would get cold. But he kept driving, ignoring her frantic pleas. When they got home, Eileen went straight to her room and climbed into bed.

After she finished telling her story, the detectives questioned her closely, and she answered with more astonishing details. Were there a lot of trees around? It was "moderately dense," she answered, with three narrow trees in a "zig-zagged row" and more trees over to her right. What kind of a road had they been driving on? A dirt road, unpaved. Hadn't she mentioned something about a ring in one of her phone calls to the police? Yes, Susan wore a "silver ring with a stone in it . . . she had her hands up to her head" when the rock came crashing down.

How far away was Eileen from Susan when her father approached Susan with the rock? About twenty feet. When he was molesting Susan, did he say anything? He said "Susie." Not "Susan," Eileen added, but "Susie." Was he drinking? Yes, he was drinking a beer from "a metal can that was silver and tan and white, and had a mountain on it." What was he wearing? Tan Levi corduroy pants and a wool Pendleton shirt with a short-sleeved white crew-neck T-shirt underneath. What color was his hair? "Red going toward brown, with a little bit of gray." Did Susan say anything while George Franklin was molesting her? She said, "No"; then she said "Stop."

The interview concluded at 3:22 P.M., three hours after it began. When the tape recording was transcribed, it covered thirty-three double-spaced typewritten pages.

The detectives left Eileen Franklin's house convinced that she was telling the truth. The ring, the rock, the mattress, the wooded setting, even Susan's hands raised above her head to protect herself matched the evidence discovered at the murder scene.

"Do you believe her?" Cassandro asked Morse as they drove away.

"Yeah," Morse answered.

"I do, too," Cassandro said.

Three days later the detectives drove to George Franklin's apartment in Sacramento and informed him that they were reviewing the unsolved Susan Nason case.

"Am I a suspect?" Franklin asked. Cassandro told him he was.

"Do I need an attorney?" was his second question.

But it was Franklin's third question that cinched the matter for the detectives. "Have you talked to my daughter?" Franklin asked.

The detectives figured that an innocent man would not have asked, just like that, if he was a suspect in a murder case. Nor would Franklin have mentioned his daughter unless he feared that she might have told them something.* An innocent man would have been confused, upset,

---

*The detectives' recollections differed as to whether Franklin said the word "daughter" or "daughters." His daughter Janice had contacted the police five years earlier to discuss her suspicions that her father might have been involved in Susan Nason's murder.

frightened. But George Franklin just stood there, looking unperturbed, almost as if he had been expecting them.

On November 28, 1989, George Franklin was placed under arrest for the murder of Susan Nason. The only evidence against him was his daughter's memory.

When Doug Horngrad, George Franklin's defense attorney, called me in the summer of 1990 and asked if I would be willing to testify as an expert witness in the case, I remember thinking: This is the most bizarre story I have ever encountered. Where was the evidence? In murder cases you can usually depend on some kind of hard evidence—a bloodstain, a semen smear, the murder weapon—or on a damning array of "soft" circumstantial evidence. But this case rested solely on the credibility of a woman's memory for an event she had witnessed twenty years earlier, when she was just eight years old—a memory that had apparently been buried without a trace and was only recently unearthed. How reliable could such a memory be? How could prosecutors build a case against a man with this twenty-year-old uncorroborated memory as the only evidence?

The prosecution and defense teams would argue the two basic possibilities, Horngrad explained. Prosecutors would present their case, based on the theory that the memory was authentic; this, if accepted by the jury, meant that George Franklin was guilty. Defense attorneys would try to prove that the memory was inauthentic, a confusion of fact (Susan Nason was murdered) and fantasy (Eileen Franklin witnessed the murder). My job as an expert witness would be to explain the basic processes of memory formation and distortion. If Eileen's memory was false, where did those colorful and essentially accurate details come from? How did Eileen know all those facts about the murder scene and why was she so confident and convincing when she described what happened that day?

"Did she reveal facts to the police that could only have been known to an eyewitness?" I asked Horngrad.

"Every detail she gave the detectives can be found in the newspaper articles that appeared at the time of Susan's disappearance and two months later when her body was discovered," he said. He agreed to send me the newspaper clippings and Eileen's preliminary statement so that I could compare the details in her statement with the facts reported in the local media.

The prosecutors were arguing that Eileen knew details about the murder that she could not possibly have known unless she was an eyewitness. If the defense could prove that the critical details in her story—specifically, the rock, the ring, and the mattress—were widely reported in the media and thus available to anyone who read the papers, watched television, or listened to others who knew about the murder, then Eileen wasn't giving the police anything they didn't already know. The case against George Franklin would rest solely on the inferences and implications contained in "memories" that Eileen admitted she didn't remember until the moment she looked into her daughter's eyes and "saw" the murder scene vividly recreated. If all the details in her memory could also be found in published reports about the murder, then no solid evidence existed proving that George Franklin was the murderer . . . and how could you convict a man of murder without any proof?

The newspaper articles were revealing. The details Eileen described in her preliminary statement matched almost perfectly with the facts reported about the murder. Three months after Susan disappeared, her body was discovered under a mattress in dense underbrush at the bottom of a steep embankment on a highway pulloff above Crystal Springs Reservoir. Her skull had been crushed, and traces of blood appeared on a three-pound rock found at the site. She wore a blue print dress, white socks, and brown saddle shoes. A silver brocade ring that Susan wore on her right hand was smashed, and the stone was missing; it was later discovered by a search team.

These facts were reported in newspaper articles published when Susan's body was discovered. But several of these widely reported details were not completely accurate. Susan actually wore two rings: a silver Indian ring on her right hand and a gold ring with a topaz on her left. One newspaper account confused the two rings, stating that the silver ring contained the stone; twenty years later, in her preliminary statement to detectives Morse and Cassandro, Eileen made the same error, recalling a crushed ring containing a small stone on Susan's right hand.

Another point of confusion was the mattress covering the body. One newspaper report mentioned a mattress, while another correctly identified it as a box spring (which, it turned out, was too big to fit in the back of George Franklin's van). By the time of the preliminary hearing, six months after her original statement to detectives Morse and Cassandro, Eileen changed her description from a "mattress" to a "thing": "He was crouched over Susan's body, putting rocks on her. I thought I saw him put this thing over her body."

"Putting rocks on her" was another detail that fit the known and published facts about the murder scene. A rock was discovered in the folds of Susan's dress and a larger rock was discovered next to the body. According to pathologists, either rock could have been used as a murder weapon. Why didn't Eileen mention "putting rocks on her" earlier, when she gave her detailed statement to Detectives Morse and Cassandro?

In the preliminary hearing Eileen also changed the time of the murder from mid-morning to late-afternoon. George Franklin could not have picked up Susan Nason in the morning, as Eileen first reported, because Susan had gone to school that morning. She came home from school sometime after three P.M., said hello to her mother, who was sewing a dress for her upcoming birthday party, and asked if she could walk to a classmate's house to return some tennis shoes she had left at school. Susan left her home around three-fifteen P.M. Several neighbors remember seeing her walking along on the sidewalk.

About four or four-thirty P.M. Margaret Nason began to worry about her daughter, who was always so responsible and careful to inform her mother about her whereabouts (and who never missed her afternoon snack). Margaret rode her bike around the neighborhood, looking for Susan, and as time slipped by and her daughter was nowhere to be found, she became frantic. Around eight P.M. the Nasons called the police.

Sometime after her initial interview with Detectives Morse and Cassandro, Eileen altered the time of day to fit with the known facts about the murder. The more she thought about her father's silhouette with the sun behind him, she explained, the more she realized that the murder could not have taken place in the morning. Susan must have been murdered late in the afternoon, Eileen decided, because in her mind she could see the sun slanting through the trees at a low angle. While she claimed later that her memory was modified in late November or December 1989, she didn't inform the prosecutor about the alteration until May 9, 1990 just two weeks before the preliminary hearing.

Eileen also changed her mind about Janice being in the van. She originally told the detectives that Janice was in the Volkswagen van when her father stopped to pick up Susan, and that when Susan climbed in, George Franklin made Janice get out. But in her May 9 statement to the prosecutor, Eileen against revised her memory, claiming that she remembered seeing Janice in an open field near the place where her father stopped to pick up Susan.

"The more I concentrated on it and tried to be certain of how the event exactly happened," Eileen testified in the preliminary hearing, "the less certain I felt about whether Janice had been in the van or out of the van. And the less certain I felt about it, the more I tried to concentrate on it and remember it. After—over a period, I would say several weeks, that I just—it seemed more and more clear to me that I remembered seeing her outside the van, and that I am just unclear of—as to whether she was inside first or what. I tend to think she was outside. And I don't know why I thought she was inside before."

All these additions and subtractions in Eileen's account of the murder confirm what researchers know to be true about the malleability of memory. Over time, memory changes, and the more time that passes, the more changes and distortions one can expect. As new events intervene, the mind incorporates the additional facts and details, and the original memory gradually metamorphoses.

Eileen's memory seemed absolutely normal to me. She clearly remembered her best friend, and she never forgot that Susan had been brutally murdered. But what happened over the next twenty years to those two basic, unforgettable facts? It is at least plausible that Eileen incorporated into her memory facts gleaned from newspaper and television reports and added more details picked up from casual conversations, creating a story that made sense. According to this theory, Eileen's mind took the scattered facts of a senseless murder, mixed them with her fantasies and fears, tossed in rumors and innuendo, and arrived at the mistaken conclusion that she had been in the woods watching when her father raped and then murdered her best friend. Her mind adorned the happening-truth with the vivid details, narrative flow, and moral clarity of the story-truth.

The prosecutors argued that this elaborate "memory" was an accurate version of the past, and they invoked the mechanism of repression to explain why Eileen forgot about her part in the murder and then twenty years later recalled exactly what happened. Changes and inconsistencies in Eileen's story should not be construed as evidence that the memory itself was flawed, they reasoned, but taken as simple proof that this was an old but reliable memory in need of a few repairs.

When did this whole idea of repression first come up? In November 1989, when Eileen called the police and gave her preliminary statement to Detectives Morse and Cassandro, she never mentioned a "repressed" memory. In fact, when the detectives asked her why she was coming forward to accuse her father now, twenty years after the murder, she explained that her memory had recently become more vivid, that it was "not as vague." On the phone with prosecutor Marty Murray a few weeks later, she claimed that the details of the murder had come back to her in the course of intensive therapy. In taped telephone conversations she mentioned several times that she had kept the memory a secret because her father had threatened to kill her if she told anyone about the murder.

But at the end of December 1989, Eileen told prosecutor Murray that the memory had only recently returned to consciousness. Soon after that conversation she gave two newspaper interviews in which she explained that the memory of the murder had been "blocked out" and came back to her suddenly in a "flashback." She told a reporter from the San Jose *Mercury* that she had forgotten the crime just a few days after Susan Nason was murdered and didn't remember anything about the murder until she began having these flashbacks. She recalled that as a child she would walk past the Nason house and feel her body suddenly veer away (a "body memory"); that peculiar physical reaction, she explained, didn't make any sense to her until the entire contents of the repressed memory returned to consciousness.

Eileen told a *Los Angeles Times* reporter that the memory of the murder had been "blocked out" immediately after it happened; only after she started having flashbacks of the murder, including an image of her father standing above Susan Nason with a rock in his hands, did she decide to call the police.

What triggered the flashbacks? Eileen's brother, George Junior, had an interesting story to tell. Eileen called her brother in August 1989, inviting him to visit. Soon after he arrived, Eileen confided that she was in therapy and had been hypnotized. The next day she told her brother that while she was under hypnosis she had visualized her father killing Susan Nason. In September 1989, Eileen told her mother about the memory, confiding that it had come back to her during a hypnotherapy session.

Just a few months later, Eileen had a different story to tell. After her father was arrested and charged with the murder, Eileen called her brother to ask if he had talked to the defense team. When he admitted that he had, she quickly changed her story about being hypnotized and asked for his help in confirming the new version. The memory had come back to her in a regular therapy session, she explained; she had never been hypnotized. Please, she begged her brother, if the police call, don't mention anything about hypnosis.

Horngrad believed that sometime in the fall of 1990 Eileen had learned that her memory would not be admissible in court if it had been elicited while she was under hypnosis. He figured that either Eileen's mother, who was a practicing attorney, or a Los Angeles lawyer she had consulted before calling the police, filled her in on the legalities. California, like many other states, will not permit testimony based on memories recovered under hypnosis because of the overwhelmingly persuasive research evidence showing that hypnosis creates a highly suggestible state in which memories can be enhanced, solidified, or even implanted in a person's mind.

In the preliminary hearing, held in May 1990, Eileen admitted that she lied to her brother and her mother about being hypnotized. She had never been hypnotized, she said, and only told her family that hypnosis was involved because she wanted them to believe her. Apparently she had believed at the time that hypnosis would add credibility to the story. Eileen also denied a story told by her older sister, Kate. Kate testified that Eileen had called her one day early in November 1989, just weeks before Eileen contacted the police, and told her that the memory of Susan's murder came to her in a dream. She had been having nightmares, she told Kate, and had decided to go back into therapy. Soon afterward she had a dream in which she saw her father murder Susan Nason.

Was Eileen's mental picture of the murder a flashback, a dream, or a hypnotically induced memory? None of the above, the prosecution insisted. It was a repressed memory, pure and simple. "Repressed" means that the memory was not simply forgotten, nor was it deliberately kept secret. Because of the traumatic nature of the murder, Eileen's mind reacted by removing the memory from her conscious mind. The memory disappeared without a trace and was sealed off from consciousness for two decades. If someone had said to her at any time in those twenty years, "Eileen, is there any chance you were there when Susan was killed?" or more pointedly, "Did your father murder your best friend?" she would have reacted with shock and disbelief, denying the possibility without even a flicker of memory disturbing her conviction. The memory was gone, as good as dead, all vital signs expired; there was not even a weak heartbeat to send up shivers of potential life.

"Repression" . . . The word whispers of dark secrets and buried treasures, of rooms filled with cobwebs and dust, with a strange unearthly rustling in the corners. Repression is the most haunting and romantic of concepts in the psychology of memory: *Something happens,* something so shocking and frightful that the mind short-circuits and the normal workings of memory go seriously awry. An entire memory, or perhaps a jagged piece of a memory, is split off and hidden away. Where? No one knows, but we can imagine the crackle of electricity and the blue sparks of neurons firing as a memory is pushed underground, into the furthest and most inaccessible corners of consciousness. There it stays for years, decades, perhaps forever, isolated and protected in a near-dead, dormant state. Removed from the fever of consciousness, it sleeps.

Time passes. And then *something happens.* Sunlight slices through trees. A black leather belt lies curled up, snakelike, on the floor. A word or a phrase is dropped, or a strange but familiar silence falls. And suddenly the memory rises from the deep, a perfectly preserved entity drifting up from the still waters of a once-frozen pond.

What causes the glaciated surface of a mind to melt, permitting a buried memory to emerge into consciousness? Where had the memory been hiding all those years? And how do we know that this resuscitated memory, while it looks real, sounds real, and feels real, is not some contaminated mixture of fact and fiction, dream and imagination, fear and desire?

When I began to search through journal articles and textbooks for answers to these questions, I was confronted with an eerie silence. It was as if repression itself had gone to sleep in the nearly 100 years since Freud first proposed the theory of a defense mechanism that protects the conscious mind from painful feelings and experiences. I looked through the second edition of Roberta Klatzky's *Human Memory* and found no entry in the index for repression. Eugene Zeckmeister and Stanley Nyberg's textbook on human memory also failed to mention repression in the index.

I finally found some information about repression in Alan Baddeley's book on human memory. Baddeley, one of Britain's most distinguished memory researchers, discusses Sigmund Freud's conviction that emotions have the power to block memory. He cites the case of a twenty-year-old woman (treated by Pierre Janet, a contemporary of Freud's) who suffered from memory disturbances caused by her mother's long illness and eventual death. The question of choice and deliberate avoidance seems crucial to Baddeley, who concludes that "the extent to which the patient is totally unable to access the stressful memories, and to what extent he/she chooses not to is very hard to ascertain."

Baddeley argues that while there is evidence for the powerful effect of emotion on memory, the evidence for repression in everyday life is "rather less strong," and that "attempts to demonstrate repression under experimental conditions . . . have been surprisingly difficult to produce." While many clinicians insist that repression is a valid phenomenon, "such exhortations tell us more about the beliefs of the exhorter than the validity of the claim. If [someone] sees evidence of repression all around him, then perhaps like beauty it is in the eye of the beholder?"

I turned to the scholarly clinical field and searched through several well-known books on incest and trauma. In psychiatrist Judith Lewis Herman's highly acclaimed *Father-Daughter Incest* the term "repression" wasn't anywhere to be found in either the index or the text. I did find some references to repression in Alice Miller's classic work on the effects of childhood trauma, *The Drama of the Gifted Child.* Miller focuses on the need to discover the truth about our lives, which "remains hidden in the darkness of the past." However, Miller strongly implies that we discover this truth not by searching for literal, historical memories but by uncovering the intense needs and emotions that traumatized children block off from consciousness because they live in an unsympathetic and uncaring environment. In the introduction to her book, she writes: "Experience has taught us that we have only one enduring weapon in our struggle against mental illness: the emotional discovery and emotional acceptance of the truth in the individual and unique history of our childhood." And in the final pages she concludes: "When the patient has truly emotionally worked through the history of his childhood and thus regained his sense of being alive, then the goal of the analysis has been reached."

It seemed fair to conclude from Alice Miller's writings that whatever "truth" we discover in our repressed or unconscious memories is inherently and subjectively emotional. Sigmund Freud, who introduced the idea of repression into the psychoanalytical literature, also emphasized the emotional content of the repressed material. Freud viewed repression as a defense mechanism that serves to repudiate or suppress emotions, needs, feelings or intentions in order to prevent psychic "pain" (variously experienced as trauma, anxiety, guilt, or shame). In a paper published in 1915, Freud described the phenomenon of repression clearly and concisely: "The essence of repression lies simply in the function of rejecting and keeping something out of consciousness."

Elizabeth von R., one of Freud's most famous patients, has been cited as a classic example of repression. In her sessions with Freud, Elizabeth experienced excruciating physical pain whenever she came close to expressing an unconscious desire (eventually retrieved into consciousness) that her beloved sister would die so that she could marry her brother-in-law. Freud compared the process of uncovering the repressed ideas and desires to a "layer by layer" excavation of a "buried city." But such psychological "digs" into the territory of repressed memories were destined to proceed slowly, for with each shovelful of earth that Freud removed, his patients would struggle desperately to fill the hole back up again. The buried feelings and experiences, in Freud's imagery, were "stratified concentrically around the pathogenic nucleus . . . the deeper we go the more difficult it becomes for the emerging memories to be recognized, till near the nucleus we come upon memories which the patient disavows even in reproducing them."

Dreams and forbidden desires were viewed as signals of the impending arrival of repressed emotional material. The Wolfman, another of Freud's famous cases, suddenly remembered being seduced by his sister after some premonitory dreams. And Miss Lucy R.'s repressed sexual feelings for her employer apparently contributed to her hysterical symptoms. In a paper published in 1893 Freud described a conversation with Miss Lucy:

> "But if you knew you loved your employer why didn't you tell me?"
>
> "I didn't know—or rather I didn't want to know. I wanted to drive it out of my head and not think of it again, and I believe latterly I have succeeded."

Freud used the case of Lucy R. to demonstrate his hypothesis that "an idea must be intentionally repressed from consciousness" for hysterical symptoms to develop. Thus, according to the original Freudian definition, repression can be an intentional, deliberate process of pushing emotions, ideas, or thoughts out of the conscious mind.

I wondered what Freud would have to say about Eileen Franklin, who claimed a different sort of repressed memory—one that was driven from her mind by completely *unconscious* mechanisms. Did her reports of a twenty-year memory loss for a severely traumatic event fit logically into Freud's theory, or did her case represent a modern-day deviation from his speculative musings on the workings of the unconscious mind? As I continued searching for information on repression, I found a fascinating article titled "Let's Not Sweep Repression Under the Rug: Toward a Cognitive Psychology of Repression," by Matthew Erdelyi. Erdelyi claims that the original Freudian conception of repression as a potentially deliberate, intentional act has been completely neglected by modern-day theorists and clinicians who insist that repression always operates as an unconscious mechanism of defense.

"An almost universal consensus has emerged on this issue. . . . It is believed that the mechanisms of defense, without exception, operate unconsciously. So widespread is this belief, that by now most theorists treat the notion not as a hypothesis but as an integral component of the definition of the phenomenon."

Erdelyi conducted an informal survey of undergraduates to find out how common the experience of repression (conscious or unconscious) is perceived to be. Eighty-five of eighty-six college-age subjects reported using "conscious repression," defined as "excluding painful memories or thoughts from consciousness for the purpose of avoiding psychological discomfort." Furthermore, most of these subjects could recall the specific *unconscious* mechanisms used to reject the material from consciousness; in Erdelyi's words, "they were now conscious of previous unconscious use of defense techniques." Erdelyi concluded that there is "almost universal support for repression."

So, I thought, what have we got here? It seemed to me that what Freud intended as a free-ranging metaphor (the poetic notion of emotions and experiences buried in a secret, inaccessible compartment of the mind) had been captured and literalized. Freud used repression as an allegory, a fanciful story used to illustrate the unknowable and unfathomable reaches of the human mind. We moderns, confused perhaps by the metaphorical comparison and inclined to take things literally, imagined we could hold the unconscious and its contents in our hands. Whole memories, some argued, could be buried for years and then exhumed without any aging or decay of the original material.

While Freud was fascinated by the complex interactions of sexual and aggressive feelings, wishes, fantasies, and impulses of childhood and their ability to exert a pathogenic effect in adulthood (always emphasizing the repressed *emotional* content of the earlier experiences), modern-day analysts had gone on an expedition for literal, historical truth. We had captured a butterfly of an idea, pinned it to the wall, and analyzed it to death. No wonder some of us were wondering why it wouldn't fly.

But the serious problems began when scholarly speculation about repression was reformatted and reinterpreted by clinicians writing for a mass market audience. Thus, in E. Sue Blume's *Secret Survivors*, repression is confidently defined as a stockroom of unconscious behaviors common to all incest survivors:

The incest survivor develops a repertoire of behaviors designed to preserve the secret . . . these behaviors are not calculated or even conscious. They become automatic and, over the years, almost part of her personality. She denies that she was abused by repressing the memory of her trauma. This is the primary manifestation of "the secret": incest becomes the secret she keeps even from herself. *Repression in some form is virtually universal among survivors.*

More than half a million copies have been sold of *The Courage to Heal: A Guide for Women Survivors of Child Sexual Abuse* (called the bible of the incest-recovery movement). In the preface co-author Ellen Bass notifies readers that she is not "academically educated as a psychologist" and "none of what is presented here is based on psychological theories." Having offered that caveat the authors go on to give specific advice regarding repressed memories. "If you are unable to remember any specific instances [of abuse] . . . but still have a feeling that something abusive happened to you, it probably did." This gross generalization is followed by a section titled "But I Don't Remember," in which the reader is told that her feelings can be taken as proof that "something happened" even if the memories have not yet surfaced.

> You may think you don't have memories, but often as you begin to talk about what you do remember, there emerges a constellation of feelings, reactions and recollections that add up to substantial information. To say "I was abused," you don't need the kind of recall that would stand up in a court of law. . . .

The idea that memories of incest begin with vague feelings or images that eventually coalesce into full-fledged reminiscences is repeated in another popular book for incest survivors, *Reclaiming Our Lives: Hope for Adult Survivors of Incest.* Authors Carol Poston and Karen Lison describe the experience of a woman with "repressed memories" of incest who dreamed about a little girl ice-skating on a frozen river. In her dream, the woman tried desperately to warn the child that monsters and snakes were making their way through the ice to devour the little girl. But, as often happens in dreams, she was powerless to warn her. A few days later the client began to remember incestuous experiences from her own childhood. Now that she had "a trusted relationship with a therapist and a survivors' group that would understand and accept her," the memories began to flow. "Women usually do not make an immediate incest connection," the authors conclude this story. "They may not recall for years that the incest occurred: memories have an uncanny way of coming only when the survivor can deal with them."

In *Adult Children of Abusive Parents,* Steven Farmer links the severity of the earlier abuse with the ability to repress the memory. "The more severe the abuse, the more likely you were to repress any conscious recollection of it." He offers several exercises designed to help readers "lift the lid of repression."

As I read through these popular incest-recovery books, I found it difficult to escape the conclusion that if something *feels* real, it *is* real, and hang the fact that you don't have any memories (let alone proof). As with Freud, feelings and emotions are what count, but in this new twist on an old theme the feelings are important *because they function as symptoms* indicating that somewhere in the unconscious a memory of abuse lies dormant, waiting to be discovered. If you (the reader of these books) think you might have been abused and you feel the rage and grief that so often accompany memories of abuse, then you are encouraged to blindly feel your way along the rope hold of these emotions, rappelling down the slippery slope of the unconscious in search of hidden and long-forgotten memories.

If a patient persists in not remembering, therapists suggest numerous creative techniques to jog their memories. *The Courage to Heal Workbook,* for example, includes a written exercise for people who think they might have been abused but have not been able to locate the memories. Feelings of shame or humiliation are accessed in an attempt to trigger the forgotten memories of abuse.

> If you don't remember what happened to you, write about what you do remember. Or write about whatever you can remember that comes closest to sexual abuse—the first time you felt ashamed or humiliated, for instance . . . Start with what you have. When you utilize that fully, you usually get more.

Even scholarly writers suggest "guessing" as a means of accessing buried memories. "When the client does not remember what happened to her, the therapist's encouragement to 'guess' or 'tell a story' will help the survivor regain access to the lost material," writes therapist Karen Olio. Olio describes the experience of one of her clients who suspected that she had been sexually abused but could not recall any specific incidents. At a social gathering she became extremely anxious in the presence of a three-year-old child. She didn't know why she was so upset although she was conscious of a desire to tell the little girl to keep her dress down. When encouraged in therapy to tell a story about what was going to happen to the child, the client ultimately related with tears and trembling her first memories of abuse. She used the story, in her therapist's words, to "bypass her cognitive inhibitions and express the content of the memory." Later she "integrated the awareness that she was indeed the little girl in the story."

The curative power of memory is often emphasized in these cases of repressed memories. In one remarkable case, Betsey, a thirty-eight-year-old woman with a history of bulimia, alcohol abuse, and episodes of self-mutilation, was hospitalized after a drunken rampage. At first she denied that she had been abused as a child, but after six months of therapy, she began to "recall" her father pushing her to her knees to perform oral sex. She also remembered her father's threats to "cut her arms off" if she ever told anyone about the abuse. Her therapist believed the self-mutilation was an enactment of past trauma; as her abuse memories pushed their way into consciousness. Betsey gradually recovered and stopped mutilating herself. "Regaining the memories of her childhood incest and discussing them with another human being has improved this woman's capacity of intimately knowing and relating," the therapist concluded.

Some therapists seem willing to believe in the authenticity of recently unlocked memories, no matter how bizarre they may appear on the surface. In the nonfiction best-seller *Michelle Remembers,* Michelle Smith recounts her psychotherapy sessions in which she was regularly hypnotized; after several months she began to have "memories" of being imprisoned at age five by her mother and a fiendish assemblage of satanists. Michelle remembered bloody rituals led by a man called "Malachi," a sadistic nurse dressed in black, and dozens of chanting and dancing adults who tore live kittens apart with their teeth, cut fetuses in half and then rubbed the dismembered bodies on her stomach, penetrated her with a crucifix, and forced her to urinate and defecate on the Bible. When Michelle recalled these and other incidents of ritual abuse, she developed physical symptoms called "body memories," including a rash on her neck that she and her therapist interpreted as the imprint of Satan's tail. A black-and-white close-up photograph of Michelle's rash is included in the book, along with this graphic description: "Whenever she relived the moments when Satan had his burning tail wrapped around her neck, a sharply defined rash appeared in the shape of the spade-like tip of his tail."

These popular books rarely warn the reader that it might be advisable to seek verification or outside corroboration of de-repressed memories. In fact, the strong theme that emerges in the popular literature is that requests for proof only revictimize the patient. If the patient expresses doubts about her memories, the therapist is encouraged to identify the events as real and convince the patient of the historical reality of the abuse. No matter how outlandish the memories or how serious and potentially damaging the accusations arising from these memories, the survivor is told that she is not responsible for providing proof or validation of her memories. As Bass and Davis write in *The Courage to Heal:*

> If your memories of the abuse are still fuzzy, it is important to realize that you may be grilled for details . . . You are not responsible for proving that you were abused.

The problem for both the accuser and the accused is how to determine whether a recovered memory is a reasonably accurate representation of past reality, a mixture of fact and fiction, or a complete fabrication. Psychology, despite its many accomplishments in the last hundred years or so, has not devised a method for reading minds; in the absence of hard evidence, we simply do not know how to ascertain absolute "truth." Perhaps that is why Sigmund Freud, Alice Miller, and other theoretical psychologists forcefully and repeatedly emphasize the *emotional* story-truth of repressed memories rather than their historical happening-truth.

But in the incest-sensitive climate of the 1970s and 1980s, well-meaning clinicians began to advocate a "leap of faith" approach, presuming the accuracy of a recovered memory in order to foster the all-important therapeutic atmosphere of trust. In one scholarly paper published in 1979, for example, authors Alvin Rosenfeld et al. acknowledge the difficulty of assessing whether a patient's report of incest is fantasy or reality but suggest that therapists err on the side of belief because disbelief may drive some patients out of therapy and possibly into psychosis. While "it is difficult to know whether a report of molestation is a memory, a fantasy, or a memory of a fantasy," the authors write, therapists should be "open-minded," for "there may be more danger of dismissing reality as fantasy than vice-versa." By presuming the accuracy of a patient's report of incest, the therapist fosters "an atmosphere of trust in which the accusation can be explored thoroughly and renounced if untrue."

In clinical situations, when a patient talks privately and confidentially with a therapist, determining whether a memory is real or imagined may be relatively unimportant. If patients are cured, many therapists would argue, it doesn't really matter whether they have worked through traumatic realities or traumatic fantasies. If a memory is not real but seems real to the person remembering it, then who can say that it is not, in some basic and critical sense, real? Every personally felt experience has its emotional story-truth, which cannot and should not be denied or minimized.

But when a memory suddenly and explosively resurfaces after nearly two decades, with colors, textures, sounds, smells, and emotions remarkably preserved, and a man is charged with murder based on the details thus revealed, then the clinical import of that memory must at least share the stage with its legal ramifications. Eileen Franklin, overwhelmed by uncontrollable reminiscences, kept "seeing" the rape and murder of her best friend, reliving the horror over and over again in her mind. With the case fast approaching the courtroom and a man's freedom hanging in the balance, it became imperative that someone ask the skeptic's question: Was this abundant and terrifying memory a nightmare, was it madness, or was it a genuine breakthrough from the remote past?

Dr. Lenore Terr was scheduled to testify as an expert witness for the prosecution in the Franklin trial. I was curious to see how this psychiatrist and clinical professor who works with traumatized children (she became famous for her work with the kidnapped children of Chowchilla, California) would explain the concept of repression. I ordered her recently published book *Too Scared to Cry* and read it from cover to cover. What I found surprised me.

While I couldn't find a definition or description of the term "repression" anywhere in the book (as is the case with most scholarly publications on trauma and incest, the term didn't even appear in the index), I did find a definition for "suppression," which Terr characterized as "entirely conscious and thus not a defense mechanism." By implication, then, was repression (defined by Freud and accepted by most modern clinicians as a defense mechanism) entirely unconscious? It didn't seem that way. Terr clearly and consistently stated that sudden, fast events overwhelm a child's defenses and create "brilliant, overly clear verbal memories" that are "far clearer, more detailed, and more long-lasting than . . . ordinary memory." Only when a child is subjected to *continuing* trauma or terror are the defense mechanisms stimulated, interfering with memory formation, storage, and retrieval.

How did this trauma theory apply to Eileen Franklin's memory? It seemed clear to me that Eileen's experience would fall in the "sudden, fast event" category of trauma which, according to Terr, would leave a permanent and indelible imprint in her mind. Terr had quite a lot to say about the nature of traumatic memory, and her theories seemed to confirm that if Eileen Franklin had witnessed her best friend's murder, she would have remembered it. "Horrible experience creates permanent mental pictures," Terr writes.

> . . . traumatic remembrance is far clearer, more detailed, and more long-lasting than is ordinary memory . . . Traumatized children do not ordinarily deny the single, shocking event . . .

I was particularly struck by Terr's comparison of the traumatized mind to a camera fitted up with expensive lenses and corrosion-resistant film:

> The memory of trauma is shot with higher intensity light than is ordinary memory. And the film doesn't seem to disintegrate with the usual half-life of ordinary film. Only the best lenses are used, lenses that will pick up every last detail, every line, every wrinkle, and every fleck.

This analysis of memory didn't square at all with my work in the laboratory on the corrosive effects of stress and trauma. I've conducted more than twenty of these studies, most of which support the theory that stressful experiences eat away at memory. Borrowing Terr's camera analogy, let's assume that our memory system operates like an expensive

(stress-induced)

camera with high-performance lenses and nondisintegrating film. Let's further assume that lighting conditions are always optimum. What happens when we are under stress? Maybe we forget to close the film compartment, and as a result the entire roll is fogged. Or perhaps we rewind the film and forget to remove it, shooting the roll all over again and creating double exposures. Or we neglect to remove the lens cap. Or our hands tremble so violently that the images appear blurred and indistinct. Or we focus in on a central detail—a gun, for example—retaining that memory while forgetting many other aspects of the experience. My point is that no matter how good your memory equipment is, if you're under stress you often forget how to use it properly.

The prosecution would argue that my laboratory findings have little to say about real-life occurrences. In a psychology experiment we can't kidnap or torture our subjects. We can't point a loaded gun at them or ask them to lift a two-thousand-pound car that is crushing the life out of their child. We can't threaten them with loss of love or subject them to constant, unrelieved fear for their lives. The traumatic situations we induce in the laboratory are mild when compared to many real life traumas.

But experimental psychologists can and do study the basic processes of memory formation, storage, and retrieval, and our documented, replicable findings can be generalized to real-life situations. Furthermore, it seemed clear to me that no matter which side you chose to believe in— my experimental studies showing that stress can reduce the accuracy and detail of memories, or Terr's clinical cases showing that traumatic events create "permanent mental pictures"—both argued against the validity and accuracy of Eileen Franklin's repressed memory. If stress (and, of course, time) cause memory to decay and deteriorate, why did Eileen Franklin's memory come back to her twenty years later in such astonishing, full-color detail? If, as Lenore Terr argued, traumatic events create clear, detailed, and long-lasting memories and if, as she also argued, traumatized children do not "deny-away" their memories, how was Eileen able to push the memory of Susan Nason's murder out of her conscious mind for nearly twenty years?

More confused than ever, I called defense attorney Doug Horngrad. "Do you have any idea how Dr. Terr plans to explain away her own recently published theories about permanent, indelible memories in traumatized children?" I asked.

He did have an idea, for Dr. Terr had recently refined her theory. In a soon-to-be-published scholarly paper she delineated two distinct types of psychic traumas: Type I trauma and Type II trauma. Type I trauma was a short, single event or experience; this allegedly led to brilliant, accurate, and indelible memories. Type II trauma was caused by multiple incidents or continuing, ongoing events. Repressed memory entered the picture in this second type of traumatic experience for, Terr theorizes, children subjected to repeated abuses would learn to anticipate the abuse and defend themselves by dissociating and repressing the memory. In this way they avoided the pain of remembering the ongoing trauma and discovered a way to function "normally" in a perpetually stressful and abusive environment.

The prosecution, Horngrad continued, would attempt to match these theories to Eileen Franklin's story. They would argue that the single traumatic event in Eileen's life (witnessing Susan Nason's murder) took place within an ongoing, everyday series of traumatic events involving physical, emotional, and sexual abuse in the Franklin household. Prosecutors were lining up witnesses who would testify that George Franklin had abused his wife and children; this evidence would create a plausible scenario to explain why Eileen had repressed the memory of her best friend's murder.

The Type I and Type II theories were certainly intriguing as hypothetical material, but I was not aware of any formal study to support the idea that one type of traumatic memory could be encased and subsumed within another type so that the normal mechanisms of memory for the first type are superseded by the mechanisms commonly used in the second type. As I tried to reason through this theoretical maze, I began to understand that there was no logical way to win this particular argument. My laboratory studies and experimental findings were a thin paper shield against the twin-headed dragon of traumatic memory. How could anyone hope to fight such a creature?

I was even more disturbed by the prosecution's plan to link the alleged physical, sexual, and emotional abuse in the Franklin household with Susan Nason's murder. Not one piece of forensic or scientific evidence connected George Franklin to Susan Nason's murder. But if the prosecution could inject the idea into the jury's collective mind that George Franklin was a monster who abused his own daughters, then it was not that great a leap to imagine that he could have sexually abused Susan Nason, murdered her in order to protect himself, and then threatened to kill the only eyewitness, his own daughter, if she breathed a word of what had happened.

Was George Franklin a wife beater, a child abuser, and a general brute? In the context of this trial, the answer to that question didn't matter, because Franklin had not been accused of emotional, sexual, or physical abuse. He was charged with murdering an eight-year-old girl. A pedophile may be a monster—but that doesn't necessarily make him a murderer.

More disturbed than ever, I went back to Terr's book. Searching for the logic underlying her argument, I was diverted by some fascinating remarks about the horror writer Stephen King. After reading King's books and analyzing his interviews, Dr. Terr identified two major traumas in his life: the disappearance of his father when he was two years old and a train accident that occurred when he was just four. She believes that these traumas continue to affect him ("Steven King still suffers from the effects of a traumatic event in his childhood") as evidenced by his continuing symptoms: nightmares, fears, a "sense of futurelessness," and "active denial."

The denial is inferred from King's repeated insistence that he doesn't remember anything about the train accident. Here is his version of the trauma from his book, *Danse Macabre:*

> The event occurred when I was barely four, so perhaps I can be excused for remembering [my mother's] story of it but not the actual event.
>
> According to Mom, I had gone off to play at a neighbor's house—a house that was near a railroad line. About an hour after I left I came back (she said), as white as a ghost. I would not speak for the rest of that day; I would not tell her why I'd not waited to be picked up or phoned that I wanted to come home; I would not tell her why my chum's mom hadn't walked me back but had allowed me to come alone.
>
> It turned out that the kid I had been playing with had been run over by a freight train while playing on or crossing the tracks (years later, my mother told me that they had picked up the pieces in a wicker basket). My mom never knew if I had been near him when it happened, or if it had occurred before I even arrived, of if I had wandered away after it happened. Perhaps she had her own ideas on the subject. But as I've said, I have no memory of the incident at all; only of having been told about it some years after the fact.

King insists that he has no memory of his friend being run over by a train, but Lenore Terr believes he repressed the memory. To bolster her argument she claims that the age of four is "slightly old for total amnesia on the basis of developmental immaturity." Terr is referring to childhood amnesia, the inability of adults to remember events that occur before the age of two or three. Since King was four when his friend was killed, and childhood amnesia generally ends by the age of three, Terr was arguing that he must have remembered *something*. Furthermore, she continued, King displays several telltale symptoms of having witnessed the accident—all those years ago he came home white as a ghost and wouldn't speak for the rest of the day, and now, in the present, he continually reenacts the original trauma in his terror-laden novels featuring runaway trains, murderous cars, and exploding fire hydrants. She gathers more supporting evidence from King's fictional characters in *It* and *Pet Semetary,* who have "on-again, off again" amnesias, partial memories which perhaps are "closer to the author's actual life experiences than his autobiographical claim to total amnesia."

In other words (if I was interpreting this correctly, and I was more than willing to admit that I was somewhat confused), even though Stephen King claims he has no memory of this exceedingly traumatic event, it's clear that he was watching when his friend was run over by a train, because he displays the symptoms common to trauma survivors and he continually acts out his memories (which are too painful for him to express or to admit that he remembers) through his fictional characters, who can face the trauma for him.

Terr's theory made wonderful sense, it tied up all the loose ends, and no one could prove her wrong. Who could document that Stephen King *wasn't* there when his friend was killed? Even if King doesn't remember the event, how can he prove that he didn't witness it? The same line of reasoning could easily be invoked in the Eileen Franklin case. If Terr could state with full confidence that Stephen King saw his friend run over by a train (even though he doesn't remember it) because he has certain significant symptoms, then how much more would she have to say (and with how much more confidence) about Eileen Franklin, who not only accepted Terr's theories but requested her expertise in order to authenticate her story of a repressed memory?

Terr actually discussed Stephen King during her testimony in the Franklin trial. She told the jury about a real-life encounter: She happened to overhear a conversation at a nearby table in a hotel coffee shop. A man was explaining his need to kill lots of people in his books and movies "because it's really part of me." The man, of course, was Stephen King. Terr summed up the meaning of the anecdote for the courtroom: "The person who has been traumatized can't stop this kind of behavior; it's a behavior that has to be. And the person may not be aware of why the behavior is linked to the trauma, but it's there, and it has to be repeated."

With that entertaining anecdote, Lenore Terr made it clear that Eileen Franklin's repressed memory was not such an oddity after all. Because he hadn't yet recovered the memory, Stephen King wasn't aware that his repetitive behavior was shaped by his childhood trauma; but Eileen Franklin, who had recovered her traumatic memories, was able to see how deeply she had been affected. The writer and housewife were linked by tragic events that occurred in early childhood, experiences that were so painful that their minds shut down, pushing the memories into the unconscious. For years only the symptoms remained, obsessive behaviors that would mark them forever after with the diagnosis of "trauma victim."

With that diagnosis all the quirks and idiosyncrasies of Eileen Franklin's personality could be explained away. Yes, she lied about being hypnotized . . . but that's understandable because she is a *trauma victim*.

Yes, she used drugs and was arrested for prostitution . . . but her behavior makes sense given that she is a *trauma victim*. Yes, she repressed the memory for twenty years . . . but that's a defensive reaction common to *trauma victims*. Anything the defense might say in an attempt to undermine Eileen's credibility as a witness could be turned around and presented as an ongoing symptom of the original trauma that left a deep and indelible scar on her psyche.

I took the stand on Tuesday, November 20, 1990, and for two hours discussed my experiments investigating memory distortion. I explained to the court that memory fades with time, losing detail and accuracy; as time goes by, the weakened memories are increasingly vulnerable to "post-event information"—facts, ideas, inferences, and opinions that become available to a witness after an event is completely over. I told the jury about a series of experiments I conducted featuring a shocking film simulation of a robbery. At the end of the short film, a child is shot in the face. Subjects who watched the film with the shocking ending were able to recall details with significantly less accuracy than subjects who watched a similar film without the violent ending.

This study, I explained, tells us about the distortions that can occur in the acquisition stage of memory, when an event occurs and information is laid down in the memory system. Other studies tell us about the retention and retrieval stages of memory, after a period of time goes by and we are asked to recall a particular event or experience. Hundreds of experiments involving tens of thousands of individuals have shown that post-event information can become incorporated into memory and contaminate, supplement, or distort the original memory.

I described a study I'd conducted in which subjects watched a film of a robbery involving a shooting and were then exposed to a television account of the event which contained erroneous details. When asked to recall what happened during the robbery, many subjects incorporated the erroneous details from the television report into their account. Once these details were inserted into a person's mind through the technique of exposure to post-event information, they were adopted as the truth and protected as fiercely as the "real," original details. Subjects typically resisted any suggestion that their richly detailed memories might have been flawed or contaminated and asserted with great confidence that they saw what their revised and adapted memories told them they saw.

Elaine Tipton, the prosecutor, attempted to persuade the jury that my studies on memory distortion had little or nothing to do with Eileen Franklin's repressed memory. You study normal memory and forgetting, but so what? her questions implied. What does that have to do with this extraordinary memory?

"You've never been asked to render an opinion that a person might not be able to accurately recognize or identify their own father, have you?" Tipton asked me.

"I don't think I've ever had a case with that as the precise issue," I answered.

"You have conducted no study, have you," she continued, "in which you tested a person's ability to retrieve and describe an event that they witnessed twenty years later. Isn't that true?"

"I don't recall personally doing such a study, and there aren't very many studies with that long an interval of time in the literature," I said.

"And, in fact, none of the studies that you have done involved the subject's having repressed the memory of the event that they witnessed prior to the retrieval; isn't that true?"

I admitted that in my experiments I studied distortions of memories that were not repressed. I was tempted to ask, How can I study a memory that doesn't exist, or at least isn't available to consciousness? But I restrained myself.

Tipton kept hammering at the point that repressed memories don't fly by the same rules as ordinary memories. "Based on the fact that none of these studies have involved the effect of, for instance, post-event information on a memory that is not in the conscious mind—that is, one that is repressed—you would agree, wouldn't you, that these findings don't necessarily apply to repressed memory?"

I explained that I could only hypothesize about the effects. But it was my scientific prediction that post-event information would have the same distorting and contaminating impact on a repressed memory that it has on a nonrepressed memory.

Tipton shifted her focus to the types of distortions that occur in the experiments I conduct. My studies generally deal with the details of a given event; they do not question whether or not the event occurred at all. The details might include, for example, "Which hand was the gun in?" or "Did the robber have a mustache?" or "Was the robber wearing gloves or not wearing gloves?"

"But you've never had a response indicating that the subject thought that the man was in a baseball game rather than committing a robbery in a market, have you?" Tipton asked.

"I don't think that's ever happened, to my knowledge, in my studies," I answered.

"So your studies really focus on a person's ability to perceive more discrete details of the event, not the actual subject matter—the broad subject matter of the event. Correct?"

"That would be the primary focus of these studies, recollections of specific aspects of the event," I answered.

Once again Tipton made the point that this extraordinary memory didn't have to abide by the rules of ordinary memory. Because Eileen

Franklin's memory was repressed, apparently it could do whatever it wanted to do. Scientists couldn't study it or understand it because repression is too complex and mysterious, part of the unconscious and unknowable processes of the human mind.

I was getting frustrated. In science everything hinges on proof and evidence. We call this the scientific method. Scientists can't just pronounce that the earth is round or the force of gravity keeps our feet on the ground without offering evidence in support of their theories (not, at least, if they want to call themselves scientists.) A scientific theory has to be falsifiable, which means that, in principle at least, some other scientist can come along and create an experiment designed to prove that the earth isn't round or that gravity doesn't keep us grounded.

But how does a scientist search for evidence to prove or disprove an unconscious mental process involving a series of internal events that occur spontaneously, without warning and with no external signs to indicate that something is about to happen, is happening, or has already happened? And how can a scientist prove or disprove that a spontaneously recovered memory represents the whole truth and nothing but the truth rather than some creative blending of reality and imagination or, perhaps, just plain and pure invention?

As I sat in the witness box answering the prosecutor's questions, I began to sense the power of this thing called repression. I felt as if I were in a church arguing with the minister about the existence of God.

"You have conducted no study, have you, in which you were able to prove or disprove the existence of God?"

"No, I have not conducted such a study."

"Your findings, which deal with the real and verifiable, do not apply to the unknowable and unverifiable. Would you agree?"

"I would have to agree."

"Your studies focus on discrete details, not the larger picture, the grand idea. Correct?"

"Yes, that is correct."

I was beginning to realize that repression was a philosophical entity, requiring a leap of faith in order to believe. For those willing to take that leap, no amount of "scientific" discussion would persuade them otherwise. Science, with its innate need to quantify and substantiate, stood helpless next to the mythic powers of repression. The courtroom was awash in credulity, the jurors' and spectators' opinions seemed predetermined, and my carefully researched scientific studies were just an old-fashioned irritation, a necessary but inconsequential detour on the road to confirming Eileen Franklin's memory and finding George Franklin guilty of murder.

Nine days later, on November 29, 1990, jury deliberations began. The jury reached a verdict the next day: George Franklin was guilty of the crime of first-degree murder.

I have little doubt that Eileen Franklin believes with every cell of her being that her father murdered Susan Nason. The images of the murder were so vivid and finely detailed that she couldn't imagine they portrayed anything but the truth. Over time the strange, flickering flashbacks settled into a coherent almost tangible picture. As additional bits and pieces of memory came floating back they were grafted onto the original nucleus, and a complex, interconnected system of image, emotions, experiences, and beliefs was created.

But I believe there is a very real possibility that the whole concoction was spun not from solid facts but from the vaporous breezes of wishes, dreams, fears, desires. Eileen's mind, operating independently of reality, went about its business of collecting ambiguities and inconsistencies and wrapping them up into a sensible package, revealing to her in one blinding moment of insight a coherent picture of the past that was nevertheless completely and utterly false. Eileen's story is *her* truth, but it is a truth that never happened.

*[margin note: * Or an implanted truth?]*

Dr. David Spiegel, who also testified for the defense in the Franklin case, agrees with this scenario. A professor of psychiatry at Stanford Medical School, Spiegel believes that it is possible to lose conscious awareness of traumatic memories through the defense mechanism known as "dissociation," which works to control painful feelings by limiting the person's access to the memory. But even if a traumatic memory is lost from consciousness, certain symptoms universally occur. As Spiegel wrote in a scholarly paper published after the trial:

> Research indicates that children exposed to violent trauma almost uniformly identify the event as a stressor (87% in one sample), suffer intrusive imagery [and] fear of recurrence of the trauma, lose interest in ordinary activities, avoid reminders of the event, and are upset by thoughts of it. The lack of evidence of any of these symptoms in Eileen after the murder does little to support the idea that she witnessed it.

Spiegel concludes that "a combination of fantasy and guilt about her friend's death, coupled with images of her father's cruelty could have led her to construct a false memory which she believed."

If Eileen's memory is false (and, of course, we have to accept the unpleasant reality that in this and other cases of repressed memory we will never know for sure what really happened), what does that tell us about her psyche? Is she somehow "sick" in the sense of mentally unstable or deranged? I don't think so, unless most of the rest of us could also be labeled sick. Consider the fact that thousands of sane and intelligent people with no evidence of psychopathology speak in terror-stricken voices about their experience aboard flying saucers. They *remember*, clearly and vividly, being abducted by aliens. Or consider the fact that thousands of reasonable, normally functioning human beings relate in calm voices and with deeply felt conviction their past-life experiences. They *remember* having lived before.

Thousands more are vulnerable to spontaneous misfirings of the limbic system (the part of the brain comprising the cortex and related nuclei that is thought to relate to emotional response). When the neurons in their brains backfire, they report seeing loved ones long since dead or, even more frightening, images of God, the Virgin Mary, or Satan. These perceptions may be imprinted as memories, which are recalled with profound emotion.

The twelfth-century mystic nun Hildegard of Bingen glimpsed the city of God in her dazzling visions of flashing lights, angelic hosts, and brilliant halos. Was she really permitted a pre-death look at heaven? Modern-day observers believe that Hildegard's celestial revelations were induced by migraine headaches. As clinical neurologist Oliver Sacks writes in *Migraine: The Evolution of a Common Disorder*:

> [Hildegard's visions] provide a unique example of the manner in which a physiological event, banal, hateful, or meaningless to the vast majority of people, can become, in a privileged consciousness, the substrate of a supreme ecstatic vision.

The Seventh-Day Adventist prophet Ellen White would suddenly fall into trances in which her eyes rolled upward as she monotonously repeated certain phrases and gestures. Her "visions" revealed to her that masturbation is fatal, wigs cause insanity, and certain races evolved from intercourse with lower species of animals. Was White insane? Was she feigning her visions in order to win converts to her religion? While the faithful accept her visions as divinely inspired, her "spells" are now believed to have been caused by epileptic seizures, possibly originating from a head injury that occurred when she was nine years old.

Strange visions, bizarre apparitions, and otherworldly hallucinations do not have to be apocalyptic. An estimated 10 percent to 25 percent of normally functioning human beings have experienced, at least once in their lifetimes, a vivid hallucination—hearing a voice, smelling nonexistent flowers, or seeing a vision of a loved one, dead for many years. Carl Sagan, professor of astronomy and space sciences at Cornell University, claims that he has heard his mother and father calling out his name perhaps a dozen times since their deaths. "I still miss them so much that it doesn't seem strange to me that my brain will occasionally retrieve a kind of lucid recollection of their voices," Sagan writes.

Hallucinations are simply part of being human. What are dreams but hallucinations of the sleeping mind? Children imagine monsters and fairies; grown-ups insist they have been visited by aliens; and roughly 10 percent of Americans report having seen a ghost or two. These people are not lying. They saw, heard, felt and experienced *something*. But was that "something" real?

When patients describe scenes from their childhood in rich and realistic detail, with powerful emotions that are appropriate to the event being relived, therapists (and any others who happen to be listening) are understandably impressed. The intense emotional expressions, the physical indications of fear and panic, and the abundance of vivid detail convince the listener that something did, in fact, happen. How could anyone invent a memory and then feign such rage, fear, horror, and grief? we ask ourselves. Why would people put themselves through that kind of emotional anguish?

But even if therapists are willing to accept the possibility of a fabricated memory, they are faced with a distressing double bind. Compassionate and conscientious clinicians work hard to create a safe and trusting atmosphere for patients to express their emotions and tell the truth about their past. In fact, a therapist's skill and sagacity can be measured by his or her ability to elicit painful, deeply buried material. How can clinicians then betray their patients' confidence and trust (and call into question their own interrogation methods) by questioning whether the memories and emotions being elicited are verifiably true?

It is not difficult to understand why therapists are so impressed by the emotional anguish expressed by their patients when they recall memories of abuse, nor is it hard to deduce why they are reluctant to disbelieve, question, or seek outside corroboration for repressed memories of sexual abuse. They fear destroying trust, impairing the therapeutic relationship, and perhaps even driving the patient out of therapy or, as some therapists fear, into psychosis.

But perhaps the most compelling reason to believe these stories of recovered memories is that *not* believing is edged with painful complexities and ambiguities. Not believing shakes up our sense of our own self. In the case of Eileen Franklin we want to believe, as she clearly and persuasively believed, and as her richly detailed memory would compel us to believe, that the story she relates is both accurate and truthful. We want to believe—in fact we need to believe—her story because the belief in her memory affirms that our own minds work in an orderly, efficient way, taking in information, sorting it, filing it, and calling it back later in full and vivid detail. In a chaotic world, where so much is out of control, we need to believe that our minds, at least, are under our command. We need to believe that our memories, inherently trustworthy and reliable, can reach back into the past and make sense of our lives. As social psychologist Carol Tavris writes, our memories are the table of contents of our lives. Who has the energy or the emotional resources to rewrite the entire book?

The idea that our minds can play tricks on us, leading us to believe in a distorted reality, even in fantasy and confabulation, is deeply disturbing. If we can't trust our own minds to tell us the truth, what is left to trust? If our minds are capable of feeding us tall tales from the past with such intense, hallucinatory detail that it never occurs to us to question them, where is the boundary between truth and lie, reality and fantasy, sanity and madness?

The boundary, I believe, is permeable and unguarded, and we cross it all the time in our dreams, desires, and imaginations. Memory is the vehicle by which we transport ourselves from reality to fantasy and back again, as many times as it takes to spin coherent and colorful stories from the dry straw of real life. Our memories tell us stories, and we listen, enthralled. We want to know what happened in our past, we need our questions answered, we seek to resolve our uncertainty and ambiguity. Memory, our most loyal and faithful servant, complies with our wishes.

Why did Eileen Franklin come to believe that she saw her father murder her best friend? How did her mind construct a memory out of bits of fact and pieces of fantasy and then come to believe that that it was absolutely, one hundred percent true? On a more practical level, what possible motivation would she have for sending her father to jail for a murder he didn't commit?

In her book, *Sins of the Father,* Eileen provides some answers to these questions. She describes her childhood as extremely violent. "My father's beatings and the mean way in which he spoke to us were terrifying," Eileen wrote. She remembered that her younger brother, George, Jr., told her that he feared his father so much that he kept a baseball bat under his bed for protection. Her mother endured both physical and emotional abuse, and her sister Janice claimed that she was repeatedly sexually abused by their father.

For most of her childhood and adolescence Eileen denied that her father abused her, but after years of therapy she eventually recalled several specific incidents of abuse. In one particularly disturbing recollection, she remembered being physically and sexually abused by her father in the bathtub when she was five. As Eileen discussed her emerging memories with her therapist, he explained that the human mind is, indeed, capable of burying a painful or traumatic event in the unconscious. When the time is right the memory will surface; as the memory emerges into consciousness, it will gradually lose its power to hurt. The ability to bring back to consciousness long-buried memories, Eileen learned in therapy, is a crucial step in healing and recovery.

A few weeks after the bathtub memory returned, Eileen recovered another memory of an event that occurred when she was eight or nine years old. She was in a strange house with her father and another man. "I was on something like a table. My father was holding down my left shoulder with one hand, his other hand over my mouth. I saw the face of a black man. I heard laughing. I felt a horrible, searing pain in my lower body. I tried to scream but couldn't because of my father's hand."

For six months Eileen believed she had been raped by an unknown black man. Only when her mother suggested to her that the rapist might have been a family friend did Eileen's mind begin to reconstruct the scene, changing the assailant from a black man she did not know to a white man she knew very well.

But no matter how these memories were originally pieced together, taken apart, and reassembled, they are emotionally devastating, full of the grief and rage of an adult woman looking back at her childhood and remembering unspeakable tortures suffered at the hands of her own father. The memory most important to Eileen, however, may have been created in her adulthood. Her daughter, Jessica, was two years old. George Franklin came to visit, and Eileen left him alone in the living room with her daughter. When she returned, she found her father holding her child on the coffee table, "carefully scrutinizing her sexual organs, pushing the labia open with his finger. I was stunned. 'What are you doing?' was all I could say."

What was going on in Eileen's mind at that moment, and afterward, as the memory of her father touching the genitals of her two-year-old daughter returned again and again to haunt her? Perhaps other images began to flash into her mind, pictures of her father molesting her sister, slapping her mother, kicking her little brother. Perhaps her imagination began to draw hallucinatory future pictures in which she visualized her adolescent daughter, beautiful as she was sure to become, shy, perhaps, and ever anxious to please her adoring grandfather. Did Eileen's mind project the remembered past into the imagined future, intensifying her fears for her daughter's safety?

Certainly her pain was intense, her anxiety overwhelming. For years she had struggled to make sense of a violent and unhappy childhood that included the senseless murder of her best friend. As an adolescent, she was troubled and depressed, dropping out of high school, experimenting with drugs and prostitution, attempting suicide. In her twenties she married a controlling and domineering man, and for many years she endured a loveless marriage. The pattern, it seemed, had established itself, and she could not escape the intolerable and relentless anguish of victimhood.

Her rage and grief, so amorphous and scattered, sought a focus and an outlet. In therapy she learned that her symptoms—her recurring fears, the flashing images, the returning memories—were clear indications of post-traumatic stress. She was told that she had every right to her feelings of victimhood, for she was simply repeating the self-destructive patterns laid down in her childhood. She learned that her confusion, anger, grief, and depression could be taken as further evidence that she had been traumatized and victimized sometime in her past.

Her therapist's oft-repeated words echoed in her mind: She had every right to feel angry and grief-stricken. Only when she accepted her emotions as real and valid would she be free, finally, to express herself, to let go of her childhood hurts, to become her true self. This search for the genuine self must not be impeded, and anyone who had mistreated her in the past was a legitimate target of her rage. Anyone who questioned her memories or asked for corroboration or proof was an impediment to the healing process. Eileen was a trauma victim, but somehow she had emerged whole and intact. She had endured. She was a survivor.

Given Eileen's rage and grief, perhaps we can begin to understand the culminating scene that took place in her living room, when Jessica was six years old and suddenly turned to her mother, her expression quizzical. As Eileen remembered the event, she looked into her daughter's eyes and was struck by the child's startling resemblance to eight-year-old Susan Nason. The two girls, one dead for twenty years and the other very much alive, could have been sisters.

One brutal image overlapped another, and in that shocking instant of recognition, flesh began to creep over the skeletal remains, and Susan briefly came back to life. Eileen could see in her mind the silhouette of her father with one leg forward, his hands raised above his head, and the look of terror on her friend's face. She could hear the scream, the rock cutting into bone and flesh, the dreadful silence. She could feel the never-ending horror.

The adhesive connecting one image to another was supplied by Eileen's guilt, anger, fear, and—perhaps most important—her desperate need to protect her own children. She was not able to protect her best friend—"I could not protect her, I could not stop him. I did not know that it was going to happen"—but as a twenty-nine-year-old mother, she could, at the very least, save her own children. Her guilt and helplessness over Susan's death fueled the fire of her maternal protectiveness: "Each day when I looked into the faces of Jessica and Aaron, I knew that I had my children and that the Nasons did not have Susan. This made me feel guilty and partly responsible for the Nasons' pain. It was my fault that the murder had never been solved."

Easing the pain, ending the torment, doing the "right" thing, protecting her children . . . were these sufficient motivations to weld the horrors of the past and fears for the future into a false memory? Or did Eileen Franklin's desire for justice and revenge spring from a more personal source? Was it possible that her mind created this memory in a desperate attempt to control an uncontrollable past and give some meaning to her troubled life?

In the final two pages of her book, Eileen described the anguish created by the unearthed memory. "I look in the mirror and compare the face I see with photos taken of me before the recollection . . . All the joy has left my eyes."

"All the joy has left," but in its place, Eileen has gained a sense of control and power over her father.

> He had the power to close down a big part of my mind. . . . If I don't achieve mastery over all he has done to me, if I allow part of my memory to remain repressed, my father wins. I must bring out and successfully put to rest all kinds of horror before I can truly say I have beaten him. If I live my life terrified of remembering more, he has won.

And so, perhaps, Eileen's mind created the memory in an attempt to destroy her father's power over her and live the remainder of her life free of fear. With the inventive powers of memory as her weapon, she was able to punish her father for his cruel, abusive treatment of her family and achieve mastery over her past. But not without cost. For once the floodgates were opened, the terrifying images rushed forth, a nonstop deluge. No safe haven presented itself; no end was in sight. "I want to flee, to lose the memory, but my mind runs as fast as I do. There is nowhere to go that I can leave my mind behind."

Eileen Franklin's "memories" have claimed her, body and soul.

I have one more story to tell. I came face to face with Eileen Franklin only once, in New York City on NBC's daytime talk show "A Closer Look." After Eileen described her repressed memory of her best friend's murder, host Faith Daniels turned to me and in a disbelieving tone said, "Do you really think that what Eileen remembered is not what happened?"

"I think there is at least a plausible alternative theory that Eileen may have believed that she really saw this but it could be a created memory," I said.

Members of the audience were fidgeting in their seats and shaking their heads at me. Daniels turned to the audience and said, "I don't think you're buying that!" She pushed the microphone up to a middle-aged woman's mouth. "Why don't you buy it?"

"I just can't believe that you would have such feelings and lose moments from your life," the woman said. "Why would you want to suffer if you didn't have to? Why would you want to put yourself through it? There's no logic behind it."

Eileen, who wore an elegant black dress with pink and blue stripes on the shoulders, nodded her head, a pained expression on her face. I wore a beige suit with a long string of pearls. As the audience continued to vent their hostility toward my skeptical viewpoint, I kept what I can only call a stoic smile plastered on my face.

After the taping, I took the elevator to the first floor. In the lobby I caught a glimpse of a striking woman with long red hair walking into the NBC souvenir shop. I edged a little closer (I wasn't looking for a direct confrontation) and watched as Eileen browsed through the narrow aisles stocked with keychains, mugs, T-shirts, and other memorabilia imprinted with the NBC logo. At one point she picked up a mug, turned it upside down to look at the price tag, and then replaced it on the shelf. Then she walked over to the T-shirts and unfolded an adult-size shirt bearing the network's logo. She held it up, trying to imagine if it would fit. Too big? Too little? Just right?

I watched, fascinated by her beauty and composure. I suppose I hoped to get some sense of who she was and what made her tick, now that she was away from the television cameras and microphones. At one point she glanced out toward the lobby, as if she were expecting someone to meet her. She looked right at me but gave no sign that she knew who I was. A few minutes later I picked up my briefcase and walked outside to hail a taxi and head for home.

That is the story-truth of my encounter with Eileen Franklin. The happening-truth is not nearly so interesting. I was in New York City in January 1992, and I appeared with Eileen Franklin on NBC's "A Closer Look." I was dressed in a beige suit, and Eileen wore a black dress. The audience felt much more comfortable with Eileen's version of the story than they did with mine. They frowned and fidgeted when I attempted to explain the ways in which memory can be distorted, and I squirmed and tried to smile my way through their expressions of disbelief and outright hostility.

I can confirm all those facts because I have a videotape of the show. But the rest of the story, while clear and vivid in my mind, can't be corroborated. Did I stand outside the souvenir shop watching as Eileen Franklin picked up a mug and looked at the price tag? (Is there even a souvenir shop in the NBC building? Could it have been a magazine stand?) Did she unfold a T-shirt? (Was it, perhaps, a child-size shirt?) Did I watch her for a few minutes from the lobby, or did I catch a glimpse of her (or someone else with long red hair?) in the lobby as I rushed outside to hail a taxi? Did she look right at me and not recognize me? Could I have imagined the whole scene?

Even in this relatively insignificant encounter with my past, I'm not sure where the happening-truth ends and the story-truth begins.

7

LOST IN A SHOPPING MALL

*I thought I remembered being lost and looking around for
you guys. I do remember that. And then crying. And Mom
coming up and saying, "Where were you?
Don't you ever do that again!"*

—Chris, *University of Washington research subject*

*The flying rumours gather'd as they roll'd
Scarce any tale was sooner heard than told;
And all who told it added something new,
And all who heard it made enlargements too.*

—Alexander Pope, *"Temple of Flame"*

T he Eileen Franklin story fulfills our expectations of the way memory
should work. Our favorite and most familiar metaphors emphasize the
accuracy and efficiency of memory. Memories, we imagine, are cata-
logued in ever-expanding ultramicroscopic libraries. Or perhaps they are
carefully stored as bits of information on a limitless supply of infinitesi-
mal computer chips, or even recorded on blank videocassettes, properly
labeled and filed away for future use.

These modern, technological metaphors reveal a deep need for order
and consistency. We would like to believe that our minds work according
to a method, that there is a strategy to be discovered somewhere in the
brain's chemical stew, even if we can only begin to imagine what it might
"look" like. We would like to think that something, somehow, somewhere, is always in control.

Fifty years ago an intriguing series of brain operations appeared to
confirm that our minds are, indeed, in ultimate control, regulating with
astonishing proficiency the vast and complicated stimuli encountered in
any given day. Neurosurgeon Wilder Penfield performed over a thousand
brain surgeries on epileptic patients, lifting a portion of the skull and removing pieces of the cortex in an attempt to reduce seizure activity. Pa-

tients were anesthetized but conscious during these procedures. Before removing any brain tissue, Penfield used an electric stimulator to plot the functions of different portions of the brain.

When he stimulated the temporal lobes, forty patients reported experiencing a "flashback"—a mental image or sensory experience that they interpreted as a memory. One young woman cried out, "I think I heard a mother calling her little boy somewhere. It seemed to be something that happened years ago . . . in the neighborhood where I live." When the electrode was moved slightly, she said, "I hear voices. It is late at night, around the carnival somewhere—some sort of traveling circus. I just saw lots of big wagons that they use to haul animals in."

These reports of memory "flashbacks" were utterly convincing and seemed to offer proof that experiences and emotions are permanently inscribed in the brain. As a *New York Times* reporter concluded, "There can be little doubt that Wilder Penfield's electrodes were arousing activity in the hippocampus, within the temporal lobe, jerking out distant and intimate memories from the patient's stream of consciousness." The fishing metaphor supplies a lively and entertaining image of an electrode dangling along the calm surface of the brain when it is given a sudden, powerful tug. A memory, filled with abundant and energetic life, emerges from the gelatinous waters and flops up onto the land of consciousness: an impressive catch.

In his original writings, Penfield favored the more businesslike analogy of a tape recorder, concluding that memories leave a "permanent imprint on the brain . . . as though a tape recorder had been receiving it all."

But do Penfield's brain stimulations really prove that all our memories are accurately recorded and stored away somewhere in the recesses of the temporal lobes? A closer look shows that only a small percentage (3.5 percent) of his patients reported memory flashbacks; furthermore, no evidence exists to corroborate that these memories were indeed factual records of actual occurrences. Of the forty patients who did report memories, twenty-four claimed to have heard only the background "noise" of memory: voices, music, or some other meaningful, identifiable sound. One patient described her memory as "a kind of sound in the distance like people singing." When asked what the people were singing, she said, "I don't know. It was like a bunch of old folks in the background, probably some hymns."

Nineteen patients claimed that they could actually see a person, a recognizable object, or an entire scene, and twelve patients reported both visual and auditory experiences. But it seems likely that even this small group of patients entwined reality and fantasy, relying on imagination to fill in the holes. For example, the young woman who remembered hearing "a mother calling her little boy" recalled that it happened somewhere "in the neighborhood where I live." Later she said that it was "at the lumberyard." But when questioned, she claimed that she had no memory of ever being at a lumberyard.

This patient apparently mixed together floating bits of fantasy and reality into something she recognized as a memory, much as the sleeping mind splashes together the oil of fact and the vinegar of fiction into the extravagant salad of dream life. Indeed, in reviewing Penfield's work, cognitive psychologist Ulric Neisser concluded that the content of these reported memories "seems entirely comparable to the content of dreams, which are generally admitted to be synthetic constructions and not literal recalls."

When the wild cacophony of dreams, wishes, and desires intrudes, the elegant, linear metaphors begin to sway and topple. While it may be soothing to imagine memory as a predictable, reliable operation, the truth is not so reassuring. Recent research featuring high-tech brain mapping procedures indicates that memory is not a broad, generalized capability drawing on a centrally located storehouse of images and experiences, but a network of numerous separate activities, each carried out in a specific part of the brain.

Scientists believe that the formation of a memory begins with the visual system's identification of objects and characteristics in space. At each of the original sites of perception, brain cells are directed to store certain impressions for later retrieval; after receiving their instructions, the cells actually undergo specific physical changes. The tiny organ known as the hippocampus* (of which there are two, one on each side of the brain) links these separate localities, integrating diverse sensations into a single experience that is then imprinted as a memory. Each time a specific memory is retrieved, the connections between the brain cells are strengthened.

Thus we can imagine the brain as filled with hundreds of thousands of tiny overlapping "nets" of information connecting separate and distinct neural locations. Tug on one thread of a particular memory, and the whole net will shift position; surrounding and overlapping sheets of memory will also be disturbed. To further complicate matters, the fabric of memory is composed of blood, chemicals and electricity, a rather slippery and volatile combination. Nets get tangled, knots develop, frays and holes begin to rip apart the intricately knotted fabric. Although the mind struggles valiantly to mend these imperfections, it is not always a skilled or meticulous seamstress. Consider the following memory of an event that occurred on August 18, 1967, in Boston's Fenway Park.

---

*The hippocampus is probably essential only for "episodic" memory—memory for the events and experiences of our lives. "Procedural learning," which includes skills such as riding a bike or tying a shoe, apparently takes place with the involvement of other structures.

Twenty-three-year-old Tony Conigliaro, an outfielder for the Boston Red Sox and one of the greatest sluggers of all time, stood at the plate facing pitcher Jack Hamilton of the California Angels. Hamilton wound up for his first pitch, throwing a fast ball that crushed the left side of Conigliaro's face.

"I never hit a guy that hard," Hamilton recalled. "He went right down, he just collapsed." Conigliaro never fully recovered from his injuries, and retired from baseball in 1975; he died in 1990 at the age of forty-five. Hamilton would never be the same again, either. "I've had to live with it, I think about it a lot," Hamilton, now fifty-one years old and the owner of a Midwestern restaurant chain, told *The New York Times* after hearing about Conigliaro's death. "Watching baseball on TV, anytime a guy gets hit, I think about it. It was like the sixth inning when it happened. I think the score was 2–1, and he was the eighth hitter in their batting order. With the pitcher up next, I had no reason to throw at him." It was a day game, Hamilton recalled, because he remembered visiting Conigliaro in the hospital later that afternoon. After the accident he remembered wondering whether or not to return to Fenway Park later that year for another series of games; eventually he decided to make the trip.

Over the years Hamilton thought about this life-changing, publicly recorded experience hundreds of times. But his memory wasn't even close to the truth. The accident didn't happen in the sixth inning, but the fourth; the score wasn't 2–1, but 0–0; Conigliaro wasn't the eighth hitter in the order, but the sixth; it wasn't a day game, but a night game; and Hamilton didn't make another trip to Fenway Park that year because the tragedy occurred during the Angels' final road trip to Boston.

These are details, of course, and everyone knows that the passage of time can cloud even the most significant and salient memories of our lives. Slightly altering or revising a real memory is not the same as creating a memory of an event that never happened. And yet, in both anecdotal accounts and experimental studies, researchers have shown that it is possible for people to believe that they experienced something that never happened. One of the most famous anecdotal accounts of a false memory is told by child psychologist Jean Piaget:

> One of my first memories would date, if it were true, from my second year. I can still see, most clearly, the following scene, in which I believed until I was about fifteen. I was sitting in my pram, which my nurse was pushing in the Champs Elysées, when a man tried to kidnap me. I was held in by the strap fastened round me while my nurse bravely tried to stand between me and the thief. She received various scratches, and I can still see vaguely those on her face. . . . When I was about fifteen, my parents received a letter from my former nurse . . . she wanted to

confess her past faults, and in particular to return the watch she had been given as a reward. . . . She had made up the whole story. . . . I, therefore, must have heard, as a child, the account of this story, which my parents believed, and projected into the past in the form of a visual memory.

Of couse, Piaget was very young, and the memory, although exciting and highly dramatic, had a happy ending. Surely with older children and a more traumatic memory, the details would be more carefully preserved. Or would they?

On February 24, 1984, a sniper fired repeated rounds of ammunition at children and teachers on an elementary school playground in Los Angeles. One child and an adult passerby were killed; thirteen other children and a playground attendant were injured. Several weeks after the sniper attack, researchers from the UCLA Preventive Intervention Program in Trauma, Violence and Sudden Bereavement in Children interviewed 113 children (10 percent of the student body), hoping to better understand the nature and consequences of their traumatic memories.

One of the children remembered that she was walking out the central school door leading onto the open playground with the girl who was subsequently killed. When the shooting began, she was halfway down the stairs and immediately turned back to get her sister. She told the researchers that when she went back outside onto the staircase landing, she saw the dead child lying on the playground with the assailant standing over her body. But from the vantage point of the stairway the girl could not have seen the victim. Furthermore, the sniper was never on the playground. Several hours after the shootings, a SWAT team stormed an apartment across the street and discovered that the sniper had killed himself.

A boy who was away on vacation during the shootings recalled his vivid "memories" of that frightful day. He was on his way to school, he said, when he saw someone lying on the ground, heard some shots, and quickly ran back home. Another child told investigators that she was at the school gate closest to the sniper when the shooting began. But in truth, she was not only out of the direct line of fire but half a block away from the playground. Many of the children who had not been to school at all that day came to examine the schoolyard the next day; in reconstructing the event, they recalled that their visit occurred on the day of the shooting.

For obvious ethical reasons experimenters cannot simulate the scene of a violent sniper attack in an attempt to probe further into the workings of traumatic memory. But they can use suggestion and influence techniques in an attempt to inject a mildly traumatic memory into their subjects' minds. That's what psychologist Jeffrey Haugaard and his colleagues did in a recent experiment in which children from four to seven years old viewed a short (three-and-a-half-minute) videotape. In one version of the tape a girl is playing at a neighbor's pond, even though she had been warned not to play there. The neighbor finds her at the pond, approaches to within about four feet, tells her that he is going to report her to the police, and sends her home. At no time does the neighbor touch the girl or make any gesture indicating that he intends to hit or threaten her. After the encounter the girl leaves the pond and returns to her home.

In the next scene the girl lies to a policeman who comes to the house. While she admits being at the pond, she adds, "But he [the neighbor] hit me two times before he let me come home." The policeman responds, "He hit you? He hit you before he let you come home?" And the girl replies, "Yes, he hit me."

After hearing the girl's "lie," a number of children came to believe that they actually saw the neighbor hit the girl. Not only did they misrecall the nonexistent hitting, but they added their own details. Of forty-one false claims (29 percent of the total) thirty-nine children recalled that the man hit the girl near the pond, one moved the assault to the girl's house, and one could not specify exactly where the girl was when the man hit her.

Alison Clarke-Stewart and William Thompson at the University of California at Irvine conducted another fascinating study with young children. Five- and six-year-old children observed an incident in which a janitor (nicknamed by the experimenters "Chester the Molester") followed one of two scripts while interacting with a doll. Chester either cleaned the doll or played with it in a rough, suggestive manner. When Chester was following the "cleaning" script, he engaged in various actions with the doll while saying cleaning-related words. For example, he sprayed the doll's face with water while muttering, "This doll is dirty, I'd better clean it." Then he looked under the doll's clothing and said, "I'd better see if it's dirty here, too." Chester also straightened the doll's arms and legs and bit off a loose thread.

When Chester was following the "rough play" script, his actions were essentially the same but his words were different. "Oh, goodie," he said, "I like to play with dolls. I like to spray them in the face with water. I like to look under their clothes. I like to bite them and twist their arms and legs."

After interacting with Chester and the doll, the children were asked questions; in some cases the experimenter's questions were incriminating, accusing Chester of playing instead of doing his job. When the children were asked to describe what Chester did to the doll, those children who were not exposed to suggestive interrogation provided reasonably accurate answers. But many of the children who were questioned in a suggestive manner reported a memory consistent with those suggestions, recalling that Chester played roughly with the doll when in truth he had merely cleaned it.

In a series of studies conducted by Nicholas Spanos, adult subjects received hypnotic suggestions to regress beyond birth to a previous life. A significant number of the participants in this study actually developed past life identities that reflected the hypnotically transmitted expectations. When subjects received a suggestion that they were sexually abused as a child, they reported higher levels of abuse than subjects who were not provided with expectations of child abuse. All it took was a suggestion, and they remembered being abused in a past life. "These findings," Spanos concluded, "are consistent with anecdotal reports indicating that clients in psychotherapy sometimes confabulate complex and extensive pseudomemories that are consistent with the expectations held by their therapists."

From these and many other experiments, psychologists specializing in memory distortion conclude that memories are reconstructed using bits of fact and fiction and that false recollections can be induced by expectation and suggestion. But how could we, as scientists, convince anyone beyond our own inner circle that these studies were relevant to the phenomenon of repressed memories and recovered memory therapy? After the George Franklin case, that question became even more vexing. For the whole world, it seemed, had gone mad over repressed memories.

"A Story of Incest: Miss America's Triumph over Shame," announced the June 10, 1991, cover of *People* magazine. "People ask me why I didn't tell what was happening to me," wrote former Miss America Marilyn Van Derbur in the introduction to her four-page disclosure of childhood sexual abuse. "In order to survive, I split into a day child, who giggled and smiled, and a night child, who lay awake in a fetal position, only to be pried apart by my father. Until I was 24, the day child had no conscious knowledge of the night child."

Four months later *People* featured another cover story on repressed memories of sexual abuse: "Roseanne's Brave Confession: I Am an Incest Survivor." Roseanne Arnold's memories began with a series of nightmares, in which she dreamed that she was being molested. When she woke up screaming, her husband reached for pen and paper, quickly jotting down the details of the dream so that Roseanne would be able to recall them later. In the next months, Roseanne began to suffer from suicidal tendencies and various difficulties with trust and intimacy. She sought help in therapy; in individual and group sessions she gradually began to recover memories of her mother abusing her from the time she was an infant until she was six or seven years old, and of her father molesting her until she left home at age seventeen. "He constantly put his hands all over me," Roseanne revealed in the *People* article. "He forced me to sit on his lap, to cuddle with him, to play with his penis in the bathtub. He did grotesque and disgusting things: He used to chase me with his excrement and try to put it on my head. He'd lie on the floor playing with himself. It was the most disgusting thing you can ever imagine."*

In a sidebar to Roseanne's confession, psychiatrist Judith Lewis Herman speculated on the mind's ability to create a special place for traumatic memories. "Many kids learn to create a secret compartment in their minds where memories are stored but not readily accessed until later on. The trigger is often a specific reminder of the abuse. Once the memories are released, they can come in a flood."

Newsweek published an article on incest survivors on the same date as the *People* magazine article. In the *Newsweek* piece, Arnold explained that her memories, which were repressed for more than thirty years, came back to her as "little flicks of memory. And then they kept coming and getting bigger and bigger . . . my head burst open. It was like bad memories times 10." Still, she was filled with self-doubt. "Voices in my head say you're making this up. Maybe you took everything the wrong way. Maybe you imagined it. Maybe you're just making it up for attention."

Scores of noncelebrities added their voices to the swelling chorus of adults who, in therapy, recovered memories of sexual abuse. *Time* magazine offered the case of a thirty-six-year-old Chicago woman who was deluged with memories of abuse that took place when she was still in diapers. She claimed that she could remember her grandfather sexually molesting her while she lay helpless on the changing table. Another woman mentioned in *Time* was making love to her husband on their wedding night when she suddenly remembered being raped and sodomized by a teacher two decades earlier. She filed a lawsuit and was awarded a $1.4 million settlement from her church-run school.

Repressed memories even made it onto the best-seller lists. Jane Smiley's Pulitzer Prize–winning novel *A Thousand Acres* features Ginny, who has repressed all memory of being abused by her father even though her sister Rose frequently discusses her nonrepressed memories of abuse with her. One day, when Ginny walks up the stairs of her childhood home and lies down on her former bed, a memory comes surging back, literally knocking her over with its powerful emotional force.

> I knew that he had been in there to me, that my father had lain with me on that bed, that I had looked at the top of his head, at his balding spot in the brown grizzled hair, while feeling him suck my breasts. That was the only memory I could endure be-

---

*Roseanne's parents both deny ever having abused her.

fore I jumped out of the bed with a cry. My whole body was shaking and moans flowed out of my mouth. . . . I lay down on the wooden flooring of the hallway because I felt as if I would faint and fall down the stairs.

Betsy Petersen described her sudden recovery of repressed memories in the autobiographical *Dancing with Daddy*. Petersen was jogging one day when "a thought came into my mind as if it had been projected on a screen: I'm afraid my father did something to me." Experiencing a sense of urgency and a desire to know if something really had happened, Petersen discussed her fears with her therapist:

> "I have this story to tell you," I said to Kris, my therapist, several days later . . . "I don't know if I made it up or if it's real."
> She listened: "It feels like a story to you," she said, "because when something like that happens, everybody acts like it didn't."
> "You mean it might really have happened?" Now I wasn't sure I really did want to know.
> There was a good chance it had happened, she said.

To support her theory, the therapist pointed to Betsy's symptoms as evidence of abuse. A strained relationship with her alcoholic father, recurrent disturbing dreams, an inability to feel close to her children, and various sexual difficulties all indicated abuse, according to the therapist. When Petersen asked how it was possible to forget such significant and terrifying experiences, her therapist told her that victims of sexual abuse often repress their memories in order to survive. If she had been abused, the therapist reassured her client, the memories would eventually emerge.

But Petersen wasn't content to let the memories surface on their own; she immediately started digging, using her writing and research talents as tools. "I had no memory of what my father had done to me, so I tried to reconstruct it," she explains in her book. "I put all my skill—as reporter, novelist, and scholar—to work making that reconstruction as accurate and vivid as possible. I used the memories I had to get to the memories I didn't have."

Like the woman mentioned in the *Time* article who initiated a lawsuit against her former teacher, many of these repressed-memory cases were being argued in the courtroom. A lawyer in San Diego called me about a case involving a twenty-seven-year-old woman who suddenly recalled being molested by her father. The repressed memories, which emerged through counseling and "therapeutic intervention," included "lewd and lascivious acts, including but not limited to touching and fondling the genital areas, fornication and oral copulation." One memory recovered in therapy focused on an incident that allegedly occurred in the master bedroom when she was three years old. Her father called her into the bedroom while he was masturbating, forced her to watch him and then made her touch his genitals.

At approximately the same time this case came to trial a bizarre case of repressed memories was tried in Orange County, California. A woman in her mid-seventies and her recently deceased husband were accused by their two adult daughters of rape, sodomy, forced oral sex, torture by electric shock, and the ritualistic murder of babies. The older daughter, forty-eight years old at the time of the lawsuit, testified that she was abused from infancy until age twenty-five. The younger daughter alleged abuse from infancy to age fifteen. A granddaughter also claimed that she was abused by her grandmother from infancy to age eight.

The memories were recovered when the adult daughters went into therapy in 1987 and 1988. After the breakup of her third marriage, the older daughter started psychotherapy, eventually diagnosing herself as a victim of multiple personality disorder and satanic ritual abuse. She convinced her sister and her daughter to begin therapy and joined in their therapy sessions for the first year. The two sisters also attended group therapy with other multiple personality disorder patients who claimed to be victims of satanic ritual abuse.

In therapy the older sister recalled a horrifying incident that occurred when she was four or five years old. Her grandmother caught a rabbit, chopped off one of its ears, smeared the blood over her body, and then handed the knife to her grandchild, expecting her to kill the animal. When the child refused, her mother poured hot water over her arms. When she was thirteen and her sister was still in diapers, a group of strangers (satanic cult members, she learned later) demanded that the sisters disembowel a dog with a knife. She remembered being forced to watch as a man who threatened to divulge the secrets of the satanic cult was burned with a torch. Other members of the cult were subjected to electric shocks in rituals that took place in a cave. The cult even made her murder her own newborn baby. When asked to provide additional details about these horrific events, she testified in court that her memory was impaired because she was frequently drugged by the cult members.

The jury found the accused woman guilty of having neglected her daughters, but nothing more, and refused the requested monetary awards. Attempts to appeal the decision have failed.

A lawyer from Illinois wrote to me requesting information concerning the "unreliability" of repressed memories and bemoaning the fact that in this particular legal area the accused were automatically presumed guilty. "I have several clients involved with charges made by family members anywhere from 15 to 25 years after the fact," he explained in his letter. "Persons charged as offenders now seem to be presumed guilty, whether criminal charges are involved or not."

Guilty until proven innocent. The fear and frustration stemming from the automatic presumption of guilt permeated every letter I received from "the accused." A woman from Michigan wrote me about her thirty-six-year-old daughter who "after a year of counseling now accuses me of abuse . . . very much like Roseanne Arnold and the former Miss America Marilyn Van Derbur." An eighty-year-old man from Georgia was desperate to understand why his fifty-three-year-old daughter suddenly recovered memories that he had abused her during her early childhood and teen years. A California woman explained that her husband, who had recently died, was accused by their thirty-five-year-old daughter of sexual abuse. The charges eventually involved the accusation that the elderly couple had molested their grandson.

A retired couple from Colorado was accused by their thirty-three-year-old daughter, an only child, of sexual and satanic ritual abuse. Several months after confronting her parents, the daughter was hospitalized for severe depression. In the hospital she tried to hang herself with a bedsheet; she survived the suicide attempt but was severely brain-damaged. Her parents brought their daughter back home and assumed the responsibility for her nursing care.

A seventy-three-year-old man revealed that he had been accused three years earlier by his three daughters, ages thirty-seven, forty, and forty-two. "If it hadn't been for the complete love and devotion of my dear wife, and the support of my cherished son, I would have been completely destroyed," he wrote. The story he told was long and involved. His youngest daughter was born with a defective bladder, which resulted in repeated infections, bedwetting, and surgery during her childhood years. She began seeing a therapist after her husband committed suicide, and the therapist told her that she had all the classic symptoms of someone who had been subjected to sexual molestation at an early age. Her bladder problem was reinterpreted in therapy, changing from a congenital birth defect to the consequence of forced vaginal penetration during infancy, most likely by her father.

"I almost vomit as I write this," the father wrote. When his daughter discussed her fears with her sisters, they agreed to go into therapy; after several months they became convinced that their ongoing sexual and emotional difficulties were also the result of sexual abuse. The eldest daughter remembered hearing a step on the stairs leading to her bedroom and thinking, Oh, no, not again. After unsuccessful attempts to recover specific memories in counseling she attended a spiritual retreat; one day during the retreat she was staring at a blank wall when she suddenly "knew" that she had been abused as an infant. The middle daughter had no real memories but experienced intense feelings of rejection and alienation from her parents. In a series of hypnotic rebirthing sessions, she was "age-regressed" to the point where she, too, recovered memories of being sexually molested as an infant.

I'm not sure that in the beginning, when the epidemic of repressed memories was just starting to spread and infect the mass media, I ever asked the truly important questions: What is happening? Where is it going? Why is it going on right now, in the 1990s, in this country? How can we begin to study and understand it? Perhaps I hadn't yet recognized "it" as a phenomenon that could be studied, but even if I had been inclined to ask the questions, I had no time to search for the answers. I was too busy trying to sort through the piles of letters and phone messages on my desk, which threatened daily to grow out of control. I knew if I didn't make it through today's stack, I'd be buried beneath the rubble tomorrow. This can't last, I kept thinking, but it did, and it got worse. Day after day the requests for help flooded in, each more anguished and more desperate than the one before.

With some relief at escaping the chaos of my office and with hopes of gaining some insight into the problem of repressed memories, I flew to San Francisco on August 18, 1991, to attend the annual meeting of the American Psychological Association. That same week Mikhail Gorbachev announced the coming disintegration of the Soviet Union. As a child of the 1950s with vivid memories of covering my head while hiding under a wooden desk during air raid drills, I should have been rejoicing along with the rest of the real world. But in this strange universe that had enveloped me, I felt insulated and emotionally numb. I read the newspapers and listened to the nightly news reports, smiled and cheered and agreed how amazing it all was, and then gratefully retreated into my confused absorption with repressed memories. Everyone in the world was preoccupied with the end of the Cold War and all I could think about was buried memories of sexual abuse.

The annual APA conventions are huge, with thousands of participants and a printed program thick enough to qualify as a textbook. I looked through the program, starring the talks and panel discussions I wanted to attend, and scribbled down my schedule for the week. One talk particularly intrigued me. George Ganaway, a professor of psychiatry at Emory University and the director of a dissociative-disorders unit at a psychiatric hospital, was speaking on "Alternative Hypotheses Regarding Satanic Ritual Abuse Memories." Ganaway, I learned from the scuttlebutt that always accompanies these meetings, was embroiled in the controversy over the link between multiple personality disorder (MPD) and satanic ritual abuse (SRA) memories.* While many of his clinical colleagues had come to the conclusion that traumatic childhood experiences can lead to MPD, in which the personality fractures and alter personalities ("alters") protect the host personality by keeping the horrific memories secret, Ganaway believed that MPD was massively overdiagnosed and urged caution regarding the recovery of abuse memories. Referring to such memories as "reconstructions" and "pseudomemories," Ganaway argued that the brutal scenarios of bloody rituals and satanic tortures reflect "psychic reality" rather than historical, fact-based reality.

If the memories aren't real, where do they come from and why are patients so willing to believe them? In his talk, Ganaway blamed false memories on the overuse and misapplication of hypnosis. He held therapists accountable, expressing amazement at the large number of experienced therapists who do not understand the innate suggestibility of their own patients. Individuals with severe dissociative disorders are highly hypnotizable, suggestible, and fantasy-prone, he explained, and will spontaneously enter "autohypnotic trance states," particularly during stressful interviews (for example, therapy sessions). In their interactions with these patients, gullible therapists can reinforce the patient's delusions or even unwittingly implant memories.

Serious problems arise, Ganaway warned, when therapists get caught up in their patients' emerging "memories" and accept them as historically accurate. He listed a whole string of clinical entities that are incorporated into reconstructed memories, including fantasy, distortion, displacement, condensation, symbolization, and confabulation (a process by which a person unknowingly fills in the gaps and holes in memory with inferences, plausibilities, and guesswork). Mix into that mystifying stew a patient's suggestibility, high hypnotizability, and fantasy-proneness and you end up with, in Ganaway's words, "a potpourri of facts, fantasy, distortion and confabulation" capable of confounding even the most experienced therapists.

Poorly trained therapists and therapists who operate under a fixed belief system (for example, "All MPD patients have been ritually abused"; "Memory operates like an interior videorecorder"; "Healing comes only when the client accesses buried memories, resolving and integrating the

---

*The label "multiple personality disorder" is in the process of being changed to "dissociative identity disorder" (DID). Dr. David Spiegel, who chairs one of the American Psychiatric Association committees charged with revising psychiatry's Diagnostic and Statistical Manual III-R (revised) explains that the new label is used because patients suffering from what is now called MPD "really have less than one personality rather than more than one personality." The committee hopes that the stigma and controversy associated with MPD will be reduced by the new label.

trauma experience") are at greatest risk for confusing fact and fiction. Through tone of voice, phrasing of questions, and expressions of belief or disbelief, a therapist can unwittingly encourage a patient to accept the emerging "memories" as real, thus reinforcing the patient's delusions or even implanting false memories in the patient's mind. Ganaway warned that such therapists may be doing a great deal of harm to their patients and their profession.

He kept hammering away at the gullibility of therapists and the need for "cautious circumspection." Therapists must be careful that their interactions with patients do not create or reinforce the patients' delusional memories. They must always, at all times, try to avoid implanting memories of abuse, either through suggestion or expectation, because once a suggestion is seeded it can sprout into an elaborate "screen memory" that serves to block out the patient's ambiguously painful but relatively unremarkable childhood experiences. A trauma fantasy is gradually structured into a believed-in memory that contains clear and logical distinctions between good and evil, allowing the patient to see himself as "special" and worthy of the therapist's attention and compassion.

Ganaway illustrated his discussion with several fascinating case histories. Sarah, a fifty-year-old multiple personality disorder patient, employed "screen memories" in an attempt to shield herself from an upsetting childhood experience. One day during a therapy session "Carrie," a five-year-old "alter" who until then was completely unknown to Sarah, spontaneously emerged to describe her participation in a ritual mass murder near Sarah's childhood home. Twelve little girls from her Sunday school class were bound, raped, and brutally murdered, "Carrie" revealed, but Sarah was spared by the cult leader (who happened to be a member of her church). As "Carrie" related the grisly tale, she became deeply emotional; it was almost as if she had gone back to the past and was once again watching the ghastly scene.

After "Carrie" withdrew, Sarah sought validation for the memory. Other alters, she claimed, were telling her that "Carrie" had even more horrific tales to tell. Ganaway remained neutral, refusing to offer an opinion on the validity of the memory and allowing his patient to come to her own conclusions. Two sessions later "Sherry," a previously known child alter, came forward to confess that she made up the whole story, creating "Carrie" in an attempt to mask the terror she felt when she recalled a real childhood memory: her grandmother reading to her from detective magazines, leaving out none of the grisly and gory details.

Ganaway concluded that Sarah invented the "screen memory" of the Sunday school mass murder in an attempt to preserve her grandmother's image as a loving, protective figure. By allowing her "alter" to weave the fiction of the crime stories into the fact of her actual experiences, she was able to hide the intolerable reality of her grandmother's emotional abuse behind an elaborate latticework of fantasy and illusion. The created memory wheeled in like a gaudy movie set to cover drab background scenery.

Generated by the patient in an attempt to disguise or mask more prosaic forms of childhood abuse, screen memories are one source of ritualistic abuse memories. "Iatrogenic implantation" is an even more potent source of these memories, Ganaway explained. An "iatrogenic" ailment is one produced by or resulting from the activity of a physician (or therapist). Thus, the attitudes, expectations, and behavior of the therapist may suggest and then reinforce a patient's vivid memories of horrific abuse. The treatment creates the disease; the illness is doctor-made.

Ganaway told an amazing story about Ann, a young woman who had been unsuccessfully treated several years earlier for multiple personality disorder stemming from abuse by her psychotic grandmother. When Ann became pregnant with her second child, her dissociative symptoms returned and she immediately started therapy with a doctorate-level therapist specializing in the treatment of MPD. The therapist, who had been to several SRA seminars and appeared to have certain expectations and a well-defined agenda, began to explore the possibility that Ann's grandmother had been in league with "satanists." Was there a group or a cult? the therapist queried. Were they wearing robes? Were babies present at the rituals, and did Ann participate?

When Ann answered no to each of these questions, she was instructed to go home, think about the possibilities, and try to remember details. In follow-up sessions while she was under hypnosis, Ann eventually agreed that she had been involved in a cult. Relying heavily on yes and no answers by the use of finger signals while Ann was in trance, her therapist successfully "contacted" several satanic alters who confided that the cult intended to sacrifice the newborn baby. After emerging from the hypnotic trance and listening to her therapist's account of the alters' plans, Ann expressed skepticism, arguing that the "memories" did not seem real to her. She wondered if the alter personalities might be lying, and she asked for the therapist's help to sort out the facts from the fiction. Disregarding his patient's concerns, the therapist informed her that the rich detail and consistency of her memories confirmed that she had been involved with a satanic cult.

The sessions continued, and the therapist proceeded to reinforce Ann's memories, communicating by gestures* while asking suggestive and lead-

---

*Such nonverbal communication by hand gestures is called idiomotor signalling. One finger on the right hand is used to signal "yes," another finger on the right hand is used to signal "no," and a finger on the left hand indicates "stop" (i.e., stop the questioning procedure). When Ann was hypnotized and in a trance state, her therapist used these gestures to communicate with her.

ing questions. When Ann went into labor, her therapist insisted on setting up around-the-clock surveillance to protect the baby. Ann was permitted to see her newborn only briefly, and always under guard, because the therapist feared that a satanic alter, programmed in Ann's mind, would emerge to perform the mandated sacrifice. The hospital staff and law enforcement personnel heeded the therapist's warnings, participating in efforts to strengthen hospital security and save the baby from the murderous clutches of the satanic cult.

Ann was eventually transferred to Dr. Ganaway's psychiatric unit by her physician husband, who was understandably concerned about his wife's therapy and the bizarre protective measures surrounding his newborn child. Within two days of psychotherapy, during which the psychiatric staff neither reinforced nor attempted to extinguish the satanic abuse memories, the entire array of memories "spontaneously evaporated." Ann eventually came to the understanding that she had fabricated the SRA memories in response to the nurturing and attention her therapist offered as a reward for confessing her cult involvement. Her greatest fear was that she might be exploited again by a manipulative therapist using invasive hypnotic techniques.

I was enthralled. Ganaway was stating clearly, forcefully, and without equivocation that therapists can unintentionally plant suggestions that lead to the creation and rapid growth of false memories of abuse. A respected scholar and esteemed psychiatrist was openly and freely admitting that he had seen evidence in his clinical practice of the same processes of memory distortion and implantation that I had observed in my laboratory. He agreed that memories can be distorted, even created, in susceptible minds by the tone of voice, phrasing of a question, subtle nonverbal signals, and expressions of boredom, impatience, or fascination. In short, he believed that in some cases—in his opinion, far too many cases—therapists were creating the very problems they hoped to cure.

How generalizable were Ganaway's conclusions? If a therapist can unwittingly implant a memory in a highly suggestible patient, and that suggestion generates a whole garden of memories, wouldn't it also be possible for a patient with less severe but nevertheless significant problems to pick up on a therapist's expectations of abuse and remember events or experiences that never happened? The memories might not be so flamboyant and spectacular as in these MPD patients with their bloody, paranoid visions of torture and ritual abuse. But given the right conditions, wouldn't it be possible to cultivate discrete and detailed pseudomemories in the fertile soil of normal minds?

I introduced myself to Ganaway after the talk, briefly filling him in on my experiences with the Franklin case and the recent onslaught of letters and phone calls from accused parents.* "You encounter the extreme cases in your work with MPD patients and SRA memories," I said, feeling a little uneasy with the unfamiliar acronyms. (I was much more at ease talking with memory researchers about "STM" and "LTM," short-term memory and long-term memory.) "But isn't it possible that the same potential for contamination and implantation exists in the larger population of confused people wandering into therapists' offices in search of answers to their life problems?"

"I think there is a similar danger," Ganaway said evenly, without so much as raising an eyebrow. "Two basic sources of contamination lead to the creation of pseudomemories. We are all susceptible to influence by books, newspaper and magazine articles, sermons, lectures, films, and television. For example, exposure to docudrama television shows, which mix fact with dramatic visual reconstructions of purported crimes, can be a potent source of contamination, creating fears, expectations, dreams and imaginings in susceptible minds. The second powerful contaminating source can be discovered in the suggestions or expectations of an authority figure with whom the patient desires a special relationship."

"In other words, a therapist," I interjected.

He nodded. "Suppose a patient desires the approval of a therapist and feels the need to be interesting, unusual, or somehow special. Or perhaps the patient feels 'stuck,' as if she is getting nowhere in her therapy. Now suppose that this patient's therapist believes that sexual abuse is approaching epidemic proportions and that a great majority of the people who walk into his office have been sexually or ritually abused. Assume further that the therapist believes that memory works like a video recorder, imprinting every thought, emotion, and experience and storing it away for safekeeping. Those are precisely the right conditions for the creation of a false memory, and I believe those conditions are being met daily in hundreds of therapy sessions."

"But why would patients want to incorporate into their history and sense of self such brutal and painful memories?" I asked him the question everybody asks me. "What would motivate people to see themselves as victims and portray their loved ones as cruel and uncaring?"

"Screen memories impart a feeling of importance and specialness, even a sense of adventure," Ganaway explained. "A patient may have felt deprived or ignored as a child, or perhaps he felt unexceptional because nothing exciting or unusual ever happened to him. Any number of experiences can cause suggestible patients to retreat into fantasy. Their elaborate pseudomemories help them to feel special and worthy of a therapist's attention, even fascination. If the therapist becomes overly fascinated,

---

*My conversation with Dr. Ganaway was recreated with his help.

asking specific, suggestive questions, expressing surprise, disgust, belief, or disbelief, voicing an opinion, or becoming excited and agitated, then the patient might feel pressured to authenticate the memory. In other words, the reaction of the therapist can function as a catalyst to solidify the imaginative material into a concrete memory."

I had one final question. "As a clinician, how can you tell if a patient's memories are real or imagined?"

"Without independent corroboration, I don't know of any way for a therapist to be absolutely sure," Ganaway said. "Actual deprivation and abuse certainly affect the nature of a child's developing psychic reality, but not in a way that allows a therapist years later to differentiate with certainty what is real and what is imagined.

"Most psychodynamically trained therapists understand and respect this fact," Ganaway continued, "for it is the careful, systematic exploration and understanding of the *meaning* derived from unconscious fantasies regarding wishes and fears that has been the focus of modern psychoanalytically informed therapies, rather than determining the factual basis of recollected personal experiences. Only recently when some therapists of various theoretical persuasions and personal motives began to completely ignore the psychodynamic influence of unconscious fantasy on their patients' memories did the current epidemic of 'abuse memories' take root and the 'psychology of the victim' begin to flourish in our society. Freud would be turning over in his grave if he knew what these therapists have done to oversimplify, distort and cheapen his complex theory of the mind to suit their personal agendas. It may be years before the public's faith in the efficacy of traditional psychoanalytic psychotherapy is restored in the wake of the damage done by what I call 'McTherapy'— the fast food pseudotherapies of the 1980's and 1990's."

Extreme suggestibility. Dissociative defense mechanisms. Therapist-induced belief systems. Iatrogenic influences.

I flew back to Seattle with a sense of purpose and direction. Ganaway's clinical observations supplied all the pieces—vulnerable clients, gullible therapists, a credulous society, pervasive fear of sexual abuse. Now all I had to do was figure out how to put these pieces together in a psychological experiment. The major difficulty confronting me was how to pierce the heart of the problem—the central question about the authenticity of these lost-and-found memories. While I couldn't prove that a particular memory emerging in therapy was false, perhaps I could step around to the other side of the problem. Through careful experimental design and controlled studies, perhaps I could provide a theoretical framework for the creation of false memories, showing that it is possible to create an entire memory for a traumatic event that never happened.

The day after I returned to Seattle I sat down with a group of graduate students and psychology majors and brainstormed with them about the possibility of experimentally implanting an entire memory for a fictitious event. As dozens of ideas were generated and then discarded, we realized that we were confronted with several seemingly insurmountable problems. First, the implanted memory had to be at least mildly traumatic, because if we succeeded in injecting a pleasant memory, or even an ambiguously unpleasant one, into our subjects' minds, critics would argue that our findings were not generalizable to recovered memories of sexual abuse.

Second, in order to parallel the therapeutic process, the memory had to be implanted by someone the subject trusted and admired, either a relative, a friend, or a respected authority figure. But we couldn't be blatantly manipulative and risk endangering the relationship between the subject and the "implanter." Nor could we cause our subjects undue emotional stress, either through the creation of the pseudomemory or in the debriefing during which subjects learned that they had been intentionally deceived. The trick was to design a study powerful enough to prove that it is possible to implant a false memory while also winning the approval of the university's Human Subjects Committee, which reviews proposed research projects to ensure that they will not be harmful to participants.

We kept coming up with ideas and dismissing them as too unlikely to succeed or too traumatic. I began to wonder if it was even possible to design a false-memory experiment. Maybe the only way around this particular problem was to approach it obliquely, reporting on real-life anecdotes and evidence demonstrating that memory is malleable even in the most traumatic experiences. In fact, a friend and colleague was in the process of doing just that in his experiments with "flashbulb memories" of the January 1986 space shuttle *Challenger* explosion.

The morning after the explosion and then again two and a half years later, cognitive psychologist Ulric Neisser asked forty-four student subjects this question: "How did you first hear the news of the *Challenger* disaster?" While most subjects described their two-and-a-half-year-old memories as "vivid," not one of the memories was entirely accurate, and over a third were, in Neisser's words, 'wildly inaccurate.' Consider the following:

January 1986:
  I was in my religion class and some people walked in and started talking about the [explosion]. I didn't know any details except that it had exploded and the schoolteacher's students had all been watching which I thought was so sad. Then after class I went to my room and watched the TV program talking about it and I got all the details from that.

Two and a half years later this student forgot all about her religion class; her new memory featured a roommate, a news flash, and a phone call:

> September 1988:
> When I first heard about the explosion I was sitting in my freshman dorm room with my roommate and we were watching TV. It came on a news flash and we were both totally shocked. I was really upset and I went upstairs to talk to a friend of mine and then I called my parents.

Even more surprising than such dramatic changes in the original memories were the subjects' astonished reactions when confronted with their original written accounts. They simply could not believe that their revised memories were mistaken; even after reading and reviewing the questionnaires they had filled out the morning after the explosion, they insisted that their altered memories were more accurate and "real." "This is my handwriting, so it must be right," one student explained, "but I still remember everything happening the way I told you [two and a half years later]. I can't help it."

"As far as we can tell," Neisser concluded, "the original memories are just gone."

Neisser's study challenges popular thinking about "flashbulb memories," which holds that strong emotions create vivid and accurate memories. As psychologist William James put it more than a hundred years ago: "An impression may be so exciting emotionally as almost to leave a scar upon the cerebral tissues." The *Challenger* explosion definitely left a vivid impression on its viewers' minds, but it was almost as if the brain, in an annual spring-cleaning frenzy, kept snipping out the scar tissue and grafting it onto a new spot. What triggered these transplants?

That was the question I attempted to answer in my experimental studies on the distorting effect of post-event information. But now I was obsessed with a *Brave New World* kind of experiment. I wanted to "scar" the brain with something that never happened, creating a vivid but wholly imagined impression. I just couldn't quite figure out how to do it.

In late October I flew to the University of Georgia to give my usual talk on what I call the misinformation effect. When people witness an event and are later exposed to new and misleading information about that event, what happens to their original memory? I typically answer this question with observations from real life and laboratory experiments showing that people can be led to believe that they perceived events or objects in a way that differs from reality or even that they remembered something that did not in fact exist. Once a person adopts a reconstructed memory, he or she tends to believe in it as strongly as in genuine memories, even replacing earlier recollections with the new, invented facts.

This speech is always a good place to insert amusing anecdotes, and I told a little story about former president Ronald Reagan's habit of confusing fact and fiction. As one might expect, the fiction in Reagan's entertaining stories was supplied by popular films from his movie star days. During the campaigns of 1976, 1980, and 1984, Reagan told and retold a story of heroism and sacrifice set during a World War II bombing raid over Europe. A B-1 was hit by anti-aircraft fire, and the wounded gunner, an inexperienced young man, cried out in terror when he could not eject from his seat. His commander, older, wiser, and very brave, comforted him, saying, "Never mind, son, we'll ride it down together." Reagan ended the story with misty eyes, recalling that the commander was posthumously awarded the Congressional Medal of Honor for his heroism.

A curious journalist checked the 434 World War II Medal of Honor winners and found no such award. He did, however, turn up a scene in a 1944 movie called *A Wing and a Prayer*, in which the pilot of a Navy torpedo bomber rode the plane down with his wounded radioman after the gunner bailed out. "We'll take this ride together," the pilot said. The journalist also discovered a Reader's Digest story in which the gunner, not the pilot, went down with a wounded crew member. "Take it easy, we'll take this ride together," the last man to jump heard the gunner say.

When the White House was questioned about the accuracy of President Reagan's accounts, which were always presented as if they were factual, a spokesman said, "If you tell the same story five times, it's true." Despite the witticism, a serious debate apparently ensued within the White House over whether the President knew what he was doing when he told made-up stories—or whether he actually could not distinguish films from fact.

That story always generates a lot of chuckles, and I rode the wave of goodwill into the dangerous waters of repressed memories. I told the story of Eileen Franklin's recovered memory and ended my talk with a hypothetical question and a simple plea for help. "Could it be," I asked, "that Eileen's memory was put together by an overactive, fantasy-prone imagination, with bits and pieces of the factual story supplied by newspaper reports, television accounts, and numerous conversations that took place over the years? I'm looking for a way to study the phenomenon of false memories in the laboratory, but I haven't quite figured out how to do it. If anyone has any suggestions, I'd be more than happy to hear them."

The next morning I got a ride to the Atlanta airport with Denise Park, a cognitive psychologist who studies information processing in the elderly. Her two children, Rob and Colleen, sat in the backseat and listened politely as I explained to their mother how frustrated I was getting with the memory-implantation experiment.

"I want to implant a whole memory," I told Denise, "not just a piece of a memory. And the memory has to be traumatic, but not so traumatic that the experiment would be rejected as unethical."

Denise was quiet for a moment. Then, in a sudden burst of inspiration, she said, "How about getting lost?"

"Lost," I repeated. We happened to be driving past a huge shopping mall, and the idea just popped into my head. "What about getting lost in a shopping mall?"

"That's perfect," Denise said, "because it taps into every parent's worst fear—losing sight of your child in an immense place filled with strangers. What do you think, Rob, Colleen?" She looked at her children in the rearview mirror. "What would it feel like to be lost in a shopping mall?"

"Scary," they answered in unison.

Colleen squirmed in her seat. "I don't even like to think about it," she said.

"What if we had a parent or older sibling make the initial suggestion?" I said after watching Denise's interaction with her children.

"Yes, that's perfect!" Denise was getting excited about the idea. "You'd have all the ingredients you would need for implantation—the traumatic event, the trusted authority figure offering the suggestive comments, and the vulnerable, suggestible subject."

"It's certainly harmless enough," I mused. I was wondering if we could get the idea through the Human Subjects Committee. Maybe. "And if it worked you could argue that you had implanted a whole memory for a false childhood event. It would be even better than the Piaget anecdote."

Jean Piaget's attempted-kidnapping story, which I quoted earlier, is the best example psychologists have of a whole memory implanted into a vulnerable mind by a trusted authority figure. But it is not a perfect illustration, because the story was undoubtedly told and retold many times and became part of the family folklore. We have no idea when and how Piaget's memory began, or how many times it metamorphosed over the years. But the shopping mall idea would enable us to know exactly what was suggested to the subjects, and if the suggestion was accepted, we could watch the memory take root and grow.

The more I thought about the possibility the more excited I became. It just might work. A week or two later I was at a party, talking with a friend whom I hadn't seen for a long time. "What's new in memory research these days?" he asked. I told him about the repressed-memory controversy and my attempts to study the phenomenon in the laboratory, mentioning the new idea for the shopping mall experiment.

"Every parent's worst nightmare," he said, immediately and automatically echoing Denise Park's sentiment. "I can't imagine how frightening it would be to lose Jenny, even for a few minutes." He gestured toward his daughter, who was sitting in a corner of the room and looking bored with the cocktail conversation.

"How old is she?" I asked.

"She just turned eight."

"Do you think it might be possible to convince her that she was lost in a shopping mall when she was five years old?"

"No way," he said with a laugh. "Jenny's very logical, very rational, and she has an amazing memory." He shrugged his shoulders. "But why don't we give it a try?"

He called Jenny over, put his arm around her, and introduced us. I asked about the family's plans for the upcoming holidays. What was she going to do during the school vacation? Did she have a Christmas wish list? Her father used those questions to slide into the shopping mall suggestion.

"Hey, Jenny, remember that time when you got lost at the Bellevue Mall?"

A confused expression came over Jenny's face, as if she were trying to remember but couldn't come up with any details.

"You were five years old," her father prompted, "and it was about this time of year, a month or so before Christmas."

"That was three years ago, Dad." Jenny looked slightly embarrassed and elbowed her father in the ribs. "How do you expect me to remember that far back?"

"Don't you remember? I had to go into the Eddie Bauer store to buy a present for Mom, and you wanted to play on the tugboat." The tugboat is a familiar landmark at the center of the Bellevue Mall. "Then when I came out of the store a few minutes later, you were gone."

Jenny continued to look perplexed.

"I looked in Nordstrom's, the toy store, and a shoe store before I found you."

Jenny slowly nodded her head. "Oh yeah, I guess I do remember that," she said. "I was looking all over for you, and I couldn't find you."

"Were you scared, Jenny?" I asked. She shook her head noncommittally.

"I was scared," her father said.

Jenny smiled and snuggled up against him. "Not as scared as I was," she replied.

I couldn't believe what I had just witnessed. In five minutes, with a few suggestions and minor prods from her father, Jenny had accepted a false memory and embellished it with details of her own. She remembered being lost, she remembered looking all over for her father, and she remembered being scared. In less time than it took to cook a hard-boiled egg, we had created a false memory.

The next week in my cognitive psychology class I announced the term project. "I want you to go out and try to create in someone's mind a memory of an event or experience that never happened. You could try to convince your roommate that she had chicken last night instead of hamburger. Or you could try to convince a friend or relative that he owes you money, and it's time to pay it back."

I give the same assignment every year, but this time I included a little extra twist. "I've been thinking a lot lately about whether it is possible to inject into someone's mind a whole memory for a fictitious event. For example, would it be possible to make someone believe that they were lost in a shopping mall as a child when, in fact, they had never been lost in a shopping mall?"

My suggestion was successfully implanted. When the assignments were handed in three weeks later, two students had devised a way to create a memory for being lost. Eight-year-old Brittany was convinced by her mother that when she was five years old she and her best friend got lost in Selby Ranch, a condominium complex. This is the story Brittany's mother told her as if it were the truth:

> A kind old lady who lived in the complex found Brittany and took her into her condo and gave her a cookie. The lady had a beautiful daughter who was a model in San Francisco and the daughter gave Brittany a bouquet of balloons.

Eighteen days later a friend of the family interviewed Brittany under the pretext of getting information for a school newspaper article on childhood memories. Tape-recording the conversation, the friend inquired about several genuine memories and then asked questions about the false memory. Brittany failed to remember anything about one of the real events, her sixth birthday party at her aunt's farm.

"Don't you remember it?" the interviewer asked.

"I don't. It was in our house at Houston."

"Don't you remember what you did?"

"No," Brittany responded.

"Do you remember who was there?"

"No . . . well, I know Samantha was there. No, she wasn't. She wasn't born yet."

But when asked about the false memory, Brittany had quite a story to tell.

"Do you remember where you were?"

"Selby Ranch. . . . I can't remember like how it looked. But I think it was there. There was like hay. It was around Halloween, so there were pumpkins around. . . ."

"Who was with you?"

"Um . . . Christina, Camille . . . and me and my mum were visiting my grandparents."

"What were you doing?"

"Well, we were playing, and, but then Christina left. I think she had to make a phone call or something. And then me and Camille went off playing in the woods. And . . . um . . . I really can't remember this, but I think this happened when we went to this girl's house. Her daughter was a model. And then we made cookies at her house. And then my mum finally found us."

Brittany continued to embellish the false memory. The kind woman who took them in not only gave them a cookie but baked a whole batch of cookies with their help. The woman's home became a "small cottage outside the gates of Selby Ranch" (in reality, most of the houses in the area are 3,000- to 4,000-square-foot contemporary California-style ranch houses). And Brittany recalled the exact words her mother said when she found her: "Thank goodness I found you, I was looking all over for you."

Another student, Jim Coan, created a false memory in the mind of his fourteen-year-old brother, Chris. In the first phase of his case study, Jim presented Chris with a one-paragraph written description of four childhood events, only three of which actually happened. Chris was instructed to write about all four events every day for five days, offering any facts or descriptions he could remember about each event. If he could not recall any additional details, he was instructed to write "I don't remember."

The false memory was introduced in this paragraph:

> It was 1981 or 1982. I remember that Chris was five. We had gone shopping at the University City shopping mall in Spokane. After some panic, we found Chris being led down the mall by a tall, oldish man (I think he was wearing a flannel shirt). Chris was crying and holding the man's hand. The man explained that he had found Chris walking around crying his eyes out just a few moments before and was trying to help him find his parents.

In his five-day journal, Chris gave the following details:

> Day 1: I remember a little bit about that man. I remember thinking, "Wow! He's really cool!"
>
> Day 2: That day I was so scared that I would never see my family again. I knew that I was in trouble.

> Day 3: I remember Mom telling me never to do that again.
> Day 4: I also remember that old man's flannel shirt.
> Day 5: I sort of remember the stores.

In summarizing his memory, Chris produced a new fact, recalling a conversation with the man who found him: "I remember the man asking me if I was lost."

Was Chris simply trying to help his older brother by elaborating on this "memory"? Chris's responses to one of the true memories seemed to argue against this possibility. On the first day Chris wrote, "I can't remember." And for the next four days he wrote, "I still can't remember."

What if Jim had inadvertently tapped into a real memory?

Perhaps Chris really did get lost in a shopping mall when he was a young boy. To test for this possibility, Chris's mother was presented with Chris's "memory" of the day he got lost in the shopping mall and asked if she remembered the event. On day one she said, "I have thought about this day, but I am having trouble remembering the details." On day two she said, "I have tried and tried to remember this day. I see us looking under clothes racks for Christopher's feet, but I can't honestly say that this was that time." After five days of trying to remember, she summarized her feelings: "For some reason I feel guilty about this, that I can't remember."

A few weeks later Chris was interviewed again and asked to describe each of the four events and rate it according to how clear it was on a scale from 1 (not clear at all) to 11 (very, very clear). For the three true memories, Chris gave ratings of 1, 10, and 5. For the false shopping mall memory, he assigned his second-highest rating: 8. Asked to describe his getting-lost memory, Chris supplied rich and abundant details.

> I was with the guys for a second, and I think I went over to look at the toy store, the Kay-Bee toys and uh, we got lost, and I was looking around and I thought, "Uh-oh. I'm in trouble now." You know. And then I . . . I thought I was never going to see my family again. I was really scared, you know. And then this old man, I think he was wearing a blue flannel, came up to me . . . he was kind of old. He was kind of bald on top . . . he had like a ring of gray hair . . . and he had glasses.

In a final part of the study, Chris was informed by his brother that one of the memories was false. Did he know which memory was implanted? Chris selected one of the real memories. When told that the memory of being lost in the shopping mall was the false memory, he couldn't quite believe it.

Really? Well, no . . . 'cause I thought I was . . . I remember being lost and looking around for you guys. . . . I do remember that. . . . And then crying and Mom coming up and saying, "Where were you? Don't you ever do that again!"

I looked at my students' results and listened several times to the tape recordings in which Chris and Brittany described their false memories. With each additional review, I became more convinced that we had the idea for our formal experiment. This rough, preliminary data proved that it was possible to experimentally implant in a suggestible person's mind an entire, and entirely false, childhood memory. Not only was it possible, it was unbelievably easy.

The method used to create Chris's false memory seemed almost ideal, although we needed to smooth out some problems before putting together a formal proposal for the study. For example, we wanted to include older subjects in our study, but shopping malls weren't widespread until the 1970s. So we made a few modifications and tried out our ideas with twenty-two-year-old John and forty-two-year-old Bill.

With the help of his aunt, we convinced John that he had been lost in a large sporting goods store at the age of five or six ("I have a vague memory of being at the top of the ramp, crying"). And with his sister's help, we convinced Bill that he had been lost in a Sears store when he was five or six. "I remember what Sears looked like in Santa Monica—or was it J. C. Penney's?" Bill said, trying to put the details of his newly implanted memory in logical order. "I felt panicky—where were Mom and Linda? I felt scared . . . I remember going up or down the stairway at Sears. I remember the elevator bell at Sears. Now I remember—it was Sears, not J. C. Penney's."

These five cases offered proof—what scientists call existence proof, which is simply proof that something exists or is possible—for the fact that it is possible to create false memories for childhood events. Five people, ranging in age from eight to forty-two, were induced to develop a memory for something that never happened. Was the memory real to them? The subjects' willingness to expand on the memory and provide details that were not even hinted at in the initial suggestion seemed to indicate that the memory was very real indeed. Jenny remembered being scared. Brittany embellished her memory with pumpkins, hay, and batches of cookies. Chris recalled verbatim conversations, balding hair, and glasses. John remembered standing at the top of a store ramp, crying. Bill imagined elevator bells.

We now had a clear procedure in mind, we were optimistic that we could produce false memories of getting lost, and we were confident that the procedure would not harm the individuals who participated in our study. (In fact, all our preliminary case examples thoroughly enjoyed their part in the study, reacting with good-natured amazement to the news that experimenters had successfully tampered with their memories.) We filled out endless questionnaires, and sent our proposal to the Human Subjects Committee for approval.

The formal study would be conducted in two major phases. In phase one, subjects would be asked to write about four childhood memories. Three memories would relate to events that actually happened when they were about five years old, but the fourth would be the false memory of being lost in a shopping center or other public place. Subjects would write about the four memories over several days; one group would keep a daily journal for five days while another group would keep a journal for only two days. In phase two of the experiment, which would take place approximately two weeks later, a researcher would interview the subjects about their memories to determine whether they "remembered" the false events. Subjects would be asked to rate the clarity of their memories on a scale from 1 to 10, where 1 indicated an extremely vague memory, and 10 an extremely clear memory.

We could hardly wait to begin the study and answer some of the crucial questions about false-memory implantation. How often would we succeed in implanting a false memory? How would subjects rate the clarity of their false memories? What would the comparisons between the "true" and the "false" memories teach us? Would the real memories have more emotion in them, more details, more inherent credibility?

We waited for two months before receiving a reply. The Human Subjects Committee tore our proposed study apart. "What if your subjects are under emotional stress and became upset at the deception inherent in the experimental situation?" the Committee members asked in their written report. "How do you plan to screen out vulnerable subjects? What will you do if someone becomes seriously distressed when informed of the deception? What if a subject finds the false memory disturbingly similar to an event that actually happened? Will your subjects experience a sense of betrayal at being manipulated?"

We carefully responded to the committee's concerns, developing a procedure for screening out psychologically unstable subjects, another plan for dealing with participants who might find the implanted memory disturbing, and additional strategies for removing confusions, defusing tensions, and repairing breaches of trust. Once again, we waited, fingers crossed. When we finally got word that the Human Subjects Committee had approved a modified version of the shopping mall study, we immediately began to recruit students to help run subjects and analyze data.

*   *   *

Several months later, when the study was well underway, one of the student researchers knocked on my office door. In her hand was a copy of *Cosmopolitan* magazine.

"I don't usually read this," she laughed, holding up the cover, featuring a stunning model in a sequined and bangled bikini, "but I couldn't resist this article titled 'Questions About Sex (Even the Most Adventurous Cosmo Girls Want Answered).' Take a look at the third question."

I read the question and answer out loud.

QUESTION: My breasts are sensitive—I don't like anyone even touching them. I know this doesn't endear me to men, so should I smile my way through the displeasure? Since my breasts are small, could the sensitivity be mostly psychological?

ANSWER: Discomfort of this kind usually means there's a link between your breasts and an unpleasant experience in your past. When you were very young, perhaps someone fondled or commented unfavorably on your breasts; it was so unpleasant that you've repressed the whole memory . . . I would suggest you find out what the discomfort is all about.

I remember putting the magazine down and shaking my head, not in dismay or disbelief necessarily, but almost in an attempt to dislodge my skepticism and come back to this world that no longer made any sense to me.

"Well, what do you think?" the student asked cheerily.

"I think another repressed memory is about to be recovered," I said.

8

A FAMILY DESTROYED

*My father loved children. He'd always play with all the little
cousins when they came over. He spent a lot of time with
teenagers in the church and stuff, so! You know.
He was a good dad, too.*

—Jennifer Nagle

*In a psychotherapeutically inspired double bind typical
of our times, denial itself is evidence of denial,
the pathological indicator that makes declarations
of innocence virtual proof of guilt.*

—*Family Therapy Networker*, September/October 1993

No parent-child relationship is perfect. When we reflect back on the
past, we often find ourselves wishing that our parents had given us more
attention, more respect, more love. These are universal yearnings, and
even people who grew up in the happiest of homes experience moments
of regret and disappointment when they remember what was and consider what might have been.

The story of *Doug Nagle* and his family* raises several important
questions. Can these unresolved, conflicted longings metamorphose over
time, with suggestions, insinuations, and continued pressure from others,
into false memories of abuse? Fifteen-year-old *Jennifer Nagle* entered
therapy with no memories of being sexually abused, but after more than
ten months of intensive psychotherapy she suddenly recovered detailed

---

*This chapter is based on a true story, but to protect the family's privacy, we
have modified certain facts and used pseudonyms. (The only people identified by their real names are Doug Nagle's attorney Steve Moen and expert
witnesses John Yuille and Elizabeth Loftus.) The story is recreated from numerous legal documents including depositions, pre-trial interviews, therapists' transcripts, and trial testimony. Interviews with Steve Moen confirmed
the basic facts.

memories of abuse—where did those memories come from, and why did they appear so suddenly and with such compelling emotional force? The search for answers is complicated by the fact that in this particular case there were two accusing daughters. It would seem, then, that the skeptic's request for "proof" has been satisfied, for one daughter's accusations provide the necessary corroboration for the other's.

When I agreed to testify as a witness for the defense in Doug Nagle's criminal trial, I understood how damning the evidence appeared on the surface. But, as you will discover, the facts in this case cannot be reduced to formulas or simple conclusions. The only truth that can be stated with absolute conviction is that a family, once functioning and intact, was slowly and methodically destroyed by a system that was supposedly constructed to protect the innocent.

"They warned me you might be in denial."

"Denial means you're dangerous."

"You are deeply in denial."

Doug Nagle had the feeling he had stepped into a nightmare. He kept looking around, touching the bedspread, pushing his foot into the carpet, twisting his wedding ring. He tried blinking his eyes, sighing, coughing, holding his breath, anything to make this dream world disappear and bring the real world back. But nothing worked. This was the real world. He was in his bedroom, it was nine P.M., and his wife *Debbie,* had just accused him of sexually abusing two of their four daughters nearly a decade earlier.

Debbie's voice was unnaturally calm and distant as she detailed the accusations. Twenty-three-year-old old *Kristen,* their oldest daughter, had recently recovered memories of being sexually abused by her father. Kristen also told her sister, fifteen-year-old Jennifer, that she thought she had seen her father molesting her. When Kristen called Jennifer's counselor and discussed her fears with her, the counselor immediately called Debbie and together they made the decision to contact CPS.

"Child Protective Services?" Doug asked. He couldn't believe what he was hearing.

Debbie nodded her head. "We've been advised by Jennifer's counselor and caseworkers at CPS that you should move out of the house temporarily."

"But I never abused my children," Doug protested.

"They warned me you might be in denial."

"This can't be happening."

"Denial means you're dangerous."

"Please, Debbie, you have to tell me . . . what did I do?"

"You are deeply in denial."

* * *

Three weeks later Doug sat in a psychologist's office, trying to prepare himself for a sexual-deviancy evaluation. Debbie had given him an ultimatum: Either he be evaluated by a licensed psychologist, or she would insist that he leave the house and never see his children again. A small, slightly built man in his mid-forties, wearing a three-piece suit, with thick glasses to correct nearsightedness, Doug waited nervously, desperate to get some insight into the disaster that had befallen his family. In his position as a natural resources lawyer for a large timber company, he was accustomed to negotiating disputes, settling arguments, and recommending compromises. If everyone would just talk to each other, he kept repeating to himself, if we could just put all the thoughts, feelings and facts on the table, a compromise of some sort could be reached, and everything would return to normal.

But no one would talk to him. No one would tell him what he had supposedly done to his children. Jennifer had moved out of the house and was living with a friend. He wrote her a letter but didn't dare send it without asking Debbie to read and approve its contents; Debbie said she would pass the letter on to Jennifer but Doug had no way of knowing if she had done so. When he asked if he could join the family at church, Debbie said his presence would be "inappropriate." She wouldn't even allow him to be alone with *Anna,* twelve, his youngest daughter, who hadn't accused him of anything.

In three short weeks his whole life had unraveled. He was confused, frustrated, and distraught; without warning, he would suddenly burst into tears. He couldn't work because he couldn't keep his mind on complicated legal issues. Friends and colleagues offered solace and advice, but their suggestions only increased his misery. A criminal attorney warned him to watch everything he said and did. "A cottage industry of poorly trained and politically inspired sex abuse therapists has sprung up in the last decade," the attorney confided, "and they have at least two good reasons for not wanting to help someone accused of sexual abuse. First, they fear malpractice suits—what if you go out and molest somebody else?—and second, Child Protective Services won't have anything to do with therapists who side with the defense. It all comes down to economics. Therapists can't make a living on the defense side."

"Mr. Nagle," a deep voice broke through his reverie. *Dr. Barker* shook Doug's hand and led him into a dark office with book-lined walls and comfortable overstuffed chairs. After the introductory exchanges, the psychologist asked his new client to describe his problem.

Doug told the short story, the only one he knew. His wife had informed him that their oldest daughter, Kristen, had accused him of sexually abusing her; Kristen believed that he had also abused her younger sister Jennifer. He had not been told any specifics of the alleged abuse—

when, where, or how it supposedly happened—and he didn't know if Jennifer agreed with her sister that she had been abused by her father.

"I have no idea what I am accused of doing to them," Doug said, struggling to keep his emotions under control. "Debbie hasn't told me anything, and I have no memory of abusing my children. I'm trying to be responsible about these charges—I've even tried to convince myself that it could have happened and I've somehow repressed the memory, just as the girls apparently repressed their memories. That's what Debbie calls the process—repression. I am willing to accept that possibility. But I don't understand how I could have molested my children and not remember anything about it, not one detail. It doesn't seem possible, although Debbie tells me it happens to people all the time."

Auto-suggestion?

Doug started to cry. "I'm having a very hard time," he said apologetically, but with no attempt to wipe the tears from his face. "I'm very confused, very upset. I've been accused, but I don't know what I've done. And I have no idea what to do, where to go, who to turn to for help."

"I have two recommendations," Dr. Barker said, after giving his client a moment to collect himself. "First, I think that we should conduct a sexual-deviancy evaluation. And second, I strongly recommend that you receive some ongoing counseling to help you cope with your situation. I could perform either one of those functions but not both."

After some discussion, Doug agreed to see a female therapist for counseling. He wanted to involve his wife and daughters in the counseling sessions, and he thought they might feel more comfortable talking to a woman. He asked Dr. Barker to administer the sexual-deviancy evaluation.

"How many of these evaluations have you conducted?" Doug asked.

"Over two thousand."

Two thousand! Doug thought. That seemed like a lot of evaluations for one not-quite-middle-aged psychologist. It took some courage to ask the next question. "How many of those two thousand did you think were innocent?"

Dr. Barker hesitated for a moment. "One, perhaps two," he finally answered.

In his second session, Doug took a battery of psychological tests, after which Dr. Barker asked detailed questions about his sexual history. Doug was unaccustomed to such frank talk about private matters—he was part of the "square" generation that came into adolescence with Elvis and Sandra Dee and ended its second decade with the assassination of John Kennedy—but he struggled to overcome his embarrassment and answer every question with complete and total honesty.

When he was eleven or twelve years old he had participated in some sexual experimentation with boys in his Scout troop. "Oral or anal sex?"

Barker asked, his pen poised. Nothing like that, Doug answered, just some touching and exploring. During junior high and high school he dated sporadically and engaged in some necking and petting, but again nothing serious. For about six months in college he was involved in his first sexual relationship, and right after college he married Debbie. He had been faithful to her except for a few "accidents" with women at work. But those regrettable incidents took place many years ago.

He and Debbie had been married for twenty-three years and had a conventional sex life. He guessed that he probably wanted to make love more than she did, but wasn't that often the case? It just wasn't a major issue. Doug explained that he was a passive sort of person, willing to comply with other people's wishes, not "macho" at all. He disliked argument and contention, preferring arbitration and compromise. He would never push Debbie to be intimate if she wasn't interested. In the last year or two she did seem to have lost interest in sex. Maybe it was his fault. Maybe he wasn't the world's greatest lover.

But, still, he reasoned out loud, it's difficult to be a great lover when your partner isn't interested, never initiates lovemaking, and makes it pretty clear that she wants the whole thing over and done with as quickly as possible. Maybe Debbie wasn't interested in sex because she was tired and overstressed from raising four children and living with a husband whose career was demanding and time-consuming. When they went off by themselves for a weekend, escaping from the phone calls, homework, quarrels, crises, doctor appointments, sporting events, and deadlines, sex was just fine.

"Isn't that common?" Doug asked Dr. Barker. "Can you expect much more when you reach middle age?"

Barker regarded him noncommittally.

"Debbie is very religious," Doug said, suddenly switching gears. "Five or six years ago she became involved with a group called the Colossian Fellowship, which maintains that most people who think they are Christians are not really 'saved.' Only a few are 'true Christians' and the rest are victims of a New Age conspiracy. She came to the conclusion that she was a true Christian, and I was not. That realization seemed to cause her a lot of pain, but there was also an element of gloating to it, sort of the attitude that 'I'm sincere and you're not, I've got the faith and you don't.' Her religion frightened me because it seemed to be driven by anger, fear, and distrust. Where was the peace and the joy? What good is religion if it leaves you scared, anxious, suspicious, and angry?"

Barker shifted in his chair.

"I bring this up," Doug explained, "because after a few years Debbie dropped out of the Colossian Fellowship. We never talked about it, but I was relieved. Then, just a few days after she accused me of molesting Kristen and Jennifer, she said I took her away from the fellowship. She said she never wanted to drop out but felt she had to because of my discomfort with the group. I wonder if that might be part of the reason we started having sexual problems. Maybe it's all somehow connected to these accusations."

Dr. Barker listened respectfully, taking notes, nodding his head occasionally. But it was clear that he wanted to talk about Doug, not his wife, and about his sexual experiences, not his wife's religion. Gently, he steered the conversation to Doug's volunteer work with teenagers. During the years he worked with disadvantaged youth, were any of the boys or girls attracted to him? Was he ever attracted to them?

Doug admitted that he occasionally felt physically attracted to the adolescents he counseled, but insisted he had never said or done anything inappropriate.

"But there is a sexual element in your attraction to teenagers?" Dr. Barker asked.

"Well, I suppose it's possible," Doug said. "I do find many of these kids attractive, and I enjoy working with them. But nothing even remotely sexual has ever occurred in my interactions with them. I am very aware of the problems associated with working with teenagers, and I have always tried to be sensitive and responsible in my relationships with them."

Doug wasn't quite sure what to make of this line of questioning. He had never had a problem with what his family called the "OPKs"—other people's kids. For years he had offered advice, friendship, and emotional and financial support to troubled teenagers, runaways, foster kids, and members of his church youth group. Debbie suggested that the family set up an "OPK fund," a twenty-five-dollar-a-week allowance to spend on OPKs for pizza, burgers, bowling, miniature golf, movies, etc. The family temporarily adopted several foster kids, including *Ryan,* a runaway teenager with an alcohol and drug problem. After Ryan went on a three-day binge, spending the entire paycheck intended to reimburse his parents, Debbie threw him out of the house. But Doug kept track of him, buying him food, picking him up at the emergency room after he was beaten up, driving him to his parents' house, when he insisted drug dealers were coming after him, sending him cards, letters, and care packages to let him know that there was someone in the world who cared what happened to him.

This seemed like good, healthy work, a small but sincere effort to make the world a better place. But the sequence of Dr. Barker's questions seemed to imply that Doug had an abnormal obsession with teenagers that originated with his adolescent homosexual experiences in his Scout troop.

"I can offer some help for your problems with teenagers," Dr. Barker said at one point. "I'll give you some vials of ammonia and if you feel a sexual attraction or impulse, just break open one of the vials and sniff."

Doug tried to be deferential. The doctor was the expert here, and he didn't want to question his authority or diagnostic skill. Still, he wasn't sitting in this office, submitting to these increasingly invasive questions about his sexual history because of a problem with the OPKs. He was here because he had been falsely accused of molesting his daughters.

"Maybe we could talk about this later," Doug said. "Right now I've got a big problem with my family, and I need help. What about a lie-detector test? I'm ready and willing to take a polygraph to prove my innocence."

"I would recommend against it," Dr. Barker said. "There's too much risk of a false reading because the issues are so emotional and the charges are so vague."

"What about truth serum?" Doug was grasping at straws. He was a civil attorney, twenty years out of law school, with no criminal-law experience. But he knew that there were issues of truth and accuracy involved here and that drugs might help uncover that truth. He was willing to give anything a try.

Barker emphatically shook his head no. "Sodium amytal," he explained, "is as likely to bring out fantasy-based feelings and thoughts as factual recollections, and even skilled clinicians have great difficulty disentangling the fact from the fiction."

"What can I do to find out once and for all if I did or didn't do whatever they think I did?" Doug was aware of the twisted search for logic in his question. I'd laugh, he thought, if only my heart wasn't breaking.

"There is nothing you can do," Barker answered. "There is no way to know for sure if you have repressed this memory."

"Let me try to understand this," Doug said, struggling to control his emotions. He knew his anger was just the outward expression of the terrible fear rising within him. "I can never say, simply, 'I don't remember abusing my children,' and convince you or any other evaluator that I didn't molest them. If I can't remember these incidents, either I repressed the memories, in which case I'm guilty, or I'm in denial—and my denial is then taken as proof of my guilt."

"It is complicated," Barker admitted. He took a moment to review his notes. "When did you go through puberty?" he asked.

Doug sighed. More personal questions. "I began ejaculating shortly after my eleventh birthday."

"Early puberty is often a sign of sexual abuse," Dr. Barker said, writing in his notebook. "Did you experience any ejaculatory problems?"

"I had a slight problem with premature ejaculation in my twenties," Doug answered. "But when I made a concerted effort to slow down during intercourse, the problem disappeared."

"Premature ejaculation can also be a sign of sexual abuse," Barker said.

Doug was confused. Was Barker implying that he had been sexually abused as a child?

The psychologist looked at his watch and announced that the session was over. "Let's meet again next week at the same time," he said. "And ask your wife to come with you."

A week later Doug waited in the reception area while Debbie spent an hour and a half with Dr. Barker. When Doug was finally invited into the office, Barker told him that he had come to an important decision. It was his opinion that Doug should move out of the family home.

Doug was stunned. "Would most therapists agree with this decision?" he asked. He turned to Debbie. "Don't you think I deserve a second opinion?"

"Most qualified and reputable experts would agree with me," Barker said evenly. Debbie looked irritated with Doug for questioning Dr. Barker's opinion.

Doug considered his options. Barker came highly recommended as one of the best experts on sexual abuse in the area. If he insisted on talking to another psychologist, it might take weeks to get an appointment, and he would just have to answer the same questions, go through the same emotional turmoil, and end up in the same place. Asking for a second opinion would only delay the process of getting his family back together and further alienate his wife.

"If you think it's the right thing to do, and in the best interests of the family, I'll move out," Doug said.

Dr. Barker turned to Debbie. "Is he always impulsive like this?"

In subsequent sessions, Doug felt an ever-increasing pressure to confess. Barker seemed to believe that he could only help him remember if he would first admit that he had abused his daughters. But how, Doug wanted to know, could he confess to something he didn't remember?

"If you confess and agree to undergo long-term therapy," Barker answered his questions, "there will be no criminal charges. You will be able to see your children, and after an intensive treatment period, you can go home. Life will return to normal."

"I won't admit to things I can't remember," Doug repeated. "But I'm willing to consider the possibility that I've repressed the memories, and I'll try whatever techniques you suggest to recover them."

"Perhaps a visual imagery exercise will help," Barker suggested. Debbie had recently confided her belief that her husband had been sexually abused by *Uncle Frank*, his mother's brother, who was fifteen years older than Doug and had lived in Doug's childhood home for thirty-three years, from the time Doug was three months old until Uncle Frank died in 1987.

When Barker asked if his uncle had ever touched him in a way that made him feel uncomfortable, Doug denied it. Uncle Frank was rather strange and eccentric, Doug admitted, but he had never molested him.

"Relax and imagine that you are back in your childhood home," Barker suggested. "You are young and very vulnerable, and you have decided to visit with Uncle Frank in his room. Can you tell me what it looks and smells like there?"

"It's musty and damp," Doug said, his eyes closed. "Uncle Frank's room is in the basement and there is only one small window high up on the wall."

"What does the bedspread feel like? Can you feel it on your arms, on your legs? Can you remember any sexual stimulation there?"

"Yes," Doug answered. "I remember masturbating there when I was twelve years old."

"How do you know you were twelve?"

"The radio reported the first *Sputnik* launch. That was in 1956. I was born in 1944."

"Think back to when you were a child," Barker said, as if starting over. "Did you ever feel violated? Was there ever a time when you felt that your privacy was being invaded?"

"Yes." Doug wanted to be truthful. The truth was all he had.

"Where?"

"In the bathtub."

"Who was with you?"

"My mother."

"What happened?"

"Mother bathed me until I was ten or eleven years old. She said that I wouldn't get clean if I did it by myself. I remember that the last time she washed me I had some pubic hair. I was embarrassed about it."

"That's sexual abuse," Barker announced.

Doug disagreed, arguing that he didn't believe his mother got any "sexual stimulation" from the baths, nor did he. But in a matter of minutes Barker convinced him that his mother had abused him. By the end of the session Doug was in tears.

A few days later Doug decided to tell his wife about the deeply emotional experience of discovering that he had been sexually abused by his mother. He hoped that she would understand how hard he was trying, how willing he was to look at every possibility. But as he described the memories he had recovered during the therapy session, Debbie drew back from him, the look on her face a mixture of revulsion and triumph.

"I knew it!" she cried. "You were abused and that helps to explain why you abused your children!"

"What?" Doug was totally bewildered by her response.

"It's been proven that sexual abuse is passed on from one generation to another," Debbie said. "If you were abused by your parents or relatives, you will in all possibility abuse your own children."

Doug just stared at her. What could he do, what could he say that wouldn't be twisted around to prove his guilt?

Two weeks later Dr. Barker announced that he had enough information to complete his evaluation.

"I don't understand," Doug protested. "I don't have any idea what is going on here, and I'm one of the central characters. How can you assess my situation after a few interviews with me and my wife? You haven't talked to my children, my parents, my friends—you don't even know me! How can you possibly have enough information to evaluate me and to make recommendations that will affect the rest of my life?"

Barker tried to calm his client. He would permit Doug to read a draft of his report and fill in the missing pieces before it was put into final form.

Doug refused the offer. "How can I fill in the missing pieces when I have no memory of abusing my children?" he asked. "We need real data, hard facts, not all this guessing and speculation and talk about repressed memories. I'll do whatever I have to do to get to the bottom of this. I'll take a polygraph, I'll take truth serum, I'll do anything. Just tell me what to do, and I'll do it."

"Those procedures are too risky," Barker said, repeating his earlier advice. "I would suggest that you consult a lawyer."

"I don't have any legal problems right now, and I don't expect any. This is a medical problem, a mental health problem. My family is falling apart. We need help."

Barker stared at his client for a moment and then slowly shook his head. He reached for a notepad and wrote down the name and phone number of a polygrapher, explaining that it might take a while for Doug to get an appointment.

"What can I do in the meantime?" Doug asked.

"You need therapy to help you cope," Barker said, recommending a female colleague.

"Why don't you list for me all the reasons that might prevent you from admitting that you abused your children," the therapist suggested.

"That won't be hard," Doug said. "I can think of a whole string of reasons. First, nobody wants to hurt their kids, or admit it if they have. I could go to jail, lose my job, lose my friends, become an outcast. There are all kinds of reasons. But I don't remember abusing my children. Second, I'm not the kind of man who would sexually abuse a child, let alone my own children. I believe that child abuse is one of the most terrible crimes imaginable. I love my children and would never intentionally hurt them."

Doug wondered if he had made a mistake using the word "intentionally." Would the therapist think that he had *un*intentionally abused his kids? Would the word "intentional" give additional weight and substance to the theory of repression?

"It isn't that I don't want to admit that I abused them," he carefully explained. "I just can't remember abusing them. And I don't think I could have forgotten doing such a terrible thing. My mind doesn't work that way. Everybody keeps telling me I abused my children and repressed the memories, but I'm having a real hard time with the idea that I could completely block out an entire event or series of events."

"Haven't you forgotten many experiences in your life?" the therapist asked.

"Of course," Doug said, "I've forgotten many things that have happened in the past, just like everyone else."

"And aren't you an optimistic person who prefers to dwell on the positive and hope for the best?"

"Yes, I think that's a fair description of me."

"Do you think Debbie might have some reasons for believing that you abused your children?"

"She claims she has reasons," Doug admitted.

"Can you list them for me?"

"She says that she believes the kids, and apparently they think I abused them. She believes I was abused when I was a child, and she argues that child abuse passes down from one generation to the next. But I'm not at all convinced that I was abused as a kid. More important, I know I would never abuse my own children, and it just doesn't seem possible that I could abuse them and repress the whole memory."

"How can you say that, Mr. Nagle?" The therapist seemed exasperated with him.

Doug tried to explain his feelings for his children. He loved them more than anything, more than his work, more than his own life. He wouldn't ever betray that love by hurting them physically or sexually. His mother had been insensitive to his needs for privacy and, contrary to what Debbie believed, that had made him more, not less, sensitive to the needs of his own children.

Searching his memory for an anecdote that would prove to the therapist that he was a gentle and sensitive man—not the kind of person who would abuse his own children—he recalled the family's tradition of a "fifth-grade trip." When each of his four children was in fifth grade, he took them on a special trip, just the two of them alone for a week. He and Kristen went to Washington, D.C., staying part of the time in a hotel and part of the time with friends. He took *Alison* to Washington, D.C., and to Orlando, Florida—to Disney World, Circus World, Cypress Gardens, and Marine World. He and Jennifer went to Washington, D.C., and

Williamsburg, Virginia. He took Anna to the Shakespearean festival in Ashland, Oregon. On each of those trips he remembered feeling self-conscious about checking into a hotel with an eleven-year-old girl. He remembered trying to give the girls privacy, allowing them plenty of time to shower, dress, and fix their hair. He explained to the therapist that he always tried to be sensitive to their needs.

"Mr. Nagle, you only remember what you want to remember," the therapist said. "You probably rearranged all your memories to be consistent with what you want to believe about yourself."

"Are you saying that the only memories that count are the ones I don't have?" Doug asked. "Are you implying that any good memories I have of time spent with my children are probably false?"

"Yes," the counselor said, emphatically shaking her head, "that's exactly what I'm saying."*

For the month of April, Doug tried to "remember" abusing his children. But no matter how hard he tried, his memory was a complete blank. Finally, he appealed to his wife. "How can I recover these memories without any idea what I'm supposed to remember? What exactly have Kristen and Jennifer accused me of doing?"

Debbie said she couldn't reveal any details without talking to Jennifer's counselor first. A few weeks later Doug called to see if she had any information for him.

"Jennifer's counselor and I are trying to help her remember," Debbie said.

"Remember what?" Doug asked.

"I can't tell you the specifics," Debbie said. "Jennifer's therapist says that you need to remember on your own. She does not want to contaminate your memories."

"Did you know that Dr. Barker interviewed Kristen, and she is no longer claiming to be an eyewitness?" Doug decided that it was time to play a trump card—his only trump card. "She admitted that she never actually saw me touching Jennifer. She only saw me lying on the bed with Jennifer, fully clothed, with both of my hands visible. Jennifer was underneath the covers, while I was lying on top of the covers.

"I used to lie down with the kids all the time when they went to sleep, Debbie. You remember that, don't you?" He couldn't keep the sarcasm out of his voice. "That's what I was doing, just lying down with Jennifer, talking to her, trying to help her fall asleep. Nothing in Kristen's descrip-

---

*A year later this therapist admitted to Doug Nagle's attorney that she pressured Doug to remember in an effort to "help" him. She believed that if Doug confessed, he would escape imprisonment and eventually be permitted to return home and be reunited with his family.

tion suggests any sexual contact. I want you to tell Jennifer exactly what Kristen told Dr. Barker and then let her come to her own conclusions."

"I won't do that," Debbie said. "It would only confuse Jennifer to suggest that maybe the abuse didn't happen."

"The truth won't confuse her!" Doug suddenly lost his temper. "You and her therapist are confusing her by trying to get her to remember something that never happened! If you don't tell her, I will."

On May 10, 1990, Debbie scheduled a meeting with Doug at his office. The moment she walked in, he knew that something fundamental had changed; the ground seemed to shift, becoming unstable underneath his feet. Feeling dizzy and light-headed, he suggested they take a walk.

"Something has happened," he said after they walked along in silence for a moment.

"Jennifer has recovered her memories," Debbie said. She seemed abnormally calm, completely in control. "Now we can prosecute you."

"Prosecute? You're going to prosecute me?" Doug felt as if he were sinking fast. He reached out for a rescue, appealing to his wife's love for her children. "Think about the kids, Debbie. Think what a court battle would do to our children."

She glared at him and hitched her purse higher on her shoulder. The look on her face expressed her thoughts more clearly than any words could: *We've got you now.*

"A court battle will tear us apart. Debbie, please, I don't want to fight you over this. I want to work things out."

Hearing the pain in his voice, she seemed to soften. "I'm sorry it worked out this way," she said. When they returned to his office, she made an appointment to talk to his supervisor. Doug learned later that his wife asked for assurances that he would not be fired until the trial was over.

On May 19, twenty days after Jennifer had recovered her memory, a detective with the Special Assault Unit called Doug.

"We want you to take a polygraph," the detective said.

"I've been advised to retain a lawyer," Doug responded.

"There's no reason you can't take a polygraph first," the detective said.

"I want to take a polygraph," Doug said, "but I need to understand the ground rules. Will I be asked about specific incidents of abuse? Nobody has told me what I've been accused of doing, and I was advised that the test may not be accurate if the questions aren't specific."

When the detective didn't respond immediately, Doug rephrased his concerns. "If the questions are not sufficiently specific, the results may be inconclusive or possibly incriminating."

"We won't reveal the specific allegations until you're officially charged," the detective said.

"Will I have any say in selecting the polygrapher or determining how the test is administered?" Doug asked.

"Look, Mr. Nagle, I'm the detective and you're the suspect. I run the show, not you."

"In that case, I will hire a lawyer and get back to you," Doug said.

"That's your choice, of course," the detective said, getting in the last word. "But I know you're guilty. You agreed to a sexual-deviancy evaluation, and no innocent person would ever do that."

Doug called his attorney friends, asking them to recommend a criminal lawyer. At the top of everyone's list was Steve Moen, variously described as "methodical," "cautious," "extremely careful," and "cerebral." Doug interviewed Moen, who agreed to represent him.

"The detective says he's convinced I'm guilty because I was evaluated for sexual deviancy," Doug explained to his lawyer.

"That's a logical conclusion," Steve said. "Accused offenders normally don't agree to sexual-deviancy evaluations unless they plan to plead guilty and hope to speed up the sentencing process."

The lawyer's matter-of-fact response unnerved Doug. This was his life they were discussing; his family, his reputation, and his career were all on the line.

"I don't understand," Doug said. "Debbie told me I had to have an evaluation. She said I couldn't visit with the kids unless I did. Nobody ever told me that being evaluated would be taken as proof of guilt."

"You should have hired a lawyer months ago," Steve said evenly.

"But this is a mental health problem, not a legal problem," Doug said, unable to contain his anger.

"Not any more." Steve's tone reminded Doug of the time he was called into the vice principal's office for some minor infraction in junior high school. "This isn't elementary school," the vice principal had warned, his voice low. "This is the big time, and *now you're really in trouble.*"

"I would advise you to stop Dr. Barker from completing his evaluation," Steve said. "I can take care of that for you, if you want."

"But if Debbie learns about that, she'll say it's just more evidence that I'm guilty."

"It doesn't make any difference what she thinks."

"It does to me," Doug said. "My first priority is to save my marriage and get my family back together."

"Our first priority is to keep you out of prison—if we can," Steve said. "I'll call the detective from the Special Assault Unit and tell him you won't take the police lie-detector test. A polygraph is too risky in these cases. There's no reason to take that risk at this point. I'd also advise you to keep a low profile. Don't talk to anyone about these accusations."

Something in Doug's expression made Steve add, "How many people have you told about your situation?"

"Dozens," Doug admitted. "My colleagues at work, family, friends, church members."

Steve sighed. "From now on, lie low. Don't do or say anything, because anything can be used against you."

Just like the *Miranda* warning, Doug thought bitterly. But when people are accused of a crime, don't they usually know what they're supposed to have done? When would he find out what he was accused of doing to his children? How could he go on living in the meantime?

"I can't lie low," he told his lawyer. "I'm in too much pain. I have to talk about my situation, as you call it, or I'll fall apart. I've lost my wife, my kids, and my main hobby, helping other people's kids. I could lose my job."

"You know, don't you, that you would lose your license to practice law if you're convicted?" Steve rummaged around in his bookshelf, brought out the rules on disbarment, and thumbed through the document.

"I never thought of that. My job is all I have left right now." Doug stopped talking and visibly tried to pull himself together. "I'm scared of prison. But worse than that is the thought of what my children are going through right now. My kids believe I hurt them. They are in pain. I can't bear to have them suffer like this. How can I keep quiet, how can I lie low when my family is being ripped apart?"

Steve was deeply concerned about his client's emotional stability. Doug needed psychological help that Dr. Barker, in his role as a sexual deviancy evaluator, could not offer him. "Let me suggest someone who might be able to help you deal with your pain and confusion," Steve said. "As a forensic psychiatrist, *Dr. Carson* has a great deal of experience with sexual abuse cases. But I'm not referring you to him for matters of jurisprudence. He's extremely perceptive, and I think he may be able to help you understand the conflicts and tensions in your family. Maybe he can help you with your efforts to get your family back together again."

Dr. Carson listened to Doug's story and then asked questions about his medical and sexual histories. It was the same territory Dr. Barker had traversed, but Doug felt more comfortable this time around. Maybe, he thought to himself, I'm just beaten down and exhausted. Or maybe I'm in such big trouble that my privacy and dignity don't matter anymore.

In their third session, Carson asked him point-blank, "Did you do it or not?"

"I don't think so."

"Yes or no. Either you did or you didn't."

"I don't know. I don't think so."

"Don't say that." Carson was impatient, tapping his pencil against the desk. "That answer confuses everybody; it makes everybody think you did it. Either you did it or you didn't do it."

"I don't think I did it."

"You didn't, then?"

"I don't think so."

"Don't say that anymore." Carson raised his voice in irritation. "You know if you did it or not. Nobody else knows but you. Did you do it or not?"

"I don't think so. No. No, I didn't do it."

Why is it so hard to say the word "no"? Doug asked himself. He thought back to that first night, when Debbie confronted him with the accusations. "I never abused my children," he told her, and she became angry, accusing him of being "in denial." "Deep denial," she called it. After that his life spiraled out of control. Jennifer left the house, and eventually he was asked to move out. He wasn't even allowed to see his youngest daughter without a chaperone present. And soon he would be facing criminal charges.

What good had it done him to deny the accusations? No good that he could see. Why couldn't he just say, "I don't remember." Debbie and all the therapists would either have to accept that statement or call him a liar. He was trying to be responsible; he was struggling to stand up and face his accusers. If he said "No, I didn't abuse my children," he would be pointing his finger at his wife and daughters and calling them liars. He could not do that. His wife and children meant more to him than anything in the world. He would not betray them. He was willing to face the possibility, as unlikely as it seemed, that he had abused them and repressed all memory of his actions. Thus, in good conscience and with absolute honesty, he could say, "No, I don't remember," or "No, I am not lying about my memory."

He regarded Carson with some confusion. Why couldn't this man, a psychiatrist after all, understand what was going on in his mind?

"If these events happened, you would remember them," Dr. Carson was saying. "Either you are lying, or the abuse never occurred. Are you lying?"

"No. I am not lying."

Are you lying? Carson must have asked that question a hundred times, and Doug always responded with a soft but sincere "No." Still, the constant repetition of the question irritated him. Just when he was struggling hardest to understand or explain his feelings, Dr. Carson would inter-

[handwritten marginal note: The "Denial on both sides" trap]

rupt: "Are you lying? Did you do it or not?" The questions began to make him mad. He was getting sick and tired of this inquisition.

"Back off," he said at one point. "I'm not lying, I'm not going to change my story, and if you don't believe me, there isn't much I can do about it. I'm fed up with these stupid games."

Carson looked at him, apparently indifferent to his anger and frustration. Was Carson using the questions as psychological cattle prods to goad him into some kind of action?

"Are you deliberately trying to make me mad?" Doug asked the psychiatrist. "Is that what's going on here?"

"You don't get angry easily, " Dr. Carson said impassively.

Doug admitted that it was difficult for him to express his anger. He told Carson about his recurring problems with indigestion and insomnia—caused, he guessed, from putting the lid on his emotions. In 1971 he had a prostate infection that wouldn't clear up. A psychiatrist friend persuaded him that he was depressed and would not recover from the infection until the causes of the depression were uncovered and treated. He had agreed to see a psychiatrist, who suggested that perhaps he was angry with Debbie.

"I know I was frustrated with her," Doug told Dr. Carson, "and at various times in our marriage I've had trouble communicating with her. She seems to think she understands me better than I understand myself, and she is always telling me that I'm an angry, hostile person. But I don't think of myself as angry or hostile, and my friends and colleagues don't see me that way."

"Perhaps Debbie recognizes emotions and patterns in you that are really going on inside her," Dr. Carson said.

Doug thought about that for a moment. Maybe it wasn't as farfetched as it seemed. Debbie claimed he was "manipulative" and "controlling," but other people saw her that way, not him. She claimed he was distant, but then she would be the one to stare blankly past people and lose the thread of the conversation. Did she feel abused as a child and then project her feelings onto her own children? Perhaps she hadn't been literally abused but only *felt* abused, and those painful, ambiguous feelings later influenced her relationships with her husband and children. Years earlier Debbie's younger sisters told Doug that Debbie helped raise them; during her teenage years she had been more her father's companion and confidant than his daughter. Was Debbie's relationship with her father somehow unhealthy? Doug wondered. Could that explain why she became so jealous whenever he was playful and affectionate with their kids?

"You need to start fighting back," Dr. Carson was saying.

"Fight what? I still don't understand what I'm supposed to be fighting!"

"If you didn't abuse your children, tell them that clearly and forcefully.

Don't give in, don't whimper and moan about your problems—stand up and fight!"

During these counseling sessions, Dr. Carson seemed to take on his patient's anger. At times he would raise his voice, pound the table for emphasis, or wave his hands around in a gesture of frustration. Watching these expressions of annoyance and irritation, Doug tried to figure out what was going on. Was Dr. Carson modeling anger for him, showing him how to get mad, how to *be* mad? Was his anger an act, or was it real—and if it was real, what was he angry about? Was he angry before Doug ever walked into his office, or did Doug's predicament somehow affect him personally? Who was the therapist here and who was the patient?

"I feel like you want to teach me how to express my anger," Doug said one day. "That may be important in my personal therapy, but this isn't just personal. My wife and my kids are involved. I'm worried that you might be pushing me to do something that will hurt my family."

"I'm here to help you," Dr. Carson said simply.

"I need your help. But I also need the best possible advice about how to help my wife and my children. I have to know when you're trying to help me and when you're trying to help my family. Let's keep clear about which is which."

"I'm afraid I can't always divide it up that way," Carson said.

Doug put his head in his hands. Of course. Carson was a psychiatrist, not a mind-reader—how could he know what was best for his patient and what was best for his patient's family? Only the patient could make those decisions. But how can you make decisions if you don't have any information? What *was* best for the children? Doug felt more dazed and confused than ever. Yes, he would agree to stand up for himself and profess his innocence, but he needed to understand the risks first. How would his actions affect his family?

Doug realized that he was starting to think more like his lawyer: Be careful, lie low, don't make any move without thinking it through first. But he didn't always agree with the cautious approach, because while there were certainly good reasons to be wary and restrained, there were also good reasons to express anger and frustration. But when to do what, when to feel what, when to say what?

He knew he was caught in a no-exit double bind. He was learning caution from his lawyer, who was afraid to have him do or say anything, and he was learning emotional spontaneity from his therapist, who wanted him to do and say things he feared might hurt his children. Which was the right approach, and in what situation and in what proportion?

Despite Doug's confusion he was grateful to both men for teaching him to think and react in new ways. Steve Moen was a meticulous fact-finder and solid thinker. If facts and reason rather than feelings were going to decide the outcome of this trial, Steve would win. But Steve was so cautious and overprotective of his client, Doug feared that following his advice might further estrange his family.

Unlike his lawyer, his psychiatrist was almost reckless, urging him to stand up for himself even at the risk of harming his relationship with his family. And yet, under Dr. Carson's guidance Doug was feeling stronger, learning how to express his anger in more appropriate ways, and beginning to throw off the heavy cloak of victimhood that had weighed him down since the first day he was accused. He was also becoming more adept at anticipating his wife's next move. Because Debbie was so intent on keeping the children as far away from him as possible, they never got to hear his side of the story. Maybe Dr. Carson was right. Maybe he should find a way to let his children know that he was innocent.

He was not allowed to see Jennifer, but every few weeks he was permitted to spend several hours with Anna. During one of those visits, Doug decided to tell his youngest daughter that the accusations against him were false; he had never abused her sisters, and he would never, ever hurt any of his children. A few weeks later Doug was eating dinner alone in his apartment and experienced an intense longing for his family. He called home, and Anna answered. They talked for a few minutes, and at the end of the conversation Doug told her how much he loved her.

The next day Debbie called in a rage. "Anna told me about your conversation," she said accusingly. "These manipulative attempts to confuse her have to stop."

"I miss her," Doug said, trying to stand up for himself as Carson had advised. "I need to see her."

"Only under my rules," Debbie said, slamming the phone down.

Doug wrote his wife a letter that evening, explaining his intention to call home more often, not less, and expressing his desire to negotiate more liberal arrangements for seeing Anna. Then he waited for Debbie's response. A week later Debbie called to arrange a meeting with him and the pastor of his church.

"I'm filing for divorce," she announced. "It's not that I really want a divorce, but I'm afraid CPS will come and take the kids away."

"I don't understand," Doug said.

"You threatened to see the kids, you refuse to stay away from them. I have to protect them somehow."

"But you wouldn't let me see Anna!" Doug struggled to keep his voice calm. "You wouldn't allow me to talk to her, write her, or visit with her. Your rules don't allow me any contact with my children, even the child who has not accused me of anything. I only wanted the rules to change so I could see Anna again."

"The prosecutors aren't moving fast enough," Debbie said, refusing to look at her husband. "Your actions have forced me to file for divorce so I can get a restraining order against you. I want you to leave the children alone."

Restraining order? Doug wanted to tell Debbie that she didn't have to file for divorce to get a restraining order, but what good would that do him? Either way he would not be allowed to see his children.

Debbie's expression changed. "Jennifer wants to see you," she said. "She's waiting outside in the car."

"Jennifer wants to see me?" Doug couldn't figure out what was going on. They had just been discussing a restraining order to prevent him from seeing Anna, who had never accused him of anything, and now Debbie was going to let him meet with Jennifer, who was accusing him of terrible things. Doug hadn't seen or talked to Jennifer since Debbie first told him about the accusations, five months earlier.

Debbie left the room and a few minutes later Jennifer walked in.

"Jennifer." Doug could barely find his voice. He wanted desperately to put his arms around her, to hug her and hold her close, to never let her go. "Do you want the pastor to stay?"

"Either way," she said, shrugging her shoulders and smiling at her father. "It doesn't matter."

Doug remembered Steve Moen's advice—be cautious, don't do anything unusual or remotely suspicious—and asked the pastor to chaperone their meeting. Doug asked Jennifer about school, friendships, plans for the summer. Eventually he ran out of questions, and they sat for a few moments in awkward silence.

"I think you did it, Daddy," Jennifer finally said. "But I've forgiven you. I went to a church camp and my friends prayed with me. I don't feel angry or afraid anymore."

Doug couldn't take his eyes off his daughter. *I love this kid so much,* he kept saying to himself, *I love her so much, so much, so much. . . .*

"I'd like to see you again," he said.

"I'd like that, too."

Doug tried not to show how desperate he was to spend time with her. He didn't want to frighten her or influence her in any way. "Maybe we could get together for pizza or burgers or something, you, me, Mom, and Anna," he suggested.

"That would be neat," she said. "I'd like that."

A week later he called Debbie to arrange a get-together. "Absolutely not!" Debbie said.

"But why?"

"I promised the prosecutors I'd never let the children see you," she said.

On September 14, criminal charges were filed against Doug Nagle—one count of first-degree rape occurring sometime between December 8,

1984, and December 7, 1985, when Jennifer was ten, and four counts of indecent liberties, one in each year from the time Jennifer was eight until she was eleven. All five counts were felony offenses; a conviction on any count would result in immediate disbarment and imprisonment.

On September 22 Doug Nagle pleaded not guilty and agreed to an order prohibiting any contact with his wife and their four children. He was booked in the county jail and placed in a holding cell. The toilet, spattered with dried vomit, was plugged with paper and feces.

When the booking officer filled out the paperwork, he commented, "This looks like a hell of a messy divorce." Doug was surprised: Nothing in the paperwork mentioned divorce. He felt tears welling up. Here, in the most unlikely of places, he had encountered a measure of kindness and understanding.

Released from jail a few hours later, Doug met with Steve Moen and began to plan his defense. "I want a cooperative approach," he told his lawyer. "We should talk to the prosecutors and agree to bring in neutral experts to interview everyone involved, evaluate the situation and give the same report to both sides. I'll waive all privileges."

Steve Moen took a deep breath and let it out slowly. He had never encountered a client like Doug Nagle. The man was extremely bright, a graduate of the Stanford Law School, one of the most respected natural resource attorneys in the Northwest, and he was just like a little kid: naïve, gullible, trusting, innocent. He was almost *unworldly*.

"What will it take to get some cooperation?" Doug said, expressing astonishment at the lack of discovery rights in criminal law. The first task in civil cases was to gather all the opposition's documents, assemble a list of their witnesses, and take depositions to find out exactly what the witnesses and experts intended to say. In civil law it's all show-and-tell, he thought; in criminal law it's more like hide-and-seek.

Doug didn't wait for Steve's response to his question. "I'll take a lie-detector test," he announced. "It will show I'm telling the truth, and maybe the prosecution will be more willing to consider the possibility that none of this happened, it's all just a terrible mistake."

"A lie-detector test is too risky," Steve said. "There's no guarantee that you'll pass."

"I'll pass," Doug said, "because I'm telling the truth."

"Polygraphs measure physiological responses to focused questions relating to the dispute," Steve explained carefully. "Just because you're telling the truth doesn't mean that you'll pass. And even if you pass, the polygraph is not admissible in court, so it won't solve your problems in and of itself."

Doug wondered how he could convince his attorney to see things his way. "We need to open up some communication here, right now, or this thing will end up in court," he said. "My family will get torn apart. We'll never recover. Let me take the polygraph to prove my innocence."

"I'll agree only if you understand the limitations," Steve said. "First, you must understand that even if you pass, the prosecution won't accept that as proof of innocence. We may be able to persuade the prosecutors to look at other evidence in the case, but again there's no guarantee that they will proceed with more care or caution. Second, if you insist on taking a polygraph, I strongly suggest that you go to a reputable examiner in private practice who has no current law enforcement connections. That way, if you do happen to fail, the police investigators and prosecutors won't be able to use the information against you."

Doug agreed to the conditions, and scheduled a polygraph with a private examiner. He failed the test. When the polygraph examiner gave him the results, Doug was stunned.

"Something is wrong here," he said. "I don't know why I failed this test, but I never abused my kids. I want to take another test."

A few days later they met again; despite Doug's entreaties, the polygrapher refused to administer another test. "You're too emotional, too confused, and you'll just fail it again," he said, offering Doug some advice. "Look, you have to understand that this is war. Your kids will destroy you if you don't fight back."

"I can't fight my kids," Doug said, wondering why everybody was telling him to get angry and fight back. "I'm not mad at my kids. They're victims, too. I blame the counselors and sometimes I blame my wife. But I love my kids and most of the time I still love my wife. I want to save our marriage."

"That's very noble in theory," the polygrapher said, "but you will go to prison if you don't change your attitude. Either attack your kids, or they'll destroy you—it's one or the other."

Doug went home, got down on his knees, and prayed for several hours. Afterward he felt calm. The so-called experts were all wrong. He would continue to love his children. He would have faith that love is stronger than hate.

But the next morning he woke up very early and very angry. How could my kids let themselves be talked into believing these things? he asked himself. Can't they see what they are doing to me, to themselves, to our entire family? Alone and miserable, he screamed, raged, sobbed, and wailed. Then, just as suddenly, his anger disappeared. He felt exhausted, but calmed by sudden insight. Maybe he was angrier at his kids than he realized; maybe it was this deep and unresolved anger that the polygraph picked up. He wrote Dr. Carson a letter, informing him that he had failed the polygraph test and sharing his new insights.

When Doug told Steve Moen that he had a long conversation with the polygraph examiner and had written to Dr. Carson, his lawyer was furious. "If the prosecutors discover that you failed the polygraph, your wife will certainly hear about it, and then everybody in this emotionally-driven case will leap to the conclusion that you're guilty," Steve fumed. "We won't be able to resolve the case in any reasonable way other than a battle royal in the courtroom."

"But I can't lie about these results," Doug responded. "I have to be absolutely honest about everything. All I have left is my honesty."

Steve made an effort to speak calmly. "You have to understand, Doug, that people who are already convinced of your guilt will use the polygraph results to confirm their suspicions."

"I can't do anything to convince people of my innocence who have already made up their minds that I'm guilty," Doug said.

"Your first priority should be to protect yourself and strengthen your legal case," Steve argued.

"No, my first priority is my family," Doug shot back. But in that disagreement over priorities, he understood the depth of his ambivalence and the meaning of his anger. He did not want to go to prison for something he didn't do. At what point would he sacrifice his family to save himself? If it came to that most terrible choice—his freedom or Jennifer's love and respect—could he stand up in court and say, "My daughter is lying"? Could he do that to Jennifer? He had lost so much already; would this tragedy descend into betrayal, with father and daughter standing in court, denouncing each other as liars? Would he have to give up everything he believed in?

"We need to stop communicating with the other side," Steve said. "I'm going to cancel Dr. Carson's appointment with the prosecutors."

"No," Doug said. "We need to keep the lines of communication open."

They argued. Steve called in his partner, and the two men tried to impress Doug with the gravity of his situation. "This is not civil law," they argued with him, "this is a criminal trial. The prosecutors think you're a pedophile, a man who would rape his own daughters. They don't want to communicate, they want to convict. They want you in jail."

When Doug refused to budge, Steve called Dr. Carson. To everyone's surprise, Carson agreed with Doug: They should keep trying to communicate with the other side.

"It won't work," Steve said.

"I'm the client, damn it," Doug said, losing his temper. "It's my life. I'm willing to take the risk."

Steve and his partner tried a different strategy. "You're a very difficult client," they said. "You are naïve, credulous, over-trusting. You should not be making these complicated legal decisions."

"And you are patronizing," Doug retorted. "You don't understand me, and you don't give a damn about my family. You just want to show off your legal skills by getting me acquitted. You don't care if my family is destroyed in the process."

In the end, the lawyers won, and Dr. Carson's appointment with the prosecutors was canceled.

"Now, what do we do about the letter he wrote Carson telling him that he failed the lie-detector test?" Steve asked his partner. "If the prosecution finds out about this, all Dr. Carson's attempts to get the different psychologists, psychiatrists and therapists working together to solve this case and bring the family back together again will be destroyed."

"I don't care," Doug interrupted their dialogue, once again feeling like the small child whose naughty actions have put his elders in a compromising position. "What's the point of going to a psychiatrist if you can't tell him what's on your mind?"

Finally, the lawyers decided that Carson could continue to counsel Doug, but that it was too risky to use him as an expert witness.

"Have you told anyone else about failing the lie-detector test?" Steve asked.

"My mother, my sister, thirty or forty people at the office Christmas party, some people from church." Doug felt combative, his chin jutting out as if to say, So sue me.

"Do you and Debbie go to the same church?" Steve asked.

"We used to, but now I go to a different church."

"So you told the people at your new church?"

"No, I told people at both churches."

From the expression on Steve Moen's face, Doug knew exactly what he was thinking: This man is hopeless.

"Look," Doug said, trying to mollify him, "I'm having a hard time getting through this. I do what I have to do to keep going, I talk to people, I listen to their advice, I try to reason my way through things. It's not easy being accused of molesting your own children. How would you handle it?"

"I would have kept my mouth shut about the polygraph," Steve said.

A month before the trial Steve requested a conference with his client. "We're in trouble," he said, handing Doug a transcript of the conversation between Jennifer and *Dr. Stein,* the forensic psychologist retained by the defense. Stein was well-known and respected in legal circles for his fairness and neutrality in child custody cases.

Steve read out loud from the transcript:

> *Jennifer Nagle:* I remember being in the shower, maybe nineish. Ages are very hard. And then, all of a sudden, my father was in the shower with me with no clothes on. And then he started to

wash me with soap and then he was washing down by my crotch and all of a sudden I started to bleed. I don't know how I started to bleed, I don't remember that, but then I don't know how or when he left or anything. I just remember crying and there being blood in the bathtub.

Steve stopped reading and looked at Doug, trying to gauge his reaction. "I'm afraid that's a fairly specific memory," he said finally.

Doug felt a shiver of fear. Was his own lawyer doubting him? "We used to take baths and showers together," he tried to explain. "I used to soap her body. But she was little then, maybe one or two, at the oldest three. I don't remember ever bathing with her when she was older. I would have been sensitive to that kind of a situation because my mother bathed me when I was older, and it upset me. I would never do that to a kid." He wondered if Jennifer was mixing up her memories. Maybe she was taking an early memory of bathing with him and putting it together with a later memory of being cleaned up after she hurt herself. How could she come up with all those details of something that never happened?

"Kristen enters the picture on page twenty-four," Steve said. "When Kristen was in Europe a few years ago, she wrote Jennifer a letter. Apparently Kristen claimed she was abused by your uncle. And she believed somebody else abused her, too. Jennifer told Stein: 'She said that she remembered being abused by somebody else, but that she didn't remember who. And that if I had any ideas I should let her know. But I didn't.' And Stein responded: 'You didn't let her know or you didn't have any ideas?' Jennifer answers, 'I didn't have any ideas.' "

Steve flipped the page. "Now we get to Jennifer's first memory of abuse. 'I was just ready to end therapy. . . . Then Kristen came in and she told me about our father. What he had done to her and she thought he had done this to me, too, but she wasn't positive. And then that was just it. That was just—I don't know how to explain what happened. It was just a gut thing. Like a cannonball hit my stomach . . . it was just very clear that what she said was true.' "

Doug thought Debbie, not Kristen, was the key. "Don't you see?" he asked Moen. "She was the first one to believe I abused the kids. Then everybody just reinforced each other. Jennifer had no suspicion of abuse until Kristen suggested to her that she might have been abused. Once the suggestion was planted, the 'memories' started developing, and Kristen, Debbie, and the counselor repeatedly told Jennifer that they believed her new memories were literally true. This whole thing begins and ends with Debbie—she led the rest of the family into delusional beliefs that I was abused as a child and then convinced Jennifer and Kristen I abused them. The note proves my theory."

Steve had received a handwritten note, dated February 22, 1991, from a therapist Doug and Debbie had consulted when they were having marital problems. The therapist indicated that two years earlier, well before Kristen or Jennifer mentioned the possibility of sexual abuse, Debbie had been "contemplating the allegations against Mr. Nagle. . . . Of the two, I would be inclined to find Mr. Nagle more credible." But the psychologist's note was not admissible in court because he had ethical concerns about testifying and discussing his sessions with Debbie. Even if he agreed to testify, Debbie would invoke the patient-therapist privilege to exclude his testimony.

To further complicate matters Dr. Stein, the forensic psychologist who had interviewed all the family members, disagreed with Doug's theory that Debbie was the dominant player. When Kristen wrote to Jennifer in 1989 and revealed her newly recovered memories of being abused by Uncle Frank, she added that she thought she might have been abused by someone else. She didn't remember who the perpetrator was, but she wondered if Jennifer had any ideas. Jennifer told Dr. Stein that she "didn't have any ideas." Later, however, when Kristen remembered that it was her father who had abused her and suggested that Jennifer might also have been abused by him, it was suddenly "very clear" to Jennifer that what her sister said was true.

Steve knew that Doug desperately wanted to discover what had happened to his family and prove his theories in the upcoming trial. But any good criminal attorney knows that the <u>defense never proves anything</u>; the prosecution is charged with proving its case beyond a reasonable doubt. If Steve made any effort in court to unravel the complex psychological crosscurrents in this troubled family, he would be providing the prosecutor with more ammunition while obscuring the defense's main point: Nobody could know for sure what really happened.

We'll never know whether it began with Debbie or Kristen, Steve thought to himself. He cleared his throat. "It is my job as your attorney to convey an offer from the prosecution," he said. "This morning the prosecutors offered to settle for a guilty plea on one count. They agreed to recommend no jail time, but of course any felony conviction involving moral turpitude would involve disbarment."

Doug couldn't believe what he was hearing. My own lawyer wants me to plead guilty! he thought. "I will not agree to a guilty plea," Doug said, his voice shaking with anger. "I simply won't do that. Someday my kids will realize that this didn't happen. It just did not happen. And when they do, it is going to be important that I never caved in. If I plead guilty, my kids will be messed up forever. I'll sit in prison for the rest of my life if I have to, but I won't plead guilty. I will not do that," he added, as if he feared Steve hadn't understood him.

Doug slammed the door on the way out of the office. He was deeply shaken by his lawyer's calm delivery of the prosecutor's offer. He knew that if he entered a guilty plea to escape imprisonment, his children would never believe that he was innocent. He would be branded for the rest of his life as a pedophile, a man who raped his own children. The reality of his situation suddenly hit him full force: He was going to prison.

Steve Moen flinched when his door slammed shut. He sat for a moment, trying to collect his thoughts. I wish I'd never heard of the word "repression," he thought. Picking up the transcripts of Dr. Stein's court-ordered sessions with Jennifer, he read through them again. Then he reached across his desk and picked up a black notebook containing the photocopied notes written by Jennifer's personal therapist. As he read through the therapist's notes for perhaps the tenth time, he was struck by the difference between her brief, three- or four-sentence summaries and the word-for-word typewritten transcripts of Stein's sessions with Jennifer.

Jennifer's first session with her personal therapist took place on June 21, 1989, two days after she attempted suicide by overdosing on the over-the-counter stimulant Vivarin. When questioned about her depression, she mentioned some sources of recent unhappiness—she didn't like the "rich snobs" at school, her best friend had just moved to California, and another friend lived too far away—but she was unable to name any specific reasons for her suicide attempt.

When the therapist asked Jennifer to describe her parents, she characterized her father as hardworking and unselfish. He often acted, she said, "like a little kid." She portrayed her mother as extremely well organized, unemotional, and insensitive.

Steve was struck by Jennifer's description of her father as "a little kid." That's also what came out in the sessions with Dr. Stein, he thought, picking up the transcript of the April 15 session. About halfway through the session, Jennifer told Stein: "My father loved children. He'd always play with all the little cousins when they came over. He spent a lot of time with teenagers in the church and stuff, so! You know. He was a good dad, too. A lot of people—um he was very absent-minded, didn't always remember things."

And on the next page: "He did spend a lot more time with us than a lot of my friends' dads did. He'd take us places and do things with us, and—he wasn't like one of those kinds of dads that expected you to be perfect and get straight A's and stuff like that. He wasn't *that* kind of dad."

When Stein asked Jennifer if her father had ever humiliated or embarrassed her, she said he did "just normal dad things. Singing in the car with my friends and things like that . . . he's a very strange person. . . . He used to sing, what did he sing? 'Clementine' . . . He used to try and dance, which was very embarrassing."

"Did your friends think he was silly?" Stein asked.

"Yes," Jennifer answered.

Steve found himself smiling at the thought of Doug Nagle—thick-spectacled, middle-aged corporate lawyer—singing and dancing in front of his adolescent daughter and her friends. He hadn't had the privilege of seeing that side of his client.

Toward the end of the session Jennifer said, "During the daytime, he was—probably an ideal father, but in the nighttime he did horrible things."

Steve returned to the therapist's notes, and again he was struck by the difference between Stein's verbatim transcripts and these summary notes, perhaps written hours after the therapy session ended. Three entire sessions were frequently summarized on a single page. It was impossible to discover from these notes what the therapist said to elicit a particular response, how she framed her questions, or what her expectations might have been. Did she make leading or suggestive comments? How did Jennifer respond to the therapist's questions—did she hesitate, stammer, rephrase the question, refuse to answer, or in some way challenge the therapist's assumptions? These questions couldn't be answered by looking at the notes.*

Steve couldn't help wondering how different this whole case might have been if the therapist's sessions had been taped. What if every therapist audiotaped or videotaped every session with every single client? Even then, would we be able to determine exactly what went on in these sessions? How much can a therapist shape the thinking of her patients by the way she phrases a question, what gestures she makes, when she pauses to reflect, or whether she regards the patient silently and without comment?

On September 20, 1989, Jennifer's therapist continued collecting information on the Nagle family history and temperament. Jennifer again described her father as a workaholic, often preoccupied and forgetful, but also good-natured and affectionate.

On October 4, the therapist noted that she continued to gather information about the patient's history and was beginning to focus in on the possibility of past abuse.

The possibility of past abuse. When Steve read those words, he frowned. Who brought up the possibility of past abuse—the therapist or her client? Once again, the answer was not to be found in these sparse, cryptic notes.

On October 11, 1989, Jennifer discussed her feelings of loneliness and alienation from her parents. As the weekly sessions continued through October and November, the therapist's most frequently repeated comment was "Progress is slow." From the notes, it seemed clear to Steve

---

*This is a common problem. Therapists' notes are very often too brief to give a full picture of what happens during the sessions.

And amateurs don't make ANY!

that she was trying to help her client become more assertive. Jennifer began to report "progress" with her self-esteem, and client and therapist continued to explore the possible causes of her depression.

On December 13, the therapist mentioned Jennifer's continued "slow progress." While her client was finding it easier to assert herself and express her feelings, she still could not isolate the reasons for her depression.

The January 24, 1990, entry stated only that Jennifer was continuing to progress.

On February 20, 1990, the therapist noted that she had received a phone call from Kristen, who thought she might be able to help her sister by sharing her memories, newly recovered in therapy, of being sexually abused by their father. The therapist discussed Kristen's phone call with Jennifer, who was concerned about her sister but could not provide any "specifics." Jennifer agreed that Kristen could join them for the next therapy session.

The word "specifics" struck Steve as somewhat strange. Did the therapist ask Jennifer if she knew anything specific about Kristen's alleged abuse, or did she suggest that perhaps Jennifer might be able to identify some "specifics" of her own? Had Jennifer initiated the search for specifics, or was the therapist searching for specific memories that did not, as yet, exist? Once again, it was impossible to know.

On March 7, 1990, for the first time since Jennifer's initial session eight months earlier, the therapist's notes covered a full page. The session had been called in response to Kristen's February 20 phone call in which, the therapist now revealed, Kristen not only discussed her memory of being abused by her father but disclosed that she had observed certain "incidents" that led her to believe Jennifer was also molested. During the joint therapy session, Kristen did not divulge the details of these incidents, but Jennifer became confused and distraught, expressing her fears that this was the reason Kristen had contacted her therapist.

On March 13, the therapist noted that she consulted a colleague, who advised reporting the case to Child Protective Services, the state agency responsible for investigating allegations of childhood sexual abuse, even though sexual abuse was not presently taking place. Two days later, Debbie Nagle called the therapist to ask if Jennifer should remain in the home with her father. Although she said she was certain her children were completely safe, the therapist recommended finding a temporary placement for Jennifer.

Later that same day the therapist reported the case to CPS.

On March 26, Debbie called to report that Dr. Barker recommended that Doug move out of the house for at least six months so that Jennifer could return to her home. That same afternoon, all four sisters met in the therapist's office to share their feelings and experiences. Alison, the second-oldest daughter, was openly hostile to Kristen and to the therapist, refusing to believe that her father was capable of abusing any of his children. Anna was distraught. Jennifer supported Kristen. The therapist hoped the session would promote additional communication between the sisters.

Two days later Jennifer expressed ambivalence about continuing with the therapy sessions. Her reasons were explored, and the therapist concluded that she wanted to avoid the pain involved in examining past sexual abuse.

For the next month, Jennifer was depressed and uncommunicative, although she agreed to continue with counseling. Another session was scheduled with Kristen, and the therapist described it in five words: "Kristen supportive, Jennifer still depressed."

A week later, on April 25, Jennifer was still depressed and continued to express ambivalence about the possibility of sexual abuse.

But on May 9, the ambivalence and confusion came to an abrupt end. Jennifer had discovered her memories, and they were astonishingly clear and finely focused. She remembered being raped by her father in fourth or fifth grade. She remembered that when she was four or five years old, her father grabbed her wrists and lay down on top of her. She remembered crying, kicking, and yelling whenever he was near her. She remembered that he kissed her on her neck and chest, that he forced her to touch his penis, and that he put his hands between her legs.

The abuse began, she recalled, when she was very young. She was certain of that fact because her mother's sister told her, just two days earlier, that she believed Jennifer was abused before she was two years old. Her aunt remembered laying down on the bed with Jennifer, who started crawling and squirming around on top of her. The baby's precocious "sexual behavior" convinced her aunt that Jennifer had been abused by her father.

In June, Jennifer, Kristen, Anna, and Debbie traveled to Europe for three weeks, and Jennifer's therapist attended a workshop led by Laura Davis, co-author of the self-help book *The Courage to Heal*.

On July 2, Jennifer told her therapist that she recognized the importance of talking about her past abuse. The therapist offered her *The Courage to Heal* and shared her insights from the workshop presentation. Many survivors think they made up the memories, she confided, and many believe they might be going crazy. The question of forgiveness came up, and the therapist told Jennifer that she did not have to forgive her father.

A week later Jennifer recovered another memory of being abused, this time an occasion when she was four years old. Her father ejaculated in her mouth. She threw up, and he hit her.

On July 11, Jennifer requested an extra session because she was feeling overwhelmed with guilt and shame, and she feared that she was to blame for what had happened to her. The therapist reassured her that the abuse was not her fault and noted that more work was needed on this issue.

Jennifer and her therapist met for twenty-three additional sessions between August and January 1991; the therapist's notes of these sessions covered only ten pages. Their conversations seemed to broaden out into discussions of friendships, boyfriends, and problems with self-esteem. Art therapy helped Jennifer confront her rage and grief. She continued to "progress," although she often expressed feelings of sadness about her memories.

The notes ended on January 29 with a short statement that Jennifer was distressed about the upcoming trial and particularly dreaded a court-ordered interview with a psychologist whom she feared didn't care about her side of the story.

Steve Moen put the therapist's notes back in their folder and reached once again for the black notebook containing the transcripts of Dr. Stein's conversations with Jennifer. Stein was the psychologist retained by the defense whom Jennifer discussed in her final sessions with her therapist. As Steve read through Stein's transcripts for perhaps the tenth time, he concluded that Stein not only cared about Jennifer but strongly empathized with her feelings of anger and betrayal.

In their second-to-last session, held on May 29, just a month before the trial, Stein asked Jennifer to describe her father.

> Stein: What was he like?
>
> Jennifer Nagle: He wasn't affectionate . . . He was gone a lot. He was absentminded. I missed having a father. . . . He was just busy with work. . . . He worked hard.

Later, at the very end of the session, this conversation took place:

> Stein: Was your dad selfish?
>
> Jennifer Nagle: I don't think so. He didn't give to the family, but he gave to other people. Boys.
>
> Stein: He said the same thing. Frankly, I don't think either of you are correct, but that's my perception.
>
> Jennifer Nagle: That he's not selfish?
>
> Stein: No, I think he is.
>
> Jennifer Nagle: How?
>
> Stein: I don't think he's anywhere as near as giving to anybody.

Jennifer Nagle: I don't know. He wasn't giving to the family, I would have to say. But there were a lot of kids that looked up to him, you know, quite a lot.

Stein: You needed more than presents, or being taken somewhere. . . . You were emotionally hurting. And that's particularly what I think he did not give you.

Jennifer Nagle: I don't think anybody in my family gave emotional support.

Stein: That's my perception as well. Anything else that you could tell me that would shed light on the way particularly you and your dad related as part of the family or the extended family, before we stop?

Jennifer Nagle: I don't think we were a family. At least I wasn't part of the family. Maybe they were a family without me. I don't know.

Stein: I don't think that was true. But even if it was, it was not through any fault of yours.

Jennifer Nagle: That's what they tell me.

Stein: I wish you'd believe it.

Jennifer Nagle: I'm working on it.

Steve Moen believed that the secret of the whole case was contained within that one-page conversation, neatly typed, photocopied, three-hole punched, and placed in a black notebook for perusal by legal types like himself. Jennifer was a sensitive, lonely girl who experienced deep emotional pain throughout her childhood. She perceived her mother to be cold, uncaring, and insensitive, and so she turned to her father for love and support. But her feelings about her father were deeply conflicted. Steve remembered a conversation in which Doug attempted to sort out his family's complex emotional dynamics. "I tried to be friends with Jennifer," Doug told Steve, "but she always kept her distance with me. I think she was trying to protect her mother, who was jealous because I was close to our two oldest daughters." Doug described a letter he had written to Jennifer when she was visiting her grandfather on the east coast. "I want to get to know you better," he wrote.

Jennifer wrote back, explaining that she did not want to be close to her father because she needed "her own space" but that he could drive her and her friends around whenever he wanted. Doug respected Jennifer's desire for "space" and whenever he could, he drove Jennifer and her friends to their various activities. But when he continued to have difficulties communicating with his daughter, he tried to talk with her about their strained relationship. "I feel bad that we're not close to each other," he said, "but I'm glad you feel close to your mother."

"But I'm closer to you, Dad," Jennifer said.

Recalling Doug's memory of those conversations and all the other privileged details he had learned about this family, Steve knew that something had gone very wrong. Perhaps things had never been wholly "right" between Doug, Debbie and their children. But from every document Steve had read, every person he interviewed, everything he knew about human nature, he simply did not believe that Doug Nagle was guilty of sexually abusing his children.

The trial lasted three weeks. Doug waived his right to a jury and left the final decision on his fate to Judge *Malcolm Ward*.

Debbie testified that she didn't want to believe that her husband had abused her children, but after listening to their stories could reach no other conclusion. On the stand she was cool, calm, and in total control, "an excellent prosecution witness," as Steve whispered to Doug. But Doug was troubled by her relaxed behavior on the witness stand. Before the judge entered the courtroom, she would tell jokes and trade stories with the deputy prosecutor. It's almost as if she's enjoying herself, he thought. Was it normal behavior for a woman whose husband was on trial for sexually abusing their children to laugh and joke around on the witness stand? What kind of strange world had he entered, and what would happen to him here?

After Debbie testified, it was Jennifer's turn. She told the court that she had very strong feelings about the "possibility" that her father might have abused her, and she interpreted those feelings as evidence that the abuse must have happened—even though she could not, at first, remember any specific incidents. Most of her memories came back in the summer and fall of 1990, and she carefully described the process used to "generate" them. Whenever she was feeling anxious, nervous, or restless and unable to sleep, she knew that a traumatic memory was about to emerge from her unconscious. After making sure that a strong support system was available, she would try to relax and let her mind wander, allowing the memories to break through to consciousness.

Throughout her testimony, Jennifer carefully avoided looking in her father's direction. At one point, when she became upset and emotional, the prosecutor moved over to block her view of the defense table. It was a dramatic moment with equally dramatic implications: Try to imagine what life must have been like for this child, the prosecutor's gesture indicated, when just the sight of her father causes her pain.

Judge Ward ruled at the beginning of the trial that the only evidence he would consider from Kristen was a description of her role in the development of her younger sister's memories; he knew that any discussion of Kristen's alleged memories of abuse would only complicate an already tangled case. Kristen testified that she telephoned Jennifer's therapist, offering to share her memories of abuse and her suspicion that Jennifer might have been abused. Her phone call, she explained, was motivated by her desire to help her sister progress in therapy. In his cross-examination Steve Moen tried to show that Kristen interfered with her sister's therapy and contributed to the development of false memories of abuse when she suggested that Jennifer might have been abused by her father.

Alison, the second oldest daughter, testified that she was initially shocked by the accusations and completely supported her father. But by the time the case came to trial, she felt that she could no longer side with her father against her mother and her sisters. When asked to describe her mother, Alison characterized her as "depressed." And without any prompting from the defense, Alison discussed an argument that erupted with Kristen during the March 26 meeting of the four sisters in Jennifer's therapist's office. Alison testified that she and Kristen quarreled about Kristen's "lying." Kristen "lied about a lot of things," Alison testified, and her lies had inflicted damage on the family many times before.

Debbie's sister *Marge* testified that she believed Doug had been abusing Jennifer "since she was less than two," because of an incident that occurred in 1976. Marge was twenty-one years old when she stayed with the Nagle children for a month while Debbie and Doug traveled to Europe. One night Jennifer, just twenty-one months old, was fussing in her crib. When Marge picked her up and lay down on the bed with her, Jennifer "wiggled around" in a way that her aunt interpreted as sexually suggestive. Marge believed that Jennifer learned this "sexual behavior" from her father.

In cross-examination, Marge admitted that she told Jennifer about the baby-sitting incident on May 7, 1991, two days before Jennifer "recovered" her memories.

The final prosecution witness was Jennifer's therapist who supported the basic authenticity of her client's recovered memories. In his cross-examination, Steve Moen confirmed that Jennifer's therapist made no attempt to critically assess the "historical truth" of her client's story. While psychotherapists have the obligation to concern themselves with "what is on the patient's mind," Moen conceded, don't they also have a duty to address the historical accuracy of any memory involving accusations of abuse? If therapist's don't make these assessments, if they refuse to use their critical thinking skills in an attempt to ascertain the facts, isn't it possible that they might end up treating patients for conditions they don't actually have?

* * *

Doug took the stand and testified that he had never abused his children or any other children. His early adolescent sexual experiences with the boys in his Scout troop were reviewed by the prosecution in detail.

Numerous character witnesses testified that Doug Nagle had a reputation for telling the truth. *Scott Jensen,* a fifteen-year-old member of a church youth group whom Doug had befriended, testified that he accompanied Debbie and Jennifer on a mission trip to Mexico in April 1990. According to Scott's testimony, Jennifer told him in three different conversations during that trip that her therapist, her mother, and her sister all believed that her father had abused her, but that she had no memories of being abused. In an interview with Steve Moen, Scott quoted Jennifer as saying, "Mom keeps telling me it's true. The counselor and Mom keep telling me it happened, but I don't remember, they won't listen to me."

The Nagle family's pediatrician testified that it was a normal part of his standard physical examination to look for signs and symptoms of sexual abuse. In all the years that he had been treating Jennifer and her sisters, he never found any reason to suspect abuse. Four expert witnesses testified for the defense. Dr. Stein reported the results of his forensic evaluation and interviews with Jennifer Nagle. Dr. Yuille, a psychology professor from Canada, discussed a controversial method designed to discriminate between true and false accusations. As an expert on child sexual abuse, Dr. Carson testified that Doug's adolescent homosexual experiences were within the range of "normal" and could not be used to support the accusations that he raped his daughters 35 years later. Dr. Loftus offered evidence about the power of suggestion to influence memory.

Closing arguments took place on Monday, July 1, 1991; that same day Judge Ward announced his verdict. After a lengthy verbal review of the testimony, Ward announced that Doug Nagle was acquitted of all charges.

Doug watched as Debbie, Alison, and Anna hurriedly left the courtroom. *Acquitted.* What did that mean, exactly? Was he innocent or just not guilty? Would an acquittal give him back his life, put his family back together again? An acquittal would keep him from going to jail, and for that he was grateful. But what else would it do?

Jennifer was surrounded by a group of people he didn't recognize. Approaching the prosecutor's table, he asked if he could talk to his daughter.

"I can't stop you now," the chief prosecutor snapped at him.

He walked over to the group surrounding his daughter. "Jennifer, will you talk to me?" he asked.

Several people whispered to her. He heard the words "You don't have to talk to him," and one woman took Jennifer by the shoulders and physically turned her around so that she would not have to face her father. But Jennifer suddenly pushed through the group. "This is my dad," she said, walking toward her father.

"I love you," Doug said. "I'll always love you."

Jennifer put her arms around her father, buried her face in the hollow of his neck, and said the only words that could truly break his heart. "I love you, too, Daddy."

For the next three days Doug tried to get through to his family, but no one was answering the phone. On the fourth day he reached Debbie. When he asked if he could speak to Anna or Jennifer, Debbie told him never to call the house again. From now on, she continued, all communication with the family would have to go through their divorce lawyers.

The lawyers arranged for Doug to meet with Jennifer, but at the last moment Debbie canceled the meeting. She told Doug that she and Jennifer's counselor were urging Jennifer to cut off all communication with her father, at least temporarily. Allowing Jennifer to meet with him would give her a "mixed message." *?? [so she was being given a message]*

Doug left messages for Jennifer's counselor, but she never returned his phone calls. Finally, when he refused to get off the line until she talked to him, the therapist admitted that she had advised Jennifer and Debbie not to cooperate with his attempts to obtain an independent evaluation of their situation. She added that she would refuse to read any letters or literature he sent to her office, she would not agree to meet with him, and she did not want to hear from him again, ever. Period.

Anna and Alison informed Doug's divorce lawyer that they were not emotionally prepared to see their father; at some point in the future they might be willing to seek a reconciliation. Jennifer refused to see Doug after, in her words, he "attacked" her therapist on the telephone. She was apparently under the misconception that Doug planned to sue the therapist.

In mid-January 1992, Jennifer was admitted to a hospital psychiatric ward. Doug didn't find out about her hospitalization until two weeks later, when he received a bill from his insurance company.

On March 1, a friend called to tell Doug that Jennifer was back in the psychiatric ward. She refused to go back home to live with her mother and was looking into other living arrangements.

Ten days later Jennifer was discharged from the psychiatric unit. She moved in temporarily with friends.

Doug and Debbie Nagle were divorced soon after the criminal trial, and Doug has since remarried. His wife, who has two grown children from a previous marriage, works as an occupational therapist. For her sake, and for his own sanity, Doug tries to stay immersed in the present. Sometimes it works. For hours at a time, he is free of the agonized longing for his children. But then, without warning, the pain and anguish return. He thinks back to his life with Debbie and tries to recall the good times they shared. Their marriage failed and somehow, for some reason, enormous damage was done to their children. But we are not bad people, and we did not intentionally hurt each other or the kids, he reassures himself over and over again. Something happened, something terrible, incomprehensible, and out of our control. Once it began it could not be stopped.

Doug doesn't ever expect to understand how or why this particular tragedy befell his family. Disasters just happen, he reasons, without any kind of logical pattern. Wars, hurricanes, car crashes, trains jumping the tracks, masonry falling from buildings—these things just happen. This time, for some unfathomable reason, it was his turn to suffer.

He prays, in formal, down-on-his-knees entreaties and in quick, whispered appeals throughout the day, that Jennifer will be released from her pain and find a sense of healing and closure on her past. He lives in terror of the phone call that might come at any time—*Jennifer tried to kill herself again*—and he will not allow himself to think that someday, somehow, she might succeed. He writes his children letters, which he keeps in a special place, waiting for permission to communicate with them again. He longs for the day when he will be able to see them again, put his arms around them, tell them how much he loves them and how desperately he has missed them.

He is learning how to reconstruct his memories by pushing the accusations, therapy sessions, and trial scenes from his mind. While the recent, painful memories continue to intrude, he is becoming more skillful at fixing the earlier, happier memories in his mind and calling them forth when he needs to remind himself that his family was together and happy, once upon a time. Given what Doug Nagle knows about the unreliability of memory, he understands that his "pleasant" memories also contain distortions and exaggerations. But the details, however magnified, minimized, or even created, comfort him and give him hope that a happy ending might still be possible.

One of the memories he likes to recall is particularly vivid. He knows from the transcript of Dr. Stein's conversations with Jennifer that this is a clear and pleasant memory for her, too, and he likes to think that sometimes when he travels back to the past and feels flooded with the rich colors and sensory detail of his memories, Jennifer is also remembering the same event, with a similar pleasure. He feels close to her in these moments, as if he could sense her presence, share her feelings, understand her longings. In the memory they share a common soul.

They are edging a wooden rowboat into the calm, cold water of Puget Sound. The clouds above are puffy and turning pink as the day nears its end. The water rises and falls beneath them as they row out a hundred yards or so from shore. Just seven or eight years old, Jennifer wears her reddish-blond hair in a ponytail. She watches him bait the hook with slices of herring, her nose crinkling up. "Yuck, Daddy," she says, giggling. It's clear that she admires him for his courage.

The boat rocks gently. After a while, her rod bends, and she calls out in her clear child's voice, "Fish! Fish!" This is her favorite part, reeling in and getting her first peek at the catch—a rockfish or dogfish, most likely, although sometimes she hooks a small salmon—but it is quickly followed by her least favorite part. She closes her eyes and puts her hands over her ears as her father takes the small wooden bat and whacks the fish on the head.

They row back to shore, surprised at how fast the sun is disappearing over the mountains to the west. Jennifer seems anxious as they hold hands on the narrow path lined with tall, thick-needled trees. A foghorn bellows as a ship plows south toward Tacoma, and Jennifer jumps.

"It's dark, Daddy," she says, looking apprehensively into the darkness beyond the trees.

"I'll take care of you," he assures her.

"Promise?" she asks.

"Always and forever," he answers.

DIGGING FOR MEMORIES

*It may take considerable digging on the part of the therapist
to discover incest as the source of the symptoms being
experienced by the client.*

—Wendy Maltz and Beverly Holman, *Incest and Sexuality:
A Guide to Understanding and Healing*

Before Jennifer Nagle recovered any memories of her father abusing her, she was exposed to two books, one thin and one fat, on the subject of incest survival and recovery. Jennifer's school counselor handed her a ten-page pamphlet, published by a rape relief organization, titled "Incest: A Book for Survivors," and her therapist gave her *The Courage to Heal*. Despite the 485-page difference in their length, the two books share the core ideas fundamental to the concept of repression and repressed memory therapy:

- Incest and child sexual abuse are epidemic. The rape relief pamphlet states that one in four women and one in six men were sexually abused as children, while *The Courage to Heal* cites statistics declaring that one of three girls and one of seven boys are sexually abused by the time they reach age eighteen.

- Many symptoms of adult psychopathology—including but not limited to anxiety, panic attacks, depression, sexual dysfunction, relationship difficulties, abusive behaviors, eating disorders, loneliness, and suicide attempts—reflect long-term reactions to childhood sexual abuse.

- A significant percentage of adult survivors completely block out their traumatic memories through the defensive and unconscious mechanism of repression.

- Accessing and accepting the memories as real and valid is a critical step in the recovery process.

- Individual and group therapy can offer healing, resolution, and renewal.

To sum up the central message in a few words: Incest is epidemic, repression is rampant, recovery is possible, and therapy can help.

In this chapter we'll examine these general themes in detail and then describe the specific techniques used to recover repressed memories. When we use the word "repression," we are referring to more than "ordinary forgetting," which is the act of not thinking about an event or experience for a period of time and then having the memory come back to mind. Repression refers to the active banishment into the unconscious of a traumatic event or series of traumas. Repressed memories are typically recovered in therapy, when the patient is exposed to extensive "memory work"—suggestive questioning, guided visualization, age regression, hypnosis, body-memory interpretation, dream analysis, art therapy, rage and grief work, and group therapy.

While we are skeptical about the truth-finding function of these and other aggressive therapeutic techniques, we are not challenging the reality of childhood sexual abuse or traumatic memories. We do not question the trauma of the sexually abused child, nor do we doubt the experiences of men and women who suffer silently with memories of abuse they have never forgotten. We are not expressing reservations about the skills and talents of therapists who work hard, with compassion and great care, to elicit memories that for many years were too painful to put into words.

Many tortured individuals live for years with the dark secret of their abusive past and only find the courage to discuss their childhood traumas in the supportive and empathic environment of therapy. We are not disputing those memories. We are only questioning the memories commonly referred to as "repressed"*—memories that did not exist until someone went looking for them.

---

*Because the controversy over repression has become so heated and contentious, clinicians and child-protection advocates often use synonyms such as "lost," "buried," or "dissociated" to describe repressed memories. But, as psychologist David Holmes writes, "repression by any other name is still repression and the absence of evidence applies to all of the synonyms."

GENERAL TENETS

INCEST IS EPIDEMIC

The first and most forcefully stated principle of the incest-survivor move-ment is that incest occurs much more frequently than any of us ever imagined. Psychiatrist Judith Lewis Herman has referred to incest as a "common and central female experience" while therapist and popular writer E. Sue Blume claims in her book *Secret Survivors* that "incest is so common as to be epidemic. . . . At any given time *more than three quar-ters of my clients* are women who were molested in childhood by some-one they knew."

Statistics are immediately gathered to fortify these alarming claims of ubiquity. Beverly Engel introduces her book *The Right to Innocence: Healing the Trauma of Childhood Sexual Abuse* with statistics gathered from three sources: an August 1985 *Los Angeles Times* survey estimating that nearly 38 million adults were sexually abused as children; Dr. Henry Giaretto's survey of 250,000 cases referred to the Child Sexual Assault Treatment Program, indicating that one in every three women and one in every seven men are sexually abused by age eighteen; and sociologist Diana Russell's 1986 study of 930 San Francisco women, 38 percent of whom revealed that they had been molested before the age of eighteen. When nonphysical contact (i.e., genital exposure) was factored in, over half of Russell's subjects reported abuse.

The statistics are frightening, but in another sense they are meant to be comforting. As Engel writes, "Be reassured. You may have felt isolated with your pain, but you no longer have to be. Many others like you have suffered from the same pain, fear and anger. You are not alone."

Definitions and expositions of incest quickly follow the statistics. Questions are raised and forcefully answered. As Blume writes:

> Must incest involve intercourse? Must incest be overtly genital? Must it involve touch at all? The answer is no. . . . Incest is not necessarily intercourse. In fact, it does not have to involve touch. There are many other ways that the child's space or senses can be sexually violated. Incest can occur through words, sounds, or even exposure of the child to sights or acts that are sexual but do not involve her."

Blume illustrates her discussion with several examples of incestuous abuse: a father hovering outside the bathroom while a child is inside, or barging into the room without knocking; an older brother coercing his sister to undress; a school bus driver ordering a student to sit with him; an uncle showing pornographic pictures to a four-year-old; a father's jealous possessiveness or suspicion of the young man his daughter dates; a relative's repeated requests to hear the details of an adolescent's sexual experiences. The event itself is not considered as important in determining whether incest occurs as the child's subjective experience—the "way" in which she is treated or touched. Thus, sexual abuse can be inferred from the "way" a priest kisses a child good-bye or the "way" a babysitter handles a child when bathing her.

Bass and Davis, authors of *The Courage to Heal,* agree that the crucial factor determining whether or not an act is incestuous is the child's or adolescent's subjective physical, emotional, or spiritual experience. They also provide examples of nonphysical incestuous activities or "violations of trust":

> Some abuse is not even physical. Your father may have stood in the bathroom doorway, making suggestive remarks or simply leering when you entered to use the toilet. Your uncle may have walked around naked, calling attention to his penis, talking about his sexual exploits, questioning you about your body . . . There are many ways to be violated sexually. There is also abuse on the psychological level. You had the feeling your stepfather was aware of your physical presence every minute of the day, no matter how quiet and unobtrusive you were. Your neighbor watched your changing body with an intrusive interest. Your father took you out on romantic dates and wrote you love letters.

Beverly Engel offers a personal memory to reinforce the point that it is the child's level of discomfort, signaled by uneasiness or embarrassment about a specific encounter, that determines whether or not the incident was abusive. The degree of discomfort can be assessed through hindsight, many years later:

> On several occasions during my high school years, my mother would get sloppy drunk and would get very sentimental. Sometimes she would plant a big "wet" kiss on my mouth. Now I have reason to believe my mother was unconsciously being sexually seductive.

But—the skeptic in the back of the room raises her hand—isn't this the adult Beverly reconstructing and analyzing a decades-old memory? Was the adolescent Beverly aware of such feelings as she was being kissed, or soon afterward? Could it be that she was more distressed by the fact that her mother was "sloppy drunk" than by the kiss it self? Were Beverly's adult interpretations, clarified and refined by years of clinical training and experience with incest survivors, grafted onto an ambiguously disturbing but relatively "harmless" experience?

These skeptical questions apparently miss the point. The adolescent feelings and perceptions aren't really at issue here, because Beverly was young and immature and thus incapable of adequately assessing and understanding her situation. Only when she grew up and looked back at the past could she understand the meaning of her earlier experiences. And if, in the process of reviewing her memories, she had the *feeling* that she was abused, then she probably was abused. She doesn't even have to have the memories.

Non-
Sicuce

REPRESSION IS RAMPANT

"Something in the neighborhood of 60 percent of all incest victims don't remember the sexual abuse for many years after the fact," proclaims self-help author John Bradshaw in his monthly *Lear's* magazine column. While Bradshaw doesn't cite a source for this statistic, a similar figure is offered by Blume in her book:

> It is my experience that fewer than half of the women who experience this trauma later remember or identify it as abuse. Therefore it is not unlikely that more than half of all women are survivors of childhood sexual trauma. . . . Literally tens of millions of "secret survivors" carry the weight of their hidden history of abuse.

Later in her book Blume announces that "repression in some form is virtually universal among survivors."

Therapist Renee Fredrickson agrees that the numbers are staggering. At first suspicious of the sheer volume of clients reporting repressed memories of sexual abuse ("I thought that this must be some form of contagious hysteria") she eventually came to believe that these buried and unearthed memories were accurate representations of the past. As her conviction grew, she searched in the scholarly journals for information on the subject of repression. To her dismay she found only Freudian speculation about patients' "fantasies" of abuse. "I was forced to rely on my own observations and the clinical experiences of my colleagues to learn about repressed memories."

It wasn't long before Fredrickson understood the magnitude of the problem and decided to write a book (*Repressed Memories: A Journey to Recovery from Sexual Abuse*) in order to help the "millions of people" who have "blocked out frightening episodes of abuse, years of their life, or their entire childhood. They want desperately to find out what happened to them and they need the tools to do so."

Bass and Davis agree that repression is a common occurrence among survivors. In a chapter entitled "Remembering," readers are told: "If you don't remember your abuse, you are not alone. Many women don't have memories, and some never get memories. This doesn't mean they weren't abused."

Scholars tend to be slightly more circumspect about the numbers, although they agree that repression is a common reaction to trauma. Psychoanalyst Alice Miller offers a generalized, universalized statement about the mind's ability to store away disturbing thoughts and emotions: "Every childhood's conflictual experiences remain hidden and locked in darkness, and the key to our understanding of the life that follows is hidden away with them."

Many psychiatrists, psychologists, and social workers believe that the reality of the "hidden-awayness" known as repression is finally being rediscovered. In a scholarly article frequently cited by trauma therapists (sometimes called traumatists) titled "The Intrusive Past: The Flexibility of Memory and the Engraving of Trauma" authors B. A. van der Kolk and Onno van der Hart provide some history. For nearly a hundred years, the authors contend, psychoanalysis (defined as "the study of repressed wishes and instincts") "virtually ignored the fact that actual memories may form the nucleus of psychopathology and continue to exert their influence on current experience by means of the process of dissociation." But in the 1980s and 1990s, psychiatrists are at long last acknowledging

> the reality of trauma in people's lives, and the fact that actual experiences can be so overwhelming that they cannot be integrated into existing mental frameworks, and instead, are dissociated, later to return intrusively as fragmented sensory or motoric experiences.

If memory blocks are protective, as every popular author and scholarly writer seems to agree, why do we expose ourselves to the risks of digging up the buried material? Because the shards and fragments of the past will continue to penetrate our present-day lives, causing piercing pain and grief. Not until we unearth the memory, file down its jagged edges, and carefully slide the smoothed-out pieces into our expanded sense of self will we experience relief and release from the past. As Van der Kolk and Van der Hart explain:

> Traumatic memories are the unassimilated scraps of overwhelming experiences, which need to be integrated with existing mental schemes, and be transformed into narrative language. It appears that, in order for this to occur successfully, the traumatized person has to return to the memory often in order to complete it.

Popular writers use looser language and familiar metaphors to make the same point. In his *Lear's* column, John Bradshaw describes the need to face our fears: "Avoidance of the facts of our lives only harms us. Help comes when we name our demons and speak plainly even of the most fearsome things."

These "fearsome things" generally reside in the unconscious mind, a hypothetical location that is given weight and substance by many popular writers. Renee Fredrickson, for example, offers a tangled but intriguing explanation of the workings of the unconscious mind and its ability to function only in the present:

> The unconscious always operates in the present tense, and, when a memory is buried in the unconscious, the unconscious preserves it as an ongoing act of abuse in the present reality of the unconscious mind. The cost of repressing a memory is that the mind does not know the abuse ended. . . . Uncompleted memory fragments will always "come back to haunt you."

But—the skeptic's hand rises again—if you have no memories of being abused, how do you know that your present-day problems might be caused by repressed memories or "uncompleted memory fragments"? The proof is in the pudding, as it were. If your life shows the symptoms, then you were in all likelihood abused. If you think you were abused, if you have the feeling you were abused, then you were abused. Don't let anyone try to talk you out of your reality, the advice continues, because if it feels real, it is real, and that's all the proof you will ever need.

Skeptics receive a rather thorough bashing in the popular incest-recovery books. Survivors are told not to give any credence to research reports about the prevalence of incest. According to E. Sue Blume, incest research "has been used to hide truths and support lies. . . . In quantifying human experience, we may lose its richness, if not its truth." Blume then quotes Judith Lewis Herman, who argues that only clinicians can accurately gauge the extent of the incest problem: "The insight of a skilled clinician cannot be matched by any questionnaire or survey instrument presently available. Subtle forms of emotional damage, which may not be detected in broader sociological studies, are apparent in clinical reports."

Psychologist John Briere makes a similar point in a recent interview. Responding, perhaps, to critics' statements that repressed-memory therapy is a temporary fad (or, as social psychologist Richard Ofshe has termed it in his characteristically blunt manner, "one of the century's most intriguing quackeries"), Briere said: "I'm hoping that because a vast number of survivors have found a voice, no amount of what is now trendy disbelief will silence them. The 'up side' of the wide prevalence of sexual abuse is that millions of people know, deep down, that sexual abuse *is* a real phenomenon."

It is difficult to escape the intimation (lurking as accusation) that memory researchers and statistic gatherers are not only antisurvivor but antitruth when they question the reality of repressed memories. As Briere's interview continues, it becomes even more obvious that he believes certain skeptical researchers are deeply committed to the task of proving survivors' stories false:

> I find myself saddened and angered by the fact that people who otherwise show reasonable scientific probity have in this case become invested in trying to prove somehow—without persuasive data—that the memories of hundreds of thousands of survivors are not true. . . . We're ultimately talking about human beings in pain, and human beings in pain are not always going to be 100% accurate. We don't do the same kind of grilling of someone who has a car accident or some other kind of experience. It seems to be especially in the sexual abuse area that we have the greatest difficulty accepting what is told to us.

Why do skeptics have such a difficult time accepting the truth? Because (we're told) we're in denial. When psychologist Carol Tavris's critical essay "Beware the Incest-Survivor Machine" appeared in *The New York Times Book Review,* therapists and survivors fired off angry letters to the editor, accusing Tavris of being afraid to face the truth. Ellen Bass outlined the reasons for the skeptic's denial:

> It is painful to face the reality that so many children were horribly abused. It is far easier to call it fantasy, manipulation, fabrication; easier to say that someone has been brainwashed into believing he or she was abused than to face the fact that this person—as a child—endured such torments.

In this, at least, skeptics and survivors join hands, for denial affects us all, obscuring the light of truth. Denial is presented as tangible and physical, like an artichoke whose sharp-tipped leaves must be stripped away to reveal the "heart" of truth. How do we peel away our denial?

"Some things have to be believed to be seen," writes Renee Fredrickson, quoting one of *Reader's Digest*'s "Quotable Quotes." For researchers who follow the scientific method, relying on faith to arrive at facts is simply against the rules. But Fredrickson and other popular writers aren't particularly interested in dislodging the stubborn skepticism of the science types. Their primary purpose is to help survivors overcome their denial, and the most efficient way to defeat denial is to jump right in and "do" memory work. Once the survivor embarks on memory work— a tool box full of exercises and techniques designed to excavate buried memories—the sheer volume of memories retrieved will conquer denial. As Fredrickson explains:

> When you have retrieved enough memories, you will reach critical mass, which is a sense of the overall reality of your repressed memories. . . . After enough memories, debriefed enough times, you will suddenly know your repressed memories are real. It is the opposite of the maxim that if you tell a lie long enough, you will believe it is real. . . . if you talk about your repressed memories long enough, you will intuitively know they are real.

RECOVERY IS POSSIBLE

Once a survivor reaches "critical mass," the road to recovery straightens out, and healing begins. Recovery is a land of triumph and renewal where we become, in Fredrickson's words, "wiser and more beautiful" than we were before we began the journey. On the road to recovery, the survivor reclaims herself, taking her power back, shedding guilt and self-blame, regaining her lost pride, experiencing new energy and vitality, healing the wounds of her childhood.

Healing must not be confused, however, with the end of a journey or the absence of pain. Recovery is a lifelong process full of painful and bewildering ups and downs, detours and backtracks. Psychologist John Briere tells a story to convey this point about the perennial nature of health and healing:

> A survivor I saw a while back ended our consultation by asking me, "Will I ever be cured?" It seemed to me that she was really asking, "Will I ever not hurt?" The sad, weird answer—and what I said to the survivor—was "No, probably you will never not hurt, at least never stop hurting completely. I understand that in your desperation not hurting is the best thing you can think of that could happen for you, but maybe that's not all of what this [therapy] is about."
>
> "Then what is it about?" she asked.
> "Freedom?" I suggested.
> And she smiled.

Freedom. Truth. Justice. The American Way.

Recovery gradually takes on the shine of truth, of the righteous fight, the global battle to end oppression and join hands with all who suffer, not just from sexual abuse but from any kind of fear or prejudice. Survivors are assured that their cause goes beyond their own healing, for by healing themselves, they contribute to the healing of the world. As therapist Mike Lew writes in *Victims No Longer:* "From where I look it's all about the same thing. Children. The ocean. Fish. The earth. We either care about them or we don't. . . . In short, how can we heal the world unless we heal ourselves?"

You don't even have to be a victim or survivor to become part of this privileged and empowered group. It does help, however, to be a woman. "Though I was not personally raped, I am a woman. I am the mother of a daughter," writes Ellen Bass in her introduction to *I Never Told Anyone: Writings by Women Survivors of Child Sexual Abuse:*

> I share in the pain, in the anger, in the healing, and in the creation of a world where children are encouraged and empowered to control their own bodies, to protest, and to ask for help, knowing they will get it. Ultimately, I am sharing in the restoration of a consciousness where the rape of children—as well as the rape of women, of forests, of oceans, of the earth—is a history to be remembered only to assure it will not begin again.

In *The Courage to Heal,* Bass and Davis make the theme even more explicit and, of course, politically correct:

> Although your responsibility toward healing begins with yourself, it does not stop there. Child sexual abuse originates from the same fear, hatred, deprivation, selfishness, and ignorance that lead people to abuse and assault in other ways. These attitudes are woven into the very fabric of our society and oppress on a large scale. We get nuclear waste, inhuman conditions for migrant farm workers, the rampages of the Ku Klux Klan.

The Courage to Heal then goes on to imply that the victims of oppression are the chosen few who can heal not only themselves but the world at large:

> Part of your healing is the healing of the earth. If you don't make it a priority, there is little hope for the world. By and large, it is not the abusers who are going to write letters to our government, imploring them to stop funding slaughter in El Salvador. It's not the mothers who are too terrified to hear your pain who are going to fight for changes in the legal system to make it easier for children to testify. And how many pedophiles care about toxic waste?

It is you—who know something about both justice and injustice, about abuse and respect, about suffering and about healing—who have the clarity, courage, and compassion to contribute to the quality, and the very continuation, of life.

Perhaps we doubters and disbelievers do have reason for concern, for this kind of warm and fuzzy survivor-speak creates an obvious polarization of the field: an us-versus-them mentality, a self-righteousness that separates and divides, a black-and-white dichotomizing of the world by people who should know better.

Just consider the implications in that one short sentence in *The Courage to Heal*: "How many pedophiles care about toxic waste?" Is the world so easily reduced to good and evil? A parallel can be drawn with a scene in Arthur Miller's *The Crucible*, in which Deputy Governor Danforth announces to the bewildered townfolk of Salem, Massachusetts:

> But you must understand . . . that a person is either with this court or he must be counted against it, there be no road between. This is a sharp time, now, a precise time—we live no longer in the dusky afternoon when evil mixed itself with good and befuddled the world. Now, by God's grace, the shining sun is up, and them that fear not light will surely praise it. I hope you will be one of those.

Miller drew parallels between the Salem witch-hunters and the McCarthyite red-baiters. He feared their shared "parochial snobbery," born and bred in the belief "that they held in their steady hands the candle that would light the world." In our zeal to end child sexual abuse and help ease the pain of adult survivors, have we been blinded by the light of what some choose to call the truth? Have we fallen prey to the same misguided and moralistic beliefs that in times past divided the world into purely good and purely evil?

SPECIFIC TECHNIQUES

There is never only one path up the mountain . . . Techniques
for memory recovery are as unlimited as human creativity.

—Renee Fredrickson, *Repressed Memories*

Having explored the general framework supporting the concept of repressed memory therapy (or simply "memory work") we come to the specifics: the various and sundry tools used by therapists to unearth buried memories.

THE DIRECT QUESTION

When clients walk into therapy and describe a history of depression, anxiety, suicidal feelings, sexual problems, eating disorders, or various addictions, many therapists automatically suspect sexual abuse as the underlying cause of their problems. What actions should a therapist take regarding her suspicions? The authors of *The Courage to Heal* suggest a direct approach.

> When you work with someone you think may have been abused, ask outright, "Were you sexually abused as a child?" This is a simple and straightforward way to find out what you're dealing with. It's also a clear message to your clients that you are available to work with the issue of sexual abuse.

Therapist Karen Olio agrees that the clinician must be experienced in the area of sexual abuse and willing to bring up this sensitive and formerly taboo subject:

> Probably the most important factor in the identification of sexual abuse among clients is the clinician's willingness to consider it as a possibility. . . . Unfortunately, because of inexperience and ignorance, many therapists do not ask the right questions or recognize the indicators of sexual abuse. . . . Unless asked directly . . . survivors may not disclose a history of abuse.

In her book *Betrayal of Innocence* Susan Forward, a therapist who claims that she has treated more than fifteen hundred incest victims, discusses her method of approaching clients:

> You know [she says to them], in my experience, a lot of people who are struggling with many of the same problems you are have often had some kind of really painful things happen to them as kids—maybe they were beaten or molested. And I wonder if anything like that ever happened to you?

Other clinicians profess to know of colleagues who say to their clients, "Your symptoms sound like you've been abused when you were a child. What can you tell me about that?" or even "You sound to me like the sort of person who must have been sexually abused. Tell me what that bastard did to you."

If a client cannot remember any specific incidences of abuse, the therapist is advised to consider the possibility of repressed memories. For repression is not only the method by which memories are banished from

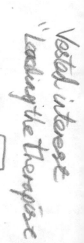

vested interest

"Leading the therapist"

consciousness, but an indication in and of itself that abuse exists. "When survivors can't remember their childhood or have very fuzzy memories, incest must always be considered a possibility," authors and therapists Maltz and Holman *(Incest and Sexuality)* advise their clinical colleagues. Psychotherapist Mike Lew echoes the theme: "When an adult tells me that he can't remember whole chunks of his childhood, I assume the likelihood of some sort of abuse."

"Vague feelings" are another indication that repressed memories of abuse may be seeping out of the unconscious and into the conscious awareness. "If you have any suspicion at all, if you have any memory, no matter how vague, it probably really happened," therapist Beverly Engel advises her patients. "It is far more likely that you are blocking the memories, *denying* it happened."

Suspicion, apparently, always leads to confirmation. "In fifteen years of practicing as a psychotherapist, I have never worked with a client who initially suspected she was sexually abused but later discovered she had not been," Engel writes. Bass and Davis confirm the theory:

> So far, no one we've talked to thought she might have been abused, and then later discovered that she hadn't been. The progression always goes the other way, from suspicion to confirmation. If you think you were abused and your life shows the symptoms, then you were.

THE SYMPTOM LIST

1. Do you have trouble knowing what you want?

2. Are you afraid to try new experiences?

3. If someone gives you a suggestion, do you feel you ought to follow it?

4. Do you follow other people's suggestions as if they were orders to be observed?

This diminutive symptom list, published in John Bradshaw's July 1992 column in *Lear's,* is part of a larger checklist titled "An Index of Suspicions" from Bradshaw's book *Homecoming.* After presenting these four questions in *Lear's,* Bradshaw offers a quick analysis:

> If you answered even one of these questions in the affirmative, you can count on some damage having been done to you in your early developmental stage, between the 9th and 18th months of your life, during the period when you began to crawl and explore and follow your innate curiosity wherever it led you.

In his August 1992 column, Bradshaw presents a slightly more specific inventory of traits that he considers "typical of adult victims of incest." The list includes nine items with an obvious sexual bent ("You have little or no interest in sex," "You are sexually promiscuous without enjoying it much," "You displayed unusually precocious sexual behavior before the age of ten," "You have never to your knowledge had sex with anyone"), with a few questions thrown in about apathetic behaviors, eating disorders, and various physical ailments. For those readers who identify with a majority of these traits but have no memories of incest, a simple exercise is suggested: "Accept the *theory* that you were sexually abused, live consciously with that idea for six months in context with an awareness of the traits you acknowledge, and see whether any memories come to you."

If Bradshaw offers the fast food of the symptom list, E. Sue Blume extends an invitation to a gourmet feast. Her menu of symptoms, impressively titled "The Incest Survivors' Aftereffects Checklist," includes thirty-four traits or characteristics of incest survivors, most of which include several components, extensions, or, oddly enough, contradictions. For example:

> Number 3: Alienation from the body—not at home in own body; failure to heed body signals or take care of one's body; poor body image; manipulating body size to avoid sexual attention.

> Number 5: Wearing a lot of clothing, even in summer; baggy clothes; failure to remove clothing even when appropriate to do so (while swimming, bathing, sleeping); extreme requirement for privacy when using bathroom.

> Number 9: Need to be invisible, perfect, or perfectly bad.

> Number 32: Aversion to making noise (including during sex, crying, laughing, or other body functions); verbal hypervigilance (careful monitoring of one's words); quiet-voiced, especially when needing to be heard.

From just this brief sample (the actual list runs on for five paperback pages), consider this: If you have a poor body image, wear baggy clothes, feel the need to be perfect (or perfectly bad), speak softly, and don't like to make noise while making love, "You could be a survivor of incest." (The reader, by the way, is given no advice about how to score an item in which one detail fits and the others don't; presumably even a flickering of recognition invites a check mark.)

Renee Fredrickson offers in her book a checklist of symptoms that highlights "common warning signals of repressed memories." Sixty-five questions separated into seven categories ("Sexuality," "Sleep," "Fears and Attractions," "Eating Disturbances," "Body Problems," "Compulsive Behaviors," and "Emotional Signals") focus on fears, preoccupations, and behavior patterns. Some sample symptoms:

- I have had a period of sexual promiscuity in my life.

- I often have nightmares.

- I have difficulty falling or staying asleep.

- Basements terrify me.

- I do some things to excess, and I just don't know when to quit.

- I identify with abuse victims in the media, and often stories of abuse make me want to cry.

- I startle easily.

- I space out or daydream.

The symptom lists are designed to help survivors recognize the extent of the damage caused by the abuse and its continuing impact on their present life. Bass and Davis *(The Courage to Heal)* present a total of seventy-four questions organized in seven broad categories: "Self-esteem and Personal Power," "Feelings," "Your Body," "Intimacy," "Sexuality," "Children and Parenting," and "Families of Origin." The question "Where are you now?" heads each section, the point being that you may have been too busy just surviving to notice the myriad ways in which you were harmed by the abuse. Here, for example, is just a sampling from the fifteen questions in the "Self-Esteem and Personal Power" section:

- Do you feel different from other people?

- Do you have trouble feeling motivated?

- Do you feel you have to be perfect?

- Do you use work or achievements to compensate for inadequate feelings in other parts of your life?

WARNING: The problem with symptom lists is that relatively harmless parts of a "normal" personality become distorted and deviant when viewed through the microscopic lens of incest. Nonpathological aspects of our temperament become symptomatic of a dark and evil secret that we hide even from ourselves. The symptom lists toss out a net that entangles the whole human race. As psychologist Carol Tavris comments:

The same list could be used to identify oneself as someone who loves too much, someone who suffers from self-defeating personality disorder, or a mere human being in the late 20th century. The list is general enough to include everybody at least sometimes. Nobody doesn't fit it.

A related problem is that the more far-fetched items on the list (the baggy clothes and fear of basements immediately come to mind) are given greater credence and plausibility when grouped with symptoms commonly accepted as aftereffects of sexual abuse (such as an exceptionally strong startle response or hypersexuality in childhood). When normal behaviors and responses are reinterpreted as suggestive of abuse, then any behavior becomes potentially symptomatic; the more items you check off on the symptom lists, the more it looks like you're a candidate for survivorship. If one symptom doesn't fit, certainly the next one, or the one after, will.

Blume is remarkably straightforward regarding the underlying purpose of her list. "We have found that the Aftereffects Checklist can serve as a diagnostic device for *suggesting* sexual victimization when none is remembered" [emphasis added]. How do clients respond to such obvious (and obviously intentional) suggestions? Some undoubtedly persist in their denials that they were not abused, and eventually either the therapist gets back on track or the client terminates therapy. Attorney *Dennis Herriot*, for example, was severely depressed after his father's suicide and sought the help of a psychotherapist. But when he tried to talk to the therapist about the problems he was facing, she kept intimating that something else was happening that he either could not or would not face. The mystery of that "something else" haunted Herriot, and his depression deepened. What was wrong with him? His therapist stunned him with her diagnosis: "I don't know how to tell you this, but you display the same kinds of characteristics as some of my patients who are victims of satanic ritual abuse." Herriot, who had never alluded in any way to satanism or ritualistic abuse, immediately terminated therapy.

But other clients, perhaps more vulnerable and less self-confident, get caught up in the quest to find those buried memories and put an end to their misery, once and for all. A woman from Oregon who heard about my work with memory distortions and the experimental implantation of false memories, wrote a long letter requesting my help. With her permission, I include a section from her anguished letter:

Three years ago, I began individual therapy to deal with symptoms which included depression and anxiety. Within a few months, my therapist suggested that the cause of my emotional distress could be a history of childhood sexual abuse. Since that time, he has become more and more certain of his diagnosis. . . . I have no direct memories of this abuse. . . . The question I can't get past is how something so terrible could have happened to me without me remembering anything. For the past two years I have done little else but try to remember. . . . Still, I am left wondering if anything really happened. . . . The guessing has become unbearable.

What can a therapist do to make the guessing less unbearable? While all the popular books on incest survival and recovery mention different therapy techniques, and several include specific methods for recovering repressed memories, the most specific and detailed advice is offered by Renee Fredrickson in her book *Repressed Memories: A Journey to Recovery from Sexual Abuse.* Fredrickson, who has a doctorate, has appeared on National Public Radio, Cable News Network, "Oprah," and numerous other radio and television talk shows to discuss her very specific techniques for uncovering repressed memories. Her book has been widely disseminated to "survivors" by therapists who practice repressed-memory therapy.

Fredrickson includes seven basic techniques designed to excavate buried memories and breathe life into the mummified remains of repressed memories: imagistic work; dream work; journal writing; body work; hypnosis; art therapy; and feelings work. Because these and similar techniques are employed by many clinicians, particularly "memory work" therapists, we'll examine them in some detail.

IMAGISTIC WORK

Sarah was haunted by a flashback of a child's body slamming violently into a wall. Because the "memory" was presenting itself as an image, Fredrickson suggested that Sarah try "imagistic work," a process of describing in great detail every sight and sensation relating to the image and adding, whenever appropriate, subjective interpretations. As Sarah focused in on her internal reality, she began to tell the story evoked by the image, always using the present tense. (Fredrickson explains that imagistic memory is located in the unconscious, where everything takes place in the present tense.)

As one image was added to another, the "memories" created a moving picture of a child—Sarah at age two—with her grandfather in an outhouse. Sarah "sees" her grandfather leading her to the outhouse and latching the door; she watches as he takes out his penis and rubs it between her legs.

"I feel like I'm just making this up," Sarah says, suddenly interrupting the "slide show" of images.

But Fredrickson urges her client to continue, explaining that "truth or fantasy is not of concern at the beginning of memory retrieval work. What is important is what was in her [Sarah's] mind and what seemed true at this moment in time." Sarah obligingly develops the image. She recalls that her grandfather ejaculated on her. Then, holding on to her by one hand, he lowered her into the toilet hole, where her body banged painfully against the side beams.

Sarah's memory is astonishingly clear and vivid as she recalls bits and pieces of conversation ("He tells me no one cares about me"), sounds ("He laughs a funny little laugh"), smells ("The smell is awful"), emotions ("I'm really scared"). After she emerges from the outhouse, she describes the sensation of being outside again (still speaking in the present tense): "I'm surprised at how sunny and pretty the world looks."

When Fredrickson summarizes Sarah's imagistic work, she leaves no doubt that these images represent real memories surfacing from the unconscious.

> The images that surface from your unconscious to your conscious mind are fragments of a traumatic memory ready to emerge. These blips flashing across your mind may be mystifying or obscure at first glance, but they are an incomplete scrap from an abuse incident that you have buried. A piece of that incident has broken through and is poking into your conscious mind. Follow it down into your unconscious and you will retrieve a repressed memory.

Nor does Fredrickson leave any doubt that, in her opinion at least, these images represent real memories. Her client, she writes, "had completed the process of imagistic retrieval of an abuse memory.... The memory that had been stalking Sarah's life was finally fully exposed."

Fredrickson insists that these images from the unconscious, while often exaggerated or cartoonlike, represent "an accurate slice of the abuse." But once again she reiterates that the truth doesn't really matter, at least not at this point in therapy: "Whether what is remembered ... is made up or real is of no concern at the beginning of the process; that can be decided at a later date."

Renee Fredrickson is not alone in suggesting imagistic work as a means of exhuming and resurrecting buried memories. In *The Courage to Heal*, Bass and Davis include an exercise that relies on a process called "imaginative reconstruction," allowing the survivor "to piece together things you can't possibly know about your history or the history of your family":

> Take an event in your family history that you can never actually find out about. It could be your father's childhood or the circumstances in your mother's life that kept her from protecting you.

Using all the details you do know, create your own story. Ground the experience or event in as much knowledge as you have and then let yourself imagine what actually might have happened.

WARNING: "Create your own story" and "imagine what actually might have happened" are important strategies for the development of fictions. But do they lead to the unearthing of lost or misplaced facts? Cognitive psychologists know that when people engage in exercises in imagination, they begin to have problems differentiating between what is real and what is imagined. And forensic psychologists have concluded that guided imagery promotes a dissociative state similar to that produced by hypnosis; as a result, it may be equally unreliable as a tool for recovering memories.

Thus, in the process of creating our own stories, we run the very serious risk of mistaking imagined events for memories of actual experiences. We end up believing in the stories we tell.

DREAM WORK

The theory is that when we dream, "the channel is open" to the unconscious mind, and all we have to do is look for the symbols and "indicators" of repressed memories. Fredrickson suggests that survivors keep an ongoing written list of memory fragments and "access symbols" (defined in the following list). Using the dream symbol as a focal point, they can then work to retrieve repressed memory fragments. Fredrickson lists six types of "repressed-memory dreams" that contain vital information from the unconscious about buried memories:

- Nightmares. The distinguishing feature of a nightmare is the intensity of fear engendered by the dream. If your nightmares include certain symbols or indicators, they may reveal sexual abuse. These symbols might include rapists, murderers, psychopaths, and stalkers; bedrooms, bathrooms, basements, closets and attics; penises, breasts, and buttocks; bottles, broom handles, and sticks; bloody sacrifices, dismemberment, cannibalism, black-robed figures, and Satan.

- Recurring dreams. These are "an emergency signal from your unconscious" and can either be nightmares or nonthreatening dreams that return over and over again with the same characters, setting, and action.

- Sexual-abuse dreams. These contain a specific, clear-cut act of sexual abuse and are always repressed-memory dreams, according to Fredrickson. The specific act may be rape, oral or anal sex, the abuse of a child or teenager, voyeurism, or bestiality.

- Dreams containing access signals. Such dreams point to the existence of buried memories of abuse. Some common access signals are closed or locked doors, mysterious passageways, anything stored or hidden, a child who cannot communicate or who needs protection, water (especially, frightening water), snakes, or phallic symbols.

- Any dream you have a strong feeling about. Even uninteresting or trivial dreams can contain fragments of repressed memories. If you have a particularly vivid dream that makes a strong impression on your conscious mind, Fredrickson advises that you consider dream work, which involves the following steps:

- Sifting through your dreams for themes or symbols of sexual abuse

- Sharing your feelings, thoughts and interpretations regarding these symbols

- Clarifying the dream by seeking more information, expanding on details, or free-associating

- Identifying the general outlines of the abuse as it has been interpreted and clarified through "dream work."

Many therapists agree that dream work is a powerful tool. "Conscious thought can be controlled; conscious awareness can be altered by defenses," writes Blume. "But in sleep realities that are carefully masked during wakefulness can leak out." And Beverly Engle claims that dreams can be "very revealing, exposing memories you have been unwilling or unable to face during waking hours." To illustrate her point she tells a story about *Judy,* who knew all along that her brother had sexually abused her but had a dream one night that her father had also molested her. "She awoke to a terrible pain in her vagina and a flood of memories. Indeed, she realized, the dream was true."

WARNING: Were these dreams "true," or did they "come true" as therapist and client worked together to explain away or resolve the client's fears, anxieties, and uncertainties? Once again, as with exercises in imagination, psychologists are questioning claims that dreams provide a reliable map to reality. Psychologist Brooks Brenneis recently completed an extensive review of the literature on the relationship between dreams and traumatic events. His findings indicate that even when someone dreams about an event that can be corroborated (for example, an actual car accident), the dream often bears little resemblance to the actual event; in fact, the dream clearly portrays the trauma *metaphorically*. Brenneis concludes:

> There is no empirical evidence and very little clinical evidence to substantiate the idea that specific traumatic experience predictably passes untransformed into dream content. Consequently, the idea that a dream may be identical to, or isomorphic with, a traumatic experience is questionable.

Given the fact that dreams often consist of "residue" from the day's events, it is not surprising that patients involved in therapy and memory work sometimes dream about abuse-related experiences. Therapists' interpretations of these dreams may reflect their own biases and beliefs, and clients may be too willing to accept their therapists' interpretations—especially if they have been told by their therapists that their dreams are direct messages from the unconscious about repressed childhood abuse.

JOURNAL WRITING

Fredrickson theorizes that there are five different types of memory: recall memory (the only type that resides in the conscious mind), and imagistic, feeling, acting-out and body memories (all of which are found in the unconscious mind). While imagistic work and dream work utilize imagistic memory ("memory that breaks through to the conscious mind in the form of imagery") and feeling memory ("the memory of an emotional response to a particular situation"), journal writing accesses acting-out memory, "in which the forgotten incident is spontaneously acted out through some physical action."

In journal writing the idea is to start with a focal point—a body sensation, image, or symbol from a dream or nightmare—and record in words the images and messages arising from the unconscious. Fredrickson suggests three basic techniques for retrieving repressed memories using the technique of journal writing.

The first technique is that of free association, in which you write whatever comes into your mind, including images, feelings, and body sensations, with no attempt to sort out or categorize. Sorting out is a right-brain process and, according to Fredrickson "will impede the left brain from accessing what you want to know."

To employ the second technique, you begin with an abusive incident, either real or imagined, and write a story about it. In storytelling, the important point is to write the story as quickly as possible: "The unconscious can be relied on to select traumatic incidents from your own past for most or all of the 'story,'" Fredrickson writes, "since it is easier to rely on experience rather than imagination when you do something quickly."

The third technique is the quick list: You jot down your immediate responses to a focal point or prompting question, resisting any urge to think, screen, edit, or organize.

Fredrickson illustrates the "quick list" journal-writing technique with a fascinating case history. On the basis of a few scattered memories and some convincing dreams, *Ann* believed that she was abused by her grandmother, but the details of the abuse eluded her. Ann's therapist provided her with pen and paper and asked her to list, without pausing to think or worry about accuracy, five abusive acts her grandmother had committed. Ann immediately jotted down eight very specific items, including a memory of her grandmother hanging her cat, another memory in which her grandmother tried to suffocate her with a pillow, and other memories involving specific sexually abusive acts. After reading the list to her therapist, Ann experienced feelings of grief and shock, but felt comforted by the fact that at least now she knew the "basics" of what had happened to her.

Fredrickson suggests a little trick to make access to the unconscious a little easier: If you write in your journal with your left hand, it will facilitate access to the right brain, the creative, intuitive, synthesizing part of the brain. In his book *Homecoming* John Bradshaw gives similar advice, urging readers to write with their nondominant hand, a technique that apparently bypasses the controlling, logical side of the brain and "makes it easier to get in touch with the feelings of your inner child."

WARNING: The technique of journal writing strikes many cognitive psychologists as a potentially "risky exercise,"* particularly when therapists suggest that their patients strive for a noncritical, stream-of-consciousness flow, writing down whatever comes to mind without stopping to evaluate the content. The possibility that this technique will lead nonabused people to create false memories and beliefs is compounded when journal writing is accompanied by other therapeutic techniques and/or the therapist's expressed beliefs about memory recovery—for example, telling the client that her current symptoms reflect childhood sexual abuse, that healing depends on recovering memories, or that accurate memories are likely to emerge from journal-writing exercises.

Same as dream work

---

*Lindsay, S. and Read, D. (in press). Psychotherapy and memories of childhood sexual abuse, *Applied Cognitive Psychology*.

Furthermore, the massive body of scientific literature on the workings of memory contains no evidence that different kinds of memories exist in the unconscious mind. Thus, "imagistic," "feeling," "acting-out," and "body" memories must be viewed as interesting but unprovable theories of how the intuitive and impulsive part of the mind works. The "inner child" is obviously a metaphor (is it really possible to "get in touch" with the "feelings" of a metaphor?), and no evidence exists that writing with the nondominant hand will gain access to this "inner child." Nor is there any evidence that sorting out, categorizing, or thinking—the cognitive acts of reflecting, reasoning, and analyzing—will impede the accessing of memories from the unconscious.

A final note on the "quick list" technique: Most psychologists would agree that any theory of the mind that suggests doing away with "thinking" should probably be reevaluated.

BODY WORK

The theory behind "body work" is that the body remembers what the mind unconsciously chooses to forget. When a traumatic or abusive event occurs, our minds may react by shutting down and stuffing the memory into the drawers of the unconscious, but our bodies will always remember the feeling of being abused. Through massage therapy or body-manipulation techniques we can access these "body memories" and begin to uncover the truth about our past.

Fredrickson delineates three stages in the process of uncovering memories through body work:

- Energy. The body stores memory as energy; when certain parts of the body are touched or massaged, the blocked energy can be accessed and the memories stimulated.

- Emergence. The stored memory emerges through any of the five senses.

- Resolution. As the memories begin to flow, rage and grief are also released, and the survivor surrenders to the truth about her past.

Body memories apparently can be stimulated through any of the five senses. Some examples of body memories include: the smell of Clorox or new leather, the sight of mouthwash or toothpaste, the sound of a door creaking or pants being unzipped, the taste of alcohol or cigarettes, feelings of sleepiness, tingling sensations, or extreme sensitivity in the lower back, arms, toes, shoulders, or other body parts. When a body memory emerges, the experience can be intensely uncomfortable, as one survivor, quoted in The Courage to Heal, testifies:

I would get body memories that would have no pictures to them at all. I would just start screaming and feel that something was coming out of my body that I had no control over. And I would usually get them right after making love, or in the middle of making love, or right in the middle of a fight. When my passion was aroused in some way, I would remember in my body, although I wouldn't have a conscious picture, just this screaming coming out of me.

Clinicians cite the intense physiological reactions experienced by clients recalling memories of abuse as impressive evidence of the body's gift of recall. In a paper published in the *Journal of Child Sexual Abuse,* clinical psychologist Christine Courtois explains that memories

can return *physiologically,* through body memories and perceptions. The survivor might retrieve colors, specific visions or images, hear sounds, experience smells, odors, and taste sensations. His or her body might react in pain reminiscent of the abuse and might even evidence physical stigmata as the memory of a particular abuse experience is retrieved and worked through. . . . Memories might also occur *somatically* through pain, illness (often without medical diagnosis), nausea, and conversion symptoms such as paralysis and numbing.

E. Sue Blume sums up the general theory of body memories and body work:

The body stores the memories of incest, and I have heard of dramatic uncovering and recovery of feelings and experiences through body work. . . . This therapy has been around for a long time but never taken seriously by talk therapists. It should be. It can release memories and feelings that talk therapy cannot touch.

WARNING: While it is theoretically possible for unconscious memories to influence behavior and create physical symptoms, no evidence exists to support the claim that muscles and tissues respond in a way that can be interpreted reliably as a concrete episodic memory. Scientists point out that it is impossible to determine whether the symptoms associated with body memories are caused by real, historical memories, by current problems and fixations, or even by chance. As psychologist Martin Seligman explains: "In science we have to set up a null hypothesis to prove something. It has to be shown that it can be disproved in order to achieve scientific credibility." But the theory of body memories refuses the possibility of a null hypothesis—you can't prove the theory, and you can't disprove it either.

HYPNOSIS

According to Fredrickson, hypnosis taps into the unconscious via "imagistic memory," thus facilitating the retrieval of buried memories of abuse. The most common hypnotic technique used for retrieving repressed memories is "age regression." Once trance is induced, the therapist encourages the client to move backward in time, stopping at an age that seems significant. The client, now "age regressed," describes the scenes, images, and feelings that come into her mind, and "abuse memories that are ready to be faced emerge from the unconscious."

Fredrickson cautions that hypnosis is not a magical truth serum and is effective only if the client is prepared to face "the truth." Other clinicians extend the warning, even arguing that hypnosis is contraindicated with incest survivors. The misuse and misapplication of hypnosis carries "the potential of harm," writes Mike Lew in *Victims No Longer*, arguing that "memories are blocked for a reason," and questioning "the benefit of dragging out memories before you are ready to deal with them." Lew is also skeptical about the "quick fix" mentality of memory recovery work:

> I don't think it makes sense to set recovery of specific abuse memories as the primary goal. Doing this gives the misleading impression that if you recover the memories everything will be all right. If you adopt this mistaken notion, you will be deeply disappointed when you discover that there is still much work to be done after the memories are in place.

ADDITIONAL WARNINGS: In a recent paper, psychologists Steven Jay Lynn and Michael Nash point out that

> features of the hypnotic context, taken individually and in combination, may conspire to elevate the risk of pseudomemory creation. This observation is reinforced by the 1985 report by the American Medical Association* and by subsequent research

---

*The report of the Council on Scientific Affairs of the American Medical Association is entitled "Scientific status of refreshing recollection by the use of hypnosis." It was published in full in the *Journal of the American Medical Association,* April 4, 1985, Vol 253, pages 1918–1923.

that underscores the fact that hypnosis can increase the confidence of recalled events with little or no change in the level of accuracy.

Repeated questioning "tends to freeze or harden memories, regardless of the historical accuracy of the memories," Nash and Lynn warn, and the problem is intensified if the therapist believes in the historical accuracy of the memories: "When clinicians communicate that clients' memories are accurate, clients may place an unwarranted degree of trust in their memories."

In a paper presented in 1992 at the annual meeting of the American Psychological Association, Nash discussed cases in which hypnotized subjects were age-*progressed* to seventy or eighty years old and recalled events they had yet to experience. He also described a patient from his own practice who believed he had been abducted by aliens and provided copious details about the high-tech machines the aliens attached to his penis in order to obtain samples of his sperm. "I successfully treated this highly hypnotizable man over a period of three months, using standard uncovering techniques and employing hypnosis on two occasions," Nash summarized.

> About two months into this therapy, his symptoms abated: he was sleeping normally again, his ruminations and flashbacks had resolved, he returned to his usual level of interpersonal engagement, and his productivity at work improved. What we did worked. Nevertheless, let me underscore this: he walked out of my office as utterly convinced that he had been abducted as when he walked in. As a matter of fact he thanked me for helping him "fill in the gaps of my memory." I suppose I need not tell you how unhappy I was about his particular choice of words.

Nash compared this patient's abduction story with memories recovered by adult survivors of sexual abuse:

> Here we have a stark example of a tenaciously believed-in fantasy which is almost certainly not true, but which, nonetheless, has all the signs of a previously repressed traumatic memory. I work routinely with adult women who have been sexually abused, and I could discern no difference between this patient's clinical presentation around the trauma and that of my sexually abused patients. Worse yet, the patient seemed to get better as he was able to elaborate on the report of trauma and integrate it into his own view of the world.

In his concluding remarks, Nash advised clinicians to proceed with care and discretion regarding their patient's traumatic memories, for "in the end we (as clinicians) cannot tell the difference between believed-in fantasy about the past and viable memory of the past. Indeed there may be no structural difference between the two."

Hypnosis researcher Campbell Perry agreed, suggesting that therapists may be responsible for creating and then validating their clients' "pseudomemories":

> Any memory that might turn up in age regression might be a fact, a lie, a confabulation, or a pseudomemory caused accidentally by inappropriate suggestions by the hypnotist. Most of the time, an expert can't even distinguish between these. She or he can only hope to validate with facts one of these possibilities.

In his book *Suggestions of Abuse,* clinical psychologist and hypnosis expert Michael Yapko emphasizes that formal hypnotic techniques do not have to be used to make a patient susceptible to suggestion. Just being in therapy creates a vulnerability to directly stated or merely implied beliefs and suggestions. Yapko describes an "unthinkable" event that occurred in his own practice.

> A woman called me and asked if I would hypnotize her in order to determine whether she had been molested as a child. I asked where she got the idea that she might have been abused. She told me she had called another therapist about her poor self-esteem, and the therapist told her—*never even having met her*—that she must have been abused and should be hypnotized to find out when and how.

This case, which Yapko insists is not unique, represents in his words "foolishness of the worst sort," and is "tantamount to professional malpractice."

ART THERAPY

According to Renee Fredrickson, art therapy accesses two types of unconscious memory—acting-out memory (forgotten memories spontaneously and physically enacted) and imagistic memory (memory that appears in the conscious mind as images). By creating a visual representation, the survivor is able to recreate the memory or memory fragment, or she can use the completed artwork to trigger the recovery of repressed memories.

Fredrickson describes three basic methods of accessing or elaborating memories through artwork:

- Imagistic recall. The client is instructed to select an image as a focal point, draw the image, and then portray whatever she thinks might happen next. Guesswork is often involved. "The key is to draw whatever your best guess is about what happened," Fredrickson advises.

- Already retrieved memories. The client adds details to an already retrieved memory in an attempt to make it more specific and concrete.

- Interpreting your artwork. In this final stage, the client tries to determine if certain symbols, themes, or objects reappear. Discovering and then interpreting these recurring symbols may help to uncover repressed memories.

Bea, one of Fredrickson's patients, loved to draw and turned to art therapy as a means of exploring her feelings. Her drawings always featured the same frightening symbols: blood, pentagrams, people dressed in robes, the devil, and "huge penises ripping through young children." Bea eventually came to believe that she was recreating factual scenes from memory. After staring at a painting of a goat and a small child surrounded by robed figures, she recognized that the scene represented an actual memory: "I painted a memory even before I knew it was a memory!" she exclaimed.

Drawing exercises are often used by therapists to help their patients "generate" memories about childhood sexual abuse. "The simple reconstruction of a bedroom can allow blocked feelings to surface if the client is able to draw what he or she imagines the room to look like," writes therapist Catherine Roland. "The bed may engender feelings of which the client is not yet aware, especially if the abuse took place in or near the bedroom." "Probing questions" can then be used to uncover the family's general attitude toward sexual activities, and specific references to the details in the artwork will help the client "begin to explore the deeper nuances of suspicion and fear."

WARNING: While drawing pictures might access blocked feelings, is it wise to use those feelings to explore "the deeper nuances of suspicion and fear"? Where, we have to ask, will those nuances lead? If memories are triggered by a client's drawings or visual representations, the therapist has no reliable way of determining whether these memories are accurate or inaccurate. Once again, caution is advised.

[margin handwriting: Same as Journal writing]

FEELINGS WORK

Feelings work is designed to tap into "feeling memory," which Fredrickson defines as the memory of an emotional response to a particular situation. The memory itself may be repressed, but the orphaned feelings haunt the mind, restlessly seeking their memory "home." Thus, feelings of being abused exist without the matching memories, and the survivor is deeply affected by intense emotions and sensations that seem unconnected to any present-day reality. If a survivor says, "I think I was sexually abused, but it's just a feeling," she is experiencing a feeling memory.

Survivors experience many feelings, of course, but two are considered universal and form the basis of "feelings work": grief and rage. If a survivor can get in touch with her emotions, the theory goes, she can begin the painful process of releasing them; when the feelings begin to emerge, the repressed memories often come with them. Fredrickson explains how structured grief work proceeds:

> You curl up or lie down and begin a slow, relaxed breathing. Whenever you feel any sense of sadness, try to express a noise with the feeling. Slowly, over time, the grief will start to build. Grief usually comes in waves, so do not be discouraged if it fades, for it will surely return. As each wave of grief is felt, let yourself moan, cry out, or sob. As the grief deepens, the related memories may also begin to surface.

Grief work often turns into rage work (and vice versa). The purpose of rage work is to focus the survivor's anger, resentment, and hostility where they belong: on the perpetrator. Clinicians suggest a variety of techniques for rage work, including whacking the floor, the walls, an old sofa, or a pile of cushions with a tennis racket, rubber hose, rolled-up towel or newspaper, or an "encounter bat" (a soft foam-rubber club); stomping on old egg cartons or aluminum cans; practicing karate kicks; shredding a phone book with your bare hands; or simply screaming as loud and as long as you can.

In *The Courage to Heal*, a survivor describes the emotional release experienced during her rage work:

> Doing the actual rage work wasn't scary. In fact, it was very exciting. It's such a safe environment with so much love, you have the feeling you can do or say anything. It's okay if you bash in your stepfather's face with a rubber hose. I remember thinking, "This isn't so bad. This isn't going to kill anybody." Every once in a while I'd stop, look around the room, and think, "No way, that didn't come from me!" I had totally shredded a Denver phone book, just obliterated it, and still more to come. I'd have to catch my breath or blow my nose, and I remember looking at

the devastation and thinking, "My God! That was all inside!" I was flabbergasted at how much rage there was.

WARNING: Because there is no evidence that feelings work leads to the recovery of real, historical memories, as opposed to imagined, invented, or fabricated memories, it seems prudent to repeat psychoanalyst Alice Miller's conclusions regarding the "goal" of therapy: "When the patient has truly emotionally worked through the history of his childhood and thus regained his sense of being alive—then the goal of the analysis has been reached."

After that goal is reached, Miller continues, it is the patient's responsibility to make his own life decisions. "It is not the task of the analyst to 'socialize' him, or 'to bring him up' (not even politically, for every form of bringing up denies his autonomy), nor to make 'friendships possible for him'—all that is his own affair."

Therapy is, or used to be, about helping people become *responsible* human beings. But some therapists argue that with its emphasis on venting emotions, therapy has the potential to become abusive. Psychologist Margaret Singer puts the problem in perspective:

> In the end, if therapy works well, the patient ends up more autonomous, more responsible, more mature and more in charge of her life. But today patients are expected to display emotions in a way the therapist approves of. Many patients tell me they were urged by their therapist to be in a continuous rage. So how could therapy help them become more mature, and more independent, functioning citizens? I feel very embarrassed that a healing profession could have strayed so far from the standards of care and practice that demand, "Do not harm the patient."

GROUP THERAPY

Group therapy is considered a powerful adjunct to individual therapy and a crucial part of the recovery process. Mike Lew stresses the benefits of community and solidarity that accrue in groups where other incest survivors can "listen to what you're saying," "believe you," and "*know* that you're telling the truth about the abuse and its effects, *because they have had similar experiences.*"

Listening, believing, and knowing the truth act as the rock salt that allows the survivor's memories to gel, eventually taking solid shape. "Your memories, which for so long have seemed unreal, gain substance each time you share them with others," Fredrickson advises survivors.

Group therapy is also considered an effective method for accelerating the memory-retrieval process. A "chaining" of recollections and feelings occurs, as one member of the group after another identifies and then connects with the memories vocalized by the others. As Bass and Davis counsel: "If you're still fuzzy about what's happening to you, hearing other women's stories can stimulate your memories. Their words can loosen buried feelings."

In her book *Trauma and Recovery,* Judith Lewis Herman extols the memory-stimulating function of the group process, claiming that it virtually guarantees the recovery of memories:

> The cohesion that develops in a trauma-focused group enables participants to embark upon the tasks of remembrance and mourning. The group provides a powerful stimulus for the recovery of traumatic memories. As each group member reconstructs her own narrative, the details of her story almost inevitably evoke new recollections in each of the listeners. In the incest survivor groups, virtually every member who has defined a goal of recovering memories has been able to do so. Women who feel stymied by amnesia are encouraged to tell as much of their story as they do remember. Invariably the group offers a fresh emotional perspective that provides a bridge to new memories.

WARNING: While many psychologists and psychiatrists consider the stimulation and triggering of associated memories to be an important function of group therapy, they warn that the chaining process can suddenly spiral out of control. Psychiatrist Paul McHugh warns that it is particularly dangerous to mix people who have memories of abuse with people who believe they may have been abused but have no memories. The pressures of such "mixed" groups can lead to the creation of pseudomemories—as one survivor, who eventually recovered memories of being molested on the changing table when she was twelve months, attests: "There was a lot of peer pressure in the group. You weren't well accepted unless you were coming up with a lot of memories."

Psychologist Christine Courtois believes that group therapy can be a valuable source of "safety, support, and understanding," but counsels that a therapist should be available to "carefully monitor and pace the group process so that members are not continuously emotionally overwhelmed." Judith Lewis Herman agrees that the memories may come so fast that it is necessary "to slow the process down in order to keep it within the limits of the individual's and the group's tolerance."

The primary focus of any trauma-based group, Herman concludes, should be on the task of establishing safety:

If this focus is lost, group members can easily frighten each other with both the horrors of their past experiences and the dangers in their present lives. An incest survivor describes how hearing other group members' stories made her feel worse: "My expectation going into the group was that seeing a number of women who had shared a similar experience would make it easier. My most poignant anguish in the group was the realization that it *didn't* make it easier—it only *multiplied* the horror."

CONFRONTATIONS

Once the repressed memories have been "retrieved," the survivor is told she has a choice: She can either continue with therapy, working to resolve her grief and rage in a private, noncombative way, or she can choose to stand up to the abuse (and stand up for herself) by confronting her abusers. The decision to confront is never promoted as easy or risk-free. Most incest-survival authors warn that confrontations should be considered only if and when the survivor is fully prepared and well along the road to recovery. Furthermore, the survivor is assured that confrontation is a choice that one can choose *not* to make. As Mike Lew writes in his sensitive chapter on confrontation, "Confronting the perpetrator is a difficult and complex issue . . . a highly individual, personal decision. For some people it is a logical next step in recovery; for others it could be a dangerous and self-destructive act."

But there is also much talk in these books about the healing power of speaking the truth. "Telling the people in your family how you were hurt is the most expedient form of healing. Now you are finally free to speak the truth," writes Fredrickson. Not only are you "free" to speak the truth, but you have the right to do so. "Everyone has a right to tell the truth about her life," write Bass and Davis at the beginning of their chapter titled "Disclosures and Confrontations."

When we speak the truth, we gain a sense of "empowerment," which Fredrickson defines as "spiritual, physical, and emotional strength." Confrontation is presented as a rite of passage, a painful but momentous step in the metamorphosis from victim to survivor. "Confronting the abuser . . . is the ultimate reclaiming of power for the survivor; it declares that she is not silenced, is not controlled," writes E. Sue Blume. "To confront is an opportunity to declare, '*I know what you did,* and you had no right.' "

Specific advice on preparing for the confrontation is sometimes offered in the incest-recovery literature. Support systems must be shored up, motivations and expectations carefully analyzed, and rehearsals undertaken. Collins Wilsden
The survivor can begin by telling her story to her supporters—her thera-

pist, group members, friends, spouse, or lover. She can explore her feelings by writing letters and asking her friends and therapists for feedback. She can create fantasy pictures of the confrontation, in which she imagines herself as strong, confident, and completely in control. Or she can engage in role-play or psychodrama, rehearsing with her therapist or group members various confrontational scenarios.

Then, when she is fully prepared, she can "tell the truth" to her family. In the actual confrontation, she should always avoid expressing doubts or uncertainties, stating clearly what she knows to be true and specifically describing how she has been affected by the abuse. "Avoid being tentative about your repressed memories," Fredrickson advises. "Do not just tell them; express them as truth. If months or years down the road, you find you are mistaken about the details, you can always apologize and set the record straight."

Survivors should expect protestations of innocence and expressions of outrage when they confront their abusers. "Be prepared to encounter denial," Mike Lew writes.

> Don't let the situation turn into an argument or a debate. Don't allow a perpetrator to talk you out of your memories. Remember that she has lied to you before. Stick to your guns and don't get involved in an exercise in frustration.

If the abuser continues to disavow and repudiate the survivor's story, it may be time to bring up the subject of repression. "You may want to suggest that the abuser has repressed all memory of the abuse," Fredrickson counsels. But at all costs survivors should avoid a reality war. It is not the survivor's job to convince or convert her perpetrator. The sole purpose of disclosure and confrontation is to free yourself, to take back your power, to prove to yourself that you will not be frightened or controlled any longer, and thus to guarantee that you will never be a victim again. Confrontation, in Lew's words, is "an act of self-respect."

The Courage to Heal offers several dramatic examples of successful confrontations:

> Twenty years ago, a woman went to her grandfather's funeral and told each person at the grave site what he had done to her. In Santa Cruz, California, volunteers from Women Against Rape go with rape survivors to confront the rapist in his workplace. There they are, ten or twenty women surrounding a man, giving tangible support to the survivor, as she names what he has done to her. . . . One survivor told us the story of a woman who exposed her brother on his wedding day. She wrote down exactly what

he'd done to her and made copies. Standing in the receiving line, she handed everyone a sealed envelope, saying "These are some of my feelings about the wedding. Please read it when you get home."

WARNING: The effect of deathbed, receiving-line, or one-on-one confrontations extends beyond the accused, who may or may not be guilty as charged. The damage to the survivor must also be considered. What if "months or years down the road," the survivor discovers that she was, indeed, "mistaken about details"? The promise that she can "always apologize and set the record straight" denies the disastrous impact of the accusation on the lives of everyone involved. Families are torn apart, relationships are irrevocably altered, and lives are destroyed.

A thirty-five-year-old woman told her mother, a widow who was dying of cancer, that she had recovered memories of being sexually abused by both parents. Two days later the accused mother drove her car off a cliff and killed herself. She left a note behind explaining that she had "nothing left to live for." Who can gauge the long-term effects of this confrontation and its aftermath on this woman who now believes her memories are false?

SUING THE PERPETRATOR

The Courage to Heal includes a five-page section written by Mary Williams, an attorney who represents adult survivors. Williams briefly describes recent changes in the statute of limitations, citing California's enactment of a three-year statute for civil actions based on childhood sexual abuse when the abuser was a family member. Under the new statute, victims can choose to bring suit up until their twenty-first birthday. When delayed-discovery laws are applied to the new statute, survivors have three years from the date of discovery to file suit. Thus, if a survivor repressed the memory of abuse and as a result was unaware of the alleged injury for many years or even decades, she would be granted three years from the date of discovery (presumably somewhere in the midst of therapy) to initiate a lawsuit. (Since *The Courage to Heal* was published in 1988, over twenty states have revised their statutes of limitations regarding childhood sexual abuse.)

An entire page in *The Courage to Heal* is devoted to the subject of "Getting Money." Williams discusses the potential range of settlements ("I have had settlements ranging from $20,000 to nearly $100,000") and includes a footnote indicating that average settlement amounts will most likely rise in the future.* The possibility of tapping into homeown-

---

*Indeed, survivors claiming repressed memories have been awarded settlements of $1 million and more.

er's insurance policies for damages caused by "negligence" is also reviewed.

In a final section, a cost/benefit analysis of lawsuits is presented. While "there's often a feeling of letdown and disappointment" after the case is settled and "emotional reconstruction still has to be done," the benefits of suing are alleged to be substantial:

> In my experience, nearly every client who has undertaken this kind of suit has experienced growth, therapeutic strengthening, and an increased sense of personal power and self-esteem as a result of the litigation. . . . A lot of my clients also feel a tremendous sense of relief and victory. They get strong by suing. They step out of the fantasy that it didn't happen or that their parents really loved and cared for them in a healthy way. It produces a beneficial separation that can be a rite of passage for the survivor.

A list of lawyers specializing in adult-survivor lawsuits, complete with addresses and phone numbers, is included at the end of the section.

In *Secret Survivors*, E. Sue Blume includes a two-page section titled "Suing Perpetrators," in which she praises the ideological benefits of lawsuits, which offer survivors "an opportunity for some validation from the system that abandoned them; a positive outcome is the system's acknowledgment that yes, something happened, and yes, he had no right." Blume also reviews the practical reasons for suing. Settlements can be used to help pay for "large medical and psychotherapy expenses for women whose earning ability (low because of their gender) is reduced by the damage done by the abuse."

And so we have reached the logical late-twentieth-century ending to the strange and mystifying problem of repressed memories of sexual abuse. When all else fails (or, preferably, *before* all else fails), hire a lawyer and sue for damages.

SOME FINAL WORDS OF CAUTION

Buried in the middle of Renee Fredrickson's book is one small sentence containing twenty-one words of caution. We would like to repeat this cautionary advice here, believing that its truth should be balanced against the oft-repeated claim that "getting your memories back is the most healing process of all."

> Neither you nor your therapist want to accept a false reality as truth, for that is the very essence of madness.

If only we had a surefire way to separate false realities from the truth. But we don't, and in most cases involving "repressed" memories, we never will. Belief is at the root of the problem. If we believe something is true, it becomes our truth, and there is little anyone can say that will shake our faith in our own reality.

Therapists, unfortunately, are no better equipped than the rest of us to discern the genuine light of truth. Perhaps it would be worthwhile to repeat here psychologist Michael Nash's conclusions regarding the ability of clinicians to distinguish between fantasy and reality: "In the end we (as clinicians) cannot tell the difference between believed-in fantasy about the past and viable memory of the past. Indeed there may be no structural difference between the two."

10

ALL I EVER WANTED

When someone asks you, "Were you sexually abused as a child?" there are only two answers: One of them is "Yes," and one of them is "I don't know." You can't say "No."

—Roseanne Arnold, *on "Oprah"*

Toward the end of March 1992 I got a phone call from a man named *Mike Patterson* in Cedar Rapids, Iowa. His daughter, he began, had accused him of heinous acts of sexual abuse on the basis of repressed memories recently recovered in therapy.

"Heinous," he repeated. "I've talked to lots of experts in the last six months, and I keep hearing that word. So I looked it up in the dictionary. It means 'grossly wicked, deserving strong condemnation.' Well, sexual abuse is heinous and false accusations are heinous, and we've got to put an end to both."

He explained that he was contacting everyone he could find who might have something to tell him about the workings of memory, the nature and reality of this "thing called repression," and what parents could do to defend themselves when they were falsely accused. "Dr. Loftus," he said earnestly, the sharp Midwestern twang carrying his words loud and clear across the telephone lines, "how can you prove a negative? How can I prove that I didn't do something?

"Well, I can't," he said, answering his own question, "so I decided to do something else. Things began to go downhill for my daughter—her name is *Megan*—when she started seeing a therapist who specializes in such things as psychospiritual concerns, victimization recovery, and dysfunctional families. I figured I'd better find out what exactly was happening in these therapy sessions, so I hired a private investigator to pretend she was a patient with problems similar to my daughter's. She was wired, and I have audiotapes of her therapy sessions. I understand you've done some experiments with suggestion and the creation of false memories, and I thought you might be interested in listening to those tapes."

"You have tapes of the therapy sessions?" I asked. This was exciting news. If Mike Patterson had tapes of therapy sessions in which the therapist was unaware that the conversation was being recorded, then he had something no one else had. While critics of repressed-memory therapy suspected that therapists' suggestions, expectations, and pressure to remember might be influencing the memory-retrieval process, they had no proof. All they had were therapists' and patients' subjective recollections of what went on in therapy, and these reports are subject to what psychologists call "retrospective bias." Retrospective bias occurs when we think back to the past and change certain facts or fill in the gaps in our memories with exaggeration, speculation, or plain wishful thinking. We are inclined to recall details that make us look "good" (happy, intelligent, generous, compassionate, tolerant, forgiving, and so on) and ignore those behaviors, thoughts, or emotions that might make us look "bad" (uncaring, thoughtless, manipulative, rude, sad, stubborn, selfish, etc.).

This lack of objective reporting is one reason memory research is so difficult. When people recall past events (and when no videotape or audiotape is available to confirm or disconfirm the truth), how can we ever know what *really* happened? Suppose, for example, that you are a researcher interested in the relationship between fat in the diet and the development of breast cancer. You decide to interview a group of women who have developed breast cancer and a group that is cancer-free, asking questions about their diets and eating habits. Although the women might try to answer your questions honestly and accurately, they may inadvertently give wrong or distorted answers because they forgot exactly what they ate on a given day. Or they might exaggerate the amount of healthy foods they ingested and minimize the quantity of unhealthy, fatty foods that also made up part of their diet.

Whatever the reasons for the inaccuracies in your subjects' recollections, you would be led to the wrong conclusions. But suppose instead that you anticipate the problems of retrospective bias and normal memory-distortion processes and engage in a little subterfuge, surreptitiously concealing videocameras in the kitchens and dining rooms of your subjects. (The Human Subjects Committee, by the way, would never approve this part of the study.) Now you could match up the subjective, retrospectively biased responses with the objective videotaped recordings and arrive at a more accurate version of the "truth."

That's what Mike Patterson claimed to have: An objective, verifiable version of the "truth" of one therapist's method of questioning and interacting with one client. While Mike Patterson's tapes couldn't be used to determine whether his daughter's memories were real or false, they could, at the very least, help us understand what might have gone on in his daughter's therapy sessions.

"I have four tapes in all," Mike was saying. "I don't know what the legalities are, but I am beyond worrying about legal issues. I believe that my daughter is the victim of suggestive therapeutic techniques. I believe that she had the misfortune of looking for psychological help from a well-meaning but inexperienced therapist who thinks that every problem in the world can be explained by sexual abuse. I did what I had to do to try to prove my hypothesis." His voice softened. "My purpose is not revenge, Dr. Loftus. My only hope is to get my daughter back."

A few days later I received a heavy package via Federal Express. In addition to the four audiotapes of the therapy sessions, Mike had sent me a blue spiral notebook divided into five neatly labeled sections, filled with hundreds of pages of correspondence, notes, research articles, and legal documents. I read every paper in that notebook and asked one of my students to transcribe the tapes of the therapy sessions. A few months later I flew out to Cedar Rapids to speak before the Iowa Bar Association and spent an afternoon with Mike and his wife, Dawn. They took me into their home, brought out stacks of photo albums and videotapes ("That's Megan when she was two," "Here's Megan winning an award at graduation," "This picture was taken the last time we saw Megan. . . ."), and sent me home with several hundred additional pages of correspondence and resource material.

I believe Mike Patterson is innocent of the accusations that have destroyed his family. But I would add that even if he is innocent and falsely accused, his case is not proof of anything but itself. His story does not prove that large numbers of therapists make suggestions to their patients, nor does it demonstrate that clients necessarily incorporate these suggestions into the creation of a false memory. This is only one case—unique, individual, and filled with many different versions, some verifiable, some not, of the "truth."

On November 15, 1985, twenty-year-old Megan wrote a cheery letter to her parents on six-by-nine-inch dime-store stationery. The script is rounded and flowing, conveying a sense of excitement and enthusiastic innocence. Most of the sentences end in exclamation marks, and every paragraph contains at least one word that has been underlined twice.

"Dear Ma and Pa," the three-page letter began, "How are you two? I'm great!" Megan breezed on, expressing her gratitude for the long-distance phone call from her parents the night before ("*I felt so loved!*") and her relief at having only one exam that week. Would her parents please deposit some money in her checking account so that she could pay her rent? She feels tired but otherwise okay and she can't wait to come home for Thanksgiving. She signed the letter "Lots of love, Megan."

Sixteen months later, on March 27, 1987, Megan wrote her parents another loving letter from graduate school, where she was working on her master's degree in social work. "I've been so busy that I haven't had time to tell you how much I love you," she wrote. In the next paragraph she thanked her parents for all their expressions of love and support—buying her a car, paying for her college education and graduate school, taking her on family vacations, and giving her money to take trips by herself. But it was their unquestioning love and willingness to help her work through her problems that she appreciated the most. "I haven't always been the perfect daughter," she wrote, "but I love you so much, and I could never pay you back for all the love and support you have given me or the lessons you have taught me. The most I can do is say thanks and I love you—more than I could ever express in words alone."

In November 1987, Megan wrote a long and revealing letter to *Teresa*, a fifteen-year-old runaway who was temporarily adopted by the Patterson family. During Thanksgiving vacation an argument erupted between Megan and her mother, and Teresa mistakenly assumed that she was at fault. Megan was writing to explain what really happened—her mother was deeply upset with her because she discovered that she was living with her boyfriend.

On the second page of her letter, Megan confessed that she and her father sometimes had trouble getting along because they were two different kinds of people. "I'm an affectionate person who needs to be hugged all the time," Megan wrote. "I need to hear Dad say, 'I love you.' But Dad isn't the same kind of person—he doesn't seem to need hugs or words of affection. (Although he does seem to like it when I tell him that I love him.)"

For years, Megan continued, she had turned to God with this problem and he always helped her. But once college began she was too busy and stopped asking for God's help. Her relationship with her father steadily deteriorated as she acted out her frustration and anger. "I've done many things I regret, hurting other people and myself. While I might look happy and self-confident on the outside, on the inside I am begging for help. I'm in so much pain, and I've felt this way for nearly three years. My life is a mess. With God's help, and with Mom and Dad's help, I'm going to pull myself together."

She ended the letter with these words: "Everyone makes mistakes, and sometimes we hurt each other unintentionally. But we can make things better talking to each other and telling each other how much we care. We all need love!"

Three months later Megan met her parents at her older sister's house in Des Moines to celebrate the birth of their first grandchild. Mike and

Dawn held the infant in their arms, tears streaming down their faces, while Megan stood apart, subdued and preoccupied. Later that evening Megan confessed to her parents that she had been sexually abused.

"Who abused you?" her astonished parents asked.

"*Patrick,*" Megan answered, naming her foster brother, who was fifteen years old when he came to live with the family. They had kissed and petted, Megan explained, but stopped short of intercourse. Although the fondling had been consensual, Megan believed that the sexual interactions constituted abuse because she was only twelve years old, three years younger than Patrick.

Dawn was devastated. How could this have happened without her knowledge? It broke her heart to think that her youngest child had carried the burden of this memory for more than a decade, feeling so ashamed that she couldn't even share her terrible secret with her parents. But despite her concern for her daughter, the timing of the announcement struck her as rather odd. Why had Megan chosen this moment, the birth of her sister's child, to reveal such a painful and disturbing memory? Why had she taken such a joyful experience and twisted it inside out?

Four months later, in June 1988, Megan received her master's degree from the University of Iowa. She settled in Des Moines, a two-hour drive from her parents' home, and was immediately offered a job working with the homeless. Her caseload was heavy, and the work was emotionally draining. In her weekly phone calls to her parents, she complained bitterly about the constant, unrelenting stress of her life. When her live-in boyfriend broke up with her that August, she seemed depressed, anxious, not herself. Mike and Dawn worried that she might be drinking too much. Neither of them had ever taken a drink in their lives, and the only pills in the house were Mike's "heart pills," which he took for angina, and a bottle of aspirin Dawn used for intermittent sinus headaches. They knew they were a little "square" when it came to drugs and sex and tried not to be overbearing with their concerns.

But they couldn't stop worrying about their youngest child. In their weekly phone conversations, Megan was becoming increasingly negative and pessimistic. She seemed grimly determined to prove that her extended family was "sick" and in need of expert help, diagnosing her cousin as having "attention deficit disorder," another relative as a "borderline personality," and a third as "paranoid."

When her mother was alone on the line, Megan constantly berated her father for his "emotional absenteeism." "He just doesn't seem to care about what's going on inside me. He's always so damn busy, always so involved with some project or some person who needs him more than he thinks I need him."

"Megan, your father worships the ground you walk on!" Dawn wondered how she could get through to Megan and help her see the cup as half full rather than half empty. "Sweetheart, I know your life is difficult and stressful right now, but try to remember how much we love you and all the good times our family has had, the trips, the vacations, the holidays . . . "

"What good times? They may have been fun for you, Mom"—Megan spat out the word "Mom" as if it were an accusation—"but did you ever stop to think what they were like for me?"

Dawn decided not to push it. Megan had a good head on her shoulders, and she would pull through this crisis in her life just as she had pulled through that time in junior high school when she was hanging out with a troubled group of teenagers who smoked pot and dabbled in New Age religions. They were worried then, too, but Mike finally had a long talk with Megan, and she "got her act together," as she put it, making new friends, devoting many hours to her church youth group and committing herself to a life of "service."

"This, too, shall pass." Dawn repeated the words she had said to herself many times over the years, whenever she wondered how she would make it through a particularly demanding stage with one of her children. She trusted Megan, and she knew her daughter would use good, old-fashioned common sense to get her life back in order. Life threw some tough curves at you, Dawn continued telling herself, no doubt about it, but you can't live your children's lives for them. All you can do is love them, raise them with good moral values, and then trust them to make their own decisions. They'll make mistakes, but if you do a good job for the first fifteen or twenty years, everything will work out just fine.

Dawn's optimism was confirmed in a September 1988 letter in which Megan apologized for making life so difficult for her parents and repeatedly expressed her gratitude for their constant love and devotion. "I know I've been a pain," she wrote. "Thanks for understanding and sticking with me."

A year and a half went by. In January 1990 Megan broke up with another live-in boyfriend. "He was a heavy drinker," she told her parents, "and I just got tired of being in a codependent relationship." Although Dawn never liked the young man, she was surprised at how casually Megan dropped him out of her life, anchoring him with a few labels and then tossing him overboard.

"By the way," Megan was saying, "did I tell you that I switched therapists? My new therapist is closer to my age—she's in her mid-thirties—and she specializes in victimization recovery, incest survival, dysfunctional families, that sort of thing."

"That's quite a list," Dawn said, trying to keep her voice cheery and supportive. But the therapist's string of specialties concerned her—was it really possible for one therapist to "specialize" in all those diverse areas?

And what was this about "victimization recovery" and "dysfunctional families"?

"Yeah, she's amazing," Megan said, her tone suddenly solemn. "We're moving really fast."

On February 10, 1990, her father's birthday, Megan called and announced that she was an alcoholic. As a birthday present to her father she decided to quit drinking and attend meetings of Alcoholics Anonymous. Mike and Dawn were surprised—their image of an alcoholic was the bum on the street corner begging quarters and drinking cheap wine from a brown paper bag—but as teetotalers themselves they enthusiastically supported Megan's decision to stop drinking.

On Mother's Day, three months later, Dawn received a heavy package in the mail from Megan. Inside was a five-hundred-page book titled *The Courage to Heal: A Guide for Women Survivors of Sexual Abuse*. "What in heaven's name is this?" Dawn asked Mike, who flipped through the pages and read off the chapter titles: "The Decision to Heal," "Believing It Happened," "Anger: The Backbone of Healing," "Disclosures and Confrontations."

"Don't you think she's going a little overboard with this idea of sexual abuse? Does that two-week period of fondling with Patrick really qualify her as"—Dawn glanced at the book's subtitle again—"a 'survivor of child sexual abuse'? Maybe she's angry with us for not knowing and not helping her out with Patrick all those years ago. What do you suppose she's trying to tell us?"

Mike was philosophical. "Megan is a very intelligent and sensitive young woman who is going through a difficult time," he said. "Let's just support her and let her know that we're here when she needs us. Everything will turn out just fine."

On October 15, 1990, a letter from Megan addressed to "Dawn Patterson" arrived in the mail. The writing sprawled dark and heavy across the page, a visual testament to the anger and haste with which it was written. Just looking at the strange, brooding script Dawn knew that her daughter was in deep trouble. Megan had never before written a letter on yellow legal paper. And she had never before written a letter addressed only to her mother.

"I've been going through a very difficult time since I quit drinking," Megan wrote. "In the past few months, I've been plagued by memories coming to the surface." While Megan didn't elaborate on what the memories revealed, she repeatedly emphasized the need to keep "safe" by not drinking, by going to A.A. meetings, and by meeting with "other incest survivors."

Safe? What does she mean by 'safe'? Dawn wondered. The more she repeated the word to herself the less sense it made. Megan explained that she was keeping herself "safe" by playing with her cats and hugging her stuffed bear. At this point in the letter the handwriting thickened and hardened, as if Megan were bearing down on the page with all her strength. Dawn could almost imagine her gritting her teeth.

> I feel like I'm inadequate, that by myself I'm never enough, and perhaps if I became someone else, I'd be worthy of love. My therapist is offering me lots of support for who I am, and helping me to learn to like myself. You and Dad have always given me lots of space to think things through on my own, but I'm feeling the need for even more space in order to get through this. I'm just trying to make it through, one day at a time.

"Space." "Safe." "Survivors." "Memories." "One day at a time." Dawn wondered what all those words meant . . . what did they signify? She tried to calm herself down with the thought that Thanksgiving was just four weeks away. As soon as Megan walked in the door, they would all sit down and have a good long talk.

Three days before the Thanksgiving holidays another letter arrived. Mike and Dawn would always, forever after, refer to it as "the Thanksgiving letter." Dawn left work early that day to go home, pick up the checkbook and grocery list, and rush to the store before the crowds descended. They were expecting their three children, two foster kids, spouses, grandchildren, Grandma, *Aunt Jenny* and her family—more than twenty people all together. Dawn was thinking about the turkey, hoping a twenty-five-pounder would be big enough (she liked sending everyone home with some leftovers) when she noticed the Federal Express package on the front doorstep. She recognized Megan's handwriting, but there was no return address.

Dawn took a deep breath. She knew this was going to be bad news. Why would Megan, who always complained about being broke and on a budget, spend the money to send an express package when she was coming home in two days? She opened the envelope with trembling hands.

The letter was dated November 15. Megan must have written it a week earlier and delayed sending it so that it would arrive just before Thanksgiving.

"I'm sick of trying to get you to understand what I'm feeling and experiencing," she began, in the same dark, angry script she had used in the October letter. More memories of sexual abuse had surfaced, memories that specifically concerned her mother and her father. These emerging memories confirmed her decision to "take a break" from the parent-daughter relationship. She didn't want anyone to contact her—and that included her parents, her brother and sister, her foster siblings, her grandmother, her aunts, her uncles, and her cousins. "I will do anything necessary to protect myself and remove myself from your influence. I've talked at length with my therapist and she agrees completely with my decision. We both feel that I am moving in the right direction."

Megan explained that she had moved but would not disclose her new address; she also had a new, unlisted phone number. Friends and colleagues at work were instructed to screen her calls. If an emergency arose, her parents could contact her through her therapist.

"I know that the timing is bad," Megan concluded her letter, "but I'm not sure that there's ever a good time to terminate a relationship."

"Remove myself from your influence." "The timing is bad." "No good time to terminate a relationship." Dawn believed that this letter had been constructed in the therapist's office, with the therapist offering direction and advice. These were not her daughter's words. These were the words of a stranger.

Two days later the Pattersons' oldest daughter, *Kathy,* arrived for the holidays, bringing with her a letter she received from Megan. Because Kathy refused to "validate" Megan's memories, Megan was writing to inform her that she could no longer stay in contact with her. While she respected Kathy's "need to not remember," she hoped her sister would understand that she needed to surround herself with people who would listen to her, identify with her story, and believe her. Megan ended the letter with a warning: "Please always listen to your children, and please, never, ever leave them alone and unattended with Mom and Dad."

Dawn was sick with grief. She couldn't eat, she couldn't sleep, all she could do was cry. After reading the letters, Mike picked up the phone and tried to call Megan, but as she had threatened, he could not get through to her. They wrote to Megan at her old address, but the letters were returned, marked "no forwarding address." Mike wrote a letter to Megan's therapist and received no response. Dawn sent the therapist a ten-page letter, begging her to help them understand what was going on with their child. This plea also went unanswered. For ten months the only contact they had with Megan was through her lawyer, who informed them that she wished to revoke her father's power of attorney and take over the responsibility of managing her trust fund.

Then, on September 9, 1991, another letter arrived. The envelope was addressed to Mike, and the letter began with the words "Dear Michael Patterson." It was time to tell the truth, Megan wrote, because now she remembered everything her father had ever done to her. The memories had recently come back to her during age-regression therapy. She remembered being a tiny child, only eleven months old, hysterical with fear that her father would come into the room and kill her. Her mother, she recalled, gave her Valium to calm her down.

Recently, she had experienced a "body memory" while she was lying in bed. Her whole body went numb. She knew "something important" was trying to surface, but she was frozen, incapable of movement. Her body convulsed suddenly with waves of memories and terrible, indescribable pain that began in her vagina and coursed up through her body and out of her mouth. She was "bleeding" from the pain. The memories were disgusting, revolting, vile. She remembered being a small child when she was brutally, repeatedly raped. Was it her mother? she asked herself after waking up from a vague dream. But her mother's face didn't fit in with the images. The knowledge came back to her slowly but with the inescapable sensation of knowing the truth: Her father had raped her repeatedly and continually from the time she was eighteen months old until she left for college.

Why? It was both question and accusation. Why did you rape me? How could you assault your own child, your own flesh and blood? Why did you feel you had the right to invade my defenseless body? Why, why, why, why? The details of the abuse were carefully and painstakingly elaborated. Megan remembered her father's penis in her anus. She remembered the feeling of wanting to throw up as she felt him thrusting against her. She remembered her father taking her right hand and forcing her to rub his penis until he ejaculated.

Did he still wonder why she was angry at him? Did he wonder why she wanted to tell him to go away and leave her alone forever? All she ever wanted from him was love and affection. All she ever needed was protection, nurturing, guidance. But instead she had been violated and humiliated. She would no longer give him the honor of being her father. She didn't need him anymore. There were other people in her life who loved and respected her. She would not only survive without him, she would thrive.

"All I ever wanted . . ." Mike put the letter down and opened his arms to his wife, who was sobbing inconsolably. "I'm so sorry," she said, over and over again. They held on to each other for a long time. Dawn cried against Mike's chest while he stared dry-eyed out the back window of their four-bedroom house. Beyond the neatly landscaped backyard was a wire-mesh fence and beyond that were the high school playing fields. A memory suddenly flashed into his mind, and the long-forgotten images temporarily disoriented him. He remembered coming home from work unexpectedly, just before lunch on a school day, to discover Megan and a friend playing in the back yard. He rapped hard at the kitchen window, and the two teenagers panicked, scrambling over the five-foot fence and tearing across the field toward school. To make up for her transgression, Megan spent an entire Saturday pulling weeds.

Mike brought his mind back to the present. It was the beginning of a new school year, and the playing fields were freshly mowed. He tried to concentrate on the colors, the brilliant emerald grass and the glowing gold and orange leaves on the maple trees. Then another memory flooded through him. He could see himself standing on that clipped green field watching his son's football games, cheering along with the other parents. So long ago, he thought. And then another memory—he remembered jumping the fence (it was only six years ago, but he was much younger then) and walking across the field to watch Megan run the hurdles in an intramural track event. Megan was never a star, but she tried hard. She always tried so hard.

He closed his eyes. It was all such a long, long time ago, but the pictures brought back by the memories were still so clear and vivid in his mind. Were Megan's bad memories—memories that included him but were not stored in his mind—filled with the same precision and detail as these harmless, everyday memories? Was this how her "memories" came back to her, suddenly and with no warning, as she discussed her fears and her pain with her therapist? Did she remember any of the good times that were still so finely focused in his memory?

Mike continued to stare out the window as Dawn sobbed. When the tears stopped, and Dawn's breathing evened out, Mike gently held her away from him and looked in her eyes. "Are you okay?" he asked. She nodded. He led her to the living room couch and sat down next to her, holding her hand.

"Something is terribly wrong with Megan," he said. He was surprised how even and calm his voice was. "I'm afraid we waited too long. We should have done something sooner. Maybe it's too late now, but we have to find out what has happened and do what we can to get her back."

"Back?" Dawn asked. Like so many words that she heard these days, this one didn't make sense.

"I think she may be in a cult of some kind," Mike said. "Somebody or something is controlling her mind and changing her memory. That letter was not written by our daughter. Megan could not have written those words and believed that I would do those things to her. Not our Megan. Something has happened to her, and I intend to find out what it is."

The September letter firmly marked the line between before and after. "Before" was the time when the bad "memories" didn't exist, and Megan was still Megan; "after" was this new, strange time when Megan became someone else and her memories held the family hostage. Before receiving the September letter, Mike had believed that Megan would come to her senses, see the harm that this "survivor therapy" was doing to her and her family, and realize that the vague and floating memories were not real at all, but fantasies, hallucinations, delusions. He believed that reason and common sense would prevail. But after he read the September letter he knew there was no hope of a simple or rational ending.

"I remember everything you did to me. . . . You raped me, your own flesh and blood. I can no longer honor you with the title 'father.' " When he read those words, Mike knew that they were past the territory of deep trouble and into the land of sick souls. Something terrible had happened. All that was good and virtuous had been wiped out by this perverse meanness, this bizarre malevolence that came from . . . where? He didn't know. He didn't understand. What insidious process had transformed a kindhearted, loving, thoughtful child into a spiteful and self-centered person? How could it be that his intelligent, compassionate daughter did not fathom the pain she was creating—or, worse, did not care about the grievous wounds she had inflicted because she was so consumed with her own pain and the growing, metastasizing, life-threatening "memories" of abuse? What was the nature of this twisted evil that had the power to change good to bad?

The same questions echoed in his mind in the morning, when he showered and shaved; during the day, when he tried to keep his mind focused on his work; in the evenings, when he and Dawn sat on the sofa holding hands, staring into space until they were too tired to do anything but drift off into a troubled, restless sleep. How could this have happened? How in the world could Megan have come up with these accusations after living with them for so many years, knowing him, knowing her mother, knowing how much they loved her, how their lives were centered around her, how their earth spun on the axis of her smile, her spirit, her very being? How could she be such a good and generous child for all those years, and then suddenly and inexplicably tear out their hearts with these false accusations?

Something had gone wrong in therapy. Mike knew that much. All he had to do was go back and look at Megan's letters. Everything had changed in January 1990, when she broke up with her boyfriend and switched therapists. A month later she joined Alcoholics Anonymous and started attending incest-survivor groups. Three months later she sent Dawn a copy of *The Courage to Heal* and six months after that she accused both her parents of sexual abuse, cutting off all contact with her family. Now there was this most recent letter, describing in vivid detail how her father had raped and tortured her.

Something was wrong with Megan's therapy, and something was definitely strange about her therapist. Why wouldn't the therapist talk to them? Why didn't she respond to their letters? Why had she encouraged Megan to cut off all contact with her family? Wasn't the purpose of therapy to heal and make whole, rather than to infect the client with anger and resentment and willingly, knowingly, carelessly shatter a family into tiny, unmendable pieces?

Mike couldn't understand it. He brought out his notebooks and file folders and carefully read through every one of Megan's letters. On December 6, 1990, two weeks after receiving the Thanksgiving letter, Mike had typed a one-page letter to Megan's therapist. He remembered how hard he tried to be professional, nonjudgmental, reasonable. The letter was typed on his business stationery.

> As Megan's father, I am concerned that her treatment be the best, most thorough available. . . . If she has not been seen by a psychologist or psychiatrist, then I am suggesting that she be tested and examined thoroughly to accurately determine her illness. . . . The accusations Megan made in her letter may be real to Megan, but they simply are not true. Perhaps some skilled professionals can determine what is real and true and help Megan sort out the actual from the imagined so that she can live confidently and without fear. . . . Any response, assistance or advice that you can offer will be appreciated.

The letter was signed "Very truly yours."

He remembered what Dawn had said when she read this letter. "It's too businesslike," she pronounced, and immediately sat down to write her own, ten pages long, handwritten, straight from the heart. Mike could not read this letter without feeling that the walls of his heart were cracking and swaying, about to fold in upon themselves.

"In a desperate attempt to get proper treatment for our daughter, I'm writing this letter and praying every minute that you will read it in its entirety," the letter began. Dawn spent several paragraphs describing her marriage and her abiding love for her husband. "My husband and I married in great love with one main purpose in mind, to have lots of children. . . . We are still in love after 32 wonderful years. Mike is the most wonderful man I have ever met and I would marry him all over again."

She wrote lovingly of her youngest daughter. "She was a beautiful, loving child, a treasured baby and much adored."

She searched for reasons that might explain the tragedy that had befallen them. "Looking back the only criticism I ever received from friends or relatives on child rearing was they all said I spoiled Megan. It was probably true. She was so sweet and so wonderful, and I probably gave her everything she ever wanted."

But the real problems began, Dawn surmised, with the decision to take in foster children. They didn't know until much later, she explained to Megan's therapist, that Megan and her foster brother Patrick had been sexually involved when Megan was just twelve years old. Megan had apparently consented to the kissing and petting but soon afterward experienced great guilt and shame and began to have difficulties in junior high school. "We now see this was due to trouble with Patrick but never knew it or *even suspected*. I cried so hard to think she carried that burden all those years by herself."

Dawn kept writing, searching for reasons for her daughter's pain.

Maybe Megan pulled away from the family because of a "clash of values." "Megan has slept with at least 6 men/boys (we know of) and lived with one since high school. We believe this has caused a lot of guilt since she was raised differently and we believe shared those values previously."

Perhaps, at some point in time, she was molested by a baby-sitter or improperly touched by a relative, and in her emotionally distraught state she confused the memories, imagining that it was her father who had abused her. "We don't know. We probably never will. We only know that *we didn't do anything* but love and support her. We have no idea what we have done. We were not perfect by a long shot but we did not abuse *her* or anyone."

The letter ended with an appeal to the therapist to try to understand Dawn's parental feelings and her extreme grief at losing her daughter for no apparent reason. The final paragraphs wrapped their hands around Mike's heart and squeezed.

> I asked if you were a parent in the beginning of this letter because maybe you could understand the loss we are going through. You bear a child in pain, change diapers, and feed, clothe and take care of this little infant for what seems like years. It's all worth it because you see this beautiful sweet little girl emerge. You go to choir concerts, honors night, track meets. You endure braces with endless appointments (not to mention money) tonsils and wisdom teeth out. You go through ear infections, colds, measles, chickenpox. You are there for everything. You love her with all your might and now this. Do you know the devastating effect on someone whose loved and cherished child tells them she never wants to talk to them again? She will not discuss any of these wild and nebulous accusations. We have not been able to communicate with her to get to the bottom of it . . . Mike sent an unemotional letter as that is a man's way—but he is dying inside. I worry about him as he has heart trouble and this will eventually kill him. It's only a matter of time.
>
> We love her and will do anything to keep her and mend our relationship. We do not know what happened and want to know. Her grandmother, aunts, cousins, sister and brother are all heartbroken. They have done nothing but love and cherish her all her life. Why are they being punished? We do not understand. Can you help us understand?

Mike put the letters back into the folder, making sure they were in chronological order. Then he read through Megan's letters once more, actually reaching out to touch his daughter's handwriting in the hope that he could feel her pain and understand the anguish of her soul through the ink on the paper. The words themselves didn't bother him. He didn't care if everybody in Cedar Rapids knew about these accusations, because he knew in every cell of his being that he had never sexually abused his daughter. He simply did not care what other people thought. He cared only about his wife, his older daughter, and his son, whose hearts had been broken, and about Megan, whose soul had been stolen. He was determined to find out what had happened to change her into this venomous, vindictive stranger who gave up her whole family in exchange for her therapist and her survivor group, in the process changing her identity from Megan, daughter of Mike and Dawn, to "incest survivor."

"It's only a matter of time," Dawn had written in her letter to Megan's therapist. She was worried about his heart. Mike smiled at the thought of his wife's concern; his heart would hold out as long as it took to get his daughter back. He picked up the telephone and started making the connections that would lead, he hoped, to an end to this madness and the recovery of his beloved child.

Six weeks later Mike received the first summary report from Falcon International Inc., a private investigation agency. He shook off the guilt that assailed him when he thought about what he had paid someone to do—spy on his own daughter—and tried to calm himself with rational thoughts: This is not about revenge. I want my child back, and I can't do anything to help Megan until I find out where she's living, what she's doing, who her friends are, how she looks, acts, reacts. We need to know if she's taking drugs, if she suffers from some dreadful mental illness or physical disease, if she's involved with some kind of brainwashing cult. We need details, facts, solid information. We can't proceed without knowledge.

The private investigator had discovered where Megan lived, providing the address, the property value of the rental house, the landlord's name and telephone number, and the name of the man she was living with—*Paul Winter*, "a male, white subject" who worked intermittently as a freelance photographer.

Megan and Paul, the report continued, followed no set pattern during the day and sometimes stayed home all day long. A check with the state and county Social Services departments revealed that Megan was not working for either department.

Attempts to retrieve trash at their residence were unsuccessful. On the days when the garbage was collected, Megan emerged from the house dressed in her bathrobe and deposited the trash bags directly into the refuse truck.

The two-page report concluded that

> Megan is presently not involved in any of the known, larger, religious cults. I believe that any problems you are having are a re-

sult of, directly or indirectly, the counseling and possible support group meetings, initiated or recommended by her therapist.

In numerous phone conversations over the next weeks, Mike and *Sharon,* the "undercover operative," planned their strategy for the therapy sessions. Sharon would pose as a divorced woman who was suffering from sleep disturbances and depression. She would admit to some minor problems with alcohol and a tense, strained relationship with her mother and stepfather. During the therapy sessions she would wear a "wire" for recording her conversations with the therapist. After each session she would write out a detailed narrative report and then Express Mail the report and the original audiotape to Mike.

Two weeks later Mike received the first package from Sharon. She had successfully contacted Megan's therapist and just completed her first two-hour session. "Now we're getting somewhere," Mike thought as he read the report. Dawn wasn't so sure. This was Mike's idea, and she wasn't completely convinced that its potential merits outweighed its inherent flaws. What if Megan found out about the private investigator and the surreptitious tapings—would she ever forgive them? Dawn feared that the plan might backfire and ruin any chance they had of a happy ending.

But Mike argued that it was the only way to find out with any degree of certainty what had happened to Megan. Praying that this tactic would lead to more good than harm, Dawn read the report. She was desperate for news of her daughter, even if it had to come in this way, through the eyes and ears of a stranger. At least they could picture Megan now, in a real room, with a real person, having real conversations. At least they had some solid information instead of all the wild guesses and fear-filled speculations. Just reading the report, Dawn felt closer to Megan. She could at least reassure herself that her daughter was still alive, walking on this earth, breathing, speaking, communicating with other human beings.

Sharon entered the one-story office building at 1:25 P.M. When no one appeared to greet her, she took a few minutes to look around. A central reception area contained three upholstered oak chairs and an end table with copies of *The New Yorker, Time,* and *New Republic* magazines. The place seemed deserted, so Sharon walked into a small kitchen area that was separated from the reception room by a half-wall divider. The kitchen cabinets were stocked with herbal and regular teas, cocoa, and foam cups. A narrow hallway led to several rooms; only the door to the first room, apparently a staff lounge, was open. She perused the bookshelves, quickly jotting down the titles in her notebook: *You Can Heal Yourself; Love Yourself; Heal Your Life; Memories, Dreams, Reflections; Sweet Suffering; Reclaiming the Heart; Intimacy.*

As she continued walking down the hallway, a woman emerged from

Room F and introduced herself. "Hi, are you Sharon? Greetings. I'm *Kate*." The therapist, an attractive, slightly overweight woman in her mid-thirties, was dressed casually in a turtleneck sweater and slacks. Her hair was cut short, just below her ears, and she wore no makeup or jewelry. Smiling pleasantly, she showed her new client into the therapy room and shut the door behind them.

The room was small, about eight feet by eight feet, and decorated with a love seat with loose toss cushions; a black vinyl recliner; two nondescript end tables; and a small bookcase. No certificates, degrees, or licenses were displayed on the walls. A variety of incense burners and candles decorated the tables and bookcase, along with brass bells sewn on a green felt ribbon, decorative ceramic elephants and giraffes, and a small green jade Buddha. Pictures of animals—a koala, a zebra, and a female lion—covered the walls, and several large stuffed animals were propped up against the walls and furniture.

Kate handed her new client a clipboard with a questionnaire to fill out, requesting her name, address, occupation, the name of the person who had referred her, insurance company, problem, symptoms, medications, and therapy history. After Sharon spent approximately ten minutes answering the questions and checking the appropriate boxes, they began to talk. Kate frequently referred to the clipboard, basing her questions on Sharon's written responses and comments. She asked about Sharon's former experience in group therapy (a divorce support group), drinking patterns, recent bouts with depression, sleeping difficulties, and possible hormonal shifts ("Any hot flashes or menopausal symptoms?") and then began to question Sharon about her childhood memories.

"What's your earliest memory?" she asked.

Sharon described a memory of sitting on a potty chair when she was "real small" while her father tossed a foam-rubber ball to her. "I think he was trying to get me to relax so I could go to the bathroom," Sharon said.

"Are you fairly confident in your memory?" Kate asked. "For example, do you feel that you could identify things that happened in each school grade?"

"I think there are times when my memory is faulty," Sharon admitted. "I've had some lapses, certain periods of my life where I just don't remember what happened."

Kate regarded the questionnaire for a moment. "Now, about this hyper-startle response," she said. "A lot of times when there is a response that wakes you out of a sound sleep, it has to do with some memory, something that's come up that was very startling or exciting or frightening or whatever. It's sort of a generalized body's way of remembering, and it can occur spontaneously, just coming out of nowhere. Most often, though, when people begin to try and piece things together they recognize that there's been a particularly dreadful period of time in their life and it ends up interrupting their sleep patterns."

Kate talked for several minutes about the benefits of regular and effective sleep and the detrimental effects of alcohol and drugs on REM sleep. Then she said, "If there is something that is coming from an unconscious state to a conscious state that you don't remember, seeping into your consciousness in one way or another, and you don't have any memory of it, it can be scary."

"How would one find out if something like that happened?" Sharon asked.

"The hyper-startle response itself is a suggestion that something did happen," Kate answered. "On that basis, then, perhaps you would allow me to take you back to the past. But I have to earn your trust in order to do that, because it's scary business."

To secure her new client's trust, Kate described her background—she held a master's degree in clinical psychology—and her "nontraditional" approach to therapy. Unlike many therapists, she explained to her new client, she believed in "short-term therapy," with two exceptions—people who are chemically dependent and people who have experienced "real trauma . . . incest survivors, rape victims, Vietnam veterans, or people who have been physically abused or exposed to mental cruelty."

With all clients, she preferred to "physically" work things out. ("If you have somebody who wants to learn how to water-ski, you can talk them through it but there's nothing like having them go out, get in the water, pull the skis on, and tell them how to hold the thing and then have them do it. I believe in environment work.") She always tried to spend more than an hour with her clients and was a firm believer in the value of giving homework: "You really get your money's worth that way."

"What direction would you recommend for me?" Sharon asked after Kate described her treatment philosophy.

"Well, given what I know, at least at this point, there's a possibility that alcohol is part of the problem," Kate answered. She recommended that Sharon quit drinking for sixty days to see if abstinence would affect her mood and alter her sleep patterns, and she discussed the merits of a "reasonable diet, reasonable exercise, and reasonable sleep."

The session ended on a positive note. "You asked me, where do we go," Kate said. "I'm going to ask you where do you want to go?"

"I want to get to the point where I can laugh, I can enjoy each day, where I don't feel tired all the time, I don't have mood swings," Sharon answered. "I want to let my anger out. I want to get past all this stuff and be able to enjoy life on my own."

"A worthy goal," Kate responded. They scheduled an appointment for the second session, four days later.

* * *

When they reviewed the tape and written analysis of the second session, Mike and Dawn were disappointed. Nothing unusual or particularly remarkable occurred during the session. "The therapist spent most of the session dwelling on alcohol and directed me to a Saturday morning meeting of Alcoholics Anonymous that is geared for women's needs," the private investigator commented in a cover letter. "During the next appointment she will work with me on dealing with the sleep interruptions that leave me fearful and panicked."

Sharon called a few days later to discuss a potential problem. "The therapist asked if she could hypnotize me during our next session," she told Mike. "She plans to work on the hyper-startle response, as she calls it, and she wants me to be in a relaxed and trusting state. I'm afraid to wear a wire because I don't want to inadvertently reveal who I am and why I'm there."

Mike agreed that it was too risky to wear the wire. "But as soon as you leave the session," he instructed Sharon, "type up everything you remember about it and send me a detailed summary report."

On November 23, 1991, Mike and Dawn received a typed, single-spaced, five-page description of the third therapy session. As they read through the narrative, they experienced alternating sensations of dread and relief. This is it, Mike thought. We've got it.

Upon entering Kate's office, I appeared to have been crying. I told her that I had had a horrible week. I told her that I had had nightmares Monday and Tuesday night and on one of those nights I awoke with a sharp pain in my arm as though my stepfather had been twisting it. On Wednesday night I awoke with a start, felt someone in the room, was terrified but my body was numb and I felt I wasn't in my body. (At this time I was crying harder and using tissues.)

She then sat back and looked at me and speaking in a much softer tone with a different cadence said, "Sharon, I feel I have to tell you something because you are so upset and I sense that you think you are losing your mind." (I never once mentioned I thought I was losing my mind.)

She told me that she was certain I was experiencing body memory from a trauma, earlier in life, that I could not remember because my brain had blocked the memory that was too painful to deal with.

Looking shocked and shakier, wringing my hands, I told her I didn't remember any trauma. She shook her head and said that is the case and many people at far later times in their lives go through this same process when the memory starts to surface.

I asked her if a lot of people go through this. She shook her head (yes) and I then asked who. She said, "Vietnam vets, earthquake survivors, and incest survivors."

I told her that I had not been in Vietnam nor had I ever been in an earthquake. She shook her head (yes) and said "Yes, I know."

At this point I started crying softly, and she went to the bookcase. She said she wanted to loan me a book she recommends (but it was not on the shelf). I asked her for the name of the book. She answered "*The Courage to Heal.*" She said she recommends it to all survivors, though it must be read in small doses as it is hard to handle all at once.

She then pulled a book titled *Secret Survivors* by E. S. Blume from the shelf, opened the hardcover copy and on the inside of the front cover began to read out loud the more than 40 symptoms of an incest survivor. With two thirds of the symptoms, she would look at me and shake her head yes as if this was confirmation of her diagnosis. She was talking in such a soft, low tone that at times it was hard for me to hear her.

She provided me with a list of incest-survivor meetings and recommended three meetings specifically.

She then went on to tell me how to make myself feel safe at night when I sleep. I should sleep with a nightlight on, put pillows down my back, open the bedroom door, and be sure to go out and buy a stuffed animal to hug when I'm afraid. I should treat myself as though a small child were with me who became frightened at night; it was my job to comfort her. Several times later, she told me to treat the small child inside myself gently.

Mike looked at Dawn. They both started to cry.

The fourth and final session was taped. Mike and Dawn listened carefully, backing up the tape and transcribing those parts of the conversation that they believed were important for their purposes. Just a few minutes after the session began, Sharon and Kate had this interchange:

Sharon: The problem I'm having is I don't have any memories. The last time we were together you seemed pretty certain, you know, that I'm an incest survivor or a victim.

Kate: The only thing I'm sure of is that it appears as though you've experienced some trauma. And most of the time that people have that particular collection of experiences, responses and reactions, it's about some form of abuse.

Sharon: The body memory I think you called it.

Kate: The body memory.

Sharon: And then the sleep . . .

Kate: The sleep disturbance.

Sharon: Yeah.

Kate: It's not for me to say I know, you don't know. I'm only sharing with you what my experience has been in the past. It's a frightening thing to consider when you don't have visual memory. . . . But it appears that something's coming to the surface.

Approximately ten minutes later, this discussion took place:

Kate: You need to allow yourself to recognize that there is a part of you that needs to really believe this hasn't happened to you and for you to know that you need that part. I hope there's a time when you get angry. You're having surges of anger right now?

Sharon: You know, if I dwell on the past, I just feel angry—like what happened, why can't I remember, did this happen? It's more of a frustration, I think, than an anger.

And at the very end of the session, therapist and client discussed the phenomenon of repression and memory-retrieval work.

Sharon: How long a process is it normally to find out? We've talked about recovering memory. I assume you mean hypnosis or self-hypnosis?

Kate: Or some people just begin to retrieve memories. It comes up, something in the environment triggers it and for some people that memory retrieval is like BOOM and all of a sudden they've got a whole load of memories.

Sharon: How does one deal with that? If it just walks up and hits them in the head like a baseball bat?

Kate: Well, usually it doesn't hit them like a baseball bat. What's happening is there is some kind of preparation for it. A big shift starts happening and under the right circumstances, it always feels like a boom when you have a memory. You feel a boom and think, "What's going on here and why is this happening?" Now it's happening on and on and on, big kinds of booms. It's pretty different, it's frightening, it's confusing.

Sharon: There's no control the way it's happening now.

Kate: Give yourself periods of time where you sit down and have an evening or an afternoon or morning whenever you can be safe. Take crayons or markers, let yourself draw what you're seeing and feeling. Show yourself what it looks like on a piece of paper. You learn a lot about what is in the periphery, in the background. You get more information and there's something you can do to control it. You can't shut the memories out. They need to come. A lot of times people don't have visual memories.

Sharon: There's a chance I may never have a visual memory. If something did happen I may never get a visual memory.

Kate: That's right.

Sharon: And I'll always wonder.

The session ended just moments later.

"There's no doubt in my mind," Mike said. "The therapist is the source of our problems."

Dawn nodded her head. She recognized the same words and phrases in the private investigator's reports and her daughter's letters—"keep safe," "hug the child within," "give yourself space," "let the memories surface," "body memories," "incest survivors." She wondered how many young women were discovering the unhappy secrets of their past in this one therapist's office. How many were accusing their parents on the basis of memories that had been buried for decades and hit them suddenly, with "big booms"? How many families were destroyed, how many parents were grieving, how many grown-up children were wondering why the past was suddenly revealing its dark and terrible secrets?

Armed with the tapes and with advice from every expert they could find on mind control, deprogramming, and repressed memory therapy, Mike and Dawn decided on their next step: intervention. The plan was to "bait" Megan with *Judy,* her best friend from high school. Judy told the Pattersons that she was willing to do anything to help them. She thought of them as her second set of parents, and she didn't believe that Mr. Patterson was capable of hurting anyone, let alone his own children. Judy expressed her fear that Megan "had gone off the deep end."

The plan was simple. Judy called Megan to tell her that she was planning a trip to Des Moines for a conference. Would Megan like to spend the weekend with her, camping out in the hotel room? Megan agreed that would be fun, and the two friends giggled on the phone . . . it would be just like old times.

The next part of the plan was carefully rehearsed. Judy would fly into Des Moines Friday morning, February 14, 1992. Four of the Pattersons' best friends would also register at the hotel that morning; they agreed to be there just in case their help was needed. Mike and Dawn would meet with the group and two professional deprogrammers who had flown in the night before from Connecticut and Florida. Over lunch the group would finalize their plans, and around five P.M. Mike and Dawn would leave the hotel to wait out the night with their oldest daughter Kathy and her family.

After dinner Judy would call Megan to let her know that she had arrived at the hotel. Megan would drive to the hotel, and the two friends would talk in Judy's room for a while. Around nine P.M. they would go down to the restaurant for a snack; there, they would "bump into" two of Judy's "friends"—the professional deprogrammers. Judy, Megan, and "friends" would go back to Judy's hotel room where the deprogrammers would reveal their real identity, tell Megan how much her parents loved and missed her, and try to help her understand that her recovered memories were not literally true but fictional creations implanted in her mind by hypnosis, age-regression therapy, body work, dream analysis, and other invasive therapeutic techniques.

As planned, Judy called Megan after dinner, but the answering machine took the call. Judy continued calling throughout the night, always getting the answering machine. The next day she drove to Megan's home, but no one answered the door, and Megan's car was gone. Later that afternoon Judy located Megan's roommate, but he refused to talk to her or tell her where Megan had gone. Judy left Des Moines Sunday afternoon without ever seeing her former best friend.

Later, when the Pattersons tried to piece together the shattered fragments of their meticulously thought-out scheme, Kathy supplied the crucial piece of information. On the morning of the planned intervention, Megan happened to call her sister, and Kathy mentioned that their parents were arriving that evening for a weekend visit.

Megan was silent for a moment. "How are Mom and Dad?" she asked.

"They're fine," Kathy said, "but they miss you. They think you've been brainwashed."

"Judy's coming into town this weekend, too," Megan said suddenly. "Don't you think that's kind of strange?"

Kathy realized then that she had made a mistake, but it was too late. Megan apparently went into hiding until everyone left town.

Mike spent $15,000 that weekend, but looking back he believes it was worth every penny because it might have saved his other daughter. Kathy admitted that Megan had pressured her to see Kate in order to overcome her "denial" and begin to recover her own "repressed" memories of sexual abuse. When Megan didn't show up, Kathy agreed to spend two days with the deprogrammers, listening to the private investigator's tapes of the therapy sessions and discussing the suggestive pressures exerted by

Megan's therapist. Afterward Kathy canceled her scheduled appointment with the therapist.

Nearly three years have gone by since the failed intervention. Kathy struggles to stay loyal to both her sister and her parents; she refuses to discuss the situation with either party or be forced into taking sides. Mike Patterson has not given up on the attempt to get his daughter back. He took and passed a lie-detector test. He has organized task forces and dinner presentations and offered his home as a gathering place for the more than two hundred Iowa families who claim that they, too, have been falsely accused. He has written letters to the National Board for Certified Counselors, the American Family Foundation, the American Association of Retired Persons, and numerous other organizations directly or peripherally involved with therapists, families, or the elderly. He has contacted producers at local and national television and radio programs, encouraging them to interview experts concerned about the dangers of "memory work" and the creation of false memories. He has consulted with literally hundreds of attorneys, judges, legislators, sociologists, psychologists, and psychiatrists.

Mike recently testified before a state subcommittee charged with revising the laws governing the statute of limitations on childhood sexual abuse. The suggested revisions would have extended the statute of limitations from one to three years, permitting survivors to sue their alleged abusers up to three years after they recovered the memory. (As we have mentioned, more than twenty states have passed such a law.) Mike proposed that the law be rewritten to require a second opinion by an independent professional who would interview the alleged victim, the victim's family, and the alleged perpetrator and then submit a written report summarizing the findings. Mike also requested that the state require psychological testing of the accuser, the accused, and family members to help ascertain the truthfulness of sexual-abuse accusations based on "repressed" memories recovered in therapy. As he testified:

> If my daughter were sexually assaulted or raped by anyone, I would prosecute the perpetrator to the full extent of the law. If a therapist using introspective therapeutic techniques creates a memory in my daughter that never happened, then that therapist is guilty of a crime equal to a real perpetrator, and justice would demand that the therapist be prosecuted to the fullest extent of the law.
>
> In the case of false accusations, which appear to be a trend across the country, there is a triple tragedy. First, the time, effort, and money spent on investigations of unabused children is stolen from another child who really has been abused. Second, the

unabused child who has been induced to believe he or she has been abused carries the trauma for a lifetime, even though abuse never happened. Finally, the falsely accused parents and family are traumatized to the extent that often innocent families are destroyed.

My appeal is for balanced legislation that would benefit the abused, those induced to believe they were abused when they were not, and those falsely accused.

Mike's testimony was emotional and persuasive. The law was tabled and sent back to committee where it is in the process of being revised to require review by outside experts, as Mike requested.

Joined by forty other accused parents, Mike and Dawn appeared before the state's board of psychology to register a complaint against Megan's therapist and several other therapists involved in repressed-memory therapy. The board concluded that it could not investigate the therapists on the basis of a third-party complaint; to do so would violate the principle of patient confidentiality.

The Pattersons considered filing a lawsuit against their daughter's therapist, charging alienation of affections, but they eventually decided against taking legal action. More anger and hatred would not solve their problem; even if a court censured the therapist's counseling approach, the victory would have no real meaning or value. For what the Pattersons really wanted, they could not attain through any court in the country.

Megan was lost. Only she could find herself and someday, perhaps, begin the long journey back home.

11

STICKS AND STONES

Sticks and stones may break my bones,
but words can never hurt me.

—familiar childhood refrain

A CNN reporter, posing as a patient and wired with a hidden video camera, walked into the office of an Ohio psychotherapist and described her symptoms. She had been depressed for about eight months, and her despondency was affecting her marriage and causing sexual problems. At the end of the first session, she was diagnosed as an incest survivor.

"It seems to me you have symptoms of someone who could have experienced sexual trauma," the therapist said.

"Do you get many women like this?" the pseudo-patient asked, after informing the therapist that she had no memories of abuse.

"Many, many."

"And they forget?"

"Yes, they forget. They have no idea. In fact, what you present to me is so classic I'm just sitting here blown away, actually."

In her second session, the CNN reporter expressed bewilderment at her total lack of memory. How could she have suffered so much and forgotten every last detail?

"I mean, if something bad happened to you, I would think you would remember it," she said.

"You're right, you're right," the therapist answered. "If something bad happens, you really remember it. But if something too bad happens to you, so bad that you can't cope with it, you forget it."

The CNN special segment titled "Guilt by Memory" represented a growing skepticism in the media about repressed memories of sexual abuse. "Phil Donahue," "Sally Jessy Raphael," "Maury Povich," "Oprah," "Sonya Live," "Frontline," "Front Page," "48 Hours," and "60 Minutes" featured stories questioning the reliability and authenticity of repressed memories and suggesting that therapists all over the country might be implanting false memories of abuse in their clients' minds.

"How could you live your whole life and not remember?" Oprah asked one of her guests who claimed to have repressed memories.

When a guest on his show described her brutal memories of satanic abuse, including the ritual murder of her newborn children, Maury Povich was obviously skeptical. "If these memories are so clear and so brutal, why all of a sudden a year ago did she remember them?" he asked the audience. "What happened to all those years?"

What began as a clear-cut moral skirmish between enlightened child-abuse advocates and entrenched patriarchal forces was turning into an untidy war with ever-changing distinctions between good and evil. Suddenly therapists were accused of being the bad guys, the hired guns, the greedy, power-hungry, ideologically inspired zealots who manipulated their clients into accepting a trendy but mistaken diagnosis, creating rather than curing their patients' psychological problems and ripping families apart. Therapists were being compared to the Salem witch-hunters and the McCarthy-era red-baiters, overturning every stone and looking under every bush in their search for a pre-identified source of evil.

Newspaper and magazine stories reflected the skeptical trend (which therapists were calling "the backlash"). Journalist Debbie Nathan wrote an article for *Playboy* magazine, detailing her experiences while attending a four-day marathon retreat for survivors of sexual abuse, physical abuse, emotional abuse and neglect. On the first morning, three dozen women clutching teddy bears or other "cuddly toys" crowded together with six therapists "in a room furnished only with mattresses." On the mattresses were thick telephone books; survivors were instructed to stand or squat on the mattresses and flail away at the telephone books, which represented their abusers, with rubber hoses.

Most of the women introduced themselves as incest survivors or satanic ritual abuse victims. When it was *"Donna's"* turn, she calmly identified herself as a survivor of emotional abuse. But then "her face contorted with sobs."

> "See," she said between tears, "I feel like I don't deserve to be here. I'm ashamed, because I have no memories of incest."
>
> The head therapist, a social worker named *Beth,* wasn't fazed. "How many of you have no memories of your abuse?" she asked. Eleven women raised their hands. "Look around you," Beth told us brightly. "Look at all the people who have no mem-

ories. You all deserve to be here. No matter if you can or can't remember. No matter what happened or didn't."

Soon it was time to plunge into the gory details. A veritable competition over satanic abuse began as one woman after another related her grisly stories, progressively upping the ante of horror. *Andrea* remembered candles used to penetrate body parts, children impaled on swords, and cannibalistic feasts. *Cathy* recalled murdering three babies—her own children—and then carving out their livers. *Teresa* claimed that her father was the king of a satanic cult practicing just a few miles down the road from the retreat; he had recently raped her, hoping to impregnate her and then sacrifice the newborn baby to Satan.*

Donna's memories paled by comparison. " 'God,' Donna said later. 'People who were sexually abused in satanic cults. After that, who wants to listen to how Dad used to criticize my school work?' "

On the final day of the retreat, Donna made an announcement to the group.

> "I had a dream last night," she said. "An incest dream." She looked calm, relieved. "Besides my father, other people were there. It felt good. But that makes me feel ashamed."
>
> Beth the therapist answered on cue. "Donna," she said, "you've made your start. When your kids inside [i.e., inner children] are ready, more memories will come." Everyone smiled.

Debbie Nathan's article appeared in the October 1992 issue of *Playboy*. That same month the *Los Angeles Times* published an article featuring the skeptic's view of repressed memories:

> Increasingly, scientists are urging caution: Seemingly long-buried memories sometimes can be pure fantasy or distortions of anything bad that happened to a child. . . .The harshest critics say repressed

---

*An obvious question that arises with stories featuring ritual abuse, torture and murder is, Where are the bodies? In most cases the allegations arise in therapy and are never discussed outside the therapy setting; as a result, no attempt is made to investigate the claims. If the case is reported to the police or if court hearings result, the FBI or another law enforcement agency may become involved. But despite numerous investigations throughout the country, law enforcement officers haven't found any evidence to support the idea of a conspiracy of devil-worshipping, baby-sacrificing cults. Kenneth Lanning, the FBI's expert on ritual abuse, concludes that due to lack of evidence, it is now "up to mental health professionals, not law enforcement, to explain why victims are alleging things that don't seem to be true." See Notes section for further comment.

memory has become a fad diagnosis, used wrongly and sometimes harmfuilly to explain all manner of psychological suffering.

And later that same month, *Time* magazine reported:

> Experiences can be altered as they are hauled out of memory. Remembering is an act of reconstruction, not reproduction. . . . Critics charge that misleading questions as well as the publicity given childhood sexual abuse frequently plant the idea of molestation in the minds of susceptible children and adults, though no abuse has taken place.

"Unfounded accusations of childhood sexual abuse are tearing apart families all over North America," a *Toronto Star* article announced. An accused parent was quoted as saying: "Some of these so-called therapists are doing brain surgery with a knife and fork."

Science writer Daniel Goleman of *The New York Times* began his story "Childhood Trauma: Memory or Invention?" with a reference to the witch trials:

> Is it Satan or is it Salem? A wave of cases in which men and women suddenly remember traumatic events from their childhood has set off a debate among psychologists who study memory and trauma. . . . Critics liken the wave of such cases to the hysteria and false accusations of the Salem witch trials.

"Recall experts say therapists create hysteria," blared the *San Diego Union-Tribune* headline.

> Psychiatrists, sociologists and memory experts from among America's most prestigious universities who have studied the mind say many of the early memory claims touted by therapists are impossible. And they criticize the therapists, who generally have master's or doctorate degrees in psychology, for subscribing to a theory that has no basis in scientific fact. The scientists further charge that these therapists, however well-intended, are injecting into the minds of their clients the idea that they were abused, that in many cases the abuse probably never occurred and that past abuse has become an unwarranted, umbrella explanation for mental unrest.

Philadelphia Inquirer columnist Darrell Sifford devoted a series of columns to criticizing therapists "who dig and dig and eventually . . . uncover what they're digging for—even if it's not there." He spoke bluntly

of the legal problems facing individual therapists and the potentially devastating impact on the psychotherapeutic profession. "I think that this
issue of false accusations will be the Big Bang that will rock therapy in
the 1990s," he wrote.

> Some of the therapists who have licenses will lose them—as pro-
> fessional organizations try to clean their houses. I think eventually
> malpractice lawsuits will be filed against some of these therapists
> when their patients figure out what's been done to them.

Sifford even suggested that therapists "who dig and dig" might have
serious psychological problems of their own.

> I can't help wondering what kinds of relationships these thera-
> pists have with their own parents. Were they, themselves, abused
> as children? Is that why they see abuse everywhere? Or is some-
> thing else involved? Is it opportunism? Is it ignorance?

Therapists were understandably angered and frightened, for their reputations, their profession, even their psyches were being shredded in public. To add insult to injury, they were forced to deal with an
unaffectionate nickname coined by a group of "retractors," former patients who believed that their "memories" had been implanted in their
minds by their therapists. The retractors, in a parody of the contraction
"perps" for perpetrators, started calling therapists "therps."

And so the counterattack began. In addition to denouncing skeptics as
antiwoman, antichild, antivictim, right-wing reactionaries in serious denial (or "bushwhackers of the backlash," as one prominent child-protection advocate phrased it), the therapists tried more conciliatory
approaches. One of their strategies was to cross the line into enemy territory, seeking understanding and support from their critics. They hoped to
win a few skeptics over to their side.

I became a primary target of their attention for several reasons: I'm a
scientist, I'm a woman, and I'm a relative moderate in a battle being
waged by extremists. Since I am a scientist who specializes in memory,
specifically the malleability of memory, my work represented valuable
booty. The therapists and child-protection advocates hoped that if they
could somehow win me over, they could maneuver around enemy lines
and win a necessary strategic advantage.

If I refused to budge as a scientist, perhaps they could appeal to me as a
woman who should know better than to line up with the macho left-
brainers. This controversy over repression was fast shaping up as a male
vs. female, patriarchal vs. matriarchal battle in the war to end child abuse.
Therapists have told me, their voices tight with emotion, anger just barely

below the surface, that skeptics (like me) will destroy the hard-won gains of the feminist movement. One therapist informed me that I should hold myself personally responsible for "the backlash against women and children" resulting from "massive denial" of repressed-memory claims. I have been told that I am not in touch with my feminine side, that I am a narrow-minded laboratory egghead who should stop sticking her nose where it doesn't belong, and that I have allowed my research to be used by those who are plotting continued male domination and victimization of women and children. In short, as a woman I had chosen the wrong side. I should stop fighting the therapists and join them.

Finally, I was potentially vulnerable to the therapists' arguments because I am a seeker of balance and compromise. Although I do not avoid confrontation or controversy, I prefer rational discussion and intelligent airing of differences, and I refuse to stand in judgment over anyone. Word spread fast when I decided not to collaborate on a paper with social psychologist Richard Ofshe, who categorically dismisses repressed memories and "memory work" as one of the "century's most intriguing quackeries," which "no human society since the dawn of time has ever recorded except a bunch of wacked-out psychologists in America." I told Richard I simply couldn't dismiss these therapists as "wacked out," nor was I prepared to label repressed-memory therapy "quackery." I admire Richard's strength of mind and purpose—he is not afraid to risk criticism, even ostracism, to make a crucial point—but I wasn't willing to attach my name to such harsh summary judgments.

Word also got around that I had collaborated with Lucy Berliner, director of research at the Harborview Sexual Assault Center in Seattle, on a paper for the *Journal of Interpersonal Violence*. Lucy is a friend, and when we got tired of arguing all the time, we set out to find some areas of agreement. In our paper we advocated an end to the simplistic division of the world into "those who care about victims and those who care about the truth.... This is a false dichotomy; ultimately we all care about the truth and about the suffering of victims." We ended the article with a suggestion to keep the lines of communication open: "Most of all, everyone will benefit if we keep this critical dialogue flowing."

And so, for these reasons and perhaps others I do not understand, the therapists, child-protection advocates, and a number of my fellow feminists came after me, writing letters, sending books, pamphlets, and scholarly articles, leaving messages on my answering machine, rendezvousing with me at professional meetings, even flying to Seattle "just to talk." They asked me to listen to their side of the story. All they wanted, they said, was a chance to be heard and understood.

Ellen Bass was one of the first to call, leaving a long message on my answering system.* Ellen didn't need to identify herself as the co-author of *The Courage to Heal,* a book that acts like a lightning rod to collect all the pent-up anger and fear of the accused parents. They have nicknamed it *The Courage to Hate.*

In her soft, pleasant voice Ellen expressed her hope that researchers and clinicians might call a truce and begin a dialogue. "Perhaps we can find some common ground," she offered, "rather than spending so much time and energy entrenched in our various foxholes, sniping at each other."

I saved the message and listened to it several times. This was an interesting development. Maybe the "True Believer" therapists and the "Skeptical" researchers and memory experts could get together and intelligently discuss our differences. Maybe it was possible to stake the boundaries of some common ground. But I must admit that I feared an ambush. Richard Ofshe believed that therapists were preparing for a final showdown. He predicted that the debate over repressed memory would become "the therapy world's gunfight at the OK Corral."

"This is not a simple scientific dispute," he warned me. "This is an ideological battle with truth and justice, right and wrong up for grabs. Therapists have put their reputations on the line, and they're going to fight like hell to protect themselves. Don't trust them, don't let them too close, because they'll shoot for the heart."

Three weeks later I met Ellen at the Bellevue Hyatt Hotel, where she had just completed a workshop designed for professionals counseling incest survivors. We shook hands hello, exchanged a few pleasantries, and sat down to a late breakfast of mushroom omelettes and croissants.

"So," I said, cutting right to the chase, "when did you first notice that you were being attacked?"

She laughed good-naturedly. Right from the start I found myself liking this congenial woman, with her naturally frizzy hair going gray and her charming smile. "After *The Courage to Heal* was published I traveled around Europe for several months," she said. "I was completely out of touch with the backlash that was developing around the book specifically and repressed memories in general."

Her expression became thoughtful. "When I returned to California a few months ago, Laura Davis, my co-author, handed me a massive stack of materials she had been collecting—newspaper clippings, editorials, scholarly articles, letters from accused parents, literature from the False

---

*The conversations with Ellen Bass have been reconstructed from my notes and recollections.

Memory Syndrome Foundation.* It was so intense and there was just so much of it, that my immediate reaction was, Oh my God, we're going to be sued! Laura looked at me and said, 'That's funny. My first reaction was Oh my God, we're going to be killed!'"

I thought about Mike Patterson and Doug Nagle and the other accused parents I knew, and I wondered if any of them were capable of murder. I didn't think so. Anger was a secondary emotion, less important than the fear and heartbreak that drove them to hope against hope that their children might come back to them. And yet the whole issue reminded me so much of the abortion debate that I felt uneasy. Pro-life activists were out there shooting the doctors performing the abortions. In what way was that situation analogous to this one? Who would be "shooting" whom and for what ideological or personal reason?

It frightened me that those of us involved in this debate were even thinking about the possibility of violence. The threats and warnings had escalated with the recent media focus on the "abuses" of therapy. Just that week I had found a message on my answering machine from a woman who claimed to know an arch-satanist with electromagnetic powers who was capable of communicating all over the globe and bending people's minds. "It might help people to cope if they knew there was a satanic force working against them rather than a force within themselves," the caller said. I listened to the tape several times, but I still couldn't figure out whose side Satan was on.

Sometimes it seemed as if the whole world really had gone mad.

"How can we cut through this anger that divides us and work together to help the victims of sexual abuse?" I asked. "You spend your days talking to survivors—"

"and nights," Ellen gently interrupted.

"Days and nights," I continued, "and on the basis of their reports, you believe that it is possible for memories to be repressed and then come back in flashbacks years or even decades later. As a scientist, I have an obligation to search for evidence. Where is the proof that these repressed memories are authentic?"

She told me a story, then, about a close friend who had suddenly recovered a twenty-year-old memory while making love. The friend had been depressed for some unknown reason, and during lovemaking her mind kept wandering. Finally her partner asked if something was bother-

---

*The False Memory Syndrome Foundation is a support group for families involved in accusations of abuse based on "repressed" memories. The purpose and function of the foundation, according to its mission statement, is "to seek the reasons for the spread of False Memory Syndrome, to work for the prevention of new cases of False Memory Syndrome, and to aid the victims, both primary and secondary, of False Memory Syndrome."

ing her. And then the memory came back, out of the blue, without any warning. Her body just floated away and her mind began to spin out of control. She was overcome with grief and shame; the images just rose up from within her and with them came a sense of knowing the truth, finally, for the first time. *Someone had hurt her a long, long time ago.* Ellen's friend shook and sobbed and the words spilled out of her, before she even knew what she was going to say: "I was molested."

The next few months were hell for Ellen's friend as the memories returned and she concluded that her grandfather had abused her. Plagued by constant, unpredictable flashbacks, she suffered from insomnia, depression, mood swings, and crying spells. But worst of all, she endured crippling doubt and disbelief: Maybe it never happened. Maybe I'm just making it up. Ellen reassured her friend that the memories had to be authentic because the pain was so intense and all-encompassing. No one would willingly choose to go through that kind of torture.

After finishing her story, Ellen appealed to me for understanding, clearly hoping to overcome my skepticism. "Survivors are in so much pain," she said. "Why would anyone invent a story that involved so much anguish and suffering?"

"Was there any corroboration of your friend's memory?" I asked.

"Yes, definitely," Ellen answered. When her friend questioned her family members, every one of her siblings remembered strange and bizarre occurrences at their grandfather's house. Even her mother, who denied that the abuse occurred, agreed that her father was "weird."

"Strange things may have gone on in her family," I acknowledged, "but is that proof that she was abused?" I remembered a line in *The Courage to Heal,* often quoted to me by accused parents: "You are not responsible for proving that you were abused . . . demands for proof are unreasonable." These men and women, typically in their sixties and seventies, do not remember having abused their children. Totally bewildered by the accusations, they always ask me the same question: "How can we defend ourselves?"

Ellen fielded my questions adroitly, managing to be clear and concise without becoming defensive. "I understand that memory is not perfect and that there will always be mistakes and errors in people's recollections of the past. But the core of my friend's memory is intact, and the feelings associated with it are appropriate and relevant. My friend physically reexperienced the terror of her abuse through body memories—she felt the pain, she endured again the fear and horror—and when the memory returned, she recalled both gross and trivial details. I don't believe that anyone could recover those kinds of details and feel that kind of pain if the event had never happened."

I told Ellen about the retractors, those whose cases we described earlier in this book, and others who told similar stories about memories created by their therapists through suggestions, expectations, and various therapeutic techniques like trance writing, age-regression, dream work and art therapy. These women recovered memories of abuse that were detailed and filled with emotional pain. Every one of them experienced what they believed at the time was a "body memory." The pain was so intense that they tried to commit suicide or were hospitalized for severe depression and heavily sedated with tranquilizers and antidepressants. And yet their memories were false. When they "escaped" from their therapists, as they put it, and found appropriate psychological help for their problems, the memories simply turned to smoke and drifted away on the stiff breeze of reality.

"Retractors," Ellen repeated. "That's the first I've heard of them. You see, my whole world is survivors. I work with them, talk to them, cry with them. My whole life is dedicated to easing their pain. Because this is my world, I have a strong sense of the massive prevalence of sexual abuse. I know that children are being abused right now, as we speak. I know how hard it is for victims to speak the truth, and I know how desperately they need to be believed. This is my reality."

"I do not deny that child abuse is a serious problem for our society," I said, "and I would not for one moment suggest that the pain and anguish of an abused child or an adult survivor be minimized or overlooked. But my reality is different from yours. I know how easy it is to distort and contaminate memory. I know that memories are reconstructions that incorporate suggestions, imaginations, dreams, and fears. I spend a great deal of my time talking to people who insist that they have been falsely accused and are desperate to understand what has happened to them and their families. I hear their stories, and I am moved by their pain. Just as you want to stop the perpetrators of the world from continuing to inflict pain on their victims, I want to stop the therapists who suggest abuse where no memories exist and who refuse to meet with family members. I want to shout at these therapists: 'Can't you see the harm you are doing?' The stories told by the accused parents are as emotionally upsetting for me as the accusers' stories are for you."

We looked at each other, trying to gauge the depth of the chasm sculpted by our separate realities.

"Perhaps we could each make an effort to understand the other side," Ellen suggested. "Perhaps you could spend more time trying to grasp the concerns of the survivors, and I could spend more time listening to the retractors and the accused parents."

"We're certainly not doing anyone much good attacking each other," I agreed. It was a serious moment but I suddenly laughed out loud, remembering a recent "attack" against me.

"What's so funny?" Ellen smiled.

I told her the story of an astonishing encounter. A few weeks earlier I was flying back to Seattle after giving a talk at a meeting in California. The woman seated next to me had just finished reading the business section of *USA Today* and was looking out the window when I asked my standard airplane opening question: "Are you headed home or away?"

"I'm returning home to Seattle from Australia and New Zealand, where I presented a series of lectures and workshops," she said pleasantly.

"On what subject?" I asked.

"Surviving childhood trauma," she said.

I must have said something like "Oh, that's interesting," but I was wondering how I had happened to get seated next to this woman when there must have been at least a hundred people on the jumbo jet who had neither repressed a memory nor counseled someone who had. Maybe there were even a handful who hadn't yet heard the word "repression." Why wasn't I sitting next to one of them?

I was feeling a bit grumpy anyway, because during the talk I'd just given to a professional audience of psychologists and psychiatrists in San Francisco, I was hissed and booed. *That* was a first. Now all I wanted to do was get back home, put my feet up, and turn on the tube. (Although the last time I'd done that, I'd tuned in to Faye Dunaway, all dyed and dressed up as Joan Crawford, inflicting horrendous tortures on her adopted child in *Mommie Dearest*.)

"And what do you do?" my seatmate asked politely.

"I teach at the University of Washington." Purposely vague.

"What do you teach?"

"Psychology."

"Are you a clinician?" she asked, turning in her seat to regard me with greater interest. "What kind of therapy do you do?"

"I don't do therapy," I said. "I study memory."

"Memory," she repeated softly. "What kind of memory?"

"I study memory storage and retrieval processes," I said, trying to use neutral language to describe my work.

"What's your name?" she asked suddenly.

I told her. How could I lie about my name? She looked at me, her eyes narrowed. "Oh no," she said. "You're that *woman!* You're that *woman!*" And—I know this will be hard to believe—she started swatting me over the head with her newspaper.

When I got to that part of the story, Ellen burst out laughing. "You're not serious!"

"It's true, the whole truth, and nothing but the truth, so help me God," I said, holding up my hand for the mock oath.

"What happened next?" Ellen asked.

"She started looking around as if she couldn't wait to get away from me, but the seat belt sign was on. The flight attendant came by a few minutes later, we both ordered drinks, and we spent the rest of the flight trying to win each other over. Just before her trip to Australia she had heard me speak on a local Seattle radio program, and she described me as strident and dismissive. She accused me of spending all my time defending the perpetrators. She believes that even if repressed memories are not literally true, they are symbolic of some terrible event or experience in the person's past. 'People in therapy are not that easily misled,' she insisted, 'and psychotherapy is not mind control.' "

"I think she's right there," Ellen said. "I just can't believe that a therapist could convince a patient who was not abused that she was abused, not just once but many times, and by someone she knew and perhaps even loved. The whole idea of implanting memories of sexual abuse strains credibility. If a therapist is on the wrong track, most patients would simply say so, and either the therapist would get back on track or the patient would look elsewhere for help. Therapy can be suggestive—suggestion is, in fact, one of the most effective tools a therapist has. Perhaps details are added that don't belong in the original memory. But it's just not possible to implant in someone's mind a complete memory with details and relevant emotions for a traumatic event that didn't happen."

"But that's exactly what we did in the shopping mall experiment," I countered.

"I've heard a lot about that experiment," Ellen said. *And not all of it good,* her tone communicated. "You were able to inject a memory for a fictitious event into the minds of several volunteer subjects. But you can't compare getting lost in a shopping mall with the experience of sexual-abuse victims."

"That's true," I acknowledged. "Being lost and frightened in a shopping mall is not the same as being molested, and I would never try to equate those very different experiences. But creating a false memory of being lost and frightened through suggestive questioning might involve a psychological mechanism very similar to that involved in the creation of a false memory of abuse. All we're trying to do in our experiment is to show how suggestion can create a traumatic or mildly traumatic memory of something that never happened."

I had been attacked before by clinicians and child-protection advocates who argued that my laboratory experiments measure distortions in normal memory and should not be generalized to the experiences of adult survivors of sexual abuse. When the shopping mall study was first reported in the press, one of my friends, Py Bateman, founder of the Seattle sexual-assault-prevention agency Alternatives to Fear and a well-known victim's-rights advocate, wrote a letter to the editor of the *Seattle Times.* "If Professor Loftus thinks that the experience of being lost in a shopping mall is analogous to incest, she needs to do her homework," Py wrote. The implication was clear: I may be an expert on memory, but I'm a mere novice when it comes to understanding sexual abuse.

Judith Lewis Herman, one of my harshest critics, wrote a long and impassioned letter to the *Harvard Mental Health Letter*, which had published a paper I wrote critical of trauma theory and repressed-memory therapy. Herman argued that I had been enlisted by defense attorneys who were "looking for new ways to challenge the authenticity of adult claims of child abuse." Despite my "lack of clinical experience and knowledge of psychological trauma," I was speculating on the psychotherapeutic process and trying to generalize my findings to patients with delayed or repressed memories of childhood sexual abuse. I had no business, Herman continued, suggesting "that therapists can implant scenarios of horror in the minds of their patients"; and indeed, by making that suggestion, I was demonstrating "common prejudices": widespread fears of manipulation by therapists; prevailing stereotypes of women as submissive, shallow, and spiteful; and "the universal wish to deny the reality of sex abuse." My laboratory research was being exploited and used to support a backlash against victims, jeopardizing future investigations into traumatic memory and increasing the social pressure on victims to remain silent, Herman concluded.

I was no longer Elizabeth Loftus, Ph.D., a specialist in the malleability of memory, but a careless academic who had allowed and even encouraged her laboratory studies to be used in a campaign against children, women, and victims. In a phrase coined by one of my graduate students, I had become the Evil Pedophile Psychologist from Hell.

"Remember," my students reminded me, "this debate is not about the prevalence of sexual abuse or the hard-won gains of the women's movement. This is a debate about memory, not ideology."

I had to keep repeating the phrase to myself. *This is a debate about memory, it's not about ideology; this is about memory, memory, memory. . . .*

Ellen was looking at her watch. "I have to leave for the airport in an hour," she said. "Why don't we go up to my room and continue to talk while I pack?"

I followed her into the elevator and up to the fourth floor to a large suite with a commanding view of the snow-covered Olympic Mountains. As I settled in an overstuffed chair and listened to her talk with such passion and intelligence about survivors and the courage they demonstrated in speaking the truth about their past, I began to wonder if maybe I *had* missed something. Certainly Ellen Bass was an expert in issues that I knew nothing about. She had practical knowledge that I would never have, insights, knowledge and wisdom that I did not possess. How could I discount her experience? How could I jeopardize the gains of the women's movement by calling into question the memories of adult survivors?

"This is about memory," I said. I was talking to myself, but I spoke the words out loud. "That's why I'm involved, that's why I'm here with you, trying to find areas of agreement. I know that incest is widespread, I empathize with the anguish of the victims, and I applaud the courage of the survivors. I am not an enemy of the women's movement, the victim's-rights movement, or the recovery movement. I don't question memories of abuse that have cogent corroboration from, for example, medical records indicating venereal disease or obvious scarring of delicate tissues. I don't question memories of abuse that existed all along, because these are as believable as other kinds of memories, positive or negative, from the past. I don't question the fact that memories can come back spontaneously, that details can be forgotten, or even that memories of abuse can be triggered by various cues many years later."

I took a deep breath. "I am only interested in this isolated subset of memories that are labeled 'repressed.' All I want to discuss, all I have the right to examine, is this relatively unexplored part of the survivor/recovery movement concerned with repression."

"But why do we even have to talk about repression?" Ellen asked. "Why can't we just get rid of that word? What if a person simply forgets about an abusive event and then remembers it later, in therapy? She's in a safe place; she feels, perhaps for the first time, that someone will believe her and validate her experience, and the memory suddenly returns. Isn't that a valid experience?"

"Of course it is," I said, "but that's simple forgetting and remembering, it's not this magical homunculus in the unconscious mind that periodically ventures out into the light of day, grabs hold of a memory, scurries underground, and stores it away in a dark corner of the insensible self, waiting a few decades before digging it up and tossing it back out again."

"But isn't it possible to redefine repression so that it falls more in line with the normal, scientifically accepted mechanisms of memory?" Ellen asked.

"But then it isn't repression," I said, "because repression isn't *normal* memory." I tried to explain the difference between normal memory processes and this exceptional, extraordinary, and empirically unproven mechanism known as repression. Researchers can demonstrate in the laboratory that forgetting, loosely defined as the failure to remember an event or the inability to recall all the details of a past experience, does in fact occur. Experimenters can demonstrate and offer verifiable evidence as proof that memories lose shape and substance as time goes by.

More difficult to prove in the laboratory, but certainly part of every human being's experience, is the phenomenon known as motivated forgetting, in which we push unacceptable or anxiety-provoking thoughts and impulses out of our conscious minds in order to avoid thinking about them. When I think about my mother's death, for example, the images and emotions are so painful that I immediately push them away, out of mind. I purposely and intentionally try *not* to think about this disturbing event. That's motivated forgetting, and it's not anything like repression, because even though I purposely shove the memories of her death out of my mind, I still know that she drowned in a swimming pool, and I remember the context surrounding the experience.

"I understand that repression is an unusual occurrence," Ellen said thoughtfully. "But isn't it similar to amnesia, where a traumatic event is encoded in an abnormal form of memory? Isn't it possible to be so severely traumatized that the memory traces are deeply and permanently imprinted in the unconscious mind? Then, years later, something triggers the memory and it returns to consciousness?"

This was trickier terrain. Human beings are affected by different kinds of amnesia, which typically follow some kind of head injury. Anterograde amnesia is a reduced ability to remember events or experiences that occur after an insult to the brain. The victim in the notorious Central Park jogger-rape case, for example, had no memory of being raped and beaten by her attackers because her brain had been injured, preventing the traumatic experience from making a biochemical impression in her mind.

Retrograde amnesia is the reduced ability to remember events or experiences that occurred before an injury or insult to the brain. An example of retrograde amnesia would be the case of a woman who leaves work to drive to a downtown restaurant for a luncheon engagement; on the way she runs a red light and is involved in a serious car accident. When she emerges from a coma two days later, she has no memory whatsoever of leaving her office, running the red light, or being broadsided by a pickup truck. The last thing she can remember is sitting at her desk on the morning of the accident, typing data into her computer.

Neither of these rare but documented types of amnesia is similar to repression, which has been proposed as a process of selective amnesia in which the brain snips out certain traumatic events and stores the edited pieces in a special, inaccessible memory "drawer." There is another kind of amnesia, however, known as traumatic (or psychogenic) amnesia, and this is the type most commonly confused with repression. A terrifying or emotionally disturbing event—a rape or murder, for example—can somehow disrupt the normal biological processes underlying the storage of information in memory; consequently the memory of the event is improperly encoded or imprinted in disconnected, unassimilated fragments.

In a paper published in 1982, Dan Schacter and his colleagues at the University of Toronto described the case of a twenty-one-year-old man, identified as "PN," who suffered from traumatic amnesia. PN approached a policeman in downtown Toronto and complained of excruciating back pains. He was taken to the emergency room, where he informed doctors that he could not remember his name, his address, or other vital personal information. When PN's picture was published in the newspaper, a cousin came forward to identify him. The cousin reported that their grandfather, whom PN adored, had died the previous week. PN did not remember his grandfather and had no memory of attending the funeral, but the next evening, while he was watching an elaborate cremation and funeral sequence in the concluding episode of the TV series "Shogun," his traumatic amnesia began to clear. As he watched the funeral scene, an image of his grandfather appeared in his mind, and his memories gradually returned.*

Traumatic amnesia typically involves a relatively large assemblage of memories and associated affects, not just single memories, feelings, or thoughts, and the unavailable memories usually relate to day-to-day information that is normally available to consciousness. The third edition (revised) of the *Diagnostic and Statistical Manual,* used by physicians and psychotherapists to diagnose psychiatric patients on the basis of their symptoms, defines psychogenic amnesia as "one or more episodes of inability to recall important personal information, usually of a traumatic or stressful nature, that is too extensive to be explained by ordinary forgetfulness." A rape victim suffering from psychogenic (traumatic) amnesia, for example, might forget her name, address, and occupation in addition to the details of the assault. But the amnesia is typically reversible, and the memories soon return.

The traumatic amnesias of PN and the rape victim described above are amnesias that temporarily affect large portions of personal memory. The cases are sufficiently interesting that they are often written up in special cases in the literature. A somewhat different type of amnesia involves the victim who, for example, gets in a serious skiing accident and loses the portion of memory that contains the actual accident but retains the context of the memory. She remembers the events leading up to the point where her memory ceased to function, and she recalls her experiences following the memory loss. Most significant of all, she knows that she is suffering from a memory loss. She is conscious, in other words, of losing her memory for a meaningful portion of her past.

Men and women suffering from repressed memories, on the other hand, allegedly lose not only the memory of the trauma but also *all awareness that they have lost it.* The whole context vanishes without a trace. Many people who claim to have repressed memories of sexual or

---

*Traumatic amnesia is to be distinguished from total "blackouts" of memory due to disease, alcoholism, or massive brain injuries that actually prevent memories from being formed in the brain. With these memory blackouts, there's nothing to retrieve, because there's nothing there.

ritual abuse grew up believing that they had a happy childhood. If asked specifically about unusual or shocking events that occurred in their past, they would answer with a statement such as "Nothing really traumatic ever happened to me." The memories simply do not exist until something happens to unlock the secret compartment and they fly out like bats released from a hidden belfry.

Twenty-five-year-old Gloria Grady's story of repressed memories is typical. On January 2, 1985, Gloria checked into the Minirth-Meier Clinic in Richardson, Texas, hoping to learn how to manage her lifelong weight problem. After a five-week hospitalization, she decided to continue weekly individual and group therapy sessions. In a meeting with her parents, her therapist encouraged her to open up and assert herself by mentioning anything that had been bothering her. Gloria's only complaint was that her father, a Baptist minister, was too quiet on Sunday mornings when the family was getting dressed for church. She also mentioned that she was considering moving out of the family home, and her parents readily agreed to help her find an apartment.

Several months later Gloria's therapist asked her to write down everything bad that had ever happened to her. When she had trouble remembering specific incidents, she asked her brother and his wife for help in sparking her memory. Her list eventually included memories of being taunted by her classmates because of her weight problem and an unhappy incident that occurred in first grade when her parents told her she couldn't square-dance with the rest of her class (she danced anyway).

Eventually Gloria began seeing her therapist twice a week in addition to two or more weekly group therapy sessions. She was combining weight-loss pills, sleeping pills, diuretics, and antidepressants, and had to be hospitalized several times for accidental overdoses. On July 24, 1987, after spending nearly two months in the hospital psychiatric ward, Gloria wrote her parents a shocking letter. During her stay in the hospital she had recovered "many horrible memories" of her childhood. Her pain had become so "unbearable" that she "literally wanted to die at the remembrance of the abuse suffered" at her parents' hands. Because family members continued to deny the truth revealed in her memories, she had decided to remove herself "from the family system."

Two years later Gloria Grady filed a request for a protective order to prevent her parents from trying to contact her. In court the Gradys learned for the first time the details of their daughter's accusations. Her father, she testified, had raped her repeatedly from age ten until she was in college, sodomizing her at various times with a knife, a pistol, and a rifle barrel. Her mother sexually abused her by inserting different items into her vagina. Her parents, her brother, her grandfather, and other family members were identified as members of a satanic cult that sacrificed her three-year-old daughter by cutting up the baby's body and throwing the pieces into a fire. The cult, she testified, ritually aborted five or six of her pregnancies and then forced her to eat portions of the fetuses.

Experts testified that Gloria displayed no scars, tearing of delicate tissues, or signs of sexual torture. Medical records, photographs, and witnesses contradicted Gloria's accusations. Police investigation uncovered no evidence of murdered babies, although testimony was presented indicating that Gloria had been pregnant. The judge denied Gloria Grady's request for a protective order.

"It all hinges on evidence," I explained to Ellen Bass. "In amnesia cases we have documentation—cogent, reliable proof that the injury occurred and that memory loss was connected to the trauma. But where is the proof in these cases of repressed memories? Can you prove to me that someone like Gloria Grady can endure numerous sexual and ritual tortures and repress all memory of every single incident, maintaining the belief that her family life was happy and unremarkable? Can you prove that it is possible, as author Betsy Petersen claims, to be raped by your father from early childhood into your twenties and repress all memory of those events and feelings? Can you prove that it is possible, as Roseanne Arnold and many others have claimed, to repress episodes of abuse that took place during infancy and then suddenly remember them in vivid and intense detail? All I ask for is proof that repression is a common phenomenon and that the brain routinely responds to trauma in this way."

I was tired of talking. "That's all I'm asking for—proof."

"But aren't these cases proof in and of themselves?" Ellen asked. "Isn't the fact that thousands of people all over this country are recovering repressed memories proof that repression exists? What kind of corroboration can you demand in cases where the event was witnessed by only two people and one of those people will never tell the truth?"

"I would like to see some kind of evidence that the brain responds to trauma in this way," I responded. "I would like to see proof for the claim that traumatic memories are engraved or encoded in abnormal ways and then stored in a separate section of the mind. I would like to see cogent corroboration for individual accusations based on supposedly de-repressed memories."

We were at an impasse. As a victim's-rights advocate, Ellen believed that *believing* is the gift that a therapist offers to her clients. For too many years, women had not been believed, and victims of sexual abuse were forced to live alone with their painful, shameful secret. By saying those three words—"I believe you"—a therapist gives her patients permission to voice their pain and to speak of their violation and outrage. Having given that permission, how can the therapist then turn around and ask for proof?

"Do you believe that repression is at least possible?" Ellen said as we prepared to leave. "Do you believe there is a possibility that it might exist as a defense mechanism?"

"I suppose it's like believing in God," I said as we walked down the hallway to the elevator. "It all depends on your definition. If God is defined as a literal, physical presence with a flowing white beard sitting on a throne in heaven surrounded by adoring angels, then I would have to say 'No, I do not believe in God.' But if God is viewed as a theory, a possibility, then I could say 'Yes, I believe in the theory that something might exist out there, but I would want proof before I'd call myself a believer.'

"The same line of reasoning could be applied to repression. If you define repression as a process in which the mind selectively picks and chooses certain memories to hide away in a separate, hidden compartment of the mind and decades later return in pristine form, then I would have to say 'No, nothing I have seen or witnessed would allow me to believe in that interpretation.' But if you define repression as a theoretical possibility, a rare and unusual quirk of the mind that occurs in response to terrible trauma, I could not dismiss the theory out of hand. I would say 'Yes, that's possible, but I would have to see some proof before I'd call myself a believer.' "

"But how can you prove that the mind buries these memories?" Ellen asked me. "How could you ever show with any scientific accuracy how the process works?"

"Then how can you justify million-dollar lawsuits and deathbed confrontations based only on a theory of how the mind works?"

"The theory *and* the memories."

"Memories that did not exist until someone suggested them."

We looked at each other across that great ideological chasm that divided and separated us. On what faith could either of us justify jumping across and losing everything we had worked so hard to achieve?

"Therapists are not priests, and repression is not theology," Ellen said gently.

I nodded my head, but I wasn't so sure.

Less than a month after I met with Ellen Bass, an essay appeared in *The New York Times Book Review* that stoked the flames of the already heated controversy over repressed-memory therapy. Titled *"Beware the Incest-Survivor Machine,"* the front-page article was written by psychologist Carol Tavris, author of the critically acclaimed *The Mismeasure of Woman.* Tavris started off with sample symptoms from *The Courage to Heal* checklist ("You feel that you're bad, dirty or ashamed"; "You feel unable to protect yourself in dangerous situations"; "You have trouble feeling motivated"). While the checklist is supposed to identify the effects of incest, Tavris pointedly remarks that the list is so generalized that "nobody doesn't fit it."

Tavris went on (it might be more accurate to say that she accelerated) to lambaste the simple-minded, greed-induced, power-hungry advocates-turned-authors of the incest-survivor recovery movement:

> The problem is not with the advice they offer to victims, but with their effort to *create* victims—to expand the market that can then be treated with therapy and self-help books. To do this, survival books all hew to a formula based on an uncritical acceptance of certain premises about the nature of memory and trauma. They offer simple answers at a time when research psychologists are posing hard questions.

Tavris's straight talk was studded with cynical witticisms. She decried the "incestuous" relationship among the incest-survivor books, claiming that one book "begat" another, which begat another and so on and so on, until the whole world was swarming with these creatures, all distantly related to one another and all programmed with the same inherently flawed genetic material. From one "generation" to another these books pass on their missing and broken chromosomes of information.

> In what can only be called an incestuous arrangement, the authors of these books all rely on one another's work as supporting evidence for their own; they all endorse and recommend one another's books to their readers. If one of them comes up with a concocted statistic—such as "more than half of all women are survivors of childhood sexual trauma"—the numbers are traded like baseball cards, reprinted in every book and eventually enshrined as fact. Thus the cycle of misinformation, faulty statistics and unvalidated assertions maintains itself.

Tavris didn't let up. She blasted the "simplistic" themes and formulaic premises appearing and reappearing in these blood-related tomes.

> Uniformly these books persuade their readers to focus exclusively on past abuse as the reason for their present unhappiness. Forget fighting with Harold and the kids, having a bad job or no job, worrying about money. Healing is *defined* as your realization that you were a victim of sexual abuse and that it explains everything wrong in your life.

Turning the tables on those who denounce the skeptics as antichild, antiwoman, and antivictim, she accused the other side of pathologizing female experience by focusing on vulnerability and victimhood rather than competence and power.

Uniformly these books encourage women to incorporate the language of victimhood and survival into the sole organizing narrative of their identity. It becomes their major story, and its moral rarely goes farther than "Join a group and talk about your feelings." Such stories soothe women temporarily while allowing everyone else to go free. That is why these stories are so popular. If the victim can fix herself, nothing has to change.

Tavris drew blood. The responses published several weeks later were razor-sharp, slashing indiscriminately in an attempt to inflict injury on the perpetrator.

"I must protest her mean-spirited and completely gratuitous attack on incest survivors," Judith Lewis Herman fumed. "If Ms. Tavris is really so tired of hearing about incest, she should stop trashing other women and join with us to try to end the epidemic of sexual violence."

"By questioning the validity of memories that are wrenched with such reluctance and with so much pain from their hiding place in the mind, Ms. Tavris has done a tremendous disservice to survivors, whose strong need to disbelieve their own stories is a common phenomenon," complained the Reverend Dorothy Greene.

Betsy Petersen voiced surprise that the attack came from within the ranks of feminism: "I never expected such charges to come from a writer I admire, one who apparently considers herself a feminist."

One letter writer compared Tavris to Sigmund Freud, who "claimed that reports of incest were merely the fantasies of hysterical women."

And therapist-turned-author E. Sue Blume actually put Tavris in the same cage with the rapists and pedophiles of the world: "Carol Tavris's essay . . . places her directly on the side of those who provide support for 'molesters, rapists, pedophiles and other misogynists,' a side one certainly should apologize for choosing."

But Tavris stuck to her guns. "I fear that the current sad and destructive impulse to see abuse in every home, and to manufacture memories where none existed, is creating a dangerous new set of problems," she replied in a letter of her own.

To raise this concern does not make me antifeminist, any more than criticizing some policies of my Government makes me anti-American. . . . Women are not helped, nor is feminism advanced, by the mindless acceptance of any doctrine that oversimplifies a complex issue. If we wish to improve the health and status of women, we need to understand not only how women are helped by the recovery movement, but also how some are harmed. Shouldn't we worry if the movement is, however unintentionally, contributing to a national mood of sexual hysteria, parents' fears of hugging and kissing their children (let alone of walking around naked in the house) and cruel condemnations of nonabusive parents who merely made normal mistakes?

Watching from the sidelines as the two opposing sides duked it out, I had one comforting thought: Now, at least, there were two Evil Pedophile Psychologists from Hell.

The attacks against me were getting personal. In a long *Seattle Weekly* article about my work and its relevance to repressed-memory therapy, the reporter interviewed two psychologists—one clinical and one cognitive—who were openly critical of my position. Interestingly enough, the clinical expert attacked my research methods, while the cognitive expert tried to psychoanalyze me.

"She doesn't study traumatic memory, she studies normal memory," Judith Lewis Herman said. "Her research is interesting and valid as far as it goes, but what is troubling is her insistence on applying it where it doesn't belong." Kathy Pezdek, a professor of cognitive psychology at Claremont Graduate School in California, wondered out loud if some difficult or traumatic experience in my past might be responsible for my unreasonable skepticism. "I just wonder if Elizabeth has been honest with herself about what went on in her past," Pezdek said. "Anyone who takes a strong stance on an issue needs to be honest about why."

But by far the most interesting comments appeared two weeks later in a letter to the editor. The letter writer, a psychiatric nurse-practitioner, expressed deep concern that my work had been given front-page coverage and worried about the "potentially devastating effects this may have on my own clients as well as the huge numbers of survivors of childhood abuse." She accused me of being hard-hearted, angry, and self-centered. I had, in her words, shut off my "feminine, instinctual side." My photo reflected "a wounded, frightened, angry woman who desperately needs to get out of her compulsive workaholism and intellectual avoiding of her own emotional pain."

(I remember looking at the photograph, which I thought was rather flattering, and wondering: Do I really look "wounded"?)

The letter ended with a reference to the fact that my work would have a "dangerous" impact on the legal system, discouraging clients from engaging in courtroom battles while leading lawyers to believe that they had the power to decide what was "therapeutic." Said the writer, "We must not give Dr. Loftus any more power or credibility. Let's continue to hear women, therapists, and men who are in touch with their feminine side speak out against this patriarchal madness!"

* * *

I have one more story to tell. I cannot reveal the real name of the therapist involved (I will call her Barbara), but I can say that she is an intelligent, articulate, and compassionate human being. I have no doubt that she cares deeply and genuinely about her clients and that her crusade to convince me of the reality of repression and the need to line up on her side against the pedophiles and rapists of the world was motivated by the best and purest of motives. Yet what happened between us taught me a great deal about the inherent and potentially abusive power of the therapeutic process.

Barbara originally called me in the late 1980s for help with an article she was preparing for a scholarly clinical journal on the retrieval process involved in repressed memories of sexual abuse. She was concerned about the difficulty of identifying adult survivors of sexual abuse and wondered if repressed memories go by the same rules as normal memories. "Are repressed memories more or less sensitive than conscious memories to the distorting effect of post-event information?" she asked.

"The answer to that completely depends on what you mean by repression," I said. "I assume you mean a memory for a real event that you haven't thought about for a very long time as compared to a memory that you have thought about periodically throughout your whole life. If this is what you mean by 'repressed,' then I would predict that such a memory would be especially susceptible to change or distortion."

For the next two or three years we communicated sporadically, a clinical psychologist and a cognitive psychologist sharing information and insights about memory-retrieval processes. Then, on August 31, 1992, Barbara called to complain about an article she had seen in that morning's edition of *USA Today*. She read me the headline and lead sentence:

SOME DOUBT REPRESSED MEMORIES

Unfounded "repressed" memories of childhood sexual abuse are splitting families and sending innocent people to jail, charges Seattle psychologist Elizabeth Loftus.

"I am extremely concerned about the effect articles like this will have on incest victims," she said. "Survivors have so much difficulty revealing their painful memories and speaking the truth about their traumatic past. They constantly question their memories and doubt their own minds. Information like this, published in a newspaper that reaches millions, will send them reeling and destroy years of productive clinical work."

"I share your concerns," I said. "I don't want to be responsible for further polarizing this already divisive issue, and I am terribly distressed by the idea that genuine survivors of sexual abuse might feel like I'm revictimizing them."

"Isn't there something you can do about it, then?" she asked. Her tone was becoming strident. "Given your reputation, these exaggerated and distorted claims seem to indicate that repressed memories do not exist, that false memories are the norm, and that repressed-memory therapy is practiced by a bunch of incompetent, fanatical quacks. You are distorting the reality of good, solid clinical work. You don't balance the stories of clinicians who say, as you put it in one of your research papers, 'Tell me what that bastard did to you!' with quotations from skilled, competent therapists. What right do you have as an experimental psychologist to criticize clinical work?"

I was sensitive to that particular argument. A psychotherapist friend had once told me that I was profoundly uninformed about clinical issues. He said he would never presume to be an expert on experimental investigations of memory, nor would he feel qualified to criticize memory research. Why, then, did I seem to have no qualms making blanket derogatory statements about psychotherapy, even to the point of telling clinicians how to do their work?

"Certainly inexperienced therapists can do a lot of harm," he continued, "just as inexperienced scientists, lawyers, surgeons, and engineers can do a lot of damage. But the implication that many, if not most therapists operate on hunches and use blatant, suggestive techniques is both disturbing and insulting. You offer a burlesque of therapy, a sarcastic parody, and as a result you distort and minimize the reality of sexual abuse, thus increasing the probability that people who have been damaged by abuse will be further damaged by a skeptical society's disbelief."

"I am concerned about the effect your work will have on the genuine cases of abuse," Barbara was saying.

"I'm also concerned about those possibilities," I said. "What can we do about it?"

"Keep talking," she said.

Two months later Barbara flew to Seattle just to "talk." We spent the entire day discussing what laboratory research can tell us about real-life experiences, exploring areas of agreement, and seeking ways to communicate our shared concern for helping genuine victims of abuse. That evening we had dinner together and shared personal stories. I told Barbara about my mother's death and my father's long, agonizing battle with melanoma.

Barbara was warm and understanding. She told me stories of her own about career setbacks, relationship problems, disappointments, and dreams. And, of course, we talked about the controversy over repressed memories. I explained how every bit of criticism wounds me, even the off-the-wall vitriol that occasionally gets thrown my way. I told her about a therapist who was in the process of writing nasty letters about me to virtually every organized group of psychologists on the West

Coast. A colleague who serves on the board of one of these organizations sent me a copy of my critic's letter with a handwritten note attached: "This fellow seems to think you have the ethics of a caterpillar swimming in beer." I laughed, but that comment hurt.

I told Barbara about a recent phone call from a former high school friend who lives in Los Angeles. Her eight-year-old son had been having problems in school; she took him to a therapist for testing and evaluation. The therapist asked to see him alone, and after a while my friend became suspicious and listened at the door.

"Were you abused?" the therapist was asking her son. "Do you remember any behaviors that made you feel uncomfortable or strange? Did anybody touch you in your private places? Can you draw me a picture of who you think might have abused you?" At this point my friend burst into the room, told the therapist she didn't think that was a productive line of questioning ("a massive understatement," she told me later), grabbed her son, and tore out of the office.

"Life is a series of daily dramas," I told Barbara. "Every day I walk into my office and think, Okay, what's going to happen now? I look to my right, and then I look to my left, and I wonder who's going to be accused next? Who will be the next person to find a repressed memory? My brother called a few weeks ago to tell me that he had a breakthrough in his therapy. His therapist hypnotized and age regressed him to eight years old, and he remembered my mother scolding him for something. He began to sob, completely overwhelmed by his emotions. He told me he didn't know the details of what had happened, but he felt like he was getting close.

"I'm sitting in my office listening to him and thinking, Don't let that therapist talk you into sexual abuse! Then I find myself thinking, Well, at least Mom and Dad are dead, and if he accuses them, they'll never know about it. And *then* I think, who else could he accuse? Who is still alive? I was in a terrible dilemma. I didn't know what to do, because my brother believed he was making incredible progress. He was getting in touch with his emotions, starting to feel things he had forgotten he had ever felt. And I'm wondering, Can I just sit back and let this therapist put these memories in his mind?"

I waved my hand at the roomful of diners. "I would bet that half the people in this room either have repressed memories or suspect they might," I said. "I just wonder sometimes—is there anything else in the world besides repressed memories?"

Barbara regarded me solemnly. "How can you treat this so lightly, Beth? You were abused as a child. Do you really feel that you can just forgive and forget? Do you really believe that you suffer no long-term consequences from being abused?"

I told her the truth. I was, in fact, deeply affected by the memory of *Howard*, a baby-sitter who molested me when I was six years old, and I had not been able to just forgive and forget. I remember waking up on my thirteenth birthday and thinking: Uh, oh. I'm thirteen, and I still don't have my period. All my friends had theirs. My second thought was filled with terror: Oh, no! I must be pregnant! (This although Howard had only fondled me.)

"I know that seems naïve," I confessed. "But that's what I thought."

"Oh, Beth. I'm so sorry," Barbara said with sincere feeling. "No one should have to enter adolescence with such shame and distress, such painful thoughts."

"I often wondered if Howard realized what he had done to me," I said, touched by her compassion. "He was fourteen or fifteen years old, certainly a narcissistic age. In his mind, I suspect, he was just taking a minor risk, experimenting with someone 'safe,' a little girl who wouldn't reject him or tattle on him. I doubt that he ever thought about the long-term effect his behavior would have on me. He wasn't cruel; he just didn't think."

"Did you ever tell your parents what happened?"

"No, I kept the secret to myself."

"That's what most abused children do," Barbara said.

"Yes, I know. But I never forgot this memory, nor did I repress it," I said. "And even though it affected me deeply, I choose to leave it in my past. I think that's where it belongs."

Barbara said she understood. When we parted later that night, we hugged.

A week later, a letter from Barbara arrived in the mail. My personal history was very painful for her, she wrote. The story about Howard made her sad; in fact, it made her angry—very, very angry. She had been trying to think of something she could do to ease my pain, my loneliness, and my sense of betrayal. On the plane trip home an idea suddenly came to her. She remembered that voodoo practitioners make a symbolic representation of the evil person and stab it with pins. That's what she decided to do for me.

On a separate sheet of paper, Barbara had drawn an outline of a male body. HOWARD was typed in extra-large bold letters and placed dead center on the figure's chest. In each of Howard's hands and through his genitals, she had inserted a straight pin; the tips of the pins were colored bright red.

I looked at that drawing for a long time, not quite knowing what to think. Barbara was trying to help me, I knew that much; but my pain seemed to have become her pain, and my anger had been swallowed up by her anger. Was this what sometimes happened in therapy? When a patient expressed her deepest fears and anxieties, did the therapist take those conflicted emotions and enlarge or symbolically recreate them?

I wasn't quite sure what it all meant, but I knew what Barbara had done—she had stolen my memory, stuck pins in it, and made it bleed.

12

CASTING OUT DEMONS

---

*There is a misty plot afoot so subtle we should be criminal
to cling to old respects and ancient friendships. I have seen
too many frightful proofs in court—the Devil is alive in
Salem, and we dare not quail to follow wherever the
accusing finger points!*

—Arthur Miller, *The Crucible*

*Whoever fights monsters should see to it that in the process
he does not become a monster.*

—Friedrich Nietzsche

I became involved in Paul Ingram's case after his conviction and sentencing, when a Seattle television producer called my office. She explained that she was working on a documentary about the case and had just reviewed some disturbing police-department transcripts.

"I can't escape the conclusion that Mr. Ingram was pressured by the investigators in this case," she said. "Would you be willing to review these transcripts and offer an expert's opinion?"

After reading several hundred pages of transcriptions of the tape-recorded police interrogations, I began to understand the significance of this bizarre case. In a mid-sized, modern American city, a law-abiding citizen was persuaded by honest civil servants to confess to crimes he had never committed. It was a modern-day Salem, and it had taken place in my own backyard.

As I attempted to unravel the story of what happened to Paul Ingram, I had the privilege of getting to know many of the major characters, including Ingram's lawyers; his former friends and colleagues Ray Risch and Jim Rabie, who were implicated by his testimony; cult expert Richard Ofshe; and journalist Lawrence Wright, who created a media sensation with his brilliant two-part article in *The New Yorker* and his book on the Ingram case, *Remembering Satan* (Knopf, 1994).

I also began a correspondence with Paul Ingram, inmate number 261446, who is incarcerated in an East Coast prison. In his most recent letter, Ingram described the "abundant blessings" in his life, including visits with his brothers and sisters and a move to an air-conditioned jail cell with a view encompassing four water towers and the new highway bypass.

When Paul Ingram looks back at the past, he engages in a bit of mind control, glossing over the traumas and focusing instead on the lessons learned. He calls the recent past "the time of my mental confusion." Others, refusing the euphemism, would call it hell. For five months, from November 1988 until April 1989, detectives from the sheriff's department in Thurston County, Washington, frequently accompanied by a psychologist and a minister, interrograted Ingram. Seeking truth, they manipulated Ingram's self-perception, inducing anxiety and guilt and undermining his self-confidence, until he confessed to sexually abusing his two daughters over a period of seventeen years.

In the beginning Ingram's confessions matched the details he had been given about the incestuous acts he had allegedly committed. But then something strange happened. Taking off from a suggestion of satanism offered by his interrogators, Ingram began to confess to increasingly bizarre and bloody deeds. In a trancelike state, with eyes closed and head in hands, he mumbled about devils and fires, blood-drinking, and infanticide. Paul Ingram, chief civil deputy of the sheriff's department, chairman of the local Republican party, churchgoing father of five children, confessed that he was a high priest in a satanic cult, a sodomizer of children, and a willing participant in the murder, dismemberment, and cannibalization of infants.

The Ingram investigation, which began as a moderately shocking case of incest involving one of the town's leading citizens, became engorged with dark passions and a blinding pursuit of the "truth." The investigation rapidly spiraled into hysteria, evoking memories of an earlier time when God-fearing citizens, gripped by fear, superstition, and religious fervor, cried witch, and a forest of stakes was pounded into the very heart of the community. The fear of evil, then as now, creates its own breed of malevolence, and the all-consuming attempt to cast out the devil from human society reveals the demons resting within our own souls.

The Church of Living Water, a fundamentalist Christian denomination located in Olympia, Washington, is an affiliate of the International Church of the Foursquare Gospel founded by evangelist Aimee Semple McPherson in 1927. The Foursquare sect teaches that the Bible is the literal word of God and that the devil is a physical presence with extensive dark powers. The fallen angel can create mental and physical illness and contribute to spiritual collapse. He can control a vulnerable person's mind, inspiring sinful thoughts and wicked deeds. Most remarkable of all, the devil can render his victims completely unaware of his pernicious influence through a method called "satanic deception." Only constant vigilance, prayer, and knowledge of God's word as expressed in the Bible can protect the human soul in the spiritual battle being waged at all times and in all ages between good and evil.

Paul Ingram and his family were "born again" into the Church of Living Water in 1975 and immediately became active members of the congregation. In the early 1980s the Ingram girls, Ericka and Julie, began attending the annual two-day "Heart to Heart" retreat sponsored by the church. Teenagers accompanied by peer counselors boarded buses and traveled to the Black Lake Bible Camp where for two days they discussed problems relating to their self-esteem, sexuality, and family problems. The group sessions were emotional and cathartic as tearful adolescents confessed the secrets of their confused souls.

Ericka and Julie Ingram were familiar with the confessional atmosphere. During a fellowship discussion held during the 1983 retreat, Ericka revealed that she had been the victim of an attempted rape. The sheriff's office was notified but dropped the investigation when it was discovered that the incident consisted of a married man offering Ericka a ride and putting his hand on her knee. Two years later Julie disclosed that a neighbor had sexually abused her; Ericka joined in the accusation, claiming that she had been abused by the same man. A complaint was filed with the country prosecutor but when Julie experienced difficulty discussing the alleged incident and inconsistencies surfaced, all charges were dropped.

The 1988 retreat, attended by sixty teenagers, was studded with shocking revelations. Karla Franko, a charismatic Christian from California, held the group in thrall with her clairvoyant visions. At one point Franko told the group that she could "see" a girl hiding in a dark closet; she could "hear" footsteps approaching and a key being inserted in the lock. Suddenly one of the teenagers in the audience called out that she was the child hiding in the closet; as counselors crowded around to comfort her, she broke down in loud, mournful sobs.

Franko was soon visited by another vision of abuse. Someone in the audience, she revealed, had been molested by a relative. A teenager stood up and raced out of the room. Counselors found her in the bathroom, where she was trying to drown herself by submerging her head in the toilet.

Twenty-two-year-old Ericka Ingram was a counselor at that retreat. After most of the participants boarded buses to return to Olympia, Ericka tearfully announced to the remaining counselors that she, too, had been abused. According to the police investigator's report, Ericka's sudden insight occurred spontaneously as she sat on the floor surrounded by a group of counselors.

But Karla Franko remembers the scene somewhat differently. At the end of the retreat, a counselor approached her and asked if she would pray over Ericka. Franko agreed, and began to pray aloud as Ericka sat on the floor at her feet. With a sudden flash of insight, Franko knew the "truth."

"You were abused as a child," she announced, her voice filled with conviction. Ericka wept bitterly but did not speak. When another vision came to Franko, she quickly translated it into words. The abuser, she said, was Ericka's father, and the abuse had taken place over a period of many years.

Ericka became hysterical, and Franko continued praying over her until the sobbing subsided. When Ericka finally calmed down, Franko urged her to seek counseling in order to uncover the traumatic memories. Ericka was so overcome with emotion that she could only nod in agreement.

After the retreat Paul Ingram and his wife, Sandy Ingram, noticed a change in their daughter's behavior. For some reason they did not understand, Ericka and Julie were withdrawn and uncommunicative. The Ingrams were concerned, but whenever Sandy tried to talk to her daughters, they avoided her with statements such as "You don't want to know." For fear of upsetting the girls and driving them even further away, Sandy and Paul decided to wait things out, reasoning that they were probably just going through a "stage."

But at the end of September Ericka abruptly announced that she was moving out of the house. Two months later Julie, a senior in high school, left home and moved in with friends. The Sunday before Thanksgiving, after evening church services, Ericka asked her mother to meet her at a Denny's restaurant. With a friend providing support, Ericka revealed that she had been repeatedly abused by her father and her two older brothers. The abuse stopped in 1975, Ericka said, when she was nine years old and her father was born again in the Church of Living Water.

"Why didn't you tell me?" Sandy Ingram asked her daughter.

"I tried to tell you, Mom, but you wouldn't listen," Ericka responded.

Later that night when Sandy confronted her husband with Ericka's accusations, he denied that he had ever touched his children in an indecent way.

"But why would Ericka make up these accusations if they weren't true?" Sandy asked.

"I don't know," Ingram answered. They looked at each other for a moment and then he added, "I don't think I have a dark side."

The next morning Sandy picked up Julie at her friend's house and drove her to school. In the car Julie told her mother that she had been molested by her father and older brother. Her abuse, she said, had stopped five years earlier, in 1983, when she was thirteen.

That same afternoon, November 21, 1988, a counselor from the rape crisis center accompanied Julie to the police station, where she gave investigators a more detailed story. The abuse began in fifth grade, she said, when her father would sneak into the bedroom she shared with Ericka and have vaginal and anal sex with one sister or the other. Her father had last raped her, she continued, amending the story she told her mother just hours earlier, three years ago, when she was fifteen.

Ericka, interviewed by police investigators that evening, also modified her story, claiming that she had caught a disease from her father just a year earlier. A few days later Ericka remembered an even more recent episode of abuse. Just before she moved out of her parents' house in late September, she awoke to find her father kneeling beside her bed, touching her vagina.

Paul Ingram woke up on Monday morning, November 28, 1988, took a shower, shaved, ate breakfast, and promptly vomited. He knew that his day of reckoning was at hand. Although his nerves were playing havoc with his intestinal tract, he went to his office at the sheriff's department, mentally if not physically prepared to deal with his daughters' accusations. Approximately fifteen minutes after he arrived at work he was called into Sheriff Gary Edwards's office. Edwards and Under-Sheriff Neil McLanahan confronted him with Ericka and Julie's accusations and read him his rights.

"I hope you are going to cooperate and not make the girls go through a trial," Sheriff Edwards said.

"I did not abuse those girls," said Ingram, immediately amending his denial with the strange reference to evil and unseen forces. "I don't think I have a dark side in me." To this day, Ingram doesn't know where the idea of a "dark side" came from; maybe he had heard those words on television, or recalled the idea from something he had read or overheard. But as a faithful member of a fundamentalist church, he was certainly well versed in the the idea that Satan inspires evil deeds in the weak and godless and then blocks all memories of such malevolent actions from conscious awareness. A primitive force of pure evil, Satan is anachronistically capable of the high-tech scrambling of human minds and memories.

Ingram's reference to a "dark side" was an acknowledgment of Satan's potential treachery and a possible explanation for the inexplicable reality that was threatening him and his family. If his daughters were telling the truth—and he had always taught them to tell the truth—then Satan must have driven him to evildoing and erased his memory.

Ingram was taken to the interrogation room, where Joe Vukich and Brian Schoenig, the detectives in charge of sex offenses, were waiting for him. Both men knew Ingram well, and both were shocked that this seemingly decent, happily married, hardworking, churchgoing man had repeatedly raped and sodomized his daughters and insisted that he had no memory of his actions. Either he was lying through his teeth, or he was one sick son of a bitch.

The first four hours of the interrogation were not recorded but, as Ingram remembers it, the detectives asked him over and over again why Ericka and Julie would make such allegations if they weren't true. Although he couldn't find answers to their questions, Ingram was willing to admit that there were problems in his family. He tried to articulate his anguished confusion through questions he couldn't answer: Why won't the girls let Sandy and me hug them? Why do I have such a hard time communicating with my children? Why did Ericka and Julie suddenly move out of the house?

The detectives gradually focused in on the specifics, asking pointed questions. They accused Ingram of raping Ericka in the middle of the night just two months earlier, days before she moved out of the family home. What was he wearing that night? Ingram answered that he usually wore a maroon bathrobe when he got up in the middle of the night. What did he say to Ericka? What did he do to her? Ingram responded that he had no memory of walking into Ericka's room in the middle of the night and raping her—not in September, not ever.

The detectives told Ingram that he was burying his memories because he couldn't face the fact that he had sexually abused his own children. They continued to offer him bits and pieces of information from his daughters' statements, hoping to stimulate his memory, and Ingram began to pray, calling out to Jesus to help him. As he prayed, the detectives hit him hard with the reality of his situation, working on his guilt and his love for his children. Over and over again, according to Ingram, the detectives said, Help us. Help your daughters. You are the only one that can help them. You were there. You gotta help us. We know you know. You're not being honest. You're holding on to it. You need to let it out. Tell us what happened.

But Ingram couldn't remember abusing his children, and how could he tell them what had happened if he didn't have any memories? The detectives met his denials by repeating three truths.

First truth: His daughters were decent and responsible human beings who would not lie about something as momentous and consequential as sexual abuse and incest. Ingram fervently agreed with this assessment. "My kids are honest," he kept repeating. "My kids always tell the truth."

Second truth: Sex offenders, unable to face the horror of their own deeds, often repress memories of their crimes. Ingram was in partial agreement with that truth, having personally witnessed denials and claims of memory loss by rapists and pedophiles and, for that matter, most people accused of brutal crimes. But, Ingram protested, he desired the truth more than he feared the horror of anything he had done, and he was ready and willing to confess his crimes . . . if only he could remember them.

Third truth: The only way to get to the facts was to admit that he had molested his daughters. If he confessed, his memories would return automatically.

The repression theory, enumerated in truths two and three, made sense to Ingram. It was simply a secular version of the church's doctrine of satanic deception: Satan attempts to destroy our memories of evil deeds so that he can continue to exert his malevolent influence. But if the afflicted can summon up the courage to confess, they will be blessed with insight into their actions and guided toward grace by the sure hand of God.

Ingram wanted desperately to be graced with the truth; he was sick with fear. Fear knotted his stomach, tied up his bowels, clouded his mind. This fear felt suspiciously like a physical presence that had lodged within him, taking root, creating a hardness that seemed to swell and grow at the very core of his being. Through his fear, he thought he could hear God's voice trying to break through. *Confess! Confess!* It was almost as if he could hear God talking to him.

After four hours of interrogation Ingram agreed to make an official statement. At 2:46 p.m. the tape recorder was turned on.

"Paul, I've talked to both Ericka and Julie," one of the investigators said, "and they have told me about specific incidences which involve inappropriate sexual contact by you with each of them. Can you tell me how you remember touching them? In what ways you think were inappropriate?"

"Well, it's, it's been hard for me to, uhm, to acknowledge this," Ingram stammered, "but I, I really believe that the, the allegations did occur and that I did violate them and abuse them and probably for a long period of time. I've repressed it. Uh, probably very successfully from myself and, and now I'm trying to bring it all out. Uh, I, I know from what they're saying that the, the incidences had to occur, that I had to have done those things."

"And why," one of the detectives interjected, "do you say you had to have done those things?"

"Well, number one, my girls know me," Ingram answered. "Uh, they wouldn't lie about something like this and, uh, there's other evidence, uh, that would point out to me that these things occurred."

"And what in your mind would that evidence be?" the detective queried.

"Well, the way they've been acting for at least the last couple years and, and the fact that I've not been able to be affectionate with them, uh, even though I want to be. I, I have a hard time hugging them or, or even telling them that I love them and, uh, I just know that that's not natural."

"If I asked you if you, and this is a yes or no answer, touched Julie inappropriately sexually, what would you say?"

"I'd have to say yes," Ingram answered.

"And how about Ericka?"

"Again I would have to say yes."

"Would this be, uh, occurrences over a long term?"

"Whew, yes."

"What would you think the age of Ericka would've been when these things first started happening between you and her?"

"I can't recall myself, but I know that the age of five has come up in a couple conversations."

"What do you remember?"

"I don't remember anything."

It was a strange sort of confession. Ingram admitted that because his daughters wouldn't lie, he must have abused them, even though he didn't have any memories of the abuse. Without the memories, Ingram was simply parroting what the detectives told him he had done to his children, and his statement could not be considered a legally sufficient confession. The detectives turned up the heat. They wanted to know about the most recent abusive episode, just before Ericka moved out of the house. Did Paul remember that incident?

"Well, I keep trying to, to recollect it and I'm still kind of looking at it as a third party," Ingram said, "but, uh, the evidence, and I am trying to put this in the first person, it's not coming very well, but, uh, I would've gotten out of bed, put on a bathrobe, uh, gone into her room, taken the robe off and, uh, at least partially disrobing her and then fondling, uh, uh, her breast and her vagina and, uh, uh, also telling her that, uh, if she told anybody that, that I would, uh, kill her."

"Now you've talked about this in the third party. I'm going to ask you directly, is this what happened?"

"Whew," Ingram sighed deeply. "I'm still having trouble getting a clear picture of what happened. I know in my own mind that these things had to happen and I'm still having trouble getting a clear picture to say that's exactly what happened."

The tape recorder was shut off at Ingram's request. Dectective Schoenig took notes indicating that Ingram frequently called out to Jesus, asking for his help. Schoenig also noted that Ingram went into "a trance type thing" and in this fugue state began to describe graphic scenes of abuse. But he discussed what he "would have done" with little or no emotion, as if he were a detached observer rather than the central character in the drama.

When the tape recorder was turned back on, the detectives asked Ingram to think back to that night when he entered Ericka's room and took his bathrobe off and put it on the end of his daughter's bed.

"Did that wake her up?" one of the detectives asked.

"Um, I don't remember."

"After you laid down the bathrobe what did you do?"

"Uh, I, I would've removed her clothing, uh, at least the underpants or bottoms to the nightgown."

"Okay, you say you would've," one of the detectives interrupted. "Now, do you mean you would've or did you?"

"I did," Ingram answered the question.

"After you pulled down her bottom, where did you touch her?"

"I touched her on her breasts and I touched her on her vagina. . . ."

"What did you say to her when she woke up?"

"I would've told her to be quiet and, uh, not saying anything to anybody and threatened her to say that I would kill her if she told anybody about this."

"Okay, you say you would've." The detectives were clearly getting frustrated with Ingram's evasive language. "Is that 'would've' or did you?"

"Uh, I did."

"What did you do when you finished? Did you do something to her clothing?"

"I, I don't remember."

"Do you remember pulling them back up?"

"No, I don't."

"Did you put your robe on, uh, when you finished?"

"Yes, I put my robe on."

"And where did you go when you left her room?"

"I would've gone back to bed with my wife."

When the interview ended late that afternoon, Paul Ingram had confessed to sexually molesting his daughters on numerous occasions. Among the specifics, Ingram claimed that he began raping Ericka when she was just five years old, and he recalled sexually abusing Julie for at least ten years. He also remembered impregnating Julie when she was fifteen years old, and arranging for an abortion.

But toward the end of his confession, Ingram once again claimed no memory. "I can't recall anything specific," Ingram said, responding to a question about what he did to Ericka after he entered her room. "I can't recall anything."

"You don't remember going into the room and touching Ericka?"

"No."

"If she says that happened, what does that mean to you?"

"It means to me that it happened. My kids don't lie. They tell the truth, and that's what I'm trying to do."

Ingram was placed in medical cell M-1, subject to a suicide watch, and given permission to call his wife. Over the phone Paul and Sandy agreed to pray for guidance, and Sandy said she would bring Paul's Bible and some underwear to the jail. That evening the pastor of his church, John Bratun, visited the county jail and prayed with Ingram in his cell.

Early the next morning, Tuesday, November 29, psychologist Richard Peterson visited Ingram. Peterson explained that he had been hired by the prosecutor's office to assess Ingram's mental state and make a "safe-to-be-at-large" recommendation. Ingram asked the psychologist to explain to him why he could not remember the events described in such detail by his daughters. Was it really possible, as the detectives kept suggesting, to completely block out the memory of such brutal and sordid events that spanned a period of nearly seventeen years?

Peterson confirmed that it is not unusual for sex offenders to repress the memories of their crimes; they can't bear to think about the horror of what they did to their victims. The more vicious and brutal the crime, the more likely it will be repressed. The psychologist then added a new layer of intrigue to the strange and twisted plot. Many sex offenders, he said, have been sexually abused themselves; thus, there was a strong likelihood that Ingram had been abused as a child—most likely around the age of five years, because that was Ericka's age when he started abusing her. If Paul had been abused as a child, Peterson continued, he probably learned to repress those memories as well. Did he have any memory whatsoever of being molested by his father, or perhaps an uncle?

Ingram carefully considered the question, but the only remotely sexual memory he could dredge up from his childhood was his mother's whispered injunction, when he was four or five years old, to stop scratching his private parts in public. "You're acting like your uncle Gerald," she said, mentioning an uncle who was visiting them at the time.

In time, Peterson assured him, he would recover a memory of his father, an uncle, or some close family friend abusing him. Peterson also reinforced the detectives' assurances that once Ingram confessed to the crimes, his memories would come flooding back. But Ingram disagreed, for that particular theory was not working out as promised. He had confessed the day before and the memories hadn't come back in either a trickle or a flood. Ingram was relieved to hear that Dr. Peterson was planning to attend the afternoon interrogation; maybe he could figure out how to remove the mental obstacles blocking the return of the repressed memories.

In the booking area, a police officer advised Ingram to hire an attorney, suggesting that he call Ed Schaller, a former prosecutor reputed to be one of the best criminal attorneys in the area. Ingram resisted the suggestion and explained his reasons in a diary he kept from the fifth day of his arrest. "My thinking was that Ed would . . . be more interested in getting me off the hook than in getting the truth out." More then anything, Ingram desired the truth. Because he firmly believed that the truth could come only from God, he decided to ask a devout fundamentalist Christian attorney to represent him.

When Paul Ingram walked into the interrogation room around 1:30 p.m. on November 29, he did not know that the detectives had just received two letters from Julie, in which she revealed that she was still being abused. "Being a Christian I supose [sic] to forgive him for what he did to me and still does to me," Julie wrote. Even more shocking, Julie claimed that the abuse involved not only her father but some of his poker buddies, most of whom worked with Ingram in the sheriff's office. When she was four years old, she remembered, the poker players would come into her room "one or two at a time" and rape her. "I was so scared I didn't know what to say or who to talk to," Julie wrote.

The detectives told Ingram they had some additional information from Julie, but they would not reveal the specifics. "What happened with Julie happened just last month," Joe Vukich said. "It's very real, it's very recent. Granted it's very hard to talk about."

"I believe it's there for you to talk about," Schoenig added.

"I, no, I can't see it," Ingram said. "I can't visualize it in my own mind. I haven't gotten to the point that I can—and I don't know any other way to say it, but I can't see it yet."

Ingram continued talking out loud, trying to figure out how he could access his lost memories. "I think it's just a matter of me getting into that part of my brain or whatever and, and give me the pieces, but they're just not there yet."

A few minutes later Ingram recalled an incident in which he had been sexually abused by an uncle when he was just four or five years old. It was just as Dr. Peterson had predicted. "When I thought about it this morning," Ingram began, "what I could see was an uncle, I believe it was Glen, coulda been Gerald, and me giving him oral sex, uh, I can't see any emotion, uh, whew, it's just, that, that came to my mind."

The detectives asked a few perfunctory questions, but they were more interested in what Ingram had done in the recent past than in what had been done to him in the distant past. They quickly zoomed ahead several decades, focusing in on the poker parties that took place in the Ingram house. Who was there? they asked. Were they friends from the department? Did they drink too much, get intoxicated, make a mess? Any raunchy conversation or loose talk about women? Where was his wife during the poker parties? Did anybody happen to go upstairs to see the kids?

"I, boy"—Ingram frantically searched his memory—"I just can't think of anything where anybody—"

"The reason I ask, Paul," Vukich interrupted, "is because Julie told me about a time or two where when there was a poker party she was molested."

"And what we're talking about, Paul, is she was molested by somebody other than you at that time, too," Schoenig elaborated. "She even remembers being—somebody tying her up on the bed and two people, at least, taking turns with her while somebody else watched, probably you."

"I just don't see anything," Ingram said, as if he were able to see the past scrolling by in his mind. "Let me think about this for a minute. Let me see if I can get in there. Assuming it happened, she would've had to have had a bed, bedroom, by herself I would think . . . uh . . ."

"I'm going to ask you to not beat around the bush about this," Schoenig put in. "This is really important. Who do you think was sexually molesting your daughter besides yourself?"

"I'm, I'm just trying to think, I'm tryin' to get into that part of . . ."

"Yeah, and she's real intimidated and she's in real fear right now because that person is still out on the street." Schoenig kept up the pressure, playing on a father's love for his child and his fears for her safety. "That person is some friend of yours that worked or works for this department."

A weak "whew" was all Ingram could manage.

"She's terrified, Paul. . . . Apparently it's somebody that's still close to you, Paul," Schoenig said.

"She's in utter fear of this person," Vukich said, "and we need to do something to protect her. . . . You need to help us protect her."

"I'm thinking," Ingram said.

"Think hard," Vukich said.

"I, I can't, I, I, I am." Ingram was getting frantic. "I can't think of anybody that I'm really close to now in the department, uh . . ."

"See, Paul, she remembers this," Vukich said.

"Well, just, just hang on a minute." Ingram scanned his mind for familiar poker buddy faces. "Jim, Jim Rabie played poker with us. Jim and I have been fairly close."

"Is Jim the person she's talking about?" Vukich asked.

"Just, just don't put words in my mouth," Ingram said in an uncharacteristic show of resistance. "Uh, I don't know . . . I'm, I'm thinkin'. I'm trying to get—to bring something up here. Uh, Uh, Jim's the only one that comes to mind. . . . I'm just trying to put some faces together. Think of anybody else . . ."

Joe Vukich gave Ingram a new mental image to consider. "In this picture you have, Paul, do you see ropes?"

"Uh, you've, you put the ropes there," Ingram said, "and, and I'm trying to figure out what I've got, uh, whew, I, I can kind of visualize a bottom bunk or even the floor, uh . . . It kind of looks to me like she'd be lying face down like she's hog-tied—maybe laying on a sheet on the floor. Uh, oh . . ."

"What else do you see? Who else do you see?" Vukich urged him on.

"I just, uh, I maybe—boy, maybe one other person, but I don't see a face, but Jim Rabie stands out, boy, for some reason."

*   *   *

From this tape-recorded exchange it's obvious that Paul Ingram was trying hard to produce something, anything, that might help the detectives in their search for the man who raped Julie and made her fear for her life. He trusted his interrogators, who were also his friends and colleagues, and he believed they were telling him the truth. Guilt and anxiety corroded his self-confidence, while religious fervor and fear for the state of his soul stoked his imagination.

Dr. Peterson asked Ingram if he had ever been involved in any kind of occult activities. "Before your conversion to Christianity, were you ever involved in any kind of black magic?"

"Uh, at one time I read a little bit of astrology but, you know, like in the paper, read your, what do you call that?"

"Horoscope," Vukich offered.

"Horoscope," Ingram confirmed. "Uh, nothing other than that."

Had he ever been involved in sacrilegious activities or participated in animal sacrifices?

"I don't know what you're driving at," Ingram said.

"The Satan cult kind of thing," Schoenig said.

Ingram denied any recollections of such activities, but inside something clicked. Maybe Satan and his demonic forces had some hold on him. Maybe the Prince of Darkness was struggling for control of his soul. Wouldn't that help to explain why a Christian man who loved his family and wanted only to do what was right was suddenly and inexplicably cast into the role of rapist and pedophile? If Satan had engineered these evil deeds and taken control of Ingram's mind and soul, he could also have erased Ingram's memory. Wouldn't that explain the strange sensations and sudden fleeting images that entered his mind like distant radio static, almost as if God were trying to get through and make known the truth? Satanic deception made sense. It was the only thing that did.

While the thought of Satan as the controlling force in this increasingly horrifying situation gave Ingram some solace, the parallel idea, that Satan might have chosen him as a likely target and at this very moment might be guiding his destiny, filled him with terror. Was he in the claws of the demon? Ingram's emotional stability cracked and swayed. Praying, sobbing, crying out in anguish, closing his eyes and rocking back and forth, he appeared to be close to a breakdown. Sensing Ingram's weakness and playing on his deep religious convictions, Peterson counseled Ingram to choose between God and the devil.

"If there's ever been a time that you've been offered a choice between the devil and God it's right now," Peterson said.

"Right. Oh, dear Jesus, Lord just help me . . ." Ingram's voice trailed off.

"So that you don't sacrifice—" Peterson began.

"You'd sacrifice your daughter," Schoenig interrupted. "I can't believe that, Paul."

"You can't come back from this, Paul, if you don't meet it and get over it," Vukich said.

"I know, I know." Ingram began to cry.

"You want somethin' to, uh, to wipe your eyes with?" Vukich asked.

"No, just keep talking, just keep talking," Ingram said.

"You need to cry and you need to let it out," Peterson counseled.

"It goes back to the poker games, Paul," Vukich said. "You're the man with the answers."

"You're not going to fall apart," Peterson said.

"Oh, dear God," Ingram said.

"Choose life over living death. A living hell," Peterson said.

"That's your responsiblity as a father," Vukich said.

"Dear God, dear God . . . Dear God help me."

"It's a clear choice between adherence to that living hell that you've been living," Peterson said, "and cleansing absolution of honesty. You have to make that decision. No one can make it for you. . . . It's your decision. You are as alone as Jesus was in the desert when he was comforted."

The detectives, recognizing that Ingram was profoundly affected by the religious references, saw the wisdom of Peterson's strategy. "God's given you the tools to do this, Paul," Vukich said.

"Oh, Jesus, merciful Jesus, help me."

"And now he's left it up to you to make the decision," Vukich continued. "You've got to show him by what you do and what you say as to whether or not you're worthy of his love and redemption and salvation."

"Oh, Jesus!" Ingram suddenly cried out. "Help me, Lord! Help me, Lord!"

Peterson took over, abandoning his formerly aggressive stance and speaking in a soft, soothing tone. "One of the things that would help you, Paul, is if you'd stop asking for help and just let yourself sit back, not try to think about anything," he said soothingly. "Just let yourself go and relax. No one's going to hurt you. We want to help. Just relax. Try not to think about anything, and ask yourself what it is you need to do. An answer will come. . . ."

Paul Ingram's eyes closed, his body went limp, and once again he appeared to enter a kind of trance. Sensing that the time was right, the detectives immediately focused in on the poker-party rape scene that Julie had described in her letter.

"Why don't you tell us what happened to Julie, Paul," Vukich said. "What happened at that poker game?"

"I see Julie lying on the floor on a sheet," Ingram said, his voice strange and faraway. "Her hands are tied to her feet, she's on her stomach. I'm standing there looking at her. Somebody else is on my left."

"Who is that?"

"But I, the, the only person that keeps coming back is Jim Rabie. He just . . ."

"Turn around and look at that person," Schoenig suggested. "Who is it? Who's standing right there?"

"What's he smell like?" Peterson asked.

"Yeah, what's he smell like?" Schoenig repeated.

"He's standing right next to you, Paul, all you have to do is just look to your left and there he is," Vukich said.

"He, he's standing up," Ingram said. "I see his penis sticking up in the air, uh . . ."

"Does he have any clothes on?"

"I don't think so."

"What's he doing to your daughter?"

"Getting down on his knees."

"Okay. Now he's there, he's in front of you on his knees?" Schoenig prompted. "Look at him. What's he doing to her? Is his penis touching her?"

"Just, just let me, uh, it's leaving." The picture in Ingram's mind was fading.

"No it's not, it's there, Paul," Vukich encouraged him.

"Come on, we have to get back there," Schoenig said, somewhat frantically. "What's he doing to your daughter? He's on his knees. Is he in front of your daughter or behind your daughter?"

"He's behind my daughter."

"Okay, is he putting his penis in her?"

"Uh, her legs are close together, but maybe she's being rolled over onto her side," Ingram said, responding to the suggestion.

"Is she clothed or unclothed?" Peterson asked.

"Uh, she, unclothed I believe, uh . . ."

"What's this person doing?"

"He's kneeling. His penis is by her stomach. Uh, he's big. Uh, I mean, broad-shouldered, big person."

"Does he have any jewelry on?"

"May have a watch on his right hand."

"What time does it say?"

"Uh, two o'clock, and I don't know why I say that, uh, I can't see him, I see his chest."

The questions keep coming, fast and furious: How close are you? Are you dressed? Are you touching her? Is anyone else touching her? Do you remember ejaculating? Are you guys intoxicated?

"Is somebody taking pictures?" Vukich asked out of the blue.

"Uh, pictures, is there somebody off to the right of me, uh, it's possible, let me look. I see, I see a camera."

"Who's taking the pictures?"

"I don't know. I don't see a person behind the camera."

"That person's very important. He's the one that holds the key," Peterson jumped in.

"Well, the person that I think I see is Ray Risch," Ingram said. Risch, a mechanic who worked for the Washington State Patrol, was a good friend of Ingram's and a regular at the weekend poker games.

"Is he saying anything?" Vukich asked.

"I don't know. Uh, I, I, I don't know . . . oh boy, where am I at, where am I at?"

At the end of that second day, after more than five hours of interrogation, Paul Ingram seemed to emerge from his trance and take stock of what had happened. "Boy, it's almost like I'm making it up, but I'm not . . . trying not to. What do I have here. What do I have here. Who am I seeing here. It doesn't make sense. . . . It's like I'm watching a movie," he concluded. "Uh, oh, it's like a horror movie."

"Paul, I'm not sure that you should go on at this point," Dr. Peterson said, expressing concern about Ingram's state of mind.

But Ingram rambled on. He was no longer talking to his interrogators; he was communing with God. "I don't have a clear picture. I . . . I'm not sure what I'm seeing. I . . . I don't know what I've got in my mind here. Doesn't make any sense to me. Uh, Lord help me. Give me . . . figure out what this is. I don't want to see things that aren't right, Lord. I mean, things that aren't true. Get me through this Lord. . . . I don't know where I'm at now. Let me just relax. Let me relax. Lord, give me a picture. Give me a picture."

When Jim Rabie and Ray Risch were confronted with the fact that their friend and colleague Paul Ingram had identified them as sexual abusers, they employed the same denials and claims of memory loss initially used by Ingram.

"I wasn't present that I know of, unless I blocked it out of my head," Risch told detectives.

Rabie insisted that he had no memory of the events and, in an eerie echo of Ingram's initial reaction, mentioned the possibility of a "dark side." When one of the detectives suggested he might be in denial, Rabie responded, "I honestly do not have any recollection of that happening, and I do not believe that I could've done it and blocked it out."

Detective Schoenig, in an obvious attempt to tease out a confession, stretched the facts. "Paul said you guys bullied him and you made him do this and he didn't want to do this," Schoenig told Rabie. "Ray [Risch] is saying basically the same thing. Only he's saying that he was the one who was the weakling, and he's saying you and Paul were the worst two."

The idea of his two good friends offering testimony against him, possibly in an attempt to secure immunity from prosecution and save themselves, was too much for Rabie. He caved in under the pressure. "Give me the responsibility, because I've blocked it out enough—I must be the worst one," Rabie confessed. "The only option is to lock me up, and you're going to have to throw away the key, because if I can't remember this, then I am so damn dangerous I do not deserve to be loose."

"I know I have a demon in me," Paul Ingram told Pastor John Bratun, begging the minister to deliver him from his "demon possession." Bratun assured Ingram that he was not possessed by demons, although he would have to be delivered of evil spirits. After the two men prayed together, Bratun told Ingram to kneel on the floor, lean over a wastebasket, and try to retch up the spirits residing deep within him. Ingram's dry heaves produced some phlegm, but not the dark mass that he felt as a massive physical presence at the center of his very being.

After this ritual, Ingram was visited by a vivid memory featuring his son Chad and his friend Jim Rabie. In his mind Ingram could see Rabie, angry and intent on his goal, pushing him down the stairs. "He wanted to do something that I didn't want him to do," Ingram said. "He said he wanted Chad. . . . Rabie shoved his way into Chad's room and ripped the boy's pants off. . . . I was powerless to do anything. He forced Chad down and had anal sex with him."

Chad was interviewed less than a week later by Detective Schoenig and psychologist Richard Peterson. At first he couldn't remember being sexually abused by Jim Rabie or anyone else, although he did recall slashing his wrists in a suicide attempt three years earlier when he was seventeen years old.

"What upset you so badly?" Peterson asked.

"Uh, probably something my dad said," Chad responded. "I can't remember . . . I can't remember specifics."

"Maybe this is the key," Schoenig suggested. "Why don't you think about it. It was something like the doctor [Peterson] said, it was something very traumatic to you that your dad said that really hurt you. Maybe it hurt your manhood . . . some abandonment reason or something . . . a put-down or something. What was it, Chad? Think about it."

"I'm thinking, I'm thinking," Chad said.

"Maybe this is the key," Schoenig repeated.

"Uh, I can remember he yelled at me for something, but I can't remember what it was for."

"The memories," Peterson said. "You remember."

"Well, all I felt . . . I felt angry," Chad said.

"But you can remember what happened," Peterson coaxed. "You need to remember what happened. You can choose to remember that if you want to."

"Like what?" Chad was bewildered. "What do you mean, remember?"

"Instead of saying I think this might have happened, but I don't know if it did or not. I can't remember," Schoenig said.

"Oh," Chad said, clearly confused by the detective's "explanation."

"The memories are there," Schoenig said. "We're trying to help you, Chad."

"I know. I know. They're there. I just can't . . . I can't put the dot on it, though. I can't."

"Well, I'm not surprised," Peterson said reassuringly. "It's not unusual with kids who have been through what you've been through to not be able to remember it the first time you go through it, because they don't want to remember. Number one, they don't want to remember. Number two, they've been programmed not to remember."

Chad responded to this rather insidious suggestion with an interested but noncommittal "Mm-hm."

"And I think something happened to you that made you not want to remember," Peterson said. "I just have to ask myself just what kind of crap have you been exposed to that you can't feel . . ."

"This may go back to what I earlier talked to you about," Schoenig said, "about something that happened to you in the fear of real death or fear for somebody else's families or death, and maybe I'm even going to suggest that it may have to do with something your dad said to you because you had said you were going to tell."

Chad was quiet for a few moments as the detective and the psychologist traded theories about his lack of memory. When asked a direct question, he answered with short, one- or two-word phrases or simply parroted back what was said to him.

"Had you been drinking?"

"No."

"Smoking pot or anything?"

"No."

"Just feeling miserable."

"Just feeling miserable."

"And alone."

"And alone."

"How about humiliated?"

"Probably."

"Come on, Chad, it's there," Schoenig said impatiently.

"I know it's there. I just can't . . . it's just not . . . it's like . . ."

"You can deal with this and you can learn," Peterson interjected. "You can choose to deal with the memories. You can choose to live. That's what it is. It's a funny little place between not feeling and learning to live with the feelings that you've got, but you've got to get them."

"Right," Chad agreed.

"You can make the choice, but you got to get them," Peterson repeated.

"Right," Chad said again.

"You can make the choice and nobody's going to destroy you because you have those feelings."

"Right."

The conversation eventually drifted toward a discussion of Chad's dreams. He described one particularly vivid dream involving "little people" who came into his bedroom and walked around on his bed. The little people's faces were painted with black, white, and red streaks of jagged lightning, like the members of the rock group Kiss.

"Those are dreams of being invaded," Peterson said.

"Yeah, I would look out my door and I would see—"

"And unprotected?"

"Yeah, I would see a house of mirrors and . . . and no way of getting out."

"Of being violated, trapped in an unescapable situation."

"Mm-hm."

"Those dreams have a key . . . being crazy at the time."

"Mm-hm."

"What happened to you was so horrible."

"Right."

"What happened to you was terrible."

"You don't want to accept what really happened to you and that's why you're seeing the ways of no escape and you want to believe it's dreams," Schoenig said, adding his two-bit analysis. "You don't want to believe it's real. It was real. It was real, Chad."

"What you saw was real, Chad," Peterson repeated.

"We know that, Chad," Schoenig said. "You weren't dreaming."

"It's no dream," Peterson said.

"No," Chad protested weakly, "this was outside my window, though."

"What you saw was real," Schoenig said. "This same type of stuff has come out of your dad, too."

"Okay," Chad said.

"So let's get into it," Schoenig said.

They "got into" another dream, in which a train went by, a whistle blew, and a witch came into Chad's window. When he woke up, Chad explained, he couldn't move his arms. It was as if somebody was on top of him.

"That's exactly real," Schoenig said. "That's the key, Chad. That's what was really going on."

"Chad, these things happened to you," Peterson chimed in.

"Okay," Chad said somewhat dubiously.

"They assaulted your ability to know what was real."

"Okay," Chad repeated. He obligingly described the witch in his dream. She was fat, and she wore a black robe like the witch in *The Wizard of Oz*. Four guys outside the window were skinny and had long curly black hair. He remembered biting someone's thigh. The witch was on top of him.

"Look at her face." Schoenig suggested. "Who does she look like to you? Somebody you know . . . it is somebody you know. Who is this person? Somebody who is a friend of your family's?"

Chad said he couldn't see the witch's face because it was dark. All he could remember was being pinned down and not being able to move or talk.

"You've got to find it inside yourself to see who this person is and what they're doing to you, Chad," Schoenig said. "You don't want to remember 'cause it's horrible and so devastating . . . something you never wanted to believe happened to you, but it did. We can stop it, Chad. We can help it from ever happening again. . . ."

"Can you breathe?" Peterson asked.

"Is there something that's keeping you from talking?" asked Schoenig. "What's in your mouth?"

"Just let the memory come," Peterson enjoined. "It's not what you think about; it's what you're trying not to think about."

The suggestive questioning and pressure to remember continued, hour after hour. At one point Chad insisted that he felt safe in his home. "I felt safe. I don't know, maybe I wasn't safe, but I did feel safe. I've always felt safe."

"Even when all this was going on," Schoenig said disbelievingly.

"Except for the dreams, because I thought they were, I put them off as dreams."

When Chad kept insisting that he couldn't remember anything, and that he thought his dreams were just that, dreams and not reality, Peterson proposed that he was suffering from a "destruction of his sense of reality," a "destruction of the sense of self," a "destruction of any ability to feel." "Total, absolute obedience and subservience to the group," he added somewhat mysteriously.

Schoenig brought the conversation back to the person sitting on Chad's chest. The detective reminded Chad that he had something in his mouth.

"And it's not cloth," he prompted.

"Right."

"It's not hard like a piece of wood."

"Right."

"What is it?"

Chad was laughing. "You just made me think, oh golly."

"What is it?"

"I don't know, I don't know."

"What were you just thinking, come on."

"I thought it was a penis, okay. I, it could be."

"Okay, don't be embarrassed," Schoenig consoled. "It could be. Then what's happening to you? Let it out. It's okay."

"I don't know what's happening to me," Chad said wretchedly.

Several minutes later Detective Schoenig chastised Chad for continuing to mistake his reality for dreams. "They were real. You know that. You've already told us that many times today you know it's not a dream. So quit trying to push it off as a dream."

"No, but it's kind of hard," Chad protested feebly. "Twenty years you been pushing off as a dream and then one day you've got to take it all as reality. You don't know what to take as reality."

"But remember, you've had time to think about it for the last couple weeks . . ."

"No, well . . . I didn't know I was a victim until I talked to you the last time."

"And what I'm saying to you, Chad, you've had time to think about it now and I'm going to believe that part of your mind is still trying to—"

"Block it out, right, right." By this time Chad knew all about the theory of repressed memories.

"Block it out because you don't want to believe it really happened to you," Schoenig continued.

"Right."

"Wouldn't it feel great to say this was real. It's not a dream," Peterson said.

"That's why I want to see faces so I can pin it on the faces," Chad agreed. "So I can say these are the ones that did it to me. I've seen the faces, I remember who you are, and go on with it from there. I've got to put a face to it."

The tape recorder was turned off, and during that time Chad found his memory. When the tape started again, Chad said that he remembered a man sitting on top of him; the man's knees were pinning down Chad's arms so he couldn't move. He was wearing jeans and a flannel shirt, and his penis was in Chad's mouth.

The dream had become reality; the witch had metamorphosed from a faceless woman into his father's good friend and poker buddy Jim Rabie.

"How certain are you that it's Jim Rabie?" Schoenig asked.

"Oh, eighty percent sure. Seventy percent. Not . . ."

"What's the part of you that feels like it isn't Jim Rabie?"

"Well, kind of the feeling that it was a dream."

"We've eliminated that it wasn't a dream, right?"

"Okay, okay. Still, confusion, uh, I don't know. It just doesn't . . . I don't know."

At the end of the seven-hour interview, Chad complained of a headache. "It's the memories coming back," Peterson reassured him.

The next day, under intense questioning, Chad reported that he had recovered another memory. Now he recalled that when he was ten or eleven years old, he had been sodomized in his basement by another friend and poker buddy of his father's—Ray Risch.

On December 16, not quite three weeks after her husband was arrested and booked in the Thurston County jail, Sandy Ingram drove to the Church of Living Water to talk to her minister. Pastor Bratun explained to Sandy, just as he had explained to her husband in his jail cell, that she was eighty percent evil and twenty percent good. The good portion controlled conscious memory, while the evil portion controlled her unconscious mind. Bratun expressed his opinion that either Sandy knew about the brutalities that went on in her own house but stayed on the sidelines, or she had been a willing participant. If she didn't confess, he counseled her, she would probably go to jail. Sandy Ingram angrily refused Bratun's suggestion that she confess. "That may work with some people, but not with me," she said in an obvious reference to her husband. After this conversation, Sandy went home, packed a few necessities, and with her youngest son Mark, drove five hours across the state in a blinding snowstorm. The next day she wrote in her diary, appealing for divine guidance. "I am afraid Jesus . . . Where have my children gone, my precious babies that I love . . ."

Three days later Sandy Ingram returned to Olympia and immediately sought out her pastor, who tried to console her with the reminder that she was still twenty percent good. The evil part—he elaborated on his earlier explanation—was trying to cover up the past and repress the memories, while the good part was bravely attempting to bring the truth to light. Bratun told her about the new, even more shocking events being recalled by her husband, involving satanism, barnyard rituals, blood oaths, and high priests and priestesses. In one of these memories Paul visualized his wife having sex with Ray Risch. Sandy began to cry.

Soon afterward, buoyed by Pastor Bratun's assurances that the remaining twenty percent good in her was struggling to remember, Sandy recovered a memory of being tied up on her living room floor with Jim Rabie. Then, in one of those strange illogical leaps so common to dreams, she recalled being in the closet with her husband, who was hitting her with a piece of wood while Risch and Rabie laughed at her. When Paul finally let her out of the closet, Risch and Rabie pinned her down and forced her to have anal intercourse.

The day after Christmas Sandy wrote a letter to her husband in which she confessed her fears and her struggle to remember the terrible events that had apparently taken place in their home. Although she had already recovered some memories with the help of her pastor, she told Paul she still could not remember what happened and was frightened because she did not know the truth. "I am not remembering anything," she wrote, "but with God's help I will remember."

The letter abruptly shifted from the recent past, with its locked store-house of repressed memories, to the easily accessed memories of the distant past, when the children were little and life was good and filled with promise. Sandy asked Paul if he remembered the children when they were babies. They were so good and so smart, she remembered, so beautiful and so tiny. When they cried, she would try to soothe them, but as soon as Paul came home and held them, they stopped crying—did he remember that? Did he remember when they met, and how shy he was? Did he remember the drive-in movie (but not, she added coyly, the movie)?

With those final appeals to her husband's happier memories, Sandy Ingram ended her letter.

On December 30, 1988, Ericka Ingram gave police and prosecutors a written statement, detailing for the first time her memories of satanic ritual abuse. "From the time I was about 5 yrs. old until the time I was bout 12 years old . . . I remember being carried from my bed, by my father, in the middle of the night," her statement began. A group of men and women, including her mother, Jim Rabie, Ray Risch, and a High Priestess dressed in a robe, waited for them by the barn. Ericka was dressed only in a nightgown, and her father wore a "gown and hat resembling viking hat with horns."

Inside the barn the group crowded around the table, and everyone took turns stabbing a six- to eight-month-old baby with a knife, continuing the bloody rite even after the infant was dead. The high priestess dressed the corpse in "something white" and then buried it in a pit in the ground. "They would tell me this is what would happen to me, also," Ericka ended her statement. "They also would say you will not remember this. They would say it over and over again like a chant."

Julie also began to remember some "satanic stuff," although her memory was not nearly so vivid or detailed as her sister's. She remembered burying animals but couldn't say for sure if the animals had been sacrificed or had died a natural death. In response to detectives' questions she said she couldn't remember attending any ceremonies other than church services. When asked if she had any scars from the abuse she suffered, she emphatically nodded her head yes, explaining that she had scars from the knife wounds inflicted by her father and Jim Rabie. But she would not permit anyone to look at the scars because, she said, they made her self-conscious . . . so self-conscious that she refused to change her clothes in the high school locker room and never wore a bathing suit without a T-shirt.

Eventually, under pressure from Jim Rabie's and Ray Risch's attorneys, both Julie and Ericka agreed to be examined by a female doctor who specialized in the treatment of sexual abuse. Although the doctor searched their bodies thoroughly, she could find no unusual marks or scars.

Less than a month after his session with Dr. Peterson and Detectives Vukich and Schoenig, Chad Ingram retracted his statement. The whole scene with the witch and the penis and the recovered memories of Jim Rabie and Ray Risch abusing him were just bad dreams. Nothing more.

Ericka's stories became increasingly bizarre and lurid. She claimed that her father had forced her to have sex with goats and dogs. Her mother also had sex with the animals, while her father took pictures. Ericka said she had been assaulted by Jim Rabie many times, perhaps as many as a hundred; after one of the assaults, she claimed that Rabie, her mother, and her father took turns defecating on her. She described satanic orgies, infant sacrifices, and gruesome abortions. She said she personally witnessed the sacrifice of twenty-five or more babies, whose tiny, mutilated bodies were buried in the woods behind the Ingram house. And once, Ericka recalled, cult members aborted her baby with a coat hanger and rubbed the fetus's bloody, dismembered body all over her naked torso.

The increasingly bizarre accusations of satanic ritual abuse and human sacrifices led the prosecution to Richard Ofshe, an expert on cults and mind control and professor of sociology at the University of California at Berkeley.

"Do you have any experience with satanic cults?" Gary Tabor, the chief prosecutor on the Ingram case, asked Ofshe in their first telephone conversation. Tabor related the basic details of the case, including the stories of satanic ritual abuse. He clearly wanted a serious answer, and Richard Ofshe had one for him.

"No," said Ofshe, "and if anyone tells you they do, they're lying, because there's no proof that baby-killing satanic cults even exist."

Ofshe knew all about the satanic ritual abuse rumors that were igniting people's imaginations in little towns and big cities all over the country. He was familiar with the theory that satanic cults "programmed" their members, a feat allegedly accomplished by secret technology known only to the high priests and priestesses of the cult. Some therapists were trying to link this devilish scrambling of minds with the creation of multiple personalities, a disorder that, if it actually appeared, Ofshe liked to quip, it did so as frequently as Siamese twins joined at the head.

Ofshe doubted if multiple personality even existed as a separate and identifiable diagnostic category; he believed it was much more likely that highly suggestible people began to display the symptoms that their therapists unwittingly suggested. And yet swarms of therapists and law enforcement officials were now claiming that repeated abuse, particularly satanic ritual abuse, caused the personality to fracture into numerous pieces. Memories of abuse then supposedly gravitated toward the alter personalities, where they were quickly buried beneath consciousness; this allowed the "host" personality to carry on with the duties and responsibilities of a normal life.

Ofshe kept close track of the burgeoning claims concerning MPD and post-traumatic stress disorder (another fad diagnosis, in his opinion), and he had a thick collection of satanic ritual abuse stories alleging blood-drinking, cannibalism, ritual abortions, sadistic tortures, and murder. He was well acquainted with the bizarre theories offered to explain why no scars, corpses, bones, or other concrete evidence could be found. Theory one: The cult is so skillfully organized that no outsider can penetrate its highest levels (some MPD experts compare the cult structure to that of the Communist party). Theory two: Talented plastic surgeons (who are also dedicated cult members) work their magic to cover up the wounds inflicted during various tortures and rituals. Theory three: Aborted babies and the bones of sacrificed victims are incinerated in mini-crematoria in the basements of the cult leaders' mansions. Theory four: Cult members' minds are emptied of all knowledge through secret, highly effective brainwashing techniques. Theory five: Police officers and other law enforcement personnel charged with finding the bodies never turn up any evidence because they are satanists themselves.

But where was the proof to support these outlandish theories? Ofshe wondered. Any scientist worth his salt would demand proof before he permitted himself to accept something that couldn't be seen. Science demands facts; science requires a hypothesis that can be disproven (many scientists believe in God, Ofshe reminded himself, but that was a personal matter); and no one, to his knowledge, had uncovered a real, practicing, baby-murdering satanic cult, just as no one had ever produced in the flesh an angel or an alien.

Ofshe had witnessed some bizarre goings-on in his work with cults and cult-inspired individuals, and there was no disputing the fact that atrocities and abominations were committed by "normal" human beings committed to bizarre ideologies. Look at Patty Hearst, a decent human being whose mind was so effectively manipulated that she identified with her captors, even protecting them in a bank holdup. But the Symbionese Liberation Army—Hearst's kidnappers—existed; the firestorm in which they died was filmed on TV; the tapes, messages, and kidnapping were all documented facts. So far there was no evidence whatsoever confirming the existence of an elusive conspiracy of blood-drinking, infant-murdering, cannibalistic satanists.

"This is real," the prosecutor was saying. "Ingram was accused by his two grown daughters, and he confessed not once, not twice, but many, many times."

Confessions didn't impress Ofshe. He had just completed a scholarly paper detailing several cases in which people caved in to police pressure, confessing to crimes they could not remember committing. In Europe three hundred years ago, tens of thousands of people confessed that they were witches, and were summarily burned at the stake for their dastardly but unproven deeds. Many of the so-called witches confessed under brutal and relentless torture, but many more spontaneously admitted their evildoings—and willingly pointed their fingers at relatives, friends, and neighbors.

For centuries a passionate belief in God and the devil contributed to the bizarre mythology of witches, just as, in modern times, a belief in the possibility of life on other planets was sending scores of people into psychiatrist's offices with tales of being abducted by aliens who experimented with their sexual organs. How many people—like Shirley MacLaine, whose books were gobbled up like popcorn—believed that they had lived before, as princesses, or pirates, or personal witnesses to the crucifixion of Jesus Christ? Were those memories real, too?

Still, Ofshe wasn't willing to automatically dismiss the possibility of an organized network of satanists. Something was happening out there, and he wanted to understand what it was and where it was coming from. If Paul Ingram really was a high priest in a satanic cult, and if the facts could be proven beyond a reasonable doubt, Ofshe wanted to be part of that investigation. If Paul Ingram confessed because he'd been influenced by coercive and suggestive tactics of a police department committed to uncovering the crime of the century, then he wanted to be part of that, too.

"What can I do for you?" he asked the prosecutor.

Paul Ingram knew that Richard Ofshe had been retained by the prosecutor's office, but he was more than willing to tell the gray-and-white-bearded professor with the dark, soulful eyes anything he wanted to know about his memories and his methods of retrieving them. By that time, early in February 1989, Ingram had endured more than two months of intensive interrogations, and his attempts to access his lost memories had developed into a regularly practiced step-by-step process.

His first step was to pray. His minister had assured him that God would fill his mind with true images if he was diligent about prayer before he began the memory recovery process. After a good long talk with God, he would sit on his bed, close his eyes, breathe deeply, and try to relax. This was easier at night when the other prisoners had settled down and the jail was relatively quiet, but Ingram tried to practice his relaxation exercises many times throughout the day.

The next stage in the process was "mind-emptying." Ingram would try to imagine that he was drifting into a warm, white fog, a visualization exercise he had stumbled across in a magazine article. Pastor Bratun also encouraged him to use his imagination in the mind-emptying process. In fact, Bratun suggested that Ingram spend a full eight hours a day trying to see with the mind's eye. "Think of it," Bratun told him, "as your full-time job." The pastor discouraged Ingram from reading Westerns or other novels and even pointed out that his Bible study should not interfere with these forays into his inner mind.

Once Ingram succeeded in entering the warm white fog, he tried to float around in there for several minutes, patiently waiting for the images to come into his mind. After a while fragments of memories would drift back into consciousness. He had little or no control over these fleeting images, and sometimes they were completely unrelated to the particular memories he was trying to reconstruct.

As Ingram described the bizarre, splintered nature of these highly visual memories, Ofshe became suspicious. Was Ingram confusing fantasy and reality? The phrase "influence machine" kept running through Ofshe's mind. Paul Ingram had a problem, a big problem, and anyone with a problem is vulnerable to people who claim to have solutions. The more uncertain and unstable the person is, the more easily influenced. And Paul Ingram was a quaking mass of uncertainty and instability. He was anxious to please, concerned about his family's safety, eager to believe in scriptural injunctions and therapeutic prescriptions, and desperate for an end to his torment.

Ofshe had no doubt that Ingram was visualizing events and that those visualizations were real experiences to him. But a "real" visualization, daydream, or hallucination is not the same thing as a memory of a real, verifiable, objective event. Ingram had been given certain facts about the abuse and encouraged to "pray on" those alleged events. Once he agreed to the basic paradigm—Your daughters say you raped them; you must have repressed the memory; if you try hard enough you can find the memories; confess and ye shall be free—he was on the road to confirming its existence. Once the folklore was established, it generated its own evidence. Ingram's confabulations became the foundation for his "memories": The more he confabulated, the more confident he became that he was guilty, and as his confidence increased, he was driven inexorably toward confession. Imagining that these events might have happened, he became increasingly sure that they actually did happen, and to account for his continuing lack of memory he invoked the mysterious mechanism that had been carefully explained to him: repression.

Sigmund Freud would turn over in his grave, Ofshe thought. All these psychotherapists spouting off about repression borrowed their ideas from some loose theoretical concepts offered by Freud nearly a hundred years earlier. Childhood trauma is the root of our problems, therapists claim (that's early Freud); traumatized children often repress their memories in order to avoid psychic pain (that's Freud stretched thin); and the primary goal of therapy is to draw out repressed memories and bring the traumas out into the light of day where their dark power can be dissipated (that's dime-store Freud). Repression had become a magical cure, and only those therapists perceptive and compassionate enough to recognize its presence could, through skillful and long-term techniques, tap into a patient's abcessed memory and allow the aching pain of a lifetime to drain away.

That was the theory, anyway. But with such oversimplification and distortion of Freud's complex theories taking place in a culture supremely sensitized to incest and sexual abuse, people were walking into therapists' offices and being asked outright if they had ever been physically, sexually or emotionally abused in childhood. If no memories came to mind, they were told not to worry: Many people who were abused don't remember what happened to them. And then began the process of excavating the buried memories through numerous invasive techniques such as age-regression, guided visualization, trance writing, dream work, body work, on and on, you name it.

Freud believed it was theoretically possible for a person to repress a traumatic event—and, particularly, the emotional associations connected to that event—but he'd have torn out whole chunks of his beard at these cowboy versions of his spare, elegant theories. Even if he surmised that a patient was employing the defense mechanism of repression, Freud would never have used such crude bulldozing techniques to dig up the lost material. In fact, Freud stopped hypnotizing his patients when he recognized that hypnosis can elicit wild confabulations bearing no resemblance whatsoever to reality. Ofshe wondered why therapists hadn't picked up on that penetrating Freudian insight, particularly since present-day experimental techniques consistently verified that formal hypnosis creates a highly suggestible state in which visualizations, hallucinations, and dreams can be confused with real events.

To complicate reality even further, hypnotized patients tend to be extremely confident that such pseudomemories represent real events and experiences. Once a patient has convinced herself that certain events occurred, she'll believe it so completely that if she took a polygraph she'd pass. All a polygraph measures is a person's conviction that something may be true or false, not the accuracy or authenticity of the event being described.

Even though most modern-day therapists understand the general idea of hypnotic suggestibility, many invest hypnosis with magical healing powers. Hypnosis is considered to function like a sort of truth serum, permitting lost material to break through the invisible but stubborn barrier between the conscious and unconscious minds. This misconception, coupled with the fact that most therapists have only a rudimentary knowledge of the reconstructive nature of memory, can lead to the creation of false memories within the therapeutic environment.

"I never use hypnosis!" a therapist might object. But as the Paul Ingram case demonstrates, you don't need formal hypnotic induction techniques to induce a trance state; all you need is a suggestible client with a problem. Ingram clearly described a process of self-hypnosis—relaxation, mind-emptying, mental imagery—and the visual, fragmentary quality of his "memories" strongly suggested that they were pseudomemories induced by his trance state rather than genuine memories accurately recovered from a traumatic past. Through well-rehearsed and studiously practiced relaxation and guided-imagery techniques, Ingram was putting himself into a trance, experiencing dissociation and heightened suggestibility.

Ofshe was aware of the phenomenon known as "the Grade 5 personality," a collection of psychological traits common to highly hypnotizable individuals. Herb Spiegel, a psychiatrist from New York who worked for a time with the multiple personality disorder patient known as Sybil, coined the phrase "Grade 5 Syndrome" to describe the five to ten percent of the population who are so hypnotizable and suggestible that they can shift instantaneously and almost imperceptibly from normal consciousness into a deep hypnotic trance state. "Grade 5s" are inordinately trusting, exhibiting in Spiegel's words, "an intense, beguiling expectation of support from others." They display a firm and steady confidence in the goodwill of their therapists, readily absorbing all suggestions, compulsively filling in the blanks in their memories, and accepting incongruent, unlikely, or even impossible information as real and valid.

Despite their confabulatory and fantastical nature, memories recalled in a hypnotic state will seem utterly real to a Grade 5; even after returning to normal consciousness, a Grade 5 will recall the memories with a compelling emotional quality, fervently affirming the truth and authenticity of the remembered experience. The memory distortions and enhancements that occur in hypnotic states are ignored or minimized by therapists who seek to reconnect their patients with forgotten memories and emotions. Therapists (or, as in the Ingram case, police interrogators) who are not aware of the "trance logic" used by Grade 5s to incorporate illogical or contradictory material into their memory systems can be hooked into believing the memories are real. Through words or gestures they can then offer the client validation and permission to permanently record the images into long-term memory.

The more Ofshe listened to Paul Ingram, the more he was convinced that Ingram was highly suggestible. The only other plausible scenario was that Ingram was lying, but Ofshe couldn't fathom why the man would purposely and consciously fabricate memories that would tear his family apart, destroy his career and reputation, and send him to jail for the rest of his life. He was confused, no doubt about that, but he was not insane.

Ofshe made a sudden and spontaneous decision to conduct a field "experiment" to test his theories.

"I was talking to one of your sons and one of your daughters," he said to Ingram, "and they told me about something that happened. It was about a time when you made them have sex with each other while you watched. Do you remember that?"

Ingram looked confused. He told Ofshe he had no memory of that particular incident.

Ofshe assured him that the event had happened; both his children clearly remembered it. Ingram was silent for several minutes, his head in his hands. Where did this happen? he asked. In the house the family currently lived in, he was told.

"Try to think about the scene, try to see it happening," Ofshe suggested, purposely using the same words and phrases Ingram employed to describe his process of memory reconstruction.

Ingram closed his eyes; after a moment of reflection he said that he was beginning to "get" some images in his mind and could actually "see" himself in the scene that Ofshe had briefly described for him.

Ofshe was struck by Ingram's use of the present tense. He seemed to be experiencing the "memory" with what Herb Spiegel called the "telescoped time sense" of the Grade 5 syndrome. When Grade 5s are asked to travel back in time to a prior moment in their lives, they typically relate the unfolding narrative in the present tense. For example, rather than saying "I was standing on the street corner when I heard the siren," a Grade 5 might say, "I am standing on the street corner and I hear a siren." This subjective experience of actually being part of the memory as it happens enhances the emotional immediacy and believability of the recalled event.

At this point, Ofshe decided to put a temporary halt to the memory retrieval process. Ingram was highly suggestible, no question about that, and Ofshe didn't want to influence his responses in any way. He asked Ingram to return to his jail cell and try to remember additional details by "praying on" the scene.

The next day Ingram told Ofshe that he could vividly recall what happened between his daughter and his oldest son, who he identified as Ericka and Paul Ross. Before Ingram elaborated any further on his memory, Ofshe asked him to return once again to his jail cell and prepare a written statement. At this point, Ofshe interviewed Ericka. "Did your father ever force you and one of your brothers to have sex while he watched?" Ofshe asked. Ericka assured him that nothing like that had ever happened.

Several hours later Paul Ingram handed Ofshe a three-page handwritten confession, complete with dialogue. Reading through the document, Ofshe was struck once again by Ingram's use of the present tense. It reads like a movie script, he thought, complete with set description.

> In Ericka's Bedroom on Fir Tree. Bunk Beds set up. Ericka + Julie are sharing the room. I ask or tell Paul Jr. + Ericka to come upstairs. . . . I tell them to undress. Ericka says "But Dad," I say "Just get undressed and don't argue." From my tone or the way I say it, neither objects and they undress themselves. I'm probably blocking the door so they could not get out. . . .
>
> I tell Ericka to kneel and to caress Paul's genitals. When erect I tell her to put the penis into her mouth and to orally stimulate him. . . .
>
> I have her lie on the floor. I caress her vagina and breasts and probably orally caress her vagina. I have vaginal sex. Paul watches all of this. If she did not have an orgasm I would have stimulated her with my fingers until she did.
>
> I may have told the children that they needed to learn the sex acts and how to do them right. That it is important that each participant have a pleasurable experience.
>
> I may have anal sex with Paul, not real clear. . . .
>
> The ability to control Paul + Ericka may not come entirely from me. It seems there is a real fear of Jim [Rabie] or someone else. Someone may have told me to do this with the kids. This is a feeling I have.

Paul Ingram had confessed with rich and abundant detail to something that never happened.

Ofshe moved on to the second and final stage in his field experiment. He needed to gauge his subject's confidence in his memories. Did Ingram believe with one-hundred-percent confidence that his visualizations were memories and not, at least in part, confabulations, hallucinations, or dream-induced imaginations? Was there any chance, for whatever reason, that he had deliberately or consciously fabricated the memories? Was he aware that his 1-2-3-4 steps of "praying on," relaxation, mind-emptying, and visualization could lead to dissociation and trance induction? And, finally, did he suspect that the detectives' leading questions and suggestive comments might be influencing and possibly creating the images that flashed into his mind?

A heated confrontation ensued, in which Ofshe told Ingram that he had invented the whole scene. Ofshe accused Ingram of lying and informed him that this was his opportunity to tell the truth and set the record straight.

Ingram became agitated and emotional. The images he had described were real, he insisted, as real as everything else he had remembered. He was telling the truth as he remembered it, and he had not intentionally or consciously padded his statement with fabricated details. No one was influencing him, he was not dissociating, and he was not trying to help the sheriff's department or protect his daughters by offering a detailed confession of something that never happened. Ingram insisted that his memories were authentic and that the scene had occurred just as he had decribed it.

Richard Ofshe returned to California with the term "witch-hunt" returning again and again to haunt him. In Salem, Massachusetts, three hundred years earlier, and in Europe during the sixteenth and seventeenth centuries, sane and rational people convinced themselves that witches were performing black magic and consorting with the devil. Now, at the close of the twentieth century, sane and rational people were getting hysterical about rumors that a murderous satanic cult had infiltrated their communities, sacrificed hundreds of aborted fetuses and newborn babies, forced young women to have sex with animals, and programmed the minds of normal churchgoing citizens to erase their memories of evildoing.

Satan—a cunning, resourceful enemy who threatened the moral order of an entire society—was alive and well in Olympia, Washington. An elaborate system of myths about the workings of evil had created its own evidence, and a community had gone daft with nonsense. Rumors and fears are often a thin cover for common prejudices. Satanists, witches, Gypsies, Jews, homosexuals, Communists—really, it didn't matter who the "demon" was as long as he encapsulated the most grotesque and terrifying images of evil. All prejudice begins with this process of stereotyping and then projecting outward onto an individual, a nonconforming group, an imagined entity, a political party, or an entire race the sense, the feeling, or the fear of diabolical malevolence.

Sane and intelligent human beings had been captured and imprisoned, once again, by a metaphor.

Ofshe was horrified at how quickly the moral outrage took fire and how rapidly the conflagration spread. This modern-day witch-hunt had begun at a church retreat, with a young woman's emotional breakdown and the suggestion by an authority figure that she had been abused. Over time, through contact with therapists and law enforcement officials, her stories solidified into an objective reality, which was enhanced by the fresh horrors offered by a sister and by a pastor's theories about satanic deception and the power of prayer to call forth God's truth. A psychologist's allusions to black magic, rampant speculations about the workings of the unconscious mind, and investigators' blind pursuit of "the truth" breathed life into the static images, creating a three-dimensional, never-ending horror show.

In the end it was all smoke and mirrors, a mass folly, a moral panic, the rumor mill gone haywire. No cult or conspiracy, no devil or priests, no blood-drinking or murdered babies could be discovered here—and for that matter, neither could the truth be discerned. Buried beneath countless layers of fantasy, smothered by speculaton, the truth had long ago died a peaceful, unremarkable death.

Ofshe sent his report to the prosecutor's office, detailing his concerns about the investigation and his conclusion that Paul Ingram was not guilty of the crimes to which he had confessed. The prosecutor, arguing that Ofshe's report did not constitute "exculpatory evidence," initially refused to hand over the report to Ingram's defense attorneys. Prodded by Ofshe's complaints, the presiding judge ordered prosecutors to share the report with Ingram and his attorneys.

On April 20, 1989, Detective Loreli Thompson, of the Lacey Police Department, examined Ericka and Julie Ingram for evidence of scarring, hoping to discover something the doctor had missed. Thompson typed up her conclusions in a memo titled "Supplemental Officer's Report, Reference: Examination of Ericka Ingram and Julie Ingram for Scars."

> On April 20, 1989, I asked Ericka to show me where she had been cut on her stomach by one of the defendants. She lifted her sweater and pointed to the midline area between her sternum and naval[sic]. I was not able to observe any scarring. I stretched the skin slightly to insure that the scar was not covered by body hair. I still was unable to see any scar. Paula Davis [Ericka's best friend] was also in the room. She stated that she thought she could observe a slight line. I noted that Ericka's torso skin was slightly darker than her face. She confirmed that she had been recently visiting a tanning booth.
>
> Later the same date, I checked Julie's shoulders, clavicle area, and upper arms for scars. I saw no marks or scars. As she was wearing a tank top, I moved the shoulder of the garment so I could see all of the shoulder area. I asked Julie if she thought she had scars in that area. She indicated that she did not.

In an April 26, 1989, letter to the prosecutor, Julie stuck to her story, insisting that she had numerous scars from wounds inflicted during satanic rituals. In one ritual, she wrote, her left arm was nailed to the floor by her father; in another her father, Jim Rabie, and Ray Risch tortured her with a pair of pliers. But these torments paled when compared to a freshly recovered memory involving her mother: "One time, I was about 11, my mom open my private area . . . and put a piece of a died baby inside me," Julie wrote. "I did remove it after she left it was an arm."

Eventually the prosecution dropped all charges of satanic ritual abuse. Despite an investigation that cost taxpayers three quarters of a million dollars, no proof could be discovered to support the allegations of devil-worshipping cults operating in the suburban back yards of Olympia, Washington.

Paul Ingram, urged by his wife and his daughters to admit his guilt and salvage what was left of the family's dignity, decided to plead guilty to six counts of third-degree rape. Two days after Ingram entered his guilty plea, the prosecutor's office dropped all charges against Jim Rabie and Ray Risch; the two men had been in custody for one hundred and fifty-eight days.

Ingram's sentencing was delayed when Julie produced a threatening letter, signed "Your ex Father Paul." "How's my very special little girl?" the letter began innocently enough. But the tone soon became sinister. "You've broke us up forever . . . there are many people that would like to see you dead and a few that are hunting for you."

The handwritten letter, it was soon discovered, was a forgery. Julie had written it herself.

Paul Ingram's world grew silent and strangely peaceful after he entered his guilty plea. Few visitors interrupted his daily routine, and the constant barrage of questions and insinuations from the detectives, lawyers, and psychologists ceased altogether. But once he was left alone with his memories, Ingram's confidence in his guilt began to deteriorate. He immersed himself in the Bible and through its teachings and scriptural pronouncements began to piece together his personal theory of what happened to him during the time of his "mental confusion." Ingram believed he had been caught up in a crisis of doubt and fear; in this state of mortal terror he had been blinded to the truth. As the Bible pronounces in 2 Timothy 1:7: "For God has not given us the spirit of fear; but of power, and of love, and of a sound mind." A spirit of fear had assailed him, and he had lost his sound mind.

From Ephesians 6:10–18, especially 6:12, Ingram understood that a battle had been waged for his very soul. "For we wrestle not against flesh and blood, but against principalities, against powers, against the rulers of the darkness of this world, against spiritual wickedness in high places." Because he had not protected himself with thorough knowledge and understanding of God's word, Ingram had not been prepared to fight that battle. He had tried so hard to hear the voice of God that he actually believed he could hear God talking to him and approving of his efforts to recall his lost and forgotten memories. But now, alone in his jail cell, he realized that God speaks in a "still, small voice" and that everything he says conforms with his word as written in the Bible.

At the April 1990 sentencing hearing held almost a year after he entered his guilty plea, Ingram stood up and announced in a clear, steady voice: "I stand before you, I stand before God. I have never sexually abused my daughters. I am not guilty of these crimes."

But Ingram had confessed, not once but many times, and the judge was not inclined to take an eleventh-hour change of heart seriously. Ingram was sentenced to twenty years in prison; after twelve years, he will be eligible for parole. All appeals have failed, as might be expected. Confessions, unlike memories, do not fade with time; tape recorded, signed and sealed, they stay on the books, uncontaminated and intact, forever.

Paul Ingram trusts that God will deliver him. He finds a precedent in the story of Joseph, who was sold by his brothers and taken as a captive to Egypt. Falsely accused and imprisoned, Joseph nevertheless prospered because he trusted God in everything he did; eventually he was joyfully reunited with his family.

"I trust God to also deliver me and to vindicate me of all the charges made against me," Ingram wrote in a letter dated February 16, 1993. With his letter he included a copy of a note from his son Chad, married now and attending graduate school. This is the first time Chad has communicated with his father in more than three years, and the note consists of four cryptic sentences. Referring to his father by his prison ID number, Chad forcefully stated his belief that his father is guilty, and expressed his hope that he will be made to suffer for his deeds. Chad ended with the statement that he never wanted to hear from his father again.

"You can see he still has a lot of bitterness and anger toward me," Ingram explained, in what can only be termed a massive understatement. He spent several paragraphs describing the activities of the rest of his family. His oldest son, Paul Ross, lives in Oregon, is married, and has a young daughter, Paul's first grandchild. Julie writes at least once a year and expresses a desire for the family to get back together; she has changed her name and works in a day care center. Ericka lives in California. Sandy, who divorced her husband and changed her name, lives with their youngest son, Mark, in a new town. She writes to Paul in prison but rarely mentions the events of the recent past.

"The entire family is still deeply affected by this situation," Ingram concludes, once again understating the impact of the trial and its aftermath.

Just before Christmas 1993, I received another typewritten, single-spaced, four-page letter from Paul Ingram. "This year of 1993 has proven to be a banner year with abundant blessings for our families, for our friends, and for the inmates," he wrote. He had been "blessed" with many visitors, including his two brothers and three sisters, who spent nearly a week with him, visiting six separate times. In October, a "major breakthrough occurred" when his youngest daughter, Julie, visited with his parents. "Julie is a beautiful young woman who seems to be doing quite well. She was reluctant to talk much about what has happened, but she did say that she wants me out of jail.

"I am truly blessed," Paul Ingram concluded his letter. Admitting that it might be difficult for others to understand how he could feel so content with his life, he explained that under the circumstances he has only two choices. "I can get angry and take it out on others, or I can thank God for all the blessings He gives me and do the best that I can in the situation forced upon me."

Paul Ingram is doing the best he can. But as I read through his letters and reflect on his situation, I can only wonder: Is it better this way? Was the Ingram family so sick and tormented that it deserved to die such a cruel, public death? It was certainly not the perfect family. Paul Ingram admits that he was not always a "good" father. He sometimes yelled at his children and verbally intimidated them. He recalls hitting Paul Ross on the back of the head and kicking him once, and he remembers slapping Julie's face when she ran the hot water for too long in Mark's bath and accidentally scalded him. Another time, when Julie ran down the driveway screaming that she was going to run away from home, Paul remembers running up behind her and pulling her by the hair.

There was also an unfortunate incident involving a roofing ax. Ingram remembers that he was standing on the deck behind their house, yelling at Chad and Paul Ross, who stood below him in the back yard. The boys had loaned the ax to a neighbor, who used it to split wood; when Ingram discovered that the blade was dulled, he became enraged and threw the ax to the ground; it landed right at the boys' feet. Ingram never intended to hurt his boys, he says; he just reacted without thinking, committing an unforgivable act of frustration that could have ended in tragedy.

Chad also remembers the incident with the ax. "Do you remember an occasion where . . . your dad got real upset with you and threw an ax at you?" Detective Schoenig asked during one of his interviews.

"Yeah. I remember that, yeah," Chad said.

"How did you feel when he did that?" Dr. Peterson asked.

"Surprised, I guess," Chad answered. "I didn't expect him to throw it."

"Surprised when somebody throws an ax at you?" Peterson asked, his tone clearly indicating that he expected a more outraged response.

"Well, I don't think he was trying to hit us," Chad explained.

Paul Ingram's memories and his self-confessed defects as a parent leave little doubt that emotional and physical abuse occasionally took place in the Ingram household. Apparently, at times, there was yelling, name-calling, a lack of communication, a dearth of affection; there were slaps, kicks, angry retorts, even an ax thrown by a father at his children.

Was there sexual abuse? Paul Ingram insists now, as he initially claimed when his wife confronted him with the accusatons, that he never touched his children, as he put it, "indecently." Sandy Ingram, whose first response to her daughters' accusations was amazement and disbelief, now believes they told the truth. Chad, who initially told investigators that he "always felt safe in his home," now insists his father is guilty and wants him to pay for his crimes. Paul Ross, who claimed that his father physically abused him but insisted that he had no memories of his father sexually abusing any of his children, refused to cooperate with the investigation; whatever he remembers, he keeps to himself. Ericka and Julie stand by their memories.

Despite the wreckage of his family and the failure of his appeals, Paul Ingram believes that he will be exonerated. "I believe that all the truth will come out and I trust God to totally vindicate me and all the others implicated," he writes. "Suffice it to say, these crimes never occurred except in the imaginations of myself and others."

Once again I am reminded of *The Crucible*'s central character, John Proctor, who realizes too late that a belief in the devil has created its own reality. A sensible man, Proctor has ventured into the Salem meeting house to confront his accusers. He demands proof of the witch-hunters' claims that his wife has hidden poppets—dolls stabbed with needles—in their house.

"Your Honor," he appeals to the governor, "my wife never kept no poppets."

"Why could there not have been poppets hid where no one ever saw them?" asks Reverend Parris, who firmly believes that he is doing his part to save the world from Satan's diabolical tricks.

Proctor is furious. "There might also be a dragon with five legs in my house, but no one has ever seen it," he protests.

Filled with the self-righteousness of one who does not need to see in order to believe, Parris pronounces the words that seal John Proctor's fate. "We are here, Your Honor, precisely to discover what no one has ever seen."

A QUESTION OF HEAVEN
AND HELL

I don't want the demons taken away
because they're going to take my angels too.

—Rainer Maria Rilke

Experience is not what happens to a man.
It is what a man does with what happens to him.

—Aldous Huxley

Toward the end of the book *We've Had a Hundred Years of Psycho-therapy and the World's Getting Worse,* psychotherapists James Hillman and Stan Passy discuss the current cultural obsession with incest and sexual abuse. Hillman suggests that incest and violence against children are "mythical, archetypal," and thus "profoundly significant." Why, he wonders, "has this particular syndrome, when there are so many other cruelties and injustices around, seized our white bread American culture just now at the end of the millennium?"

"It's a question of Hell," Passy responds.

> We've lost the place of Hell in our culture. . . . We are desperate to rediscover it, and I'm convinced that in modern culture the rediscovery of Hell emerges as: Childhood! Our childhood . . . This is why we're all priests, we're no longer psychologists. We're delivering them from the maw of Hell.

And that's why therapists have become so blind, Hillman agrees, because they're on a mission to deliver their patients from hell. But how did hell get relocated aboveground and take over a whole stage of our lives? Passy suggests that the metaphor of childhood as hell tilts precariously on the fulcrum of another metaphorical construct—the pure and innocent Inner Child. "So we have a new Hell in modern times called childhood and a priest cult, a craft designed to save you from that Hell, all with the aim of recovering one's lost innocence."

The journey to recover our lost innocence takes us deep into the land of metaphor and myth, where we encounter the divine purity of the Inner Child, the Hell of Childhood, and many other richly symbolic and profoundly imaginative archetypes. In the Myth of the Dysfunctional Family, for example, we learn that every family is dysfunctional in one way or another and that family rules and customs "kill the souls of human beings." In the Myth of Psychic Determinism we discover that our personalities, psyches, and behaviors are determined by events that occurred in our childhood. While we may think we are free to choose, the myth teaches that we are passive characters acting out a script, moved and played upon by unconscious, uncontrollable forces.

But even in this land of metaphorical excess, where Evil is personified and Innocence is inevitably perverted, there is hope of a happy ending. The Myth of Growth promises that we can "grow out of" our complexes and conflicts and "grow into" more mature, stable, understanding, and loving human beings. Salvation is possible—our wounds can be healed, our broken places mended, our impurities purged, our souls cleansed—through the Myth of Total Recall. Memory is imagined as a computerized process in which every action, expression, emotion, and nuance of behavior is imprinted into the soft tissue of the mind. If we are willing to search for the Truth, we can discover it (and in the process be cured) by going back to the past, facing our demons, and reclaiming our lost innocence.

Do the myths hold up to reality? Only if reality is molded and framed to fit the myth. When we ask hard questions about these myths and challenge their metaphorical underpinnings, the uneven fit between fact and fiction is quickly revealed and the rickety theoretical structure wobbles. Does the inner child really exist? Are human beings ever wholly "pure" or perfect? Is there such an entity as an ideal family against which dysfunction can be measured? Is our history necessarily our causation? Can therapists accurately discriminate between fact and fiction in their patients' stories? If we're constantly "growing," are we becoming more and more someone else's ideal of the mature, "together" human being—and less and less ourselves? Do traumatic memories permanently and indelibly scar the mind?

Asking these questions does not make us enemies of therapy, nor does it mean that we doubt the reality or the horror of childhood sexual abuse. We would only suggest that the "literal" and the "metaphorical" be respected as separate and distinct entities. If therapy chooses to deal with myth and metaphor (and many therapists would argue that meaning can only be discovered in symbol and imagination), it would seem wise and prudent to appreciate the metaphor for what it is—a symbolic representation rather than a literal re-creation. If therapy chooses to search for meaning in history (and many therapists believe that we cannot heal our psychic wounds without looking to the past), then memory must be recognized and appreciated as a creative mechanism in which fact and fiction are inextricably interwoven.

"Memory is a reconstructive process in which new details can be added to old images or old ideas, changing the quality of the memory," says psychotherapist Michael Yapko. "If you think about it, that's what you're doing as a therapist—changing the quality of the memory. A client says, 'This is what happened to me, this hurt, this was painful,' and you add in new perspectives, new ideas, new frames that alter the entire representation of the memory."

In this view, therapists rely on the malleability of memory to help their patients re-create or reconstruct their traumatic life histories. But what happens when both patient and therapist seek a definite answer in the indefinite past? "Therapists sometimes fall prey to the desire for certainty," writes Judith Lewis Herman. "Zealous conviction can all too easily replace an open, inquiring attitude. . . . The therapist has to remember that she is not a fact-finder and that the reconstruction of the trauma story is not a criminal investigation. Her role is to be an open-minded, compassionate witness, not a detective."

Some critics of psychotherapy believe that the profession should stop looking to the past for "truth." Marshall Edelson, psychoanalyst and professor of psychiatry at Yale University, argues that psychoanalysis should abandon attempts to re-create history, for "if a history is revived, it is the history of the acts of the patient's mind, creating through time his symbolic representation of his conceptions of the past, present and future 'reality.' " Edelson employs a lovely metaphorical construct of his own to make the point that literal and symbolic realities are not one and the same. "Between stimulus and response, between event and behavior, falls the act of the mind. It is the creation of the symbol, the 'poem of the act of the mind,' that is the object of study in psychoanalysis."

If the patient's mind is playing with symbol and imagination to create idiosyncratic poetry while the therapist is searching amidst the metaphors for literal fact, somebody is bound to be confused. Psychotherapist Donald Spence warns that therapists often misinterpret the stories patients tell because they fail to distinguish between two kinds of truth. "Narrative truth is confused with historical truth, and the very coherence of an account may lead us to believe that we are making contact with an actual happening," Spence writes. "Conviction emerges because the fit is good, not because we have necessarily made contact with the past."

Perhaps the whole idea of therapy as a vehicle for "making contact with the past" deserves reconsideration. While the stories patients tell and the interpretations therapists offer may provide insights into the meaning of an individual's experience, "meaning" should not be confused with "history." The problem is that therapists, being human themselves, bring into the therapeutic environment their assumptions, biases, and expectations. Suggestion is insidious—neither therapist nor patient knows that it is working its magic beneath the cover of authentic therapy.

"Psychotherapy offers no way to control for the preexisting assumptions of the therapist or the patient," psychiatrist Samuel Guze cautions, "nor for the effect on the patient's communications of the therapist's interpretations and suggestions. And, significantly, the psychotherapeutic process does not allow one to determine the causal relationships between phenomena of interest considered during psychotherapy and the patient's clinical problems." Guze suggests that therapists abandon claims to understand etiology—the causes of behavior—and settle for the more modest and achievable goals of helping patients "feel better, suffer less disability, and cope more effectively."

But perhaps "feeling better" is not the ultimate goal of therapy. James Hillman, trained as a Jungian analyst, suggests that therapy might consider shifting its focus from "fixing"—processing, transforming, refurbishing, or purifying—and concentrate instead on moving deeper into the patient's present pathology, which is "the window in the wall through which the demons and the angels come in." What is the meaning, the essence, the purpose of our suffering? Why do we feel abused, whether we were or were not abused in fact? What is happening now, in the present, to make us feel victimized, wounded, injured?

With the focus on the present, therapy would become less a self-centered process of withdrawal and retreat than an act of moving outward to embrace the concerns of the community, the culture, and the environment. Hillman describes the possibilities:

> Therapy might imagine itself investigating the immediate social causes, even while keeping its vocabulary of abuse and victmization . . . we don't want to get rid of the feeling of being abused— maybe that's very important, the feeling of being abused, the feeling of being without power. But maybe we shouldn't imagine that we are abused by the past as much as we are by the actual situation of 'my job,' 'my finances,' 'my government'—all the things that we live with. Then the consulting room becomes a cell of revolution, because we would be talking also about, "What is actually abusing me right now?" That would be a great venture, for therapy to talk that way.

Traumas and tribulations would no longer be viewed as "victimizations," but as "contributions to soul." "Wounds and scars are the stuff of character," Hillman insists. "The word 'character' means, at root, 'marked or etched with sharp lines,' like initiation cuts."

Because we are all "wounded" by life, the important question becomes, What are we going to do with these wounds? Recognizing that memory is a form of fiction, therapists might encourage their patients to ask themselves, What can my memory do with my experiences? Hillman quotes Freud, who said: "It's how you remember, not what actually happened," to make the point that patients in therapy can be encouraged to remember traumatic events in such a way that they are *abused by the memory.* "I'm not saying that children aren't molested or abused," Hillman explains. "They *are* molested, and they *are* abused, and in many cases it's absolutely devastating. But therapy makes it even more devastating *by the way it thinks about it.* It isn't just the trauma that does the damage, it's remembering traumatically."

By locking memory into the child's passive, powerless point of view, therapy imprisons its patients in the painful past rather than releasing them from it. When we "remember traumatically," the violations and insults are revisited over and over again, and childhood does indeed become the hell from which there is no escape.

In her book *Trauma and Recovery,* Judith Lewis Herman tells the story of a Vietnam veteran who struggled with questions of faith, loss, and grief; in his despair, he turned to a priest for help.

> I could not rationalize in my mind how God let good men die. I had gone to several . . . priests. I was sitting there with this one priest and said, "Father, I don't understand this: How does God allow small children to be killed? What is this thing, this war, this bullshit? I got all these friends who are dead . . . " That priest, he looked me in the eye and said, "I don't know son, I've never been in war." I said, "I didn't ask you about war, I asked you about God."

Few possess the wisdom of this man, who knew that his questions were both literal and metaphorical. He was in pain, and he needed help, but his questions were not about guns, bullets, horror, cruelty, injustice, or even death. He wanted to know about *God.* But even this explanation does not reveal the meaning in the metaphor, for what, we can legitimately ask, did he mean by "God"? Nikos Kazantzakis has a partial answer:

> We have seen the highest circle of spiraling powers. We have named this circle God. We might have given it any other name we wished: Abyss, Mystery, Absolute Darkness, Absolute Light, Matter, Spirit, Ultimate Hope, Ultimate Despair, Silence.

When we question our fate—when we wonder what happened in our past, when we struggle to heal the wounds of our bodies, minds, and souls, when we ask questions about God or any of the other unfathomable mysteries of the human condition—we are searching for meaning, for insight, for some way to measure the depth of our despair and the potential for hope. Explanations and answers diminish the profundity of the experiences we have set out to explore. In truth, we do not want our questions answered; we want our experiences shared.

Perhaps therapy can become the place where our pain is truly witnessed and our memories are appreciated, even celebrated, as ongoing, ever-changing interactions between imagination and history.

REFERENCES

CHAPTER 1.

Page 2: For more details on the Souza case, see the cover story of *Newsweek,* April 19, 1993.

CHAPTER 2.

For more infomation on research on the malleability of memory, interested readers can look at these sources:

Loftus, E. F. (1979). *Eyewitness Testimony.* Cambridge, MA: Harvard University Press.

Loftus, E. F. (1980). *Memory.* Reading, MA: Addison-Wesley. (Reprinted by NY: Ardsley Press 1988.)

Loftus, E. F. and K. Ketcham. (1991). *Witness for the Defense: The Accused, the Eyewitness, and the Expert Who Puts Memory on Trial.* NY: St. Martin's Press.

CHAPTER 3.

For additional stories of people who have retracted their memories and accusations of sexual abuse, see Goldstein, E. & Farmer, K. (1993). *True Stories of False Memories.* Boca Raton, FL: SIRS Books.

CHAPTER 4.

Page 21: Bass, Ellen and Laura Davis. (1988). *The Courage to Heal: A Guide for Women Survivors of Child Sexual Abuse.* NY: Harper & Row.

Page 22: Blume, E. S. (1990). *Secret Survivors: Uncovering Incest and its Aftereffects in Women.* NY: Ballantine.

CHAPTER 6.

The authors are deeply indebted to Harry MacLean, author of *Once Upon a Time* (HarperCollins, 1993), and Dr. David Spiegel for their contributions to this chapter.

Page 38: O'Brien, Tim (1990). *The Things They Carried.* NY: Penguin Books, pp. 203–204.

Page 49: Baddeley, Alan (1990). *Human Memory: Theory and practice.* Boston: Allyn & Bacon.

Klatzky, Roberta L. (1980). *Human Memory: Structures and Processes.* San Francisco: Freeman and Co.

Zeckmeister, Eugene B., and Stanley E. Nyberg. (1982). *Human Memory: An Introduction to Research and Theory.* Monterey, CA: Brooks/Cole Publishing.

Page 50: Herman, J. L. (1981). *Father–Daughter Incest.* Cambridge: Harvard University Press.

Miller, A. (1981). *The Drama of the Gifted Child.* NY: Basic Books, pp. 111–112.

Freud's definition of repression in "Repression" (originally published in 1915), in Strachey, J. (ed.) *The Standard Edition of the Complete Psychological Works of Sigmund Freud,* Vol. 14, London: Hogarth Press, 1957. Elizabeth von R. and Miss Lucy are discussed in Breuer, J., and S. Freud. (1895) "Studies on Hysteria." Strachey (1955), volume 2. "The Wolfman" case can be found in Strachey (1955), volume 17.

Page 51: Erdelyi, M. H., and B. Goldberg. (1979). "Let's Not Sweep Repression Under the Rug: Toward a Cognitive Psychology of Repression." In Kihlstrom, J. F., and F. J. Evans. (eds.) *Functional Disorders of Memory.* Hillsdale, NJ: Erlbaum, pp. 355–402.

Page 52: Blume, E. S. (1990), pp. 67.

Page 53: Bass & Davis (1988), p. 21–22.

Poston, C. & Lison, K. (1990). *Reclaiming Our Lives: Hope for Adult Survivors of Incest,* NY: Bantam.

Farmer, S. (1989). *Adult Children of Abusive Parents,* NY: Ballantine.

Page 54: Davis, L. (1990). *The Courage to Heal Workbook: For Women and Men Survivors of Child Sexual Abuse.* NY: HarperCollins, p. 217.

Olio, K. (1989). "Memory retrieval in the treatment of adult survivors of sexual abuse," *Transactional Analysis Journal, 19,* pp. 95–96.

The case of Betsey is described in Frawley, M. G. (1990). "From secrecy to self-disclosure: Healing the scars of incest," in Stricker, G., and M. Fisher. (eds). *Self-disclosure in the Therapeutic Relationship.* NY: Plenum Press, p. 255.

Page 55: Smith, M. and L. Pazder, M. D. (1980). *Michelle Remembers.* NY: Pocket Books.

Bass & Davis, p. 137.

Page 56: Rosenfeld, A., C. Nadelson, and M. Krieger. (1979). "Fantasy and reality in patients' reports of incest," *Journal of Clinical Psychiatry, 40,* pp. 159–164.

Rosenfeld et. al. state: "Litin et. al. have proposed that the therapist's insistence that a patient's memory was a fantasy may have driven some patients, who in fact had been molested, out of therapy or into psychosis because of the therapist's repeated denial of the reality of their experience." Litin, E. M., M. Giffin, A. Johnson. (1956). "Parental influence in unusual sexual behavior in children," *Psychoanal Q*, 25:37–55.

Pages 56–57: Terr, L. (1990). *Too Scared to Cry.* NY: Basic Books. Definition of suppression: pp. 111–112; "Horrible experience" quote from pp. 170–172; "The memory of trauma is shot with higher intensity light . . . " p. 170.

Page 58: Terr, L. (1991). "Childhood Traumas: An Outline and Overview," *Am J. Psychiatry, 148,* 1, pp. 10–20.

Pages 59–61: Lenore Terr's discussion of Steven King's train trauma can be found on pp. 251–260, *Too Scared to Cry.*

Page 60: King, S. (1983). *Danse Macabre.* NY: Berkley, pp. 83–84.

Page 62: Loftus, E., and T. Burns. (1982). "Mental shock can produce retrograde amnesia." *Memory and Cognition,* 10, pp. 318–323.

Loftus, E. F., and M. Banaji. (1989). "Memory modification and the role of the media." In Gheorghiu, V. A., P. Netter, H. J. Eysenck, and R. Rosenthal. (eds.) *Suggestibility: Theory and Research,* Berlin: Springer-Verlag, p. 279–294.

Page 65: Spiegel, D. (in press). "Dissociated or fabricated? Psychiatric issues in the case of the People vs. George Franklin," *International Journal of Clinical and Experimental Hypnosis.*

Page 66: Beyerstein, B. (1988). "Neuropathology and the legacy of spiritual possession," *The Skeptical Inquirer,* pp. 248–262.

Ellen White anecdote: Beyerstein, pp. 254–255, citing Clapp (1982). "Was Ellen White merely an epileptic?" *Christianity Today:* 26:56.

Hildegard is discussed on page 258 of Beyerstein's article. Beyerstein cites Sacks, O. (1970). *Migraine: The Evolution of a Common Disorder,* London: Faber & Faber, 1970, chapter 3.

Sagan, C. (1993, March 7). "What's really going on?" *Parade Magazine.*

Page 68: Franklin, E., and W. Wright. (1991). *Sins of the Father.* NY: Crown.

On page 111–112 Eileen Franklin discusses her therapist's interpretations of her repressed memories: "My main motive in telling Kirk was to learn if it was possible to forget such a powerful event. I also wanted his help in dealing with the memory, perhaps reducing its hold over me. As I told him the story, I began to cry and couldn't stop until I finished. As I expected, Kirk was soothing and understanding. He told me that now that I'd brought the memory into my consciousness, it could no longer hurt me. He urged me to believe that I had made a sizable step toward psychic health . . . Kirk did not think me crazy . . . My relief was enormous."

Page 69: On page 279 of *Too Scared to Cry* Terr writes: "In children and in the untreated children who turn out to be troubled adults, these monotonous, literal, specific repetitions—the dreams, play, reenactments, and visualizations—are the surest cues we get to childhood trauma."

CHAPTER 7.

Page 73: For information on Penfield's work, see: Loftus, E. F., and G. Loftus. (1980). "On the permanence of stored information in the human brain," *American Psychologist, 35,* pp. 409–420.

Page 75: For a discussion of the Tony Conigliaro tragedy, see Anderson, D. (1990, Feb. 27). "Handcuffed in history to Tony C.," *The New York Times,* p. B9.

Page 76: Piaget, J. (1962). *Play, Dreams and Imitation in Childhood.* NY: Norton.

Page 77: Pynoos, R. S., and K. Nader. (1989). "Children's memory and proximity to violence," *Journal of American Academy of Child and Adolescent Psychiatry, 28,* pp. 236–241.

Haugaard, J. J., N. D. Reppucci, J. Laurd, and T. Nauful. (1991). "Children's definitions of the truth and their competency as witnesses in legal proceedings," *Law and Human Behavior, 15,* 253–272.

Page 78: Clarke-Stewart, A., W. Thompson, and S. Lepore. (1989, April). "Manipulating children's interpretations through interrogation." Paper presented at the meeting of the Society for Research in Development, Kansas City, Mo. A discussion of the study can also be found in Goodman, G. S., and A. Clarke-Stewart. (1991). Suggestibility in children's testimony: Implications for sexual abuse investigations. In Doris, J. (ed.) *The Suggestibility of children's recollections,* pp. 92–105. Washington, D.C.: American Psychological Association Press. Commentaries on the chapter by Max Stellar, John Brigham, and Lucy S. McGough, also contained in the Doris volume, are worth reading.

Pages 78–79: Spanos, N., E. Menary, N. Gabora, S. DuBreuil, and B. Dewhirst. (1991). "Secondary Identity Enactments During Hypnotic Past-Life Regression: A Sociocognitive Perspective," *Journal of Personality and Social Psychology,* Vol. 61, pp. 308–320.

Page 79: The Marilyn Van Derbur story appears in an article titled "The Darkest Secret," *People,* June 10, 1991, pp. 88–94.

The Roseanne Arnold story appears in an article titled "A star cries incest," *People,* October 7, 1991, pp. 84–88 and Darton, N., October 7, 1991, "The pain of the last taboo," *Newsweek,* pp. 70–72.

Page 80: Toufexis, A. (October 28, 1991). "When can memories be trusted?" *Time,* pp. 86–88.

Smiley, J. (1992). *A Thousand Acres.* NY: Ballantine Books, p. 228.

Page 81: Petersen, B. (1992). *Dancing with Daddy: A Childhood Lost and a Life Regained.* NY: Bantam Books, pp. 64–65.

Collier, D. v Collier, J. (1991, December). Deposition of plaintiff, Case No. 711752, Superior Court, County of Santa Clara, California.

Pages 81–82: Rogers, M. L. (1992, March). "A case of alleged satanic ritualistic abuse," paper presented at the American Psychology-Law Society meeting, San Diego.

Page 84: Ganaway, G. K. (August 1991). "Alternative hypotheses regarding satanic ritual abuse memories," paper presented at the American Psychological Assocation Annual Meeting, San Francisco.

Ganaway, G. K. (1989). "Historical versus narrative truth: Clarifying the role of exogenous trauma in the etiology of MPD and its variants," *Dissociation,* 2: 205–220.

Dr. Paul R. McHugh has also written extensively on MPD and with Dr. Ganaway is one of the most articulate proponents of the "created MPD" position. See McHugh, P. R. (1993). "Multiple personality disorder," *Harvard Mental Health Letter,* vol. 10, pp. 4–7. On page 6, Dr. McHugh recommends:

"Close the dissociation services and disperse the patients to general psychiatric units. Ignore the alters. Stop talking to them [the alter personalities], taking notes on them, and discussing them in staff conferences. Pay attention to real present problems and conflicts rather than fantasy. If these simple, familiar rules are followed, multiple personalities will soon wither away and psychotherapy can begin."

For more information on the variety of views regarding MPD see:

Braun, B. G., and R. G. Sachs, (1988, October). "Recognition of possible cult involvement in MPD patients," paper presented at the Fifth International Conference on Multiple Personality/Dissociative States, Chicago IL.

Kluft, R. P. (1993, October). "Multiple personality disorder: A contemporary perspective," *Harvard Mental Health Letter,* Vol 10, pp. 5–7.

Weissberg, M. (1993). "Multiple personality disorder and iatrogenesis: The cautionary tale of Anna O," *The International Journal of Clinical and Experimental Hypnosis,* Vol. XLI, pp. 15–34.

Page 89: For another source for the difficulty of distinguishing real from imagined events see: Bonanno, G. A. (1990). "Remembering and psychotherapy," *Psychotherapy,* 27, pp. 175–185.

For similar difficulties with children's testimony, see Ceci, S., and M. Bruck. (1993). "Suggestibility of the child witness," *Psychological Bulletin,* 113, pp. 403–439.

Page 90: In a letter dated April 4, 1994, George Ganaway further elaborated on his ideas regarding the phenomenon of repression and the workings of the unconscious:

"Perhaps the most important contribution to our knowledge about memory and reality from a century of clinical psychoanalytic literature is an awareness of the existence from childhood of a realm of unconscious fantasies called 'psychic reality.' The tension created by intrapsychic and interpersonal needs contributes to the formation of wishes, worries, and unconscious fantasies, which constantly inform and influence our conscious thoughts, emotions and behaviors, distorting our perceptions and memories of personal experiences in the service of preconceived beliefs.

"Psychotherapists and others are currently involved in the argument over the existence of 'robust repression'—whether an individual can keep extensive, important, personal information outside of conscious awareness for years, only to retrieve it later during therapy sessions. Assuming our patients are not consciously lying when they say they are not 'making up' their memories—and I have rarely found them to be lying—then, in fact, pseudomemories could not be created *without* a mechanism such as repression or dissociation. Confabulated memories come to conscious awareness in such an effortless manner, especially while in trance, that they seem always to have been there, waiting to be 'discovered.' This may fool the patient and therapist alike. There must be some unconscious or 'repressed' organizing factor that strings together these bits and pieces of fact and fantasy in order to present the unconscious mind with such a convincing scenario.

"Throwing the concept of repression and/or the 'unconscious' out entirely, as some investigators in social and cognitive psychology might prefer to do, makes it much more difficult to explain the entire spectrum of pseudomemories you see in patients, especially when careful attempts are made by most therapists to avoid any leading or reinforcing suggestions. In my opinion, only the concept of an active unconscious mental life can explain some of the material that comes up spontaneously in patients during waking states of reverie and in formal dream states during the night."

Pages 91–92: Neisser, U., and N. Harsch. (1992). "Phantom flashbulbs: False recollections of hearing the news about Challenger," in Winograd, E., and U. Neisser. (eds.) *Affect and Accuracy in Recall: Studies of "Flashbulb" Memories.* NY: Cambridge University Press, pp. 9–31. For more information on flashbulb memories in general, see the entire volume.

For another perspective on memory for very significant events, see Wright, D. (1993). "Recall of the Hillsborough Disaster over time: Systematic biases of 'flashbulb' memories," *Applied Cognitive Psychology,* 7, pp. 129–138.

See also: Loftus, E. F., and L. Kaufman. (1992). Why do traumatic experiences sometimes produce good memory (flashbulbs) and sometimes no memory (repression)? In Winograd, E., and U. Neisser. (eds.) *Affect and Accuracy in Recall: Studies of "Flashbulb" Memories.* NY: Cambridge University Press.

Pages 92–93: Cannon, L. (1991). *President Reagan: The Role of a Lifetime.* NY: Simon & Schuster.

Page 100: Loftus, E. F., and J. Coan. (in press). The construction of childhood memories. In Peters, D. (ed.) *The Child Witness in Context: Cognitive, Social and Legal Perspectives.* NY: Kluwer.

Pages 100-101: "Questions about sex (even the most adventurous Cosmo girls want answered)," by Helen Singer Kaplan, M.D., pp. 150–151, July 1992 *Cosmopolitan.*

CHAPTER 8.

Page 214: Many articles, both popular and scholarly, advance the idea of the generational nature of incest. See for example, Wells, R. H. (1994, January). "There's no such thing as 'mis-remembering,' " *Adolescence.*

CHAPTER 9.

Books and articles used in this chapter are listed below:

Bass, E., and L. Thornton. (1991). *I Never Told Anyone: Writings by Women Survivors of Child Sexual Abuse.* NY: HarperPerennial (originally published by Harper in 1983).

Bass, E., and L. Davis. (1988) *The Courage to Heal: A Guide for Women Survivors of Child Sexual Abuse,* NY: Harper & Row.

Bishop-Milbradt, M. (1984; revised by Terri Platt, 1988) *Incest: A Book for Adult Survivors,* Tacoma, WA: Pierce County Rape Relief.

Blume, E. S. (1990). *Secret Survivors: Uncovering Incest and its Aftereffects in Women,* NY: Ballantine Books.

Bradshaw, J. (1990). *Homecoming.* NY: Bantam Books.

Bradshaw, J. (July 1992). "Discovering what we want," *Lear's,* 5, p. 49.

Bradshaw, J. (August 1992). "Incest: When you wonder if it happened to you," *Lear's,* 5, pp. 43–44.

Braun, B. G., and R. G. Sachs. (1988, October). "Recognition of possible cult involvement in MPD patients." Paper presented at the Fifth International Conference on Multiple Personality/Dissociative States, Chicago, IL.

Brenneis, B. (1993). "On the relationship of dream content to trauma." Unpublished manuscript.

Brewin, C., B. Andrews, and I. Gotlib. (1993). "Psychopathology and early experience: A reappraisal of retrospective reports," *Psychological Bulletin,* Vol. 113, pp. 82–98.

Briere, J. (1992). "Studying delayed memories of childhood sexual abuse," *The Advisor* (Publication of the American Professional Society on the Abuse of Children), 5, pp. 17–18.

Briere, J. (1989). *Therapy for Adults Molested as Children: Beyond Survival*. NY: Springer Pub. Co.

Briere, J., and J. Conte. (1993). "Self-reported amnesia for abuse in adults molested as children," *Journal of Traumatic Stress*, Vol 6, pp. 21–31.

Claridge, K. (1992). "Reconstructing memories of abuse: A theory-based approach," *Psychotherapy*, Vol. 29, pp. 243–252.

Courtois, C. (1988). *Healing the Incest Wound*. NY: Norton.

Courtois, C. (1992). "The memory retrieval process in incest survivor therapy," *Journal of Child Sexual Abuse*, vol. 1(1).

Davis, L. (1990). *The Courage to Heal Workbook: For Women and Men Survivors of Child Sexual Abuse*, NY: HarperCollins.

Davis, P., and G. Schwartz. (1987). "Repression and the inaccessibility of affective memories," *Journal of Personality and Social Psychology*, Vol. 52, no. 1.

Dinges, D. F., W. G. Whitehouse, E. C. Orne, J. W. Powell, M. T. Orne, and M. H. Erdelyi. (1992). "Evaluating hypnotic memory enhancement (hyperamnesia and reminiscence) using multitrial forced recall," *Journal of Experimental Psychology: Learning, Memory and Cognition*, 18, pp. 1139–1147.

Engel, B. (1989). *The Right to Innocence*. NY: Ivy Books.

Farmer, S. (1989). *Adult Children of Abusive Parents*. NY: Ballantine.

Forrest, M. (1993). "An interview with John Briere, Ph.D.," *Treating Abuse Today*, Vol. 3, no. 1.

Forward, S., and C. Buck. (1988). *Betrayal of Innocence: Incest and its Devastation*. NY: Penguin Books.

Fredrickson, R. (1992). *Repressed Memories: A Journey to Recovery from Sexual Abuse*. NY: Simon and Schuster.

Gudjonsson, G. (1985). "Comment on 'The use of hypnosis by the police in the investigation of crime: Is guided imagery a safe substitute?" *British Journal of Experimental and Clinical Hypnosis*, Vol. 3, p. 37.

Herman, J. L. (1981). *Father-Daughter Incest*. Cambridge: Harvard University Press.

Herman, J. L. (1992). *Trauma and Recovery*. NY: Basic Books.

Herman, J. L., and E. Schatzow. (1987). "Recovery and verification of memories of childhood sexual trauma," *Psychoanalytic psychology*, 4, pp. 1–14.

Holmes, D. (1990). "The evidence for repression: An examination of sixty years of research." In J. Singer (ed.) *Repression and Dissociation: Implications for personality, theory, psychopathology and health*. Chicago: Chicago University Press, pp. 85–102. Holmes has recently updated his review in a piece to be published in the *Harvard Mental Health Letter.*

Howell, R. J. (1965). A verified childhood memory elicited during hypnosis. *American Journal of Clinical Hypnosis,* 8, pp. 141–142. A psychologist hypnotized a 15-year-old girl and regressed her back to 11 months when she recalled falling down a long flight of stairs. However, even the hypnotist admitted "obviously there is no way of knowing if the subject had ever heard of this incident from her parents or her grandmother" (p. 142).

Kaminer, W. (1992). *I'm Dysfunctional, You're Dysfunctional: The Recovery Movement and Other Self-help Fashions.* Reading, MA: Addison-Wesley.

Laurence, J-R., and C. Perry. (1983). "Hypnotically created memory among highly hypnotizable subjects," *Science,* 222, pp. 523–524.

Laurence, J-R., R. Nadon, H. Nogrady, and C. Perry. (1986). "Duality, dissociation, and memory creation in highly hypnotizable subjects," *International Journal of Clinical and Experimental Hypnosis,* 34, 4, pp. 295–310.

Lew, M. (1988). *Victims No Longer: Men Recovering from Incest and Other Sexual Child Abuse.* NY: HarperCollins.

Lindsay, S., and D. Read. (in press). "Psychotherapy and memories of childhood sexual abuse," *Applied Cognitive Psychology.*

Lynn, S., M. Milano, and J. Weekes. (1991). "Hypnosis and pseudomemories: The effects of prehypnotic expectancies," *Journal of personality and social psychology,* 60, pp. 318–326.

Lynn, S., and M. Nash. (1994). "Truth in memory: Ramifications for psychotherapy and hypnotherapy," *American Journal of Clinical Hypnosis,* Vol. 36. pp. 194–208.

Maltz, W. (1992). *The Sexual Healing Journey: A Guide for Survivors of Sexual Abuse.* NY: HarperCollins.

Maltz, W., and B. Holman. (1986). *Incest and Sexuality: A Guide to Understanding and Healing.* NY: Free Press.

McHugh, P. R. (1992). "Psychiatric misadventures," *The American Scholar,* 61, pp. 491–510.

McHugh, P. R. (1993). "Psychotherapy Awry," *The American Scholar,* 62, pp. 17–30.

McHugh, P. R. (1993, September). "Multiple personality disorder," *Harvard Mental Health Letter,* Vol 10, pp. 4–6.

Miller, A. (1981) *The Drama of the Gifted Child: The Search for the True Self.* NY: Basic Books.

Mulhern, S. (1991). "Satanism and psychotherapy: A rumor in search of an inquisition." In Richardson, J. T., J. Best, and G. Bromley. (eds.) *The Satanism Scare,* NY: Aldine de Gruyter.

Nash, M. (1987). "What, if anything, is regressed about hypnotic age regression? A review of the empirical literature," *Psychological Bulletin*, 102, pp. 42–52.

Nash, M. (1992). "Retrieval of childhood memories in psychother-
· apy." Paper presented at the annual convention of the *American Psychological Association*, Washington, D.C.

Neisser, U. (1991). "A case of misplaced nostalgia," *American Psychologist*, 46, 1, pp. 34–36.

Olio, K. A. (1989). "Memory retrieval in the treatment of adult survivors of sexual abuse," *Transactional Analysis Journal*, Vol. 19, pp. 93–94.

Orne, M. T. (1979). "The use and misuse of hypnosis in court," *International Journal of Clinical and Experimental Hypnosis*, 27, pp. 311–341.

Poston, C., and K. Lison. (1990). *Reclaiming Our Lives: Hope for Adult Survivors of Incest*. NY: Bantam (originally Little Brown, 1989).

Roland, C. (October 1993). "Exploring childhood memories with adult survivors of sexual abuse: Concrete reconstruction and visualization techniques," *Journal of Mental Health Counseling*, Vol. 15, No. 4.

Root, M. (1992). "Reconstructing the impact of trauma on personality," in Brown, L., and M. Ballou. (eds.) *Personality and psychopathology: Feminist Reappraisals*, NY: The Guilford Press.

Rosenfeld, A., C. Nadelson, and M. Krieger. (April 1979). "Fantasy and reality in patients' reports of incest," *Journal of Clinical Psychiatry*, 40, pp. 159–164.

Russell, D. E. H. (1984). *Sexual exploitation: Rape, child sexual abuse and sexual harassment*. Beverly Hills, CA: Sage.

Salter, S., and C. Ness. (April 4–9, 1993). "Buried Memories/Broken Families," *San Francisco Examiner*.

Sgroi, S. M. (1989). "Stages of recovery for adult survivors of child sex abuse." Chapter in Sgroi, S. M. (ed.) *Vulnerable Populations: Sexual abuse treatment for children, adult survivors, offenders and persons with mental retardation*, vol. 2, Lexington, MA: Lexington Books.

Sherman, S. J., R. B. Cialdini, D. F. Schwartzman, and K. D. Reynolds. (1985). "Imagining can heighten or lower the perceived likelihood of contracting a disease," *Personality and Social Psychology Bulletin*, 11, pp. 118–127.

Singer, M., and R. Ofshe. (1990). "Thought reform programs and the production of psychiatric casualties," *Psychiatric Annals*, Vol 20, pp. 188–193. Margaret Singer has also co-authored a chapter with Richard Ofshe: Ofshe, R. J., and M. T. Singer. (1993). "Recovered memory therapies and robust repression: A collective error." Unpublished manuscript, University of California, Berkeley.

Smith, M. (1983). "Hypnotic memory enhancement of witnesses: Does it work?" *Psychological Bulletin*, 94, pp. 387–407.

Summit, R. (1992). "Misplaced attention to delayed memory," *The Advisor* (published by the American Professional Society on the Abuse of Children), 5, pp. 21–25.

Tavris, C. (1992). *The Mismeasure of Woman*. NY: Simon and Schuster.

Tavris, C. (January 3, 1993). "Beware the incest-survivor machine," *The New York Times Book Review*. (See also: "Real Incest and Real Survivors: readers respond," in *The New York Times Book Review*, February 14, 1993).

Terr, L. (1988). "What happens to early memories of trauma? A study of 20 children under age five at the time of documented traumatic events," *J. Amer Academy of Child and Adolescent Psychiatry*, 27, pp. 96–104.

Terr, L. (1990) *Too Scared to Cry: How trauma affects children . . . and ultimately us all*, NY: Basic Books.

Van der Kolk, B., and O. Van der Hart. (1991). "The intrusive past: The flexibility of memory and the engraving of trauma," *American Imago*, 48, pp. 425–454.

Weekes, J. R., S. J. Lynn, J. P. Green, and J. T. Brentar. (1992). "Pseudomemory in hypnotized and task-motivated subjects," *Journal of Abnormal Psychology*, 101, pp. 356–360.

Williams, L. M. (1992). "Adult memories of childhood abuse: Preliminary findings from a longitudinal study," *The Advisor*, 5, pp. 19–20. A more complete version of this research will be published by the *Journal of Consulting and Clinical Psychology*.

Yapko, M. (1988). *When Living Hurts*. NY: Brunner/Mazel.

Yapko, M. (1989). "Disturbance of temporal orientation as a feature of depression," in Yapko, M. (ed.) *Brief Therapy Approaches to Treating Anxiety and Depression*. Brunner/Mazel.

Yapko, M. (1990). *Trancework: An introduction to the Practice of Clinical Hypnosis* (2nd ed.). NY: Brunner/Mazel.

Yapko, M. (1994). "Suggestibility and repressed memories of abuse. A survey of psychotherapists' beliefs," *American Journal of Clinical Hypnosis*, 36, pp. 163–171. Readers might also be interested in commentaries by P. B. Bloom, D. M. Ewin, E. Loftus *et al.* M. Gravitz, and S. J. Lynn *et al.* that accompany the Yapko article in the same issue of the *American Journal of Clinical Hypnosis*.

Yapko, M. (1994). *Suggestions of Abuse*. NY: Simon & Schuster.

CHAPTER 11.

Page 201: CNN Special Assignment, "Guilt by Memory," Kathy Slobogin, May 1993.

Pages 202–203: Nathan, D. (October 1992). "Cry Incest," *Playboy*, Vol. 39 #10

For an alternative view on cult ritual abuse, see Rose, E.

(January/February 1993). "Surviving the Unbelievable: A first-person account of cult ritual abuse," *Ms.*, vol III, no. 4.

Page 203: Lanning, footnote: Lanning, K. V. (1991). "Ritual abuse: A law enforcement view or perspective," *Child Abuse & Neglect*, 15, pp. 171–173. The full context of Lanning's comment:

"For at least eight years, American law enforcement has been aggressively investigating the allegations of victims of ritual abuse. There is little or no evidence for the portion of their allegations that deals with large-scale baby breeding, human sacrifice, and organized satanic conspiracies. Now it is up to mental health professionals, not law enforcement, to explain why victims are alleging things that don't seem to be true. Mental health professionals must begin to accept the possibility that some of what these victims are alleging just didn't happen and that this area desperately needs study and research by rational, objective social scientists."

Wielawski, I. (October 3, 1991). "Unlocking the secrets of memory," *Los Angeles Times.*

Page 204: Taylor, B. (May 16, 1992). "What if sexual abuse memories are wrong?" *Toronto Star;* and Taylor, B. (May 18, 1992) "True or False?" *Toronto Star.*

Goleman, D. (July 21, 1992). "Childhood Trauma: Memory or Invention?" *The New York Times*, p. B5.

Sauer, M., and J. Okerblom. (Sept. 13, 14, and 15, 1992). "Haunting Accusations, *San Diego Union-Tribune.*

Pages 204–205: Darrell Sifford wrote a series of articles on the subject of false accusations, all of which appeared in the *Philadelphia Inquirer.* ("Accusations of sex abuse, years later," November 24, 1991; "When tales of sex abuse aren't true," Jan 5, 1992; "Perilous journey: The labyrinth of past sexual abuse," Feb. 13, 1992; and "Her mission: Heal families, don't blame," Feb. 23, 1992).

Page 206: Ofshe, R., and E. Watters. (1993, March/April). "Making Monsters," *Society,* pp. 4–16.

Berliner, L., and E. Loftus. (1992). "Sexual abuse accusations: Desperately seeking reconciliation," *Journal of Interpersonal Violence,* 7, pp. 570–578.

Pages 215–216: For information on anterograde amnesia, see the books on human memory mentioned in the endnotes for chapter 6. Also see Loftus, E. F. (1980). *Memory.* Reading, MA: Addison-Wesley. (Re282 282printed by Ardsley Press, 1988).

"PN" was discussed in Schacter, D. L., P. L. Wang, E. Tulving, and M. Freedman. (1982). "Functional retrograde amnesia: A quantitative case study," *Neuropsychologia,* 20, pp. 523–532.

For other research on amnesia by Schacter see: Schacter, D. L. (1983). "Amnesia observed: Remembering and forgetting in a natural environment," *Journal of Abnormal Psychology*, 92, pp. 236–242, and Schacter, D. L. and J. F. Kihlstrom. (1989). "Functional amnesia," In Boller, F., and J. Grafman (eds). *Handbook of Neuropsychology*, 3, pp. 209–231.

Page 216: Diagnostic and Statistical Manual—3rd edition, revised.

Whitley, G. (1991 October). "The seduction of Gloria Grady," *D Magazine*, pp. 45–49, 66–71.

Pages 219–221: Tavris, C. (January 3, 1993). "Beware the incest-survivor machine," *The New York Times Book Review.* (See also: "Real incest and real survivors: Readers respond," in *The New York Times Book Review,* February 14, 1993).

Page 222: Robinson, K. (August 11, 1993). "Memories of Abuse," *Seattle Weekly.* Letters to the editor appeared in the "Letters" column on August 25, 1993.

Page 223: The article on repressed memories was written by Karen S. Peterson and appeared in *USA Today,* August 31, 1992, p. D1.

CHAPTER 12.

Richard Ofshe is a professor of sociology at the University of California, Berkeley. His research focuses on extreme techniques of influence and social control. Ofshe shared in a 1979 Pulitzer Prize for an expose of Synanon.

Lawrence Wright's two-part article on the Paul Ingram case ("Remembering Satan," published on May 17 and May 24, 1993 in *The New Yorker*) has been expanded into a groundbreaking book: *Remembering Satan* (NY: Knopf, 1994). The book was reviewed in *Newsweek* on April 4, 1994. "This is a cautionary tale of immense value, told with rare intelligence, restraint and compassion," the reviewer noted, *"Remembering Satan* catapults Wright to the front rank of American journalists."

Page 252: Ofshe, R. (1989). "Coerced confessions: The logic of seemingly irrational action," *Cultic Studies Journal*, 6, pp. 1–15.

Ofshe has written extensively about the Ingram case. See:

Ofshe, R. J. (1992). "Inadvertent hypnosis during interrogation: False confession due to dissociative sate, misidentified multiple personality and the satanic cult hypothesis," *International Journal of Clinical and Experimental Hypnosis,* XL, pp. 125–126.

Ofshe, R., and E. Watters. (1993, March/April). "Making monsters," *Society,* pp. 4–16.

See also:

Watters, E. (1991). "The devil in Mr. Ingram," *Mother Jones,* 16, pp. 30–33, 65–68.

Page 255: Spiegel, H. (1974). "The Grade 5 Syndrome: The highly hypnotizable person," *International Journal of Clinical and Experimental Hypnosis,* 22: pp. 303–319.

For more information on the Grade 5 Syndrome, see:

Mulhern, S. (1991). "Satanism and psychotherapy: A rumor in search of an inquisition," in Richardson, J. T, J. M. Best, and D. G. Bromley (eds.), *The Satanism Scare,* San Francisco: Aldine.

Watters, E. (1993). "Doors of memory," *Mother Jones,* Jan-Feb, pp. 24–29, 76–77.

CHAPTER 13.

Page 264: The Passy and Hillman discussion takes place on pages 187–199 of Hillman, J., and M. Ventura. (1992). *We've Had a Hundred Years of Psychotherapy and the World's Getting Worse,* NY: HarperSan-Francisco.

Page 265: The phrase "Family rules . . . kill the souls of human beings" is attributed to self-help writer John Bradshaw in a brilliant article about the recovery movement: Rieff, D. (October 1991). "Victim's All? Recovery, co-dependency, and the art of blaming somebody else," *Harper's Magazine,* pp. 49–56. On page 51 Rieff quotes Bradshaw as saying: "What we're hearing from experts is that approximately 96 percent of the families in this country are dysfunctional to one degree or another."

Page 266: M. Yapko, Ph.D. in a Grand Rounds presentation at Charter Hospital, November 4, 1992.

Herman, J. (1992). *Trauma and Recovery,* NY: Basic Books, p. 180.

We are indebted to S. B. Guze, M.D., Spencer T. Olin, Professor of Psychiatry at the Washington University School of Medicine in St. Louis, Missouri, for his insightful chapter "Psychotherapy and the medical model" in his book *Why Psychiatry is a Branch of Medicine,* New York, Oxford Univ. Press, 1992. Dr. Guze's work introduced us to the ideas of Donald Spence, Marshall Edelson, and others who seek to expose the blind spots and weaknesses of modern psychotherapy. Quotes from Spence and Edelson are borrowed from Guze.

Page 268: The story of the Vietnam veteran and the priest is told in Herman, J. (1992), *Trauma and Recovery,* NY: Basic Books, p. 55.

Nikos Kazantzakis is quoted in Sagan, C. (1979). *Broca's Brain: Reflections on the Romance of Science,* NY: Random House, p. 281.

INDEX

McTherapy
- falls under the en vogue aspect
- Loftus part of this phenomenon.
- courage to heal because the 'standard'
  literature, why does it keep getting
  revised.
- implant memory retrieval is addictive,
  like fast food

- The En vogue aspect.
- Playboy, Oprah, Donahue, Maury
- courage to heal as standard.
- Rosanne.
- Loftus criticized for not jumping on
  bandwagon.
    - p. 206 accused for not being
      in touch w/ her feminine side.
- ppl. become blind to the truth.
    - McDonald's blind to health.

p. 202 → teddy Bears

- Is Loftus a victim to the en vogue phenomenon that Acaella refers to in her book? Only from the other side? Loftus becomes integral to the entire world of this controversy.

- what about the language + discourse used to describe these issues. Is it appropriate to use the term 'survivor' for people who merely 'survived' something fictitious? How can we use the same word if it really means nothing in this case?

Questions

• How does Loftus rely on science to discuss validity of RM/Abuse? esp. 208 quote about science

  OR: Loftus relies on science to discuss the validity or lack thereof...
  → Discuss w/ evidence from text

• McTherapy (p. 90)

• How did this phenomena come across as a cult phenomena? → very sheltered group therapy, where 'survivors' were encouraged to alienate themselves from their families